MONORAILS OF THE EARLY 20TH CENTURY

Designed by Ian Pope
British Library Cataloguing-in-Publication Data. A catalogue record for this book is available from the British Library
ISBN 13: 978 1911038 12 2

Lightmoor Press
Lightmoor Press is an imprint of
Black Dwarf Lightmoor Publications Limited
144b Lydney Industrial Estate, Harbour Road
Lydney, Gloucestershire, GL15 4EJ

Printed and bound in Poland by www.lfbookservices.co.uk

Rails across the desert: the monorail track crosses the flat bed of Searles Lake. See Chapter 6. *Searles Valley Historical Society*

MONORAILS OF THE EARLY 20TH CENTURY

Scherl envisaged railway hubs or main stations being built in each major city from which tracks would radiate out in a star like fashion at roof top level. His book, *Ein Neues Schnellbahnsystem, Vorschläge zur Verbesserung des Personen-verkehrs* published in 1909 contained route maps and illustrations of grand concourses. His work is discussed in Chapter 2.

Adrian S. Garner

Another postcard which shows the fine view over Barcelona seen by those comfortable with heights. See Chapter 5. *Author's collection*

CONTENTS

ACKNOWLEDGEMENTS

When I set out researching monorails nearly fifty years ago I had not intended to write a book, let alone a second volume, but thanks to the encouragement from Ian Pope, help from my wife and support from others this book has been completed. As with the first book, Ian has sympathetically used my text and pictures to design a book capturing the period, in this case the development of the monorail in the early 20th century.

Much of the material for this volume was captured before and during writing the first book. I would like to thank again the many librarians over the last half century who have patiently provided dusty papers, books and documents from their collections for my review. These include major libraries including, but not limited to, New York Public Library, Los Angeles Public Library, National Library of Congress, Melbourne Reference Library and the British Library. In addition help has been provided by many specialist collections including the Autry National Center of the American West, Museum of English Rural Life (University of Reading Library), Gloucestershire and Leicestershire County Archives, Maturango Museum, Searles Valley Historical Society collection and the library of the Society of Model and Experimental Engineers. I must also thank the librarians at the many libraries who have searched there collections and whilst not able to provide material have given me leads as to where else to look.

I also wish to thank individuals who have provided photographs or other material for this book or who have provided information which has enabled me to carry out further research. These include Lit Brush, Chuck Doan, Michael Guerin, Martin Griffin and the team at the rebuilt Listowel and Ballybunion Railway, David Mills, Betty Peters, Joe Powell, Alexander (Sandy) Rogers, David Smith and David Voice. My apologies go to any person not named who has helped. Your input is appreciated.

Particularly I would also record thanks to the inventors of the various digital services we now take for granted but which aid research. These include Google which has enabled me to trace libraries preserving the documentation I needed to read and Abebooks which has enabled me to purchase much original documentation, sometimes not available in libraries, and often at cost lower than visiting distant libraries.

Sadly my good friend Adrian Hall who checked through the first volume has passed on and therefore the details in this work rely solely on my ability to correctly capture the history. All errors that have crept in are my own.

Lastly, I must again thank my wife, Carolyn. She continues to put up with my obsession and indeed happily travels the world with me to see peculiar monorail and narrow gauge railways. She has also read over this book to correct my English. I am indebted to her.

Adrian Garner, August 2016

NOTES

Drawings

All drawings by the author were drawn using AutoCad LT and have been based on the dimensions quoted in the relevant chapters. In many cases, however, it has been necessary to scale from large copies of the illustrations. Wherever possible dimensions have been cross checked using more than one illustration. Cross checks for consistency have also been made between separate drawings but dimensional accuracy cannot be guaranteed.

The drawings may be reproduced to any scale for private use. The author would be delighted to see models of these fascinating railways.

Imperial and metric units

Unless otherwise stated, all weights and dimensions are quoted in the units adopted in the original sources. This policy has been adopted as both UK and US engineering journals often converted metric units to the nearest rounded imperial units convenient for publication. Retaining the original published figures avoids compounding these conversion errors. Regrettably this sometimes leads to a mixture of measurement systems e.g. lengths in feet and inches and weights in kilograms.

The current (2015) internationally agreed conversion rates between metric and imperial measures are:

Lengths
1 inch (in.) = 25.400 millimetres (mm)
12 inches = 1 foot (ft.) = .305 metre
3 feet = 1 yard = 0.914 metre
80 chains = 5,280ft = 1,760 yards = 1 mile = 1.609 kilometre

Liquid
1 Imperial (UK) gallon = 1.201 US gallon = 4.546 litre

Weight
1 UK ('long') ton = 20 hundred weight (cwt) = 2,240 pounds (lb) = 1,016 kilograms
1 US ('short') ton = 2,000 pounds = 907 kilograms
1 Tonne (metric) = 2,205 pounds = 1,000 kilograms

Monetary values

As for units of measurement, no conversion has been made from the currencies quoted in the original sources.

Updating monetary values to a single currency in today's values is not trivial; it requires both converting between currencies and uplifting by a mix of price inflation (the change in value of money) and earnings inflation relating to employment costs. The following is provided only as a guide for readers.

The Sterling to US dollar exchange rate during the period covered by this book was:

Year	Number of US$ purchased by £1.00
1900	4.86
1910	4.86
1920	3.66
1930	4.86
1940	3.83
1950	2.80

Both the UK and USA economies suffered significant price inflation and a severe economic depression during this period. This is illustrated in the following table. The values have been uplifted through to the end of 2007 to be consistent with the earlier volume.

Year	Value of £1 uplifted by UK Retail Price Index £	Value of US$1 uplifted by US Consumer Price Index US$
1900	78	26
1910	74	23
1920	29	10
1930	46	12
1940	39	15
1950	25	9

Comparable series of earnings inflation figures for the period are complex and outside the scope of this book.

In the UK, prior to decimalization, £1.00 = 20 shillings = 240 'old' pennies ('d'). Under the convention before decimalisation one shilling and five old pence, for instance, was written as 1/5d.

Before adopting the common currency of the Euro, France used the French franc (1 Fr. = 100 centimes) and Germany used the Deutschmark (1 DM = 100 pfennigs). The relative values varied significantly due to the effects of inflation, economic depression and wars in Europe. The position is further complicated by formal devaluations and the issue of 'new' francs and marks during the 20th century. The study of their relative values is beyond the scope of this book.

Reference: www.measuringworth.org Website developed by Lawrence H. Officer, Professor of Economics at University of Illinois, Chicago and Samuel H. Williamson, Professor of Economics, Emeritus, Miami University.

Above: Whilst the Sydney monorail (opposite page) has not survived, the ALWEG system monorail in Seattle which opened in 1962 continues to flourish and is seen here emerging from the EMP Museum tunnel. The metal 'A' frame structure invented in the 19th century has evolved into a concrete 'I' beam with trains running on pneumatic rubber wheels.

Right: Opened in 2004, some forty years after the original ALWEG monorail in Seattle, an ALWEG Mark VI system snakes its way through downtown Las Vegas. Each train has a maximum capacity of eighty seated and 160 standing passengers and can reach fifty miles per hour. The line skirts car parks and golf courses behind the Las Vegas Strip and joins multiple hotels on its 3.9 mile journey.

both Author

INTRODUCTION

Following writing *Monorails of the 19th Century*, published in November 2011, a natural sequel would have been *Monorails of the 20th Century*. A detailed history of every monorail railway developed during this period, however, would take many volumes as monorails have proliferated from 1950 onwards. This book therefore has the humbler objective of recording monorails invented and built during the period from 1900 through to just after the end of the Second World War and is written as a continuation of the earlier volume. This is a convenient point to stop as there then followed a period during which monorail development ceased due to the economic restraint resulting from the events of the war. For the story of the re-emergence of the monorail from 1950 onwards the reader is referred to the books by Hermann Botzow and David Voice[1].

In the first book monorails were categorized into four categories:

Post and Rail: The original monorail system patented by Henry Palmer in 1821. The weight is distributed pannier fashion over a rail raised on posts. The vehicles are prevented from toppling over by keeping the centre of gravity low.

'A' Frame: Also adopted but not patented by Palmer, this system adds two symmetrically placed guide rails below the main weight bearing rail to maintain the vehicles attitude.

Bicycle: The vehicle stands on a single rail positioned below the vehicle. Attitude whilst stationary is maintained by one or more rails above or beside the vehicle. Once in motion the bicycle effect helps maintain attitude.

Suspended: The vehicle hangs from an overhead rail.

Unique: A wide variety of designs.

For the twentieth century an additional category must be added:

Gyroscopic: A monorail system where attitude is maintained by the use of one or more gyroscopes.

Since commencing research and writing these books a number of developments have occurred to the monorails previously illustrated or described. Sadly the Sydney monorail pictured in the introduction to the first volume was closed on the 30th June 2013 after operating for twenty-five years[2]. Two carriages have been preserved in the Powerhouse Museum in Darling Harbour and uniquely two further carriages have been acquired by Google and have been built into their offices in Pyrmont to form meeting rooms[3]. Carriages have also been preserved by the Sydney Electric Train Society and by the National Transport Museum at Inverell, New South Wales.

The Wuppertalbahn, however, has continued its success and has been carrying up to 70,000 passengers every day. The line has been updated and new carriages have been delivered.

Pleasingly the Listowel and Ballybunion Railway has been resurrected as a museum line using new equipment and the long closed Feurs-Panissières line, now forms part of a fascinating country walk which includes many remaining civil engineering works. This book allows space in appendices for an update on these developments. A few additional details have also emerged about other 19th Century lines previously described and these are also included in the appendices.

References

1. *Monorails* by Hermann S. D. Botzow, Jr., 1960 and *Monorails of the World* by David Voice published 2010.
2. *The Age* 26 June 2013.
3. *Sydney Morning Herald* 9 October 2013.

A sad sign near the demolition area of the Sydney monorail. *Author*

By February 2014 only the stations remain of the Sydney monorail. Their future use is uncertain. *Author*

Louis Brennan stands proudly in front of his model seen crossing the wire rope bridge erected in the garden of his house.

National Library of Congress

CHAPTER 1
THE BRENNAN GYROSCOPIC MONORAIL

During the nineteenth century wagons, carriages and locomotives on monorails were kept upright either by arranging a low centre of gravity, as in the first monorail developed by Henry Robinson Palmer, or by combinations of side rails, such as those designed by Charles François Marie-Thérèse Lartigue, or by suspending the carriages from an overhead rail as in the Carl Eugen Langen system. Given the inventiveness of the Victorian era it might seem surprising that the use of a gyroscope to keep vehicles upright was not tried until the twentieth century.

Certainly the stabilizing effect of a spinning body was well known. The spinning top was a popular children's toy consisting of a turned pear shaped piece of wood, often brightly painted, with a steel point inserted at the smaller end and a dowel with a cross hole at the 'stalk' end. When string was wound around the dowel and quickly pulled off whilst holding the top in a wooden fork it rotated at speed and would remain upright on its steel point for some minutes.

There were hints of gyroscopic use on monorails. The most overt was by Eben Moody Boynton who realised that when travelling at speed his bicycle railway made little use of the overhead supports[1]. The large wheels on his locomotives acted like the rotating wheels on a pedal powered bicycle.

There were two key reasons why gyroscopic stabilization was not developed further during this period. First the toy spinning top loses energy due to friction and when the rotation stops it no can no longer balance on the steel point. To maintain the motion requires power to be applied and this awaited the development of the electric motor. The steam engine was cumbersome and its oscillating motion disturbed the gyroscope.

Second, whilst the spinning top is a children's toy and easily used as a play thing, a full understanding of why the top remains upright and an ability to calculate the rate of rotation and the mass of the rotating flywheel for a particular use was needed. This was not within the grasp of physicists or mathematicians at that time, albeit Leon Foucault had devised laws of rotation which provided a basis for understanding in 1852. A comparison may be made with magnets, which had been incorporated into toys and used for navigation for centuries, but a deeper understanding was only emerging towards the end of the nineteenth century following the work of James Clerk Maxwell.

By the beginning of the twentieth century, however, the electric motor had been developed along with the internal combustion engine which could be used with a dynamo to generate electricity to drive the motor and hence the gyroscope. Practical experimentation with gyroscopes together with progress in related mathematical analysis had also been made.

Enter Louis Philip Brennan

Brennan was born on the 28th January 1852[2] at Castlebar, Ireland. He immigrated with his family to Australia in 1861 and returned to England in 1880. During his period in Australia he attended Joel Eade's Technical College in Collingwood and was articled to Mr A. K. Smith a prominent civil and mechanical engineer. Whilst in Australia he was struck by the engineering problems and related costs of building railways through hilly and sparsely populated countryside and it was during this period that he, like monorail developers before him, thought of the monorail as a possible solution[3].

Little practical development took place as in 1874 he had conceived the idea of a steerable ('dirigible') torpedo which was to prove technically successful and make Brennan both famous and financially rich. At that time Australia was a UK colony and Major Ellery of the Torpedo Corps and Professor William Kernot, lecturer at the University of Melbourne, had provided encouragement in the interests of the UK military. The local Victorian Government helped provide finance and Brennan applied for a UK patent on the 4th September 1877 which was granted on the 1st February 1878 (Patent No. 3359 'Improvements in machinery for propelling and guiding vessels on land and through air and water').

Following his return to the UK, the Admiralty purchased the invention from the Brennan Torpedo Company in 1887, where he remained the factory superintendent, for the sum of £110,000[4]. The final design of torpedo adopted by the Admiralty was 24ft long, by 2ft 9in. by 2ft, weighed about 3½ tons and had 200lbs of explosive. It had a range of 1½ miles and travelled at thirty miles per hour. A description published in the *The Aeronautical Journal*, February 1973 by Robert Graham, an engineer and friend of Brennan, read:

> "It was designed to run about 12 feet below the surface. …In the body of the torpedo, two steel drums were mounted, each having wound upon it a very considerable length of high tensile steel wire, several miles in fact.
>
> The drums were connected through a differential gear to the twin in-line propellers arranged to rotate in opposite directions. If one drum were rotated faster than the other then, although the propellers continued to rotate at the same speed, the rudder was operated.
>
> The twin wires from the drums passed out through the tail shaft of the torpedo and from the tail shaft, small steel rings embracing the wires were paid out at intervals, thus preventing the wires from separating.
>
> The other ends of the wires were connected to winding engines, either in a ship or on a land base, and these twin winding engines were so arranged that their respective speeds could be varied within fine limits, thus providing sensitive control for the steering of the torpedo…"

In 1892 Brennan was honoured by being awarded Companion of the Bath, he married Anna Mary Quinn from his home town of Castlebar and moved to 'Woodlands', a large house in Gillingham, Kent. From there he commenced work on his ideas about monorails.

The gyroscope idea

In 1896 Brennan negotiated to cease his role as superintendent of the dirigible torpedo factory and instead became a consultant. His income was reduced from £1,500 per annum to £700 per annum but the new arrangement released two thirds of his time allowing him to develop the monorail and other ideas. These included a patent granted on the 16th May 1902 for a 'System and apparatus for facilitating the ascent of stairs or inclined ways', Patent No. 3415. Brennan's consultancy with the factory finally came to an end in 1907 when manufacture of the dirigible torpedo ceased. After some twenty years of success the dirigible torpedo was being replaced by 9.2in. shore line guns which had a longer range and rapid fire.

The novel idea of using a gyroscope rather than balance rails in his design of monorail, however, occurred whilst he was on holiday in Cannes when he saw a pedlar demonstrating simple gyroscopes for sale [5]. He purchased one and by the 11th December 1903 he applied for his patent 'Improvements in and relating to the Imparting of Stability to otherwise Unstable Bodies, Structures or Vehicles'[6].

It is clear from this patent that Brennan recognised the problems of precession and nutation. A rotating body, as in a gyroscope, will resist forces applied to displace its position but, as all children observe, when a side force is applied there is a motion at right angles to the plane of that force. This is precession. This and other factors cause the secondary rotation of the gyroscope ('nutation') as it slows down until it finally topples over. Brennan's patent proposed the use of two rotating flywheels running in opposite directions to compensate for these problems.

ILLUSTRATIONS OF THE PRINCIPLE OF THE GYROSTAT.

Descriptions of the action of the gyroscopes in Brennan's monorail varied from the technically precise to the loosely descriptive. This is perhaps the simplest being a cartoon published in *Railway and Locomotive Engineering* Vol. 20, August 1907.

Whilst the word gyroscope is commonly used, Brennan always referred to these devices when mounted in cages as gyrostats. In current language, the words are interchangeable.

The following extract from Brennan's patent describes his idea:

"My invention further consists in the application of two gyrostats rotating in opposite directions, and supported in frames pivoted on preferably parallel axes, the frames being connected in such a way as to ensure correspondence of the opposite precessions. This connection is specially advantageous in enabling a vehicle or vessel to move in a curved path either forward or backward without difficulty.

A further part of my invention consists in employing a mass or weight suitably disposed and connected to the gyrostat frame or frames, so as, when acted on by centrifugal force, to control the precession, and thus to compensate for the effects of centrifugal force in tilting the vehicle moving on a curved path…

…I therefore, for a vehicle intended for ordinary purposes, employ two similar gyrostats rotating in opposite directions. The carriers of the two gyrostats are pivoted on parallel axes, and I connect the carriers by means of gearing so that the rotation of the one carrier in one direction produces a corresponding rotation of the other carrier in the opposite direction. I then control the movements of the carriers by a suitable lever. When automatic control of the stability of the vehicle is desired, I provide an inverted pendulum, whose motion is communicated by means of gearing to the carriers, so that when the pendulum owing to the disturbance of the equilibrium of the vehicle tends to fall over in one direction at an increasing rate, it produces an acceleration of the precession of the gyrostats, and thus restores the balance of the vehicle. The inverted pendulum may itself be controlled by hand if desired. In passing round a curve with the vehicle the inclining effects required to compensate for centrifugal forces are obtained by the action of the centrifugal force on the inverted pendulum."

The work by Brennan on his monorail had not generated any income and despite his earlier financial success with the torpedo he needed support for the continued development of the monorail. He therefore made a model measuring about 2ft 6in. long by 1ft wide and 10in. high with gyroscopes and electric motors powered by lead accumulators. Whilst the body was a rough wooden structure and the model weighed 70lbs it showed the system worked. Brennan carried out tests for some two years on the model helped by a local ten year old boy, William Barham, who sat on the car as the payload. William was weighed by Brennan and the lad had to alter his position on the car in order for Brennan to assess the reactions of the gyroscopes. R. E. Wilkes[5] reports that these experiments were to ensure the correct flow of mercury around the gyroscopes. The mercury probably acted as the electric connector with the electric motors that formed part of the flywheel. The casings of the gyroscopes were made by a local blacksmith at

Gillingham Gas Works and were sealed and evacuated, the air being withdrawn with a bicycle pump.

With this successful model he applied to the Army Council on the 15th March 1904 for £1,000 financial support and permission to use the Brennan Torpedo Company factory to build a larger model. The Army Council visited on the 7th May 1904 and was so impressed they recommended a grant of £10,000 but their financial department refused payment. This was notified to Brennan on the 19th June 1904.

Luckily the Director of Fortifications and Works, General R. M. Rick, stepped in and, after a visit by several members of the Army Council to Brennan's home on the 23rd December 1904, Brennan was authorized on the 16th March 1905 to spend up to £2,000 and to use the Brennan Torpedo Factory together with a design team of an assistant engineer, two draughtsmen and a clerk.

The terms for this financial support were that the War Department had the right to use the invention for naval and military purposes at a royalty of 5% of the cost of the rolling stock, track etc. This financially tight approach was probably coloured by the very favourable deal that Brennan had previously managed to conclude for the use of the dirigible torpedo.

Brennan rapidly realised the enormity of the work needed to move from an imperfect model to a full size vehicle weighing many tons. By September 1905 he wrote to the Treasury to sanction more finance and in November of that year he discontinued work on the full size vehicle and opted to build a working model of the prototype. This was fortunate as on 5th January 1906 the War Office replied to his appeal for more funds stating that no more would be available until his full sized mechanism had proved successful in trials.

⅛th scale model

With the help from the Brennan Torpedo Company factory a model was built using lightweight aluminium wherever possible. The gyroscopes ran up to 8,000rpm, each in the opposite direction, the electric motors forming and being built into the flywheels. The mechanism was mounted in a box like structure with a lid enabling the air to be partly evacuated.

As shown in the accompanying illustration, the stabilizing mechanism used two contra-rotating gyroscopes mounted in separate cages. These cages were geared together and could turn about vertical pivots (A and A') on the main frame. The gyroscopes were symmetrically placed each side of the centre line of the vehicle and when in the 'neutral' position the axes of rotation of the gyroscope flywheels were in line and the vehicle was upright. The gyroscopes had protruding horizontal axles or spindles that projected over brackets fixed to the sides of the vehicle. When the vehicle was displaced from the vertical the rising bracket pressed against the adjacent axle. This upward force caused the

The ⅛th scale model painted in War Department light grey poses for a photograph in the garden of Brennan's home, 'Woodlands', in Gillingham. The top of the air tight cover of the gyroscopes can just be seen through the cab. *National Library of Congress, LC-B2-615-2*

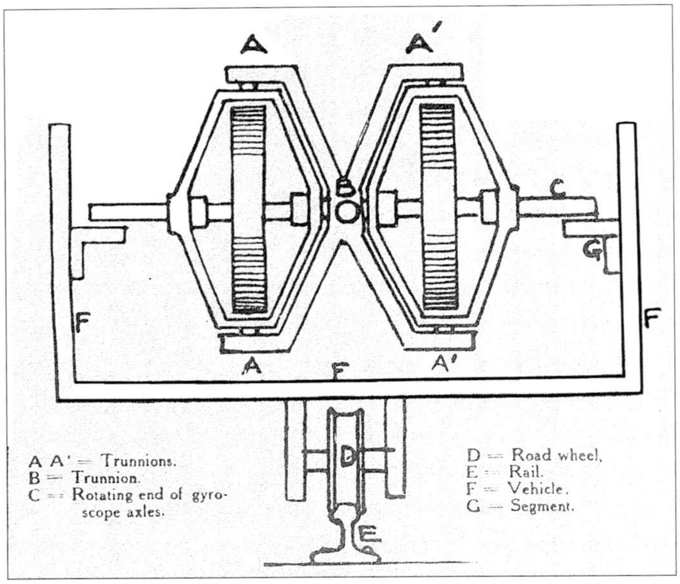

Left: Published in *McLure's Magazine* Vol. 30, December 1907, this drawing was typical of those accompanying the many articles describing the mechanism in Brennan's monorail model and prototype.

Below: The key features of the model were set out in this diagram published in *McLure's Magazine* Vol. 30, December 1907.

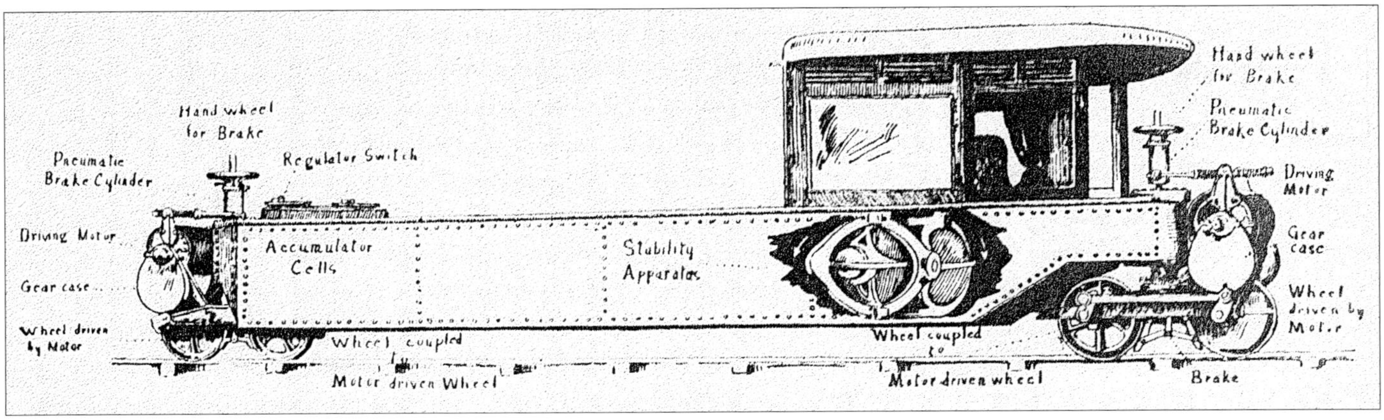

gyroscope to precess, that is to rotate about its vertical axis within the fixed frame. As the two cages of the gyroscopes were geared together, the other gyroscope also rotated about its vertical axis. Matters were so arranged (complications ignored in this description) that it also pressed down on the bracket to form the righting force required.

In practice a more complex arrangement was required to generate the needed forces and enable the gyroscopes to return to their 'neutral' central position. (For detail see Technical description)

The final design measurements were:

Length overall	6ft 0in.
Length of body	5ft 0in.
Width of body	1ft 6in.
Depth of body	6in.
Diameter of each gyroscope wheel	5in.
Weight of vehicle (unloaded)	128lbs
Weight of accumulator cells	45lbs
Maximum load	140lbs

The model was powered by twelve secondary (accumulator) cells.

The track for the model was simple and made from ½in. diameter gas pipe. About half a mile of track was laid out at Brennan's home, 'Woodlands'. The layout

Brennan fitted pneumatic brakes to each bogie of the model. The valve and cylinder can be seen at the top of this picture together with a connecting nipple as the model did not have its own pumps. The brake shoes were connected by levers to a central shaft up to the brake cylinder. *Author*

With both the cab and air tight cover removed, the two gyroscopes in their cages are visible. These cages are able rotate about vertical axes on the main frame. The extensions of the gyroscope spindles can be seen along with a number of extra unused holes in the side plates which were probably made during the experimental stages as the design was developed. *Author*

was designed to show the ability of the vehicle to cope with extremes of track work and included gradients of up to one in five, severe curves, a wire rope bridge of 50ft span and a section of rope laid on the ground without sleepers.

The model still exists. It was presented to London's Science Museum on the 8th March 1946 by Robert Graham, who was Brennan's assistant. It is currently (2015) on display at the National Railway Museum, York.

Model demonstrations

Having granted money to Brennan in 1905, the War Office pressed Brennan for a demonstration of progress. Only one day after testing the vehicle at 'Woodlands', a War Office Committee led by Sir John Wolfe-Barry, K.C.B., L.L.D., F.R.S. visited on the 23rd July 1906. The model performed perfectly but, despite repeated requests, it was not until the 5th November 1906 that Brennan was able to obtain a copy of the War Office report on their visit.

The accumulators powering the model can just be seen at the rear of the vehicle in this photograph taken at 'Woodlands'.
Model Engineer and Electrician *Vol. 16, 23 May 1907*

Brennan was delighted to find the summary by Sir John Wolfe-Barry which read:

"From all points of view I am thus of opinion that it would be wise to continue the experiment of Mr. Brennan's invention on a full-sized working example, suitable to a load of freight of about 60 tons."

The political timing, however, was unfortunate. The general election held between 12th January and 8th February 1906 had resulted in a land slide victory for the Liberal Party led by Henry Campbell-Bannerman with an austerity policy making it difficult to obtain finance for experiments such as Brennan's monorail. On the 24th November 1906 Brennan was formally informed that the Army Council did not intend to continue financing the trial.

Brennan had, however, anticipated this possible outcome and the previous year, on the 6th August 1905, he had contacted the Secretary of State for India asking if he would assist. This was probably on the basis of the adoption of the monorail for hill railways in India. On the 19th November 1906 Brennan met with Lord Morley, Secretary of State for India. He was probably already aware that the Army Council would not continue finance but he had received an indication that they would be willing to temporarily transfer the Brennan Torpedo Factory (which was ceasing production of torpedoes) to the Indian Government for the experiment.

A committee, including a number of representatives from Indian railway companies, appointed by the India Office visited 'Woodlands' for a demonstration on the 23rd November 1906. The demonstration was again successful but by March 1907 no progress or feedback had been given. The factory remained idle.

On the 25th March 1907, however, Brennan received an invitation to demonstrate the model at the Royal Society Soirée on the 8th May 1907 where many new inventions were being displayed. Both the War Department and Indian Government gave clearance for this demonstration (Brennan was careful not to jeopodise their good will or infringe military secrets) and the event was a great success. *Engineering* reported positively[7] that a track about eight feet above the ground had been erected in the meeting room at Burlington House for the demonstration. The monorail vehicle negotiated the sharp curves with ease; it ran across a tight wire rope fixed to a stout timber frame and also ran over a coiled rope on the platform.

Scientific American[8] was more skeptical, especially about the apparent claim by Brennan of the speeds that might be reached by the monorail. After questioning the type of metal needed to ensure safety in the rotating flywheel, it stated:

"Another difficulty which suggests itself is the action of centrifugal force upon the passengers in rounding curves at the 120 miles an hour speed proposed. The car would incline to the outside of the curve at an angle which would be the result of the pull of centrifugal force against the resistance of the gyroscope; but the living freight would be thrown even farther off the vertical. But perhaps the scheme involves the provision of some ingenious form of 'pocket' gyroscope to be 'carried conveniently' on the person; or it may be that the promoters are satisfied that those who would trust themselves to such means of travel already carry sufficient 'wheels' in the head to secure all the desired gyroscopic effects."

Like nearly all previous monorail inventors Brennan was inclined to overstate his case. Not only did he claim high speed but *Engineering News*[9] reported that he said that under his monorail system "...every facility can be given for the enjoyment of life while travelling, as the carriage may be fitted up with all the comforts of a first-class hotel, and separate rooms provided every purpose, such as smoking, dining, reading, writing, etc., even promenade and music rooms, will probably be provided to relieve the tedium of railway travelling."

Brennan certainly needed more publicity for his invention as the military had ceased direct funding. He had therefore arranged to give a demonstration to the press on the 1st May 1907 at 'Woodlands' prior to the above event with an embargo on reporting until after the Royal Society Soirée (i.e. the 9th May 1907). The press response was wide with articles appearing in both the specialist press such as the *Engineer*[10] and also the general press such as the *Daily Mail* in Britain, the *New York Times* in the US[11] and hobby magazines including the *Model Engineer and Electrician*[4].

In addition to the descriptions of the gyroscopic model, *Engineering News*[9] and the *Engineer*[10] also reported that Brennan was engaged on a full sized vehicle 12ft in length powered by a 100hp petrol engine with gyroscopes 2ft 9in. in diameter running at 2-3,000rpm. The vehicle was to have change gears to allow hill climbing. The use of this was aimed, so Brennan stated, at 'feeder railways to existing railways, and pioneer lines in new countries, such as the Colonies.' Brennan stated that 'notching' in the side of a hill to lay a normal two rail track would cause many tons of material to fall from higher up the hillside. His track of one rail, he said, would in no way interfere with the natural drainage of the land. Indeed experience has shown that subsidence is a regular occurrence on the Himalaya and Darjeeling Railway and other hill railways in India, but it is not clear that the monorail would have overcome this problem.

These reports of the construction of this larger model were probably premature. Brennan still needed finance and on the 28th May 1907 he demonstrated the model to Lord Morley and Andrew Carnegie, the American multi-millionaire, at the Indian Council. Impressed, the India Council granted £6,000 for further experimental development but inclusive of the cost of their appointed officer to oversee the work. The grant was also subject to an agreement with Brennan that if successful the Indian Government would be able to use the monorail system at a royalty of 5% of the cost of rolling stock involved.

Brennan was also successful in arranging the continued use of the Brennan Torpedo Factory, at the royalty of 5% if adopted by the War Department. *The Railroad Gazette*[12] reported:

"The War Department of the British Government has begun the construction of a large car of this kind. It will be propelled by a gasoline-electric generator

Keen for more publicity, Brennan demonstrated his monorail tight rope to the bowler hatted press on the 1st May 1907.
Scientific American *Vol. 96, 1 June 1907*

Outrageously steep hills for the monorail track had been built at Brennan's home which it is doubtful could have been climbed without the use of a rack. Presumably the vehicle was positioned at the top of the hill (far right) and allowed to helter skelter down then up over the smaller hump.
Model Engineer and Electrician *Vol. 16, 23 May 1907*

Left: A member of the press takes a ride, 1st May 1907. This picture is unusual in showing the vehicle with the cab removed to expose the lid of the airtight case enclosing the gyroscopes. The vehicle had no means of evacuating the air. This was done by a separate pump connected to the case before running the vehicle.
Model Engineer and Electrician *Vol. 16, 23 May 1907*

Below: To demonstrate its ability to cope with sharp curves, Brennan, seen here in the flat cap, used a rope loosely laid on the ground to form a track.
Scientific American *Vol. 96, 1 June 1907*

set. The motors on the wheels will be provided with change gears for ascending steep grades. This car will be tested for its availability in military railroad work where the monorail track construction would be especially valuable."

Interestingly Brennan's name is only mentioned once in this article (as the inventor).

Progress towards the full size prototype

By October 1907 the research for the full size prototype was underway with a wooden platform measuring 12ft long by 10ft wide. It was mounted on knife edges instead of wheels so that the top surface was 4ft 6in. above the ground and used only one gyroscope. The initial experiments were probably to assess the mass needed in the flywheel and rotation rate for a given load. The precession was controlled manually and loads of up to seven tons were tried. Unlike the model, it is recorded that trouble with the electric motor was experienced when running in a partial vacuum and serious difficulties arose with lubricating the plain bearings made of gun metal. The final solution adopted was to replace the bearings with cast iron running in white metal, the use of vegetable rather than mineral oil and a system of injecting the oil to the bearings patented in 1909[6].

A second gyroscope was ordered in May 1908 and delivered just over one month later. With the second gyroscope fitted to the platform a pneumatic arrangement was used to control the needed precession but initially the valves were manually rather than automatically operated. The addition of the second gyroscope showed that a total weight of 17½ tons could be balanced. The only serious issue that arose was controlling the electric motors which needed to rotate at the same rates, albeit in opposite directions. The first circuitry allowed one of the motors to draw more current. This was eventually overcome by compounding the field coils of the motors.

The remaining issue was the automatic control of the pneumatic arrangements to generate precession. Unlike the platform and gyroscopes, this was a relatively small mechanism and described in Patent No. 26,034[6]. After testing at 'Woodlands', it was shipped in December 1908 to the Brennan Torpedo Factory for fitting and further testing which began on the 1st January 1909. After a few days adjustment it proved to be totally successful. The platform could carry up to twenty tons and it was stable even when a one ton weight was lowered from a crane on to the extreme edge.

Financial problems were, however, never far away as the India Office grant was exhausted. Brennan's ability to promote his ideas again came to the rescue. Some two years earlier, on the 5th February 1907, Brennan had been contacted by Alain Chartier Joly de Lotbinière, then a Major and subsequently Lt. Colonel, who had proposed and carried out the first hydro-electric transmission power scheme in India at Kolar Gold Fields, Mysore. Born in Quebec, Canada, Major de Lotbinière requested the opportunity to see Brennan's monorail at 'Woodlands' as he thought it might provide ideal rail transport in Kashmir. Brennan obliged and Major de Lotbinière encouraged Mr A. Brereton, then Director of Indian Railways, and other officials to provide financial assistance to Brennan. Despite some correspondence including an acceptance by Brennan of terms for finance drafted by Major de Lotbinière, nothing transpired until the 25th October 1908 when Brennan received a telegram from Major H. A. D. Fraser RE, Agent and Engineer in Europe to the Kashmir Durbar informing him that a loan of £5,000 on reasonable terms had been granted.

The prototype is demonstrated

After considering using an external source of electric supply for the gyroscopes and propulsion via an overhead cable or side rail, Brennan decided to make the vehicle self-contained to allow for its use in rugged conditions such as in India and in hostile military environments. He therefore ordered two petrol engines, 80hp and 20hp and two dynamos. The former order was placed with the Wolseley Tool and Motor Car Company and the latter with the Siemens Bros.

With knowledge of the cost of these major items and the grant from the Kashmir Durbar, Brennan set out his final budget for completing the vehicle to the Secretary of State for India indicating that another £2,000 would be needed. On the 12th May 1909 Brennan was informed that this was granted but with the condition that the royalty originally agreed be reduced from 5% to 4% in respect of the first three hundred vehicles supplied to the Indian Government.

Construction now progressed rapidly. It is nearly certain that the prototype vehicle used the same gyroscopes that had been tested on the test platform. By the 15th October 1909 the vehicle ran for the first time under its own power but its success was not without setbacks. The frequent stopping and starting during trials took its toll on the 80hp powered dynamo and on the 1st November 1909 the armature coils burnt out. Repair required return to Siemens Bros which necessitated dismantling the cab. Siemens Bros acted appropriately with the repair and Brennan set up arrangements for a demonstration to the government bodies that had financed the prototype, notably, the War Office, the India Office and the Kashmir Durbar.

To the horror of Brennan, he learned on Tuesday 9th November 1909 that a gyroscopic vehicle was to be publicly demonstrated in Berlin the following afternoon. If the vehicle by Herr August Scherl was demonstrated first, Brennan's invention would always be considered to be second, or worse, a copy[13].

Brennan immediately decided to launch his vehicle to the press the next morning, Wednesday the 10th November 1909, despite only having the one 20hp generator in use which limited its speed. Invitations were rapidly telegraphed to journalists who congregated in the grounds of the Brennan Torpedo Factory around 11 o'clock. After a full explanation, Brennan gave the signal for the vehicle to come out of the gate. Stunned at its stability, Brennan gave them permission to stand on the platform behind the cab. It was a great success.

The event was reported widely in both the engineering press and newspapers. The *Engineer*[14] provided a detailed description:

The prototype running on the monorail track laid at the Brennan Torpedo Factory during trials. A stub type single rail point is visible lower right. The Graphic *20 November 1909*

"On Wednesday last we had an opportunity of inspecting this vehicle in operation at the Brennan Torpedo Works at Gillingham, near Chatham. Here is a circular single railway, some 220 yards round and a straight line some 440 yards in length, have been laid, in addition to sidings. The rails employed, we may say in passing, were of the Vignoles section, 5¾in. high, and weighed 70lb to the yard run. The head of the rail is rounded to a radius of 5in. The line is laid on sleepers 3ft 6in. long, placed at about 3ft centres on soft ground, the rails being held down by spikes driven into the sleepers…

…The car is carried on four wheels, mounted two and two in independent trolleys. When on the straight all the four wheels are in one straight line; but, since the centre pins of the trolleys are connected to the body of the vehicle by means of ball bearings, there is considerable flexibility in rounding curves – indeed, reverse curves of 35ft radius are readily negotiated, as we had several opportunities of observing. The four wheels are each 3ft in diameter, and one wheel of each trolley is driven by an enclosed tramway type electric motor, through reduction gearing and two coupling rods, one on each side of the trolley frame.

The car itself consists of a long platform, 10ft wide, carried on rolled joists, and at one end of it is mounted the cab which contains the propelling and controlling mechanism. The former consists of two petrol engines, practically, if not identically, of the same type as those used in motor cars. One of these engines is rated at 80 horse-power and the other at 20 horse-power, though both may develop more than these figures when called upon to do so. Each engine drives an electric generator, which supplies current for a number of purposes:- First for driving the trolley motors, and hence for propelling the vehicle; secondly, for revolving the wheels of the gyroscopes, of which there are two; thirdly, for compressing air for the brakes, and for another purpose which will be alluded to later on, and fourthly, for working a small motor which drives an oil pump.

The gist of the whole system lies, of course, in the gyroscopes. It is the office of these to correct any tendency of the vehicle to depart from a position of stable equilibrium. The two gyroscopes are mounted side by side, but some few feet apart in the cab. The wheels each weigh ¾ of a ton, and they each are driven at a speed of 3,000 revolutions per minute by a shunt-wound motor. Each wheel and its motor are contained in an air-tight casing, and they run in what is nearly a vacuum, the air pressure inside it representing only that due to a column of from ½in. to ⅝in. of mercury. It is interesting to note that as long as a vacuum of this character is maintained the motor runs quite cool, but as soon as air is admitted it runs hot."

The article then describes, in not too much detail, the action of the gyroscopes. The use of pneumatic power alluded to in the article was to provide the acceleration needed to the rate of rotation about the vertical of the gyroscopes to generate the required precession to right the vehicle. The article continued its description:

"As evidence that the vehicle is of a practical size, we may say that it measures 40ft long over its buffers – or will do so when these are fitted – that it is 10ft wide, and 13ft high. The total wheel base is 20ft, and that of each trolley is 5ft 4in. Its weight empty is 22 tons, and it can carry from 10 tons to 15 tons. At the trials some forty people were easily conveyed on the platform. As at present built it could, we are informed, surmount a short incline of 1 in 13, and with some additional motive power which would represent an added weight of 4 tons it could negotiate gradients of 1 in 6½. The two engines can be used separately or together, so that the power that can be supplied can be varied from 20 to 100 horse-power. During the trials only the smaller engine could be worked, as the generator of the larger engine had had to be returned to the makers for some alterations; but the smaller power was quite sufficient to demonstrate the working of the vehicle, though, of course, no great speed could be obtained. The actual speed developed was about seven miles per hour; but with the two motors together we understand that a speed of some 35 miles per hour can be attained on the level."

As always with monorail inventors, Brennan told the press that his system would eventually be successful in high speed passenger trains. The press reported that he envisaged carriages 25ft wide and perhaps 150ft long travelling at speeds of up 150 miles per hour, the speed being limited only by wind resistance[13 & 14].

The demonstration was repeated in the afternoon and again on the 2nd December 1909 for representatives of government departments that had not been able to attend on the 10th November 1909 which included the Royal Engineers. By this time the larger generator had been repaired and re-installed and the vehicle reached twenty-two miles per hour.

The news of the demonstration of Brennan's monorail vehicle spread worldwide and stimulated a letter to be sent to *Scientific American* by T. E. Baker of Lockwood, Ohio[15]:

"...there is one point regarding gyroscopes which I have never seen mentioned in connection with this scheme.

It may not be of much importance, but it is nevertheless interesting, to note that a gyroscope does

Brennan stands proudly in the cab window whilst the gyroscopic monorail vehicle poses with a full load of military personnel at the Brennan Torpedo Factory. The fixed side support on which the vehicle rested when the gyroscopes were not running is visible along with the front power bogie. *National Library of Congress, LC-B2-921-9*

Seen from the rear, the simple construction of the vehicle body is obvious. Just a platform built up from I and L shaped iron joists on which the bogies were pivoted below and the gyroscopic mechanism was secured above. The cab was plain sheet iron without windows necessitated by the strictly limited finance available. The regimental dog clearly did not like the ride (centre of platform) and has moved in this picture! *National Library of Congress, LC-B2-921-8*

not retain its balance relative to the earth, but relative to a fixed point in space. In other words, it would appear that on a 'mono-railroad' running north and south, a car would be tilted to the west at the rate of fifteen degrees per hour, or one degree every four minutes, due to the rotation of the earth.

Of course, this is not fast enough to inconvenience anything, and perhaps Mr. Brennan has provided a way to overcome this difficulty; but if not, it would be interesting to hear what others have to say in regard to this."

Mr. Baker then went on the congratulate Brennan for his invention. The point missed by Mr Baker was that Brennan's gyroscopes were continually adjusted to maintain the vehicle upright using a pendulum attracted to the earth by gravity. The gyroscopes were not being used as a guidance system in themselves. The slow continuous rotation of the earth, which had been demonstrated in 1852 by Foucault using a gyroscope, was taken up in the multiple corrections being made by the pendulum.

Whilst the demonstration had been a success neither the military nor railway companies were enthusiastic in taking up the invention. Brennan was also aware of Scherl, his rival inventor in Germany. As he had now exhausted the monies granted to build the prototype, Brennan opted to generate cash by selling the rights for the use of his patents in both Germany and the USA to Scherl for a substantial sum[16]. He also granted the British military rights to use his patents on a royalty basis.

The editorial of *Scientific American* reflected opinion following the initial launch of the monorail by Brennan [17]:

"Sober second thought, however, must convince any thoughtful and practical mind that, in spite of the brilliant results of the recent demonstration, the monorail gyroscopic car, in the nature of things, can only have a more or less limited application under present-day conditions."

Not deterred Brennan gave another successful demonstration at the factory in Gillingham on Friday the 25th February 1910[18]. Around two hundred and fifty to three hundred people were present in what is reported to have been decidedly unfortunate weather. Despite this, the vehicle used the eighty horse power motor to allow it to run at a speed of twenty miles per hour around the circular track of 105ft radius. Passengers were taken in groups of fifty for a trip around the circle of track which

Few pictures exist of the details of Brennan's prototype. This picture published in the *Railway Times* Vol. 97, 5 March 1910, shows the underside construction of the vehicle with pneumatic cylinders and power bogies.

No photograph has been traced of the gyroscopes used by Brennan but by 1909 gyroscopes were being developed for many purposes. This picture shows a contemporary gyroscope to stabilize a ship designed by Herr Otto Schlick.
The Graphic *20 November 1909*

must have been exciting on a wet day given the lack of side fence on the vehicle's platform. It was reported that a speed exceeding twenty-five miles per hour was reached on the quarter of a mile of straight track.

An unusual feature of the demonstration related to unloading of packing cases. As described in *Engineering*:

> "The vehicle was intentionally tilted over on to chocks on the right-hand side, and some cases unloaded. It was then righted and then tilted over towards the left side, and the other cases unloaded, being finally righted again, all these operations of tilting being performed solely with the assistance of the gyroscope gear."

The audience for this demonstration included delegates from the War Office and Admiralty as well as many well-known from the scientific world including Hon. C. A. Parsons, Sir William White, Professor Fleming and Mr Alexander Siemens. Brennan is reported to have stated to them that it was intended to build one or more trailers to be coupled to the vehicle in order to show the practicality of running such vehicles on trains.

The problems of Brennan's system were, however, becoming aired more widely. These concerns were initially financial and were set out by J. Sutherland Warner, A.M.Inst.Mech.E. in his letter to *The Times Engineering Supplement*[19] headed 'Mono-rail Fallacies'. He pointed to the concentration of the load on one rail which would, in his view, at least double the cost of the track compared to the usual bi-rail track due to the depression of the sleepers into the ballast necessitating concrete or piles being employed. He also doubted the advantages or capability of the monorail in reaching high speeds. This brought a rapid response from Brennan stating that Warner's letter was misleading and based upon a want of appreciation of the facts, followed by a long argument outlining the errors and stating that he was confident that his system "will be widely adopted wherever the initial capital outlay on track bears a heavy ratio to the cost of the rolling stock, or where the need exists for high-speed passenger transit, such as, for example, between big cities, or a city and its distant residential quarter."

Warner's letter also generated a response from F. B. Behr, who had promoted the Lartigue monorail system [1]. Behr was keen to point out that "A mono-rail is a railway on which the whole weight of the rolling stock is carried on one rail, as against a bi-rail where such weight is carried on two rails. It does not matter how many other rails such railways may possess, in the shape of guide-rails, guard-rails, or any other safety arrangements, so long as the principle above stated is strictly carried out." By stating this definition, Behr sought to distance Warner's comments from monorails in general (which would have included the Lartigue system) by suggesting the fallacies were not inherent in monorails but specific to Brennan's system. The correspondence closed in April with *The Times Engineering Supplement* editor allowing Warner to have the last response.

Brennan continued to promote the system and make some headway. In May 1910 he granted a license to an American syndicate, represented by Major J. E. Ballaine, of Seattle, Washington State, who was one of the original promoters of the Alaska Central Railroad, which had gone into receivership in 1909 after completing only about fifty miles of track. Major Ballaine was supported by an unnamed firm of New York bankers and the license was for an extension to connect the above line with the rich coal fields situated 185 miles north of Seward. Major Ballaine had undertaken to finish this extension, a length of about one hundred miles, by December 1912. The cost of rails under the Brennan system was estimated at $1,870 a mile, sleepers $280, labour, equipment and other expenses $2,750, bringing the total to about $5,000 a mile. The idea was to use two vehicles on the Brennan system each carrying fifty or sixty passengers making two journeys a day at about twenty miles per hour. Receipts were estimated at $200,000 a year[20]. The monorail was never built.

Brennan continued some further design work and on the 9th June 1910 he applied for a US patent for a retractable undercarriage that could be lowered to support the vehicle when it was at rest. This would have replaced the fixed supports on the sides of the prototype. As the patent was only taken out in the USA it is likely that this was related to the above proposal.

The last major event to publicise Brennan's monorail was the Japan-British Exhibition held at Shepherd's Bush in west London from the 14th May to the 29th October 1910. Open to the public at an entrance price of one shilling, (5p), it was run under the auspices of the Imperial Japanese Government and displayed cultural, military and industrial works of both countries. Fireworks by the British firm of Pains were shown in the Grand Stadium and a key feature in adverts was 'Marvellous Brennan Monorail'. The vehicle was the same one that had been demonstrated at Gillingham. In describing the event *The Times* reported one additional statistic not previously recorded, the clear platform space on the vehicle was 225 sq. ft[21].

One of the many parties that took a ride on the Brennan monorail at the Japan-British Exhibition. Seats and a safety fence had been added.
Author's collection

On Friday the 4th November 1910, after the exhibition had formally closed, Winston Churchill gave a luncheon party at the Hotel Ritz in honour of Brennan. This was attended by ministerial colleagues and friends following which Winston Churchill plus the seventeen guests went to see the Brennan monorail. The party included Mr Lloyd George, Mr Birrell, Sir E. Cassel, Sir E. Troup, Lord Basil Blackwood, Mr G. Cornwallis West, Mr W. Guy Granet, Mr Raymond Asquith, Miss Violet Asquith, Mrs Churchill, and Lady Gwendoline Churchill. *The Times*[22] reported that the monorail had been laid at the northern end of the grounds behind a mountain railway and the track included a circle plus a straight course of a quarter of a mile. This was probably the track previously laid at Gillingham. As at previous demonstrations, the party initially watched the vehicle circle the track and then they were invited to ride on the rear platform. Mr Asquith, Mr Lloyd George and Mr. Birrell joined Brennan in the cab.

The demonstration was briefly interrupted when the party's attention was diverted to the cruise of Mr Willows' airship, which was seen rising over the airship shed at Wormwood Scrubs. The airship passed so low that the name of Mr Willows could be seen beneath the envelope. No doubt the party had one eye on the sky as only a few minutes before a monoplane from the Blériot School at Hendon had passed over and after completing a circle had headed north east. Once the airship was out of sight and had passed into the mist that was hanging over London, the party resumed their inspection of the monorail. After their ride, the party was shown the models made by Brennan in the shed made to house the prototype vehicle.

Project abandoned

In the USA, studies were being made to analyse the operation of the Brennan vehicle, possibly with a long term view to commercial possibilities, and a working model was made by Professors Crew and Tatnall, Northwestern University.

The model made by Professors Crew and Tatnall. No power bogies were provided and rather than link the gyroscope cages by toothed wheels, a simple lever linkage system was arranged on the top of the main frame supporting the cages. It would appear that the drive for the gyroscope wheels was external. The shaft to the right of the picture has a cross peg so that it could be temporarily linked to an external motor to wind up the gyroscope wheels and then be released. This model was only for experimental purposes and thus it did not need to be able to sustain itself for long periods.
Journal of the Franklin Institute
Vol. 169, June 1910

Subsequently a paper by Henry T. Eddy based on their work, work by Prof. W. S. Franklin of Lehigh University and his own work was published in the *Journal of the Franklin Institute*[23] which provided a detailed analysis. This showed that whilst Brennan's vehicle was stable under most conditions, a rapid deviation caused by say an extremely high wind, could cause the vehicle to tilt beyond about thirty degrees in which event it would be beyond the precessional deviation from which the vehicle's gyroscopes were designed to recover. It would therefore be necessary to have some form of automatic safety system.

The press coverage of Brennan's gyroscopic monorail becomes silent after 1910. Wilkes[5] states that two monorail vehicles were built and that a local Gillingham resident reported that one went to a local scrap metal dealer from whence the chassis and motors went to the Strood Motor Company to be dismantled for parts. The cab of one of them was used as a park shelter on Jackson Recreation Ground, Rochester from about 1918 to 1930 and Tomlinson[2] states that one of the engines was sold during the First World War for use with trawler patrols.

Whatever their final fate, by September 1912 Brennan was forced to sell his home 'Woodlands' to avoid financial ruin as no railway or government body took up his invention. After his lack of success with the gyroscopic monorail his subsequent work was on the development of the helicopter. Sadly this again came to naught as, whilst the Air Ministry encouraged the work, they eventually abandoned the experiments. In the late 1920s, when Brennan was in his seventies, he reverted to his interest in gyroscopes and had constructed a gyroscopic motor car but again there was little commercial interest.

Louis Brennan died on the 17th January 1932 following a car accident in Montreaux, Switzerland where he was recovering from an illness at the age of eighty. A Requiem Mass was held at Holy Souls Chapel, Westminster Cathedral, on the 26th January 1932 following which he was buried at St. Mary's Cemetery, Kensal Green[24]. On the day of his funeral *The Times* published the following letter from Captain F. Whelford, M.Inst C.E.:

"Mr. Louis Brennan lunched with me the day after he perfected his 'mono-rail' car. He had for some time succeeded in making his car stand up and go forward on two wheels arranged 'fore and aft' but it would not go backwards without falling over. He solved the problem by having two gyroscopes running in opposite directions. The car would then do anything, and was one of the most remarkable inventions in modern times. He had a model which did gymnastics in his own garden at Gillingham, Kent. He laid a wire cable all over his lawn, straight, curved, and in fantastic loops. The model followed the cable. On curves it banked itself against the curve. Its behavior was most uncanny. If you pressed with your fingers against its side, instead of being depressed, it jumped up against you. At one place the cable spanned some 50ft. of lawn. The car took this 'Blondin' fashion, carrying Brennan's little girl who, incidentally, didn't like it. Many distinguished people came to see the model. Later, Brennan made a full-sized truck which carried 30 people round a field upon a single rail. Scores of people rode on that truck. Brennan was a most remarkable inventor, but somewhat impracticable. He told me that every railway would run upon his principle, having one rail instead of two; and in such places as West Africa it would only be necessary to cut down the trees to 3ft. from the ground and to place rails between the stumps. I had to explain to him that trees did not grow quite so regularly as that, even in West Africa. I told him that I feared that his invention, remarkable as it was, was of no real value except for exhibition purposes. I pointed out that every one of his monorail trucks would require a gyroscopic equipment, and would cost £3000 to £4000 each, at least."

The last words should probably be those at the end of the obituary in the *Engineer*:

"Louis Brennan was an Irishman of the Irish. He had all the charm of his race and was much beloved by all who knew him well. His ardour for invention never failed him, even when ill-health dogged him and drove him out of England during the winter months. He was a familiar figure in the Savage Club, of which the Bohemian atmosphere appealed to his temperament, and will be much missed by his "brothers"."

Technical description of the gyrostat balance mechanism

The First Patent: The initial design was published in Brennan's patent in 1903[6]. The first published mathematical analysis of Brennan's application of the gyroscope was given in *Engineering* on the 7th June 1907[25] which was followed by a correction published a week later[26].

In the patent Brennan envisaged that the two flywheels would be mounted in cages to form gyroscopes with their axes aligned horizontally across the vehicle when in the neutral position with the vehicle upright.

Each cage would be free to rotate about horizontal axes aligned with the length of the car but the cages would be linked by an arm with ball and socket joints at each end so that their motions opposed (i.e. as one turned clockwise, the other turned anti-clockwise). Further, the cages would be free to rotate about vertical axes but this time linked by toothed sectors fixed to the bottom of the vertical pivots of the cages. The effect of the latter would again be that if one gyroscope cage rotated clockwise when viewed from above, the other would rotate anti-clockwise.

In the original design the outer end of one gyroscope armature spindle was to be prolonged. At its extremity was a small loosely fitting wheel 'd'. This ran freely in a radial slot guide 'e' which was to be rigid with the casing or body of the vehicle as shown on Fig. 4 of the drawing opposite. The guide slot 'e' was to be stepped. In the drawing the slot on the left is slightly higher than that on the right. This is an important feature as there were also to be two rigid bearing surfaces 'g' and 'h' with which a larger wheel 'f' may come into contact. The step is such that wheel 'd' can contact the upper surface of the slot when moved to the right in Fig. 4 but cannot touch the lower surface of slot 'e' as wheel 'f' will have contacted surface 'h'. Conversely wheel 'd' can only contact the

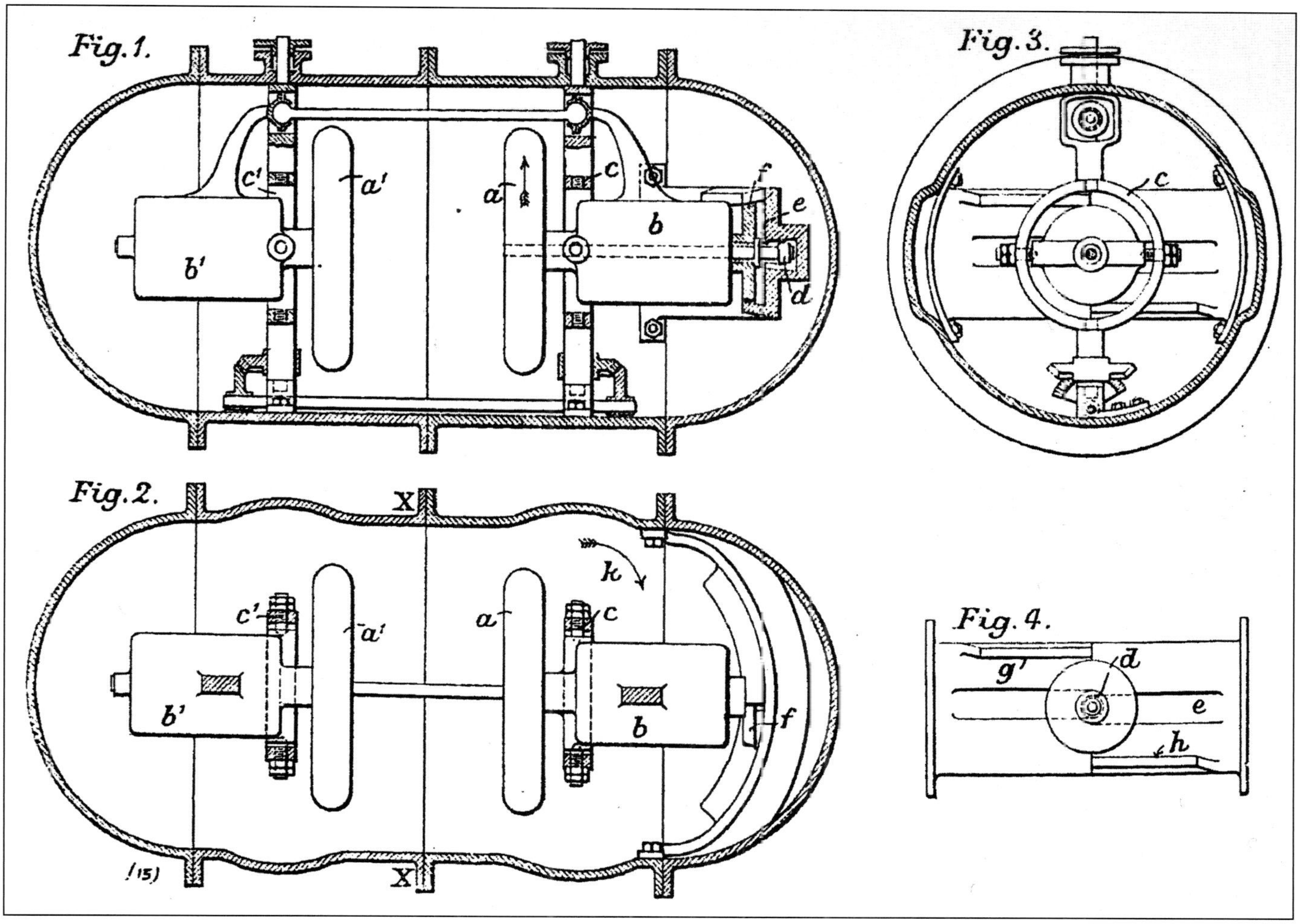

Taken from Brennan's Patent No.27,212, 1903, and subsequently widely published, Fig. 1 is a sectional view of the stabilizing mechanism which would be mounted across the vehicle, Fig. 2 is a plan, and Fig. 3 is from the side viewpoint. Fig. 4 shows the operation of the spindle extension and wheels running in the side slot. Engineering *Vol. 83, 14 June 1907*

lower surface of slot 'e' if movement causes rotation to the left as wheel 'f' will have contacted the surface 'g'. Wheel 'f' was also loosely carried on a sleeve mounted on the spindle.

The vertical distances between the upper surface of the small slot guide 'e' and the contact surfaces 'g' and 'h' were to be such that the wheels 'd' and 'f' were allowed a slight amount of movement about the axis of the horizontal pivot of the gyroscope.

As stated in *Engineering*, it will now be evident that when the vehicle tilts the wheel 'd' will come into contact with one or other of the surfaces of the guide slot 'e'. In a gyroscope, a couple ('force') applied to tilt its plane does not cause the gyroscope to tilt in the direction of the couple. Instead it tilts ('precesses') at right angles to the couple and its axis of rotation. Assume the vehicle tilts so that wheel 'd' touches the upper surface of slot 'e', a motion to the right in Fig. 4 and direction 'k' in Fig. 2. In this event the slot 'e' puts pressure on wheel 'd' due to the vehicle leaning to one side and the gyroscope will precess or swing round at right angles, the tail carrying with it the wheel 'd' and the wheel 'f'.

As the motion occurs friction is developed between the wheel 'd' and the slot surface 'e' and also between the wheel 'd' and the prolonged spindle on which it is mounted (which is rotating). This rotation will thus be partly transferred to the wheel which will cause it to accelerate along the slot surface thus increasing the precession. This acceleration, essentially a force or couple, in turn generates a precession or turning couple by the gyrostat in the horizontal plane. The effect of this is to right the vehicle to the vertical position.

When this upright position is reached, the acquired angular momentum of the vehicle will tend to cause the vehicle to overshoot and produce a tilt in the opposite direction. At this point the wheel 'f' would bear on guide 'h'. Fig. 4 This wheel 'f' was to be arranged so that there was practically minimal friction and hence the force between this wheel and the surface was essentially in the vertical plane. The effect would cause the gyroscope to swing in the horizontal plane back to its mid or neutral position.

Any overshoot of the motion beyond the mid-position will bring the wheel 'd' back into play but this time with the lower surface of slot 'e' due to the step in the slot. The acceleration will again check the new swing of the vehicle. Repetition of this action kept the vehicle upright.

The original patent also envisaged the possible use of an inverted pendulum to control the couple (in practice an acceleration on vertical rotation) to help maintain the position of the vehicle and hand controls.

The Models: The first model constructed by Brennan, demonstrated to the Army Council in 1904, probably followed his 1903 patent with the gyroscopes connected as described above. This was complicated and experience with this model probably led him to the simpler but successful design used in his second model built to $\frac{1}{8}$th scale.

At the meeting of the Physical Society in 1908 the second model was demonstrated and Prof. Perry, the President of the Society, gave a detailed mathematical analysis of the properties then known about gyroscopes and a description of the mechanism used in the model [27].

In this model the two gyroscopes were not individually pivoted about horizontal axes aligned with the length of the vehicle. The ball and socket connecting arm was thus not needed. Instead, the gyroscope cages were mounted on a single frame that could pivot about a horizontal axis aligned with the centre line of the vehicle. The cages could, however, rotate about vertical axes and the cage frames were linked by sections of gear teeth. This significantly simplified the structure.

This change also allowed a further simplification. In the original design only one gyroscope spindle was extended and this had to run in a stepped slot as described above. With the two gyroscopes mounted on a single frame which could rotate about the centre line of the vehicle both gyroscope spindles could be extended. Instead of running in slots each only had to make contact with surfaces mounted on a bracket on each side of the vehicle. The slot was effectively cut in two with a section on each side of the vehicle.

An addition to the original design, in the model constructed by Brennan was a spring connecting the two gyroscope cages. This was positioned above the frame (see photograph) and when the gyroscopes were in the neutral position its tension was aligned along the axes of the gyroscopes and thus caused no turning force and thus no precession. When the gyroscopes were displaced from their neutral position, however, the tension pulled on the cages and thus further amplified their precession.

The gyroscopes needed to run at high speed, around 7,000 to 8,000 rpm. To reduce air friction the whole mechanism was enclosed in an air tight box which was partially evacuated. No record has been found as to whether this gave rise to any issues regarding cooling of the electric motors or indeed over heating of the plain bearings.

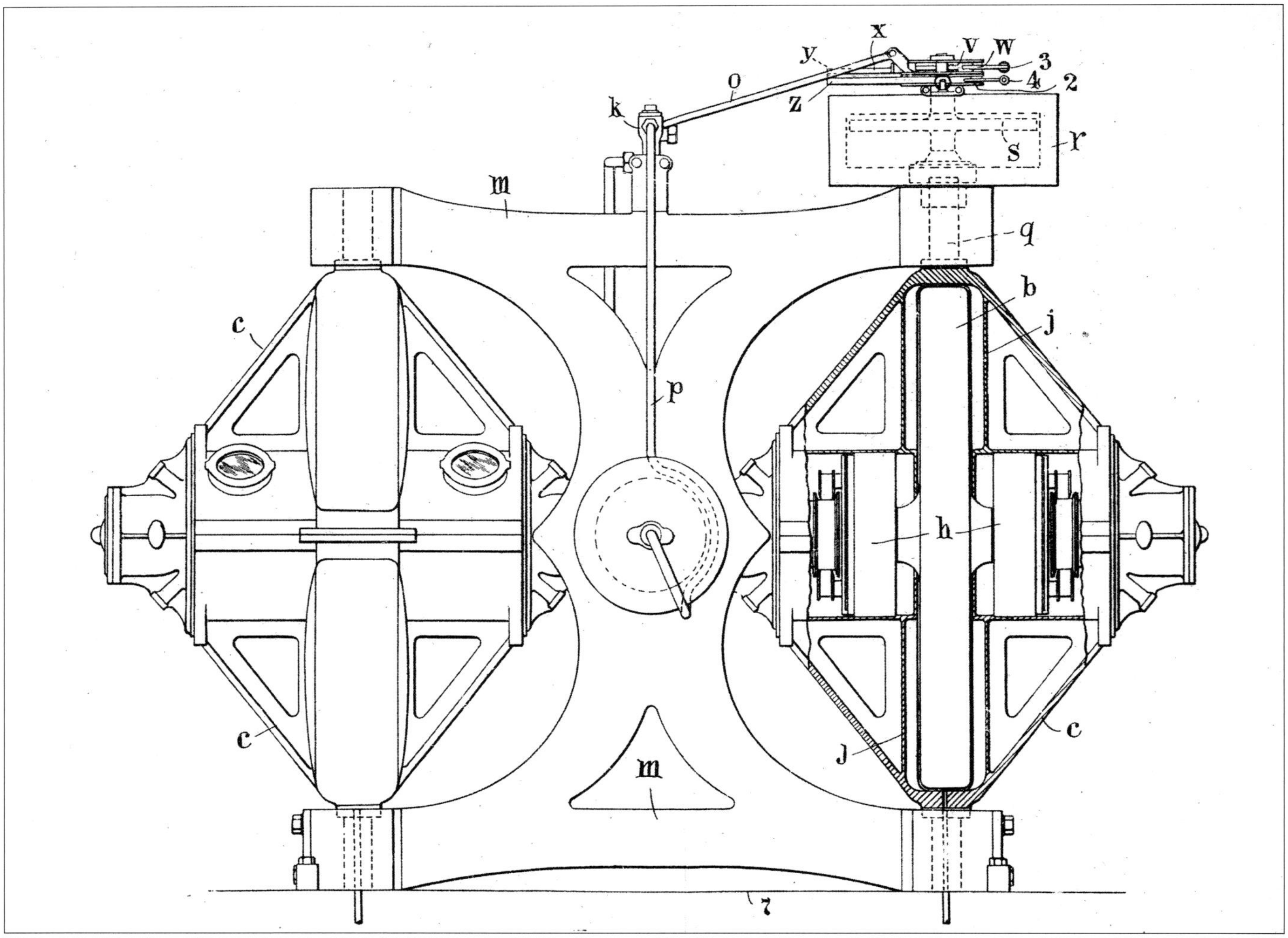

This drawing from Patent No. 26,034, 1909, shows the design used by Brennan in the full size prototype. The main frame 'm' with the two gyroscope cages each side is mounted on the chassis of the vehicle. The left-hand side of the drawing shows the gyroscope cage casing whilst the right hand side shows a section through the casing. Above the vertical pivot on the right hand side is the control mechanism to detect the position and rotation of the gyroscope cages about the vertical. This operated the valve 'k' allowing fluid (air) to flow through the pipe 'p' to the cylinder seen end on.

The Test Platform and Prototype: The final design with automatic control was described in Brennan's 1909 patent[6].

Many features incorporated into the model had to be changed due to the size and mass of the gyroscopes required. Firstly it would no longer be possible to construct a single compartment containing all the workings, including the gyroscopes and connections to external controls, that would be sufficiently air tight for it to be partially evacuated. Instead each gyroscope had to be enclosed in its own sealed casing. The sealing of these cases together with the much greater forces required to maintain a heavy vehicle and load upright meant that it was no longer possible to extend the spindles of the gyroscopes to act as both governors and the righting mechanism.

The main frame supporting the gyroscopes was also no longer pivoted about a horizontal axis along the centre line of the vehicle. Instead, this frame was fixed to the vehicle and thus the forces needed to right the vehicle and any rotational movement of the vehicle from the upright position was directly imparted from/to the gyroscopes by this main frame. The two gyroscope cages could still rotate about vertical axes but were linked together by segments of gear teeth meshing with a double sided rack connected to pneumatic pistons.

To control the balance mechanism Brennan used an inverted pendulum positioned along the centre line of the vehicle. This was connected pneumatically to the system and the result was similar to the operation in the ⅛th scale model. Assume the vehicle is upright and all aspects in the neutral position with the gyroscope armatures in line across the vehicle. The vehicle is then displaced from the vertical by, say, an off centre load being added. The couple acting on the gyroscopes directly through the main frame, due to its displacement from the vertical, will cause them to precess, that is rotate about the vertical. The pendulum will, however, try to stay upright and the effect of the change in position of the vehicle will be to open a valve causing the pistons to push on the rack accelerating the precession of the gyroscopes. This in turn generates precession, but this couple will be in the direction needed to restore the vehicle to the upright position at which point the valve operated by the pendulum closes. The inevitable overshoot due to angular momentum of the vehicle as it rights itself

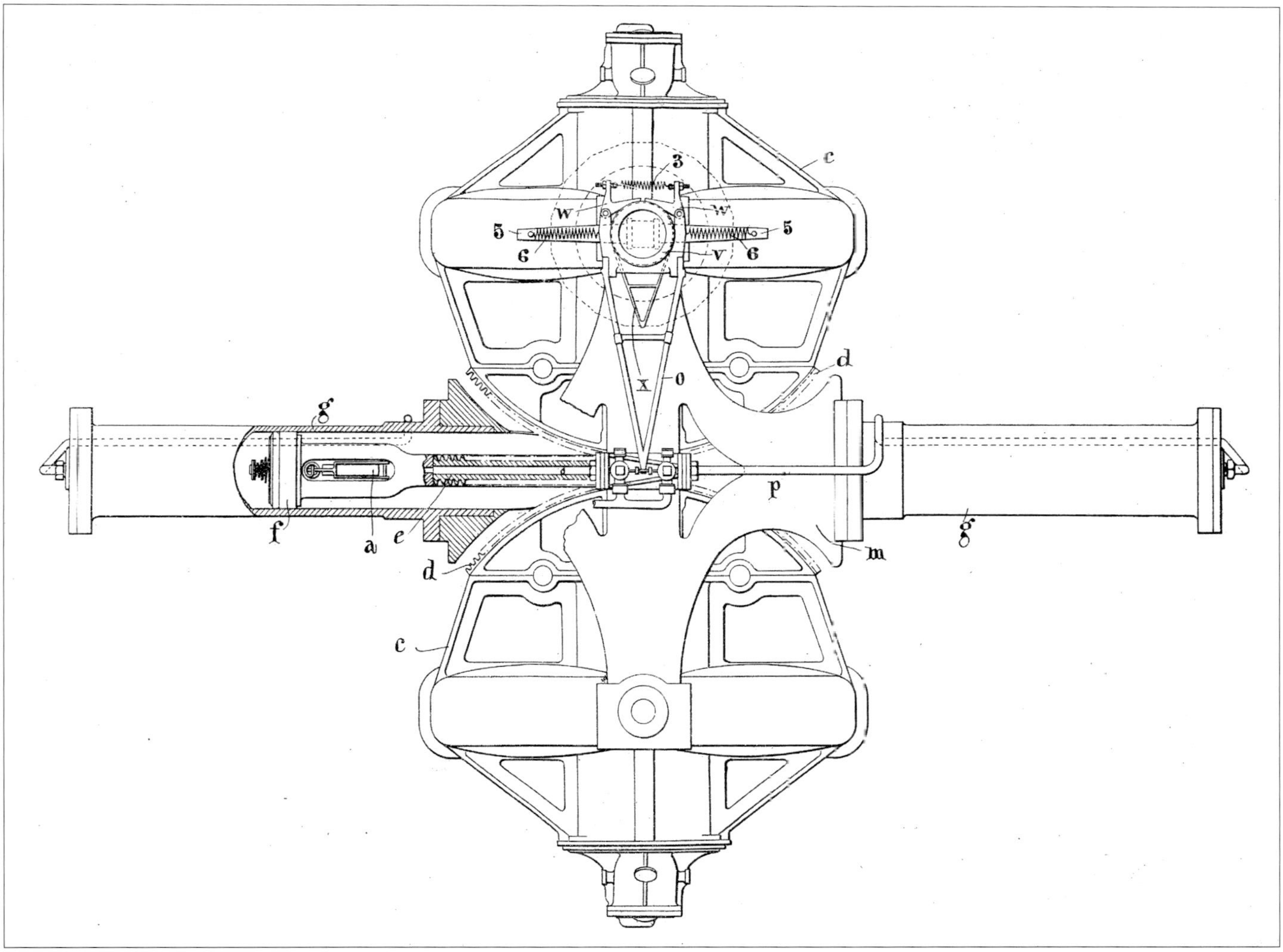

The two gyroscopes seen from above (Patent No. 26,034, 1909). The toothed sectors on the cage casing are marked 'd' and these mesh with the double sided rack marked 'e' so that the cages' rotation was linked. The rack was connected, however, to pistons running in the cylinders marked 'g'. The control mechanism allowed air to flow under pressure into these cylinders generating a force on the piston which in turn added a force onto the rack and thus accelerated the precession.

These drawings from Patent No. 29,579, 1909, show the operation of the two power bogies. The drawings are reproduced with the 3ft 0in. diameter wheels scaled to 1½in. (½in. : 1ft) On the drawing the wheel centres are then correctly spaced at 5ft 4in. as on the prototype implying that these patent drawings were very near to the general arrangement drawings of the prototype. Only a few details differ from those seen in photographs. Unlike the model, in this patent Brennan reverted to a mechanical linkage to the brake shoes.

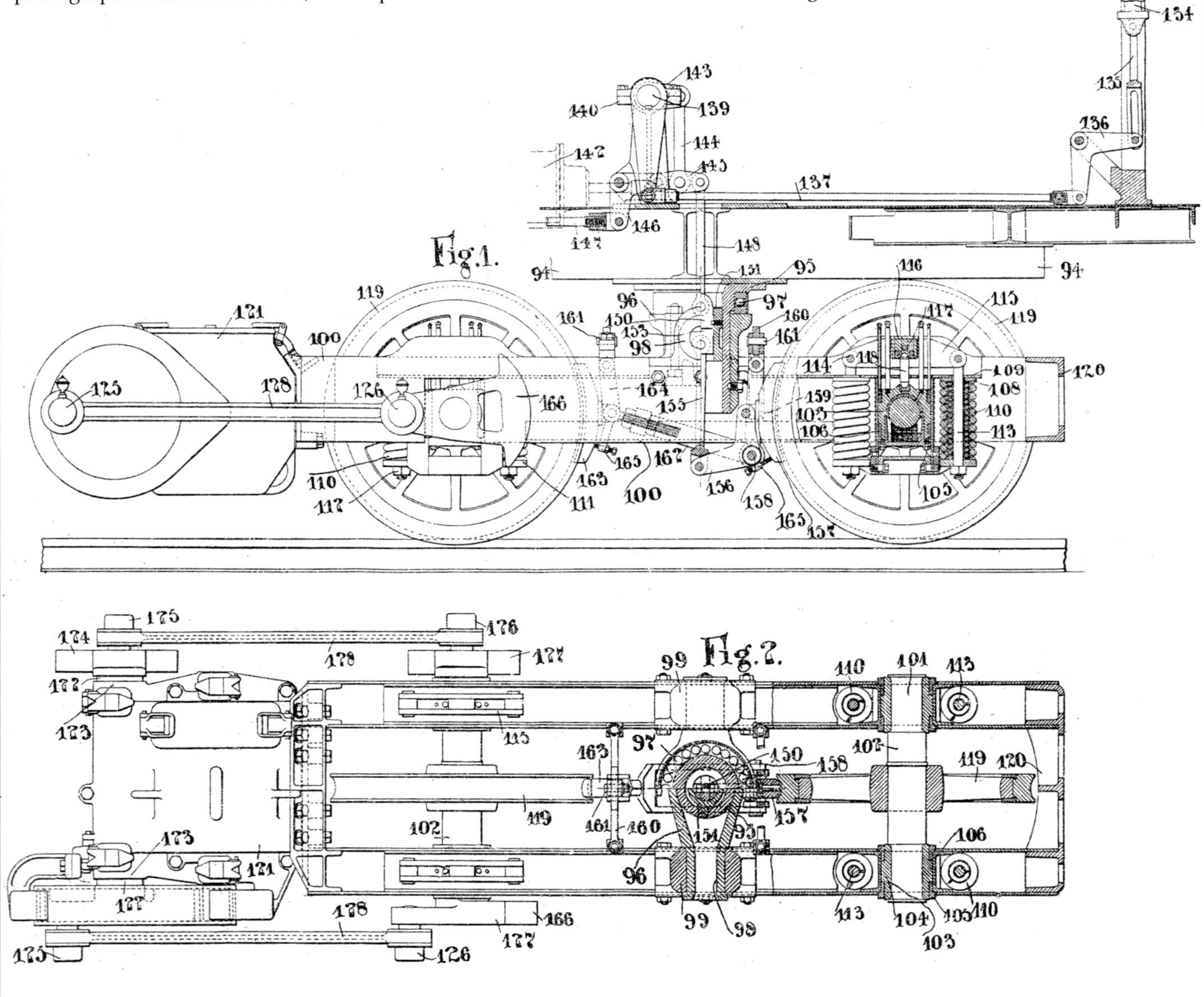

causes the gyroscope to precess but this time back to the neutral position. Once back to this position, any further displacement allows the pendulum to reopen the valves and the process is repeated.

The use of a pendulum to control the mechanism had a further advantage. When stationary it was generally desirable for the vehicle to remain upright. On curves taken at speed, however, it was desirable for the vehicle to lean into the curve to counterbalance the centrifugal force on the occupants and load. The pendulum automatically acted this way and could, of course, be overridden by hand control.

For a mathematical analysis the reader is referred to the analysis by H. Cousins, M.Sc., A.M.Inst.C.E. published in *Engineering*[28], the doctorate thesis by J. F. S. Ross[29] and the work by James B. Scarborough, Professor Emeritus of Mathematics, U.S. Naval Academy Annapolis, Maryland[30].

References

1 For details of these railways see *Monorails of the 19th Century*, 2011, by Adrian S. Garner.

2 *Metropolitan Magazine* Vol. 26, August 1907, pp611-617 and *Louis Brennan: Inventor Extraordinaire* 1980, by Norman Tomlinson.

3 *Royal Engineers Journal* Vol. 5, June 1907, pp340-347.

4 *Model Engineer and Electrician* Vol. 16, 23 May 1907, pp483-485.

5 *Louis Brennan CB: Gyroscopic Monorail*, 1973, by Robert E. Wilkes, Local History Series No. 5 Part 2, Gillingham Public Libraries.

6 UK Monorail Patents:

Patent No.	Date of Application	Date of Grant
7177	24 March 1902	26 February 1903
27212	11 December 1903	11 March 1905

Patent No.	Date of Application	Date of Grant
26034	10 November 1909	10 January 1911
29391	15 December 1909	
Combined and accepted with No. 26034		
29579	17 December 1909	19 December 1910
30417	29 December 1909	29 September 1910

Note: Patent No. 26034 expired on 10 November 1913 due to the non-payment of the prescribed renewal fee. According to the *London Gazette*, 22 January 1915, p724, Brennan applied for its extension, which was granted.

US Monorail Patents

Patent No.	Date of Application	Date of Grant
721499	16 May 1902	24 February 1903
796893	3 December 1904	8 August 1905
1019942	9 June 1910	12 March 1912
1183530	4 January 1910	16 May 1916

Patents also granted in Austria, Canada, Denmark, Finland, France and Switzerland.

7 *Engineering* Vol. 83, 10 May 1907 pp621-623.

8 *Scientific American* Vol. 96, 18 May 1907, p406. (see also 1 June 1907 pp449-450)

9 *Engineering News* Vol. 57, 30 May 1907, pp598-9.

10 *Engineer* Vol. 103, 10 May 1907, pp480-1.

11 *New York Times* 10 May 1907, p3 & 12 May 1907 pC3.

12 *Railroad Gazette* Vol. 43, 19 July 1907, p66. See also *Railway and Locomotive Engineering* Vol. 20, August 1907, pp360-1.

13 *Railway News* 13 November 1909, p855.

14 *Engineer* Vol. 108, 12 November 1909, p510. See also *Engineering* Vol. 88, 12 November 1909, p659, *The Times* 11 November 1909, p8, *Electrical World* Vol.54, 18 November 1909 p1223, *Illustrated London News* Vol. 135, 20 November 1909, pp708 & 719, *Railway Magazine* Vol.25, December 1909, p504.

15 *Scientific American* Vol. 101, 27 November 1909, p389 & Vol. 102, 1 January 1910, p9.

16 *Daily Mail* 20 December 1909.

17 *Scientific American* Vol. 102, 22 January 1910, p82,

18 *Railway Times* Vol. 97, 26 February 1910, p228, *Engineering* Vol. 89, 4 March 1910, p289, *The Times*, 26 February 1910, p6. This event was widely reported in many other journals.

19 *The Times Engineering Supplement* 16 March 1910, p15, 30 March 1910, p15, 6 April 1910, p15.

20 *Electrical World* Vol. 55, 19 May 1910, p1255 & *Scientific American Supplement* Vol. 69, 18 June 1910, p391.

21 *The Times*, 26 May 1910, p12 & 28 May 1910, p1.

22 *The Times* 5 November 1910, p9 & *New York Times* 13 November 1910, pC2.

23 *Journal of the Franklin Institute* Vol. 169, June 1910, pp469-485. Paper subsequently published in *Scientific American Supplement* Vol. 72, 18 November 1911, p334-336.

24 *The Times* 21 January 1932, p14 & 26 January 1932, pp14-15, *Engineer* Vol.153, 22 January 1932, p87 & 29 January 1932, p135.

25 *Engineering* Vol. 83, 7 June 1907, p749.

26 *Engineering* Vol. 83, 14 June 1907 pp776 & 794.

27 *Nature* Vol. 77, 12 March 1908, pp447-450.

28 *Engineering* Vol. 96, 21 November 1913, pp678-681, 28 November 1913, pp711-712 & 12 December 1913, pp781-784.

29 *The Gyroscopic Stabilization of Land Vehicles* by J. F. S. Ross, 1933. Thesis approved for the degree of Doctor of Philosophy in the University of London.

30 *The Gyroscope, theory and applications* by James B. Scarborough, 1958.

The demonstration of the Scherl gyroscopic vehicle in the hall of the Zoological Gardens in Berlin. The meaning of G. W. IV. painted on the front is not known. One of the four single wheel supports mounted to the girder frame has been lowered for safety in this picture.
The Graphic *20 November 1909*

CHAPTER 2
GYROSCOPIC MONORAIL COMPETITORS

Louis Brennan was not alone in developing gyroscopic monorails. The development of the electric motor allowed many to experiment with gyroscopes and they generated a variety of ideas for both civilian and military use. The stabilization of ships and, in particular, guns on board ships was a major line of development.

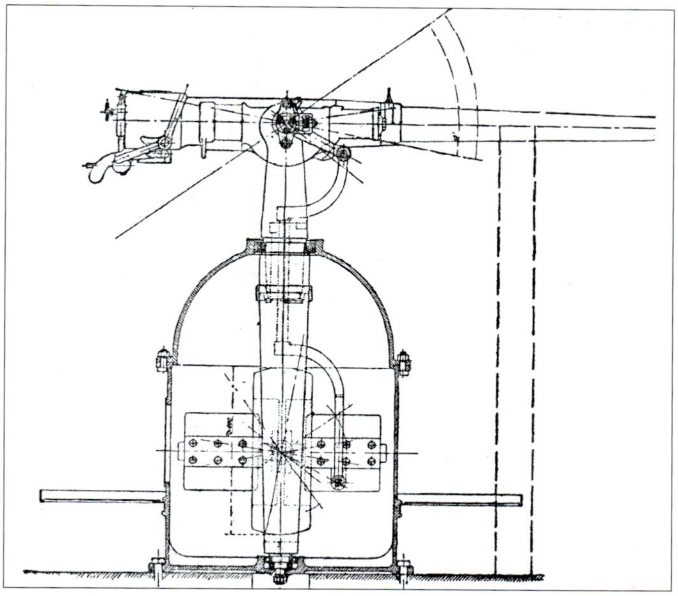

This simple diagram shows the basic method of stabilizing a gun on board a ship to mitigate the effect of roll. A key task of designers during the early twentieth century was to ensure that the firing and recoil had minimal effect. This usually led to the gun barrel being in line with the spindle axis of the gyroscope.
The Gyroscope: Its practical construction and application
by P. P. Schilovsky, 1924

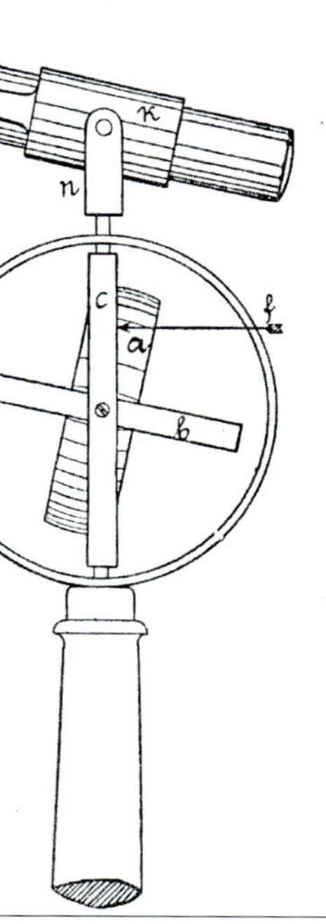

A detailed drawing of a 47mm gyroscopic Hotchkiss gun.
The Gyroscope: Its practical construction and application
by P. P. Schilovsky, 1924

Their use in ground transportation was also being developed in both Germany and Russia in parallel with the work by Brennan.

THE SCHERL MONORAIL

As mentioned in Chapter 1, Brennan seems to have been unaware of the rate of developments in Germany until the announcement that August Scherl was to demonstrate the monorail he had financed on the 10th November 1909 in the Berlin Zoological Gardens.

This is surprising as applications for patents for this system had been filed with the UK Patent Office in May 1908 and these referenced patents granted in Germany in 1907[1]. Whilst the early patents were taken out in August Scherl's name, they were not his work, he was the financier. Indeed Scherl was a wealthy newspaper magnate who supported many projects in the arts and elsewhere. Born on the 24th July 1849, August Hugo Friedrich Scherl had founded a publishing company when he was thirty four. By the early 1900s his companies' weekly and daily publications had a circulation in Germany which was larger than any of his rivals.

To design the monorail, Scherl financed Paul Frölich to work out the theory and data for the design and Emil Falcke to design and construct the monorail vehicle[2].

It is possible that the original idea for this system of monorail may have been from August Scherl's son Richard. Later patents were taken out in his son's name in the UK and in Falcke's name in the US.

Unlike Brennan, the designers decided not to make a small model followed by a full size prototype but instead to make an intermediate sized vehicle sufficient to carry six people, including the driver.

The demonstration in Berlin went well with sixty thousand people seeing the demonstration over a period of five days. To promote his system, Scherl published a leaflet and also a large book propounding the superiority of the system and how it could revolutionize the railway system in Germany and other countries. Like nearly all monorail supporters before, and indeed since, his claims went far beyond the capabilities of the system.

With an eye to commercial development of the system Scherl then shipped the vehicle and track to New York. On arrival in the USA the promotion of the monorail was overseen by Hart O. Berg, an American promoter who had launched the Wright brothers' flying machine interests in Europe on a business basis[3]. Scherl was undoubtedly using a business connection he had made with Berg when he had visited Germany. The demonstration in New York was to be followed by exhibitions of the vehicle in Philadelphia, Boston, Chicago and St. Louis.

In New York, the monorail was assembled for display on an elliptical track at the Claremont Skating Rink, Brooklyn[4]. A private viewing was arranged for Monday the 10th January 1910 followed by demonstrations on the Wednesday and Thursday for local charities. The *New York Times* stated that some of the monies raised would

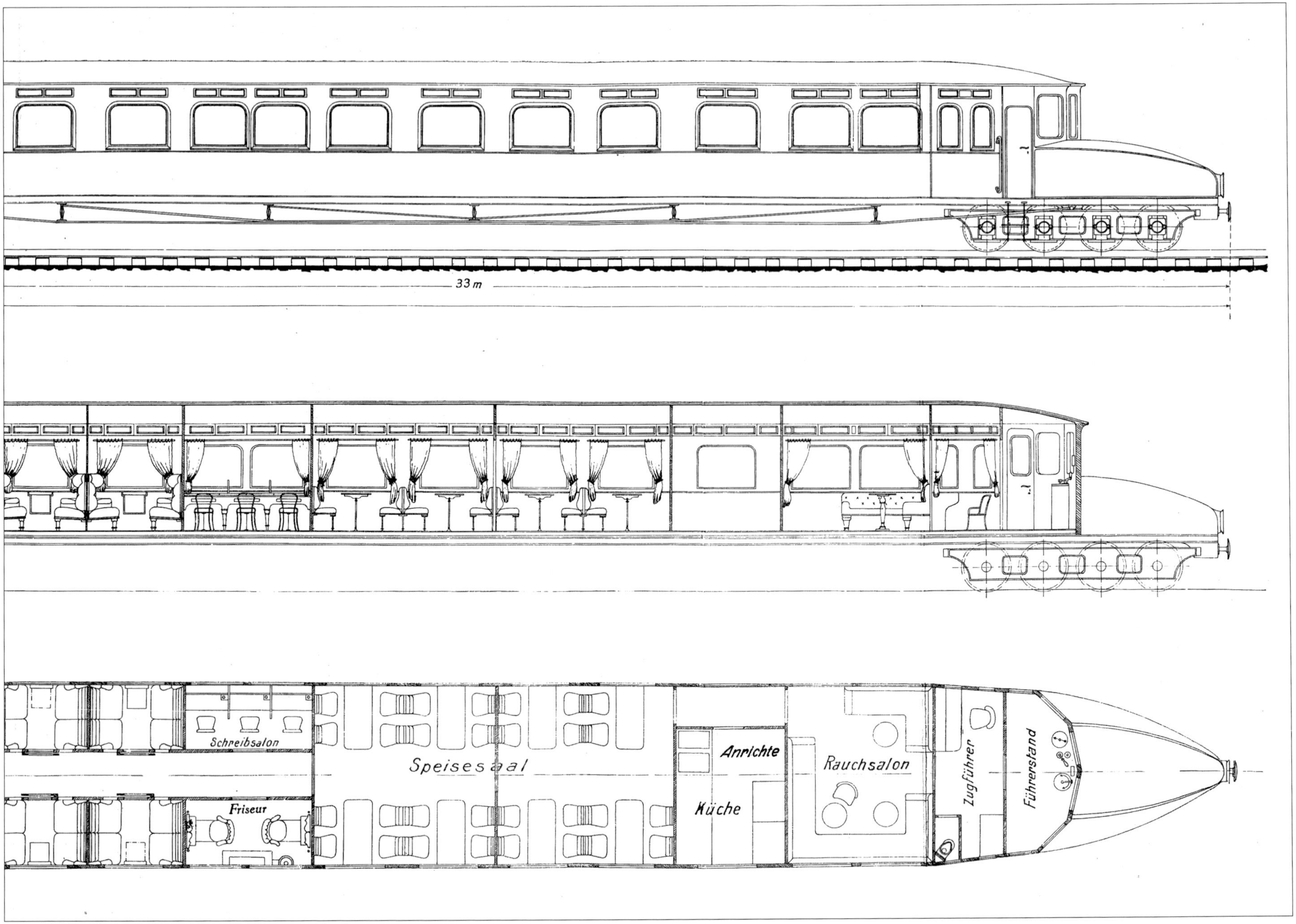

Scherl's book contained large fold out drawings of the planned express trains but there seemed to be little space to accommodate the needed gyroscopes.
Ein Neues Schnellbahnsystem, Vorschläge zur Verbesserung des Personen-verkehrs

In line with the ideas of monorail promoters both before Scherl and since, Scherl believed his monorail trains would be both fast and luxuriously fitted. Ein Neues Schnellbahnsystem, Vorschläge zur Verbesserung des Personen-verkehrs

Luggage and goods being offloaded from an express.

Ein Neues Schnellbahnsystem, Vorschläge zur Verbesserung des Personen-verkehrs

"be devoted to the benefit of the striking shirtwaist girls" (a large group of immigrant clothes workers who were striking for better conditions).

The demonstration got wide press coverage and by the 27th January 1910 it was reported that Scherl and his associates were being further assisted by Charles Ranlett Flint of 25 Broad Street, New York[5]. Flint had also been involved with the sale of Wright brothers' aeroplanes which is probably how he knew Berg. Flint had made his fortune merging several companies to form U.S. Rubber and subsequently was the founder, by the merger of smaller companies, of the Computing Tabulating Recording Company which was eventually renamed IBM.

Despite this strong commercial backing and publicity the Scherl monorail failed to appeal to any railroad and none took up the system. Both Berg and Flint moved on to their other interests but the financial commitment by Scherl to this unsuccessful venture, as well as his support of the arts, severely diminished his fortune and forced him to sell his interests in the publishing empire he had built up in Germany. He died on 17th April 1921[6].

Technical description of the Scherl monorail

Like Brennan's vehicle, the Scherl monorail used two gyroscopes rotating in opposite directions. The spindles of the gyroscopes, however, were vertical when in the neutral position and were mounted in tandem rather than transversally across the vehicle. The cages could rotate about the horizontal being pivoted to the girder frame of the vehicle. These cages were linked by a system of levers and toothed quadrants so that as one tilted forwards the other tilted backwards and vice versa.

At the demonstration in Brooklyn, New York, three men stand on one side of the vehicle to show its stability. An effect not corrected in these early gyroscopic monorail experiments was the tendency of the vehicle to rise on the side to which the weight is added. The 'landscape' was probably painted on the walls of the ice rink.

Scientific American *Vol. 102, 22 January 1910*

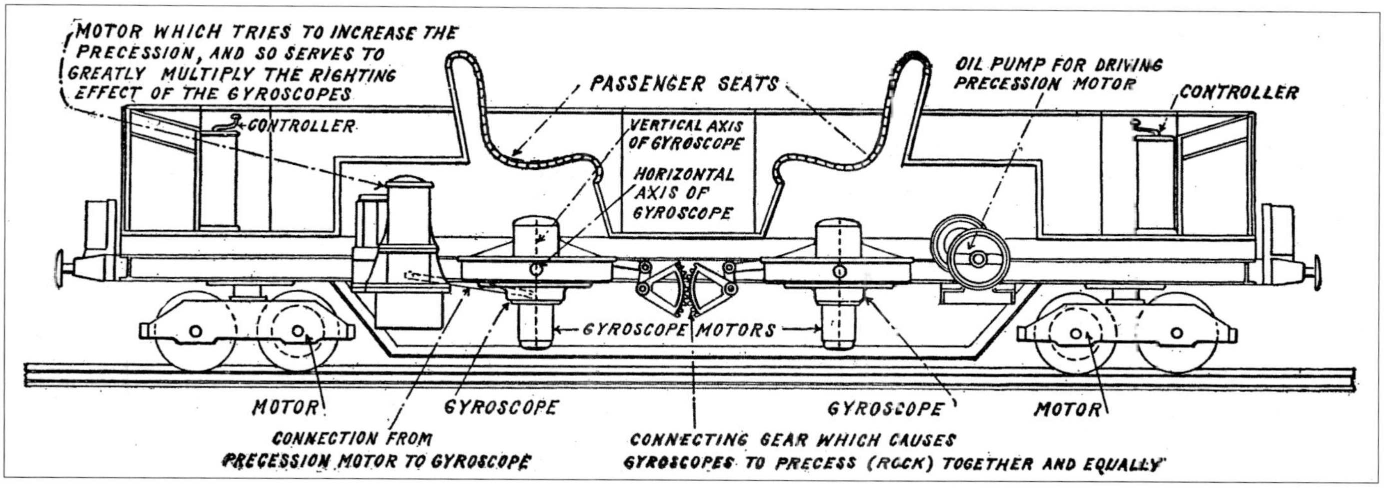

A diagrammatic view of the Scherl monorail vehicle showing the position of the gyroscopes and an outline of the linkage. Scientific American *Vol. 102, 22 January 1910*

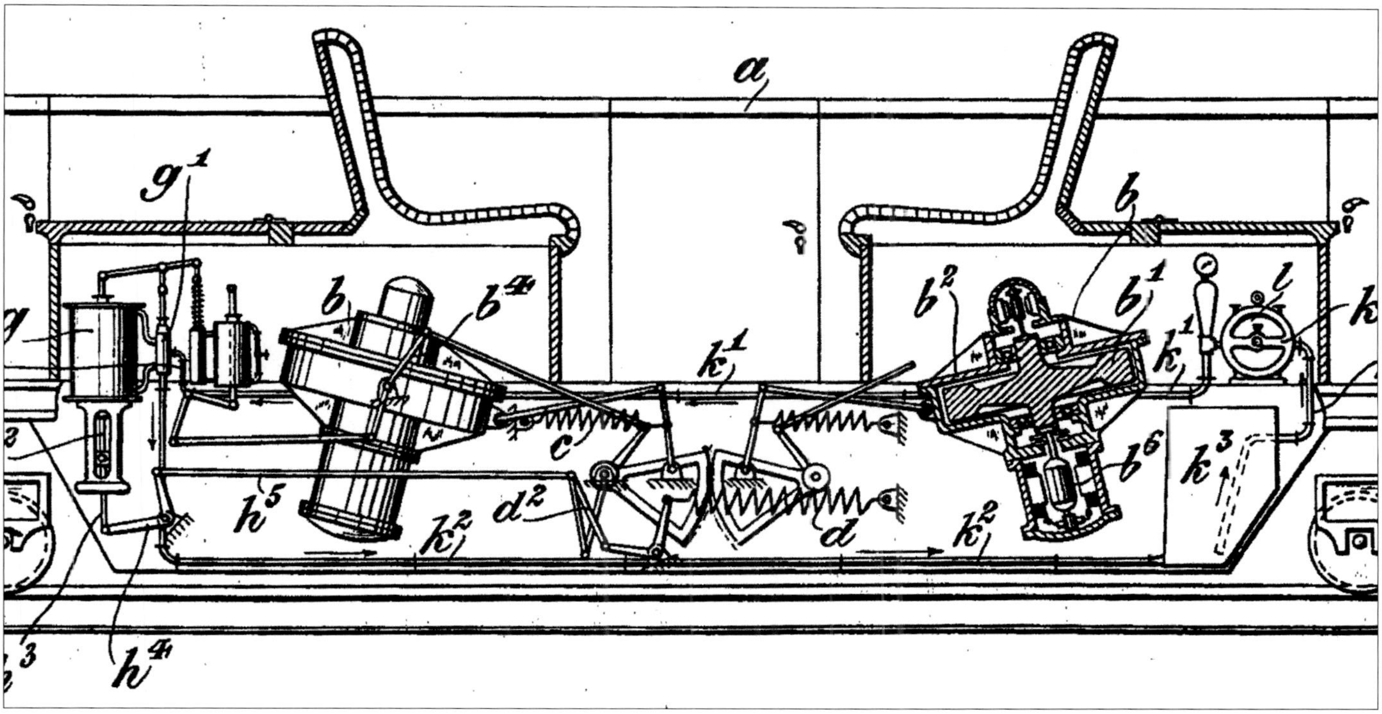

The mechanical connections within the Scherl vehicle were shown in this extract from Falcke's patent taken out in the USA in 1912. The risk of failure with this labyrinth of levers and springs must have been high. The hydraulic and electric systems were similarly complex.

In this configuration, if the vehicle began to lean over, the precession generated by the side force or couple caused the gyroscope cages to move away from the vertical. As in the Brennan monorail vehicles, a mechanism within the vehicle accelerated this precession (put simply, the movement from the vertical was given an extra push) which generated the forces needed to right the car. The 'accelerating' mechanism was hydraulically driven using an electric pump to generate the fluid pressure.

The body of the vehicle was a simple construction based on a girder frame and measured 18ft. long by 4ft. wide by 3ft 6in. high. The total weight was about 5,500lbs[7]. According to the *Railway Age Gazette*, the gyroscope wheels each weighed 110lbs but *Scientific American*[2] and *Engineering News*[5] reported them to weigh 125lbs each. The gyroscope wheels were about 18in. in diameter and ran at 8,000rpm in partial vacuums within their individual steel housings. They were driven by 115 volt d.c. shunt wound motors each generating a little less than ½hp. The mass of the gyroscope wheels was considerably less than that adopted by Brennan and hence Scherl needed to operate them at considerably higher rates of rotation. At these rates of rotation the bearings and balance of the wheels would have been critical factors in manufacture. The gyroscope wheels took about an hour to come to rest once power was removed.

The car balanced on two bogies. These had truck pin centres of 15ft and each had two double flanged 12in.

Few photographs of Scherl's vehicle were published. A little more detail of the controls is visible in this picture taken at the ice rink in Brooklyn. Scientific American *Vol. 102, 22 January 1910*

diameter wheels to rest on the 20lb rail. The bogies were driven by two 2 horse power 115 volt d.c. series wound motors according to *Railway Age Gazette* but *Scientific American* states they were only ¾ horse power each. Inside hung brakes were provided on each bogie.

Unlike Brennan's vehicle, Scherl's needed an external supply of electricity. This was supplied through two feed wires running along the sleepers a few inches below and either side of the top of the rail. The current collectors were suspended near the rear wheel of the rear bogie.

For safety, there were four emergency balance rods each carrying a small wheel or roller that could be lowered to the ground.

During the demonstrations the vehicle ran at about four miles an hour on straight track reducing to about 3½ miles an hour on curves. The reporter in the *Railway Age Gazette* commented on the 21st January 1910 that the vehicle inclined towards the centre on meeting a curve whilst the previous week on the 15th January they reported a slight swaying motion when the vehicle was standing. These, however were not the cause of its lack of appeal to the main railway companies. The system was just not economically viable[2].

THE SCHILOVSKY MONORAIL

On Wednesday the 4th May 1910 an unusual event occurred in the Westminster Palace Hotel in Victoria Street, London, His Excellency Pierre Schilovsky, the Governor of Kostroma, on the Volga, had hired space to demonstrate a model of his gyroscopic monorail[8].

This monorail was very different from those designed by Brennan or Scherl. Firstly Schilovsky decided not to use electricity as the power source but instead reverted to steam. This apparently retrograde step might have been to demonstrate that the monorail could be used in undeveloped areas. Secondly, unlike the other gyroscopic monorails, it used only one gyroscope.

Schilovsky commissioned the well-known firm of model makers, Bassett-Lowke & Co. Ltd, High Holborn, London, to make the model under the direction of Mr Henry Greenly[9]. The train consisted of a steam locomotive followed by a stabilising vehicle containing the gyroscope, a wagon, another stabilising vehicle and another carriage.

Bassett-Lowke opted to base the locomotive on a model 3½in. gauge Great Northern type model locomotive which would have been a 4-4-4T if it had run on a conventional

The model monorail train built by Bassett-Lowke & Co. Ltd to Schilovsky's design. It appears that the locomotive was not in steam for this photograph as the tables and track were only of sufficient length for a stationary train and there appear to be tapes tied to the chimney to maintain the locomotive in the upright position. Railway Magazine *Vol. 27, June 1910*

two rail track. It had a 5in. outer, and 3½in. inner, tube boiler with eight water tubes and a large superheater in the firebox[10]. The boiler was fired by a duplex 'G. B.' petrol blowlamp. The driving wheels were 3½in. in diameter and the cylinders were ¾in. diameter by 1¼in. stroke. The valve gear was Greenly-Heywood type with a straight slide-shaft, the driving point being taken from a point in the connecting rod just below the big end.

To run on the monorail the front and rear bogies had been modified to have just two central double flanged wheels. Similarly the driving wheels were just two, being central on their axles. The centre of gravity was high as the boiler appears to have been raised above its normal position to accommodate the central driving wheels. This locomotive provided the driving power to pull the train and also a supply of steam for the stabilising vehicles. It weighed 62lbs.

The Stuart Simplex engine can be seen mounted on the top of the gyroscope casing. Combined with this case it formed the gyroscope cage that could rock fore or aft on the bearings mounted on each side of the chassis frame.
Scientific American *Vol. 104, 28 January 1911*

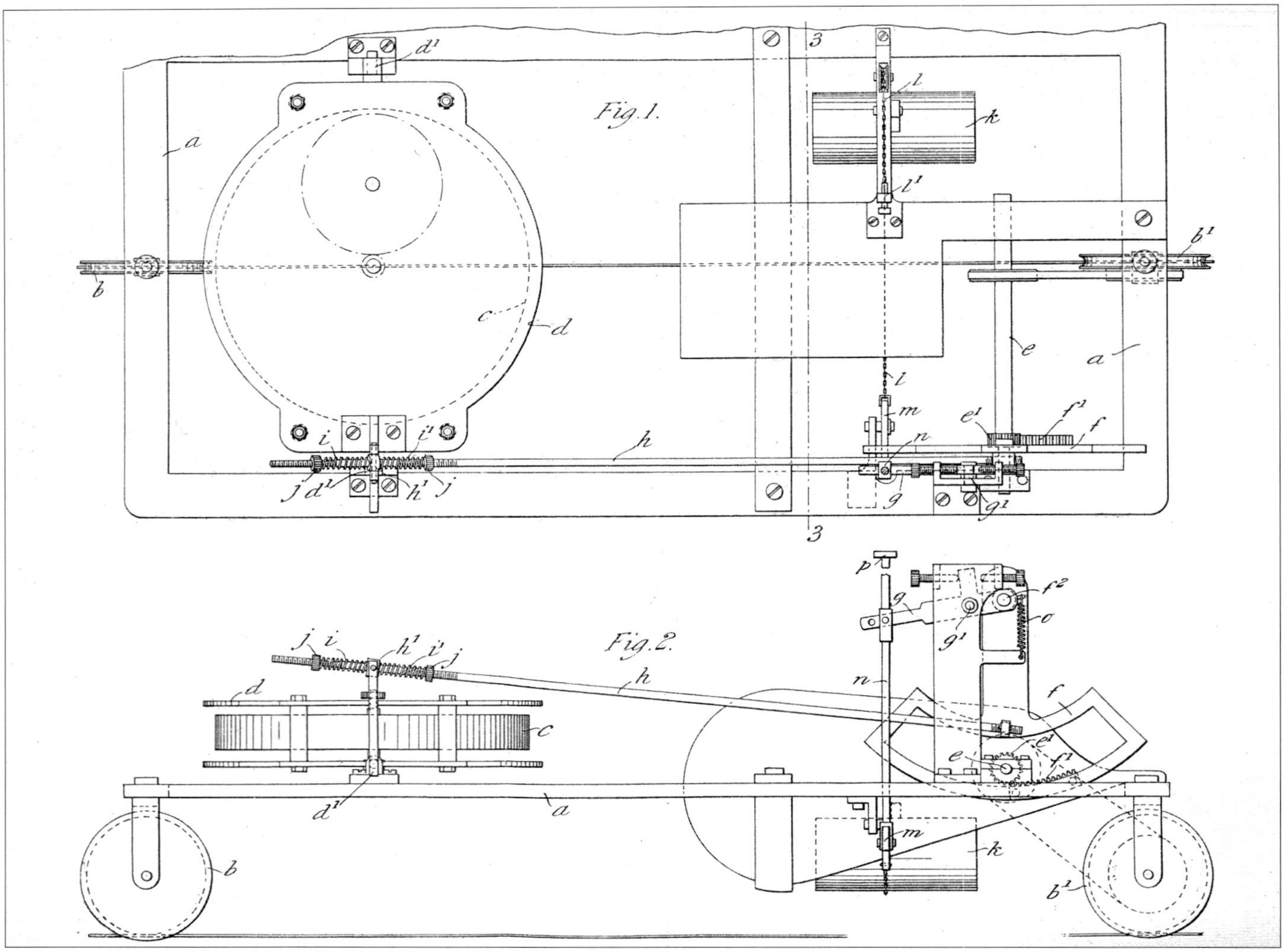

The gyroscope cage 'd' was pivoted about point 'd¹'. Rod h ran through a hole in an arm above the gyroscope cage 'd' with stops and springs either side so that movement of this arm put pressure on the gyroscope cage and thus could accelerate its precession. Movement of the pendulum 'k' caused the rod 'n' to move up or down. This in turn caused crank 'g' to rotate. On the end of crank 'g' was pivoted the sector plate 'f' at point 'f²'. The pulley drive shown as 'b¹' on this drawing was not adopted on the model.

UK Patent No. 12,021, 1909

Engineering[8] states that the steam supply to the stabilising vehicles was provided by a flexible metallic hose to drive the two small steam engines in each vehicle. The first was a Stuart 'Simplex' high speed single cylinder steam engine with a ⅝in. stroke by ⅝in. bore which was directly coupled to the top end of the axle of the gyroscope wheel. The wheel was 8in. in diameter, enclosed in an airtight casing and was reported to weigh 10lbs[9] or 12lbs[10], the latter being probably more reliable. This relatively heavy wheel was necessary as this small steam engine could only reach 1,500rpm, considerably less than the rates of rotation adopted by Brennan or Scherl in their electric powered versions.

In the neutral position with the vehicle level the spindle of the gyroscope was vertical. The gyroscope case together with the small steam engine, however, was carried on trunnions of which the axis was across the car allowing it to rock fore and aft as on the Scherl monorail. Importantly the pivot point was below the centre of gravity of the gyroscope cage so that it was top heavy i.e. it would try to fall fore or aft if the gyroscope was not running.

To one side an arm with a collar was connected to the gyroscope cage. The collar had a hole through which ran a long rod on which stops were mounted. These retained springs between them and the collar. This rod provided the needed acceleration to the gyroscope's precession to cause the vehicle to right itself. At the other end of the rod was the control mechanism. The drawing, opposite top, shows an end on view. To the left was a very heavy weight suspended from above the vehicle frame so that it could swing if the vehicle departed from the vertical. A chain or cable ran around this pendulum so that as the pendulum moved in respect to the vehicle it caused a crank to turn which lifted a connecting rod. This connecting rod operated a crank upon which a large sector plate was pivoted. The effect was to raise or lower this sector plate.

The sector plate had fine gear teeth around an internal periphery which did not engage with a nearby pinion when the vehicle and gyroscope were upright. This pinion was continually rotating at about 60-100 revolutions per minute driven by a ½in. diameter by ⅝in. stroke slide valve single cylinder marine engine through 5 to 1

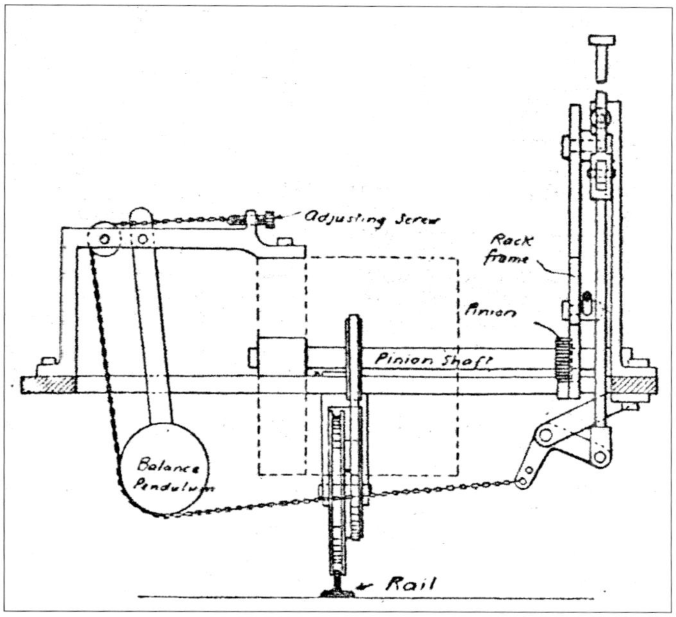

The end view of the pendulum control mechanism.
Model Engineer and Electrician *Vol. 22, 16 June 1910*

gearing. (In the patent, it was envisaged that it would be driven by a pulley from a vehicle wheel.

No attempt was made to balance the weight in the vehicle. Indeed its operation was dependent on the vehicle being heavier on the pendulum side so that it would normally topple in that direction. Both steam engines were mounted that side to ensure the weight bias.

Operation of Schilovsky's first model

Once the locomotive boiler was in steam, both of the small steam engines on each stabilising vehicle would have needed to be started by hand as each had only a single cylinder. With the gyroscopes up to speed, the model would no longer have needed to be held upright.

To understand the operation of the control mechanisms consider just one of the stabilising vehicles. The uneven distribution of weight would cause it to start to topple towards the heavier side, that is the side with the pendulum. As it did so the turning couple would cause the gyroscope to precess and, assuming the steam engine driving the gyroscope was turning clockwise when viewed from above the gyroscope cage, it would tilt aft towards the control mechanism. The pendulum, however, would remain upright as the vehicle toppled and so the connecting cranks described above would raise the sector plate. This would engage it with the rotating pinion and the resulting rotation of the sector plate would pull on the long rod and the springs at the gyroscope cage end would be compressed 'pushing' or accelerating the precession.

This additional precession would result in generating a righting force to the vehicle. Once upright, the pendulum would lower the sector plate, disengaging the pinion and thus the acceleration would cease. If the righting motion overshot, the biased weight of the vehicle would bring it back. In practice, the process was a continual series of shocks as the pinion engaged/ disengaged with the sector plate.

The stabilising vehicles had, of course, to maintain the upright position of the locomotive and rolling stock. Schilovsky therefore patented couplings[11] which were incorporated into the model.

The *Model Engineer & Electrician* reported that during the demonstrations the model worked perfectly which is a tribute to Bassett-Lowke. It is likely that it took some time to set up with the many adjusting screws, notably the stops on the long rod controlling the compression in the springs (these were nuts on a long thread), the limit stop screws on the vertical movement of the sector plate

The engine driving the pinion can be seen with its flywheel in this view of the rear of the vehicle. The flywheel was necessary as the continuous engaging/disengaging with the teeth in the sector plate would otherwise have stopped the single cylinder steam engine. The patented coupling needed to maintain the upright position of the attached carriage is visible to the right of the picture.
Model Engineer and Electrician *Vol. 22, 16 June 1910*

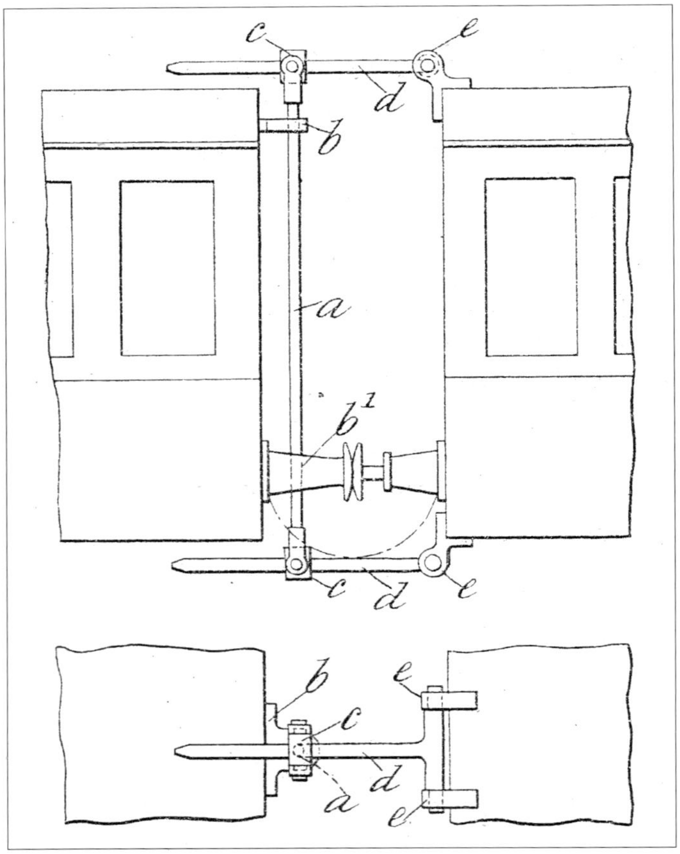

Left: Schilovsky designed a very simple way of connecting his monorail vehicles to ensure they remained in the same plane as the stabilising vehicles. It consisted of two projecting rods mounted on one vehicle which fitted into holes in collars mounted on a vertical rod free to turn on the other vehicle.
UK Patent 29,892, 1911

and the adjusting screw controlling the length of the cable around the pendulum. Further, whilst the system worked, the continuous engaging/disengaging of the pinion would have led to excessive wear if the model had been used for more than demonstrations.

The remaining story

A few days after the initial demonstrations, George Eckford of 199 Piccadilly, London, who was acting as a consulting engineer to Schilovsky, wrote to *Engineering* stating that an electrically driven model was in hand and that work on a larger scale was proceeding in Russia[12]. In January 1911 *Scientific American* reported that Schilovsky was engaged in the construction of a full sized train and track in Russia and that the Russian government had "expressed a desire to see the system in actual operation

Below: Schilovsky's second model was electrically driven and had the stabilising section in the middle of a model carriage. Both the first and second monorail models were gifted by Schilovsky to the Science Museum, South Kensington, London.
Author

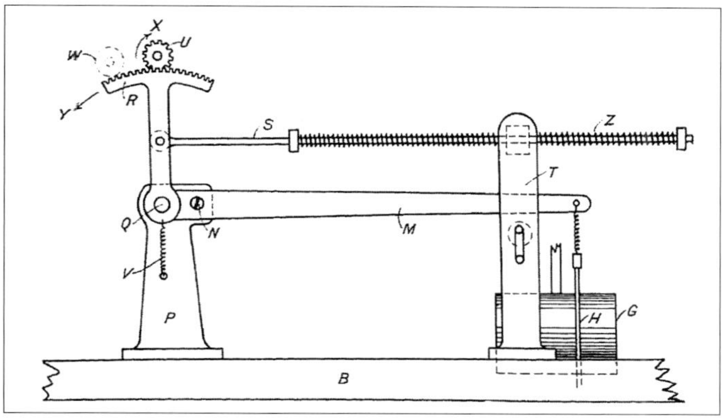

Side elevation of one of the two pendulum and sector plate mechanisms on the second model. As the vehicle toppled, the pendulum 'G' would add tension to the cable 'H' and thus pull on arm 'M'. This was pivoted at point 'N' and thus raised the sector plate 'R' to engage with the pinion 'U'.

Engineer *Vol. 117, 23 January 1914*

under normal conditions, with a view to its adoption as an inexpensive means of transportation in the sparsely populated districts of the empire"[13].

By January 1914 Schilovsky had designed and built an electric version of his stabilising vehicle. This was demonstrated on Monday the 19th January at the Imperial College of Science and Technology in South Kensington, London[14 & 15].

This vehicle used two pendulums, each about 4in. long by 2½in. in diameter, one on each side of the vehicle.

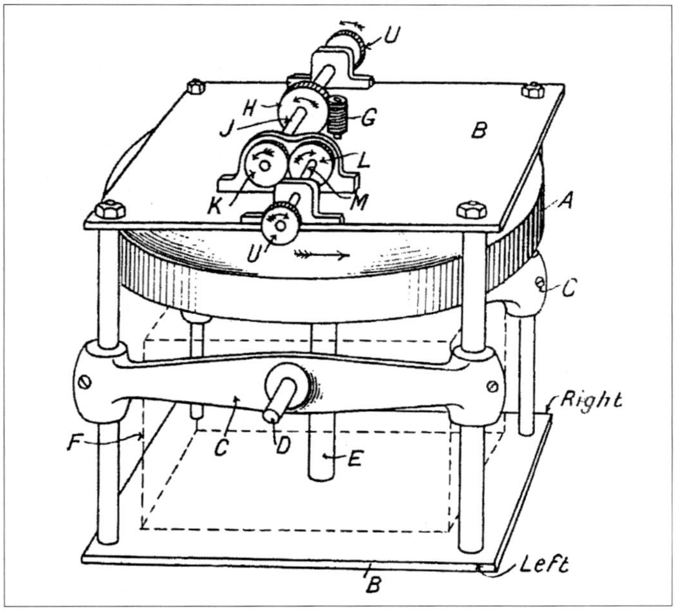

The gyroscope cage on the second model. The electric motor driving the gyroscope wheel was mounted in the dashed area 'F'. Worm wheel 'G' was mounted on an extension of the gyroscope spindle and drove the wheel 'H' continuously. This caused the pinions 'U' to turn continuously, albeit in opposite directions. When the vehicle began to topple, these pinions became engaged with the raised sector plate (either left or right). The resulting rotation of the sector plate acting through spring 'Z' in the illustration above added the needed acceleration to the precession to bring the vehicle back to the upright position.

Engineer *Vol. 117, 23 January 1914*

Each operated a mechanism to raise a sector plate when displaced from the vertical, the one on the left raising a rack when the vehicle lent to the right whilst that on the right only raised its sector plate when the vehicle lent to the left.

Unlike the first model, the second model did not rely on the vehicle being out of balance as there were two sector plate mechanisms to correct for toppling of the vehicle to either the left or right. These engaged with pinions rotating in opposite directions on the top of the gyroscope cage. These revolved continuously, as on the first model, and were driven from an extension of the gyroscope spindle on which was mounted a worm wheel.

Like the first model, observers noted that "In actual running it requires very close watching to discover that the gyroscope is continually precessing in one direction or the other. But it can be seen and at the same time it will be noticed that the racks… …are continually rising, checking the precession, and falling again."[15].

The following week *Engineering* described the vehicle but whilst praising its novelty cast doubts on its commercial success:

"The track which Mr. Schilovsky was using did not, however, admit of experiment either at high speeds or with deep curves. The model, moreover, which bore a picturesque resemblance to a passenger train, was not adapted to be loaded, and the gyroscopic mechanism in use was heavy out of all proportion to the weight of the car by which it was carried…

…Theoretical considerations suggest a doubt as to whether this mechanism would get over the practical difficulties of mono-rail traction."

The gyroscope wheel was later reported to be about 8in. in diameter and about 1¼in. thick and mounted in a vehicle about 3ft. long. One compartment contained the driving motor, a second portion of the length was devoted to the gyroscopic stabilising mechanism and the third represented passenger space.

Schilovsky's enthusiasm for the gyroscope continued, however, and, being from the wealthy aristocracy in Russia, he commissioned the Wolseley Tool and Motor Car Company Ltd., to construct a car to his design[16].

The first demonstration of the car was planned for Friday the 24th April 1914 but failure of a driving chain prevented its appearance. The repair was made by Tuesday the 28th April 1914 when it proceeded around Portman Square and Regents Park at a speed described as 'usually below walking pace'.

The car weighed about three tons and was powered by a petrol engine estimated to develop about twenty horse power. In addition to moving the car, the engine ran a dynamo to drive an electric motor connected to the gyroscope which was running at about 1,200 to 1,500 revolutions per minute. This had ball bearings and was not enclosed in a vacuum or casing. It was stated that the gyroscope took about 1.25 horse power, got up to speed in about thirteen minutes and could balance the car for about twenty minutes after the engine was shut off.

Schilovsky continued to promote his monorail model and another report of a demonstration given in

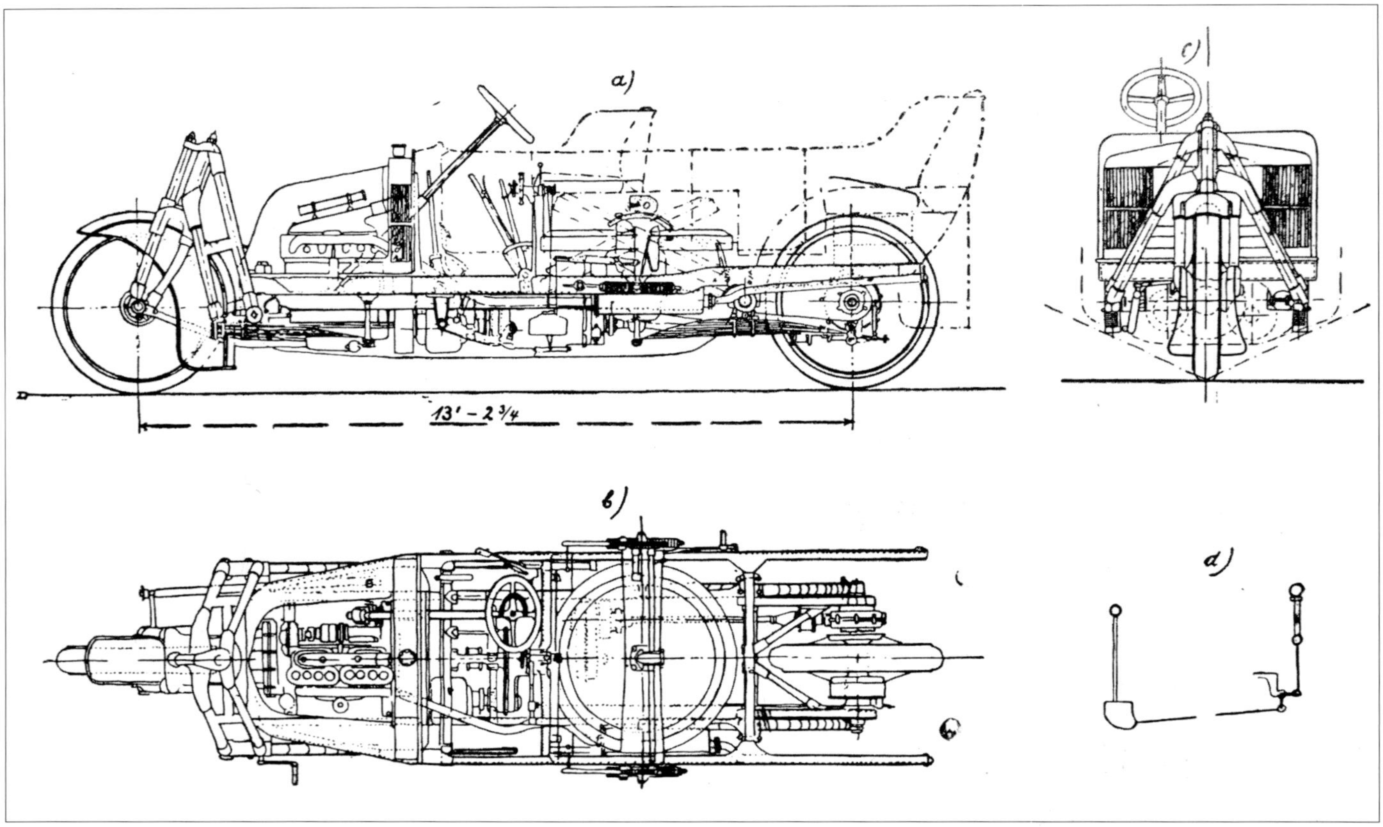

Drawing of the car built by the Wolseley Tool and Motor Car Company Ltd to Schilovsky's design in 1914.
The Gyroscope: its Practical Construction and Application *by P. P. Schilovsky, 1924*

The Schilovsky gyroscopic car. The Gyroscope: its Practical Construction and Application *by P. P. Schilovsky, 1924*

London in May 1914[17] states the he had expanded his demonstrations to include a 5ft long model ship with a gyroscope to prevent rolling and a 3ft wing span model aeroplane with the mechanism built in.

On the 28th June 1914 Archduke Franz Ferdinand of Austria was assassinated and, realising the political situation, Schilovsky rapidly returned to his home in Russia. Before doing so, Schilovsky presented his two models to the Science Museum, South Kensington, London as a gift to the nation[18]. The First World War commenced on the 28th July 1914 which temporarily stopped further promotion or development of Schilovsky's ideas.

Schilovsky must have been politically astute as he survived both the First World War and the revolution that took place in Russia during that period. Being part of the aristocracy he lost his personal fortune in the Bolshevik Revolution managing to save only his Stradivarius violin and some table ware. He was able, however, to take advantage of the shortage of steel rail in Russia to promote his system and by 1919 he was appointed to lead a group of engineers to review building a monorail between the Kremlin in Moscow and Kuncevo, a distance of about 16km. As the line was to be a trial, the cost of earthworks and other civil engineering needed to be minimised and it was therefore subsequently decided that the experimental line would run over the easier terrain from Petrograd (now St. Petersburg) to Gatchina via Tsarskoye. Trains were to consist of two articulated vehicles each seating fifty passengers powered by two engines of about 240 horse power.

By 1922 the finance for this monorail ran out and Schilovsky returned to London. In the same year he addressed the Physical Society[19]. Again promoting his inventions, including the monorail, he claimed that some fifty Russian experts (calling themselves the Gyroscopic Society, Petrograd) had under his chairmanship evolved designs for the construction of a perfectly safe and practicable monorail system for a suburb of Petrograd. Schilovsky reported that some progress had been made in constructing the monorail with about 10km of track having been laid but the scheme had got no further.

No monorail train was built but some ten kilometres of track was laid near Petrograd.
The Gyroscope: its Practical Construction and Application
by P. P. Schilovsky, 1924

Below: One of the designs by the team chaired by Schilovsky for a two car train for the monorail in Petrograd. In this design the gyroscope, mounted in front of the rear bogie of the lead vehicle, would have been enclosed and needed to run at a high rpm to balance the long vehicle. The rear vehicle was also to have a gyroscope and careful synchronisation of their effects would have been required to ensure the conventional coupling between cars did not break.
The Gyroscope: its Practical Construction and Application
by P. P. Schilovsky, 1924

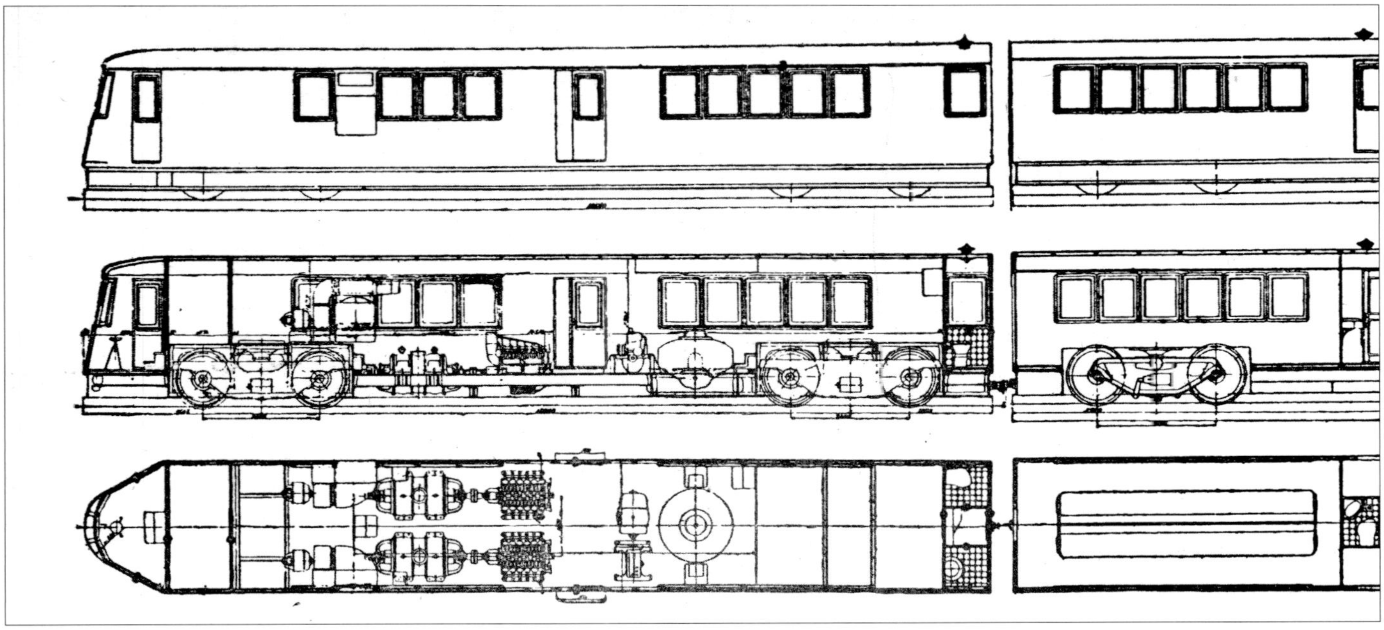

The audience included many eminent scientists and after the demonstration Prof. C. Vernon Boys expressed his pleasure at seeing a Russian scientist alive and well and sent a message to his 'confrères' in Petrograd of goodwill and sympathy.

Many of the designs for the Petrograd monorail were published in 1924 in the book by Schilovsky describing both the theory and multiple uses of the gyroscope[20]. This book was written in conjunction with J. F. S. Ross a physicist who subsequently published an authoritative paper on gyroscopes[21].

Schilovsky remained in the UK but made no further developments of the monorail. The publication of his book led to his employment by Handley Page Ltd, designing turn and bank indicators for aircraft using gyroscope technology. He subsequently worked for Vickers-Armstrong Ltd developing navigational gyroscopes for torpedoes and Sperry gyroscopes to stabilise ships.

On retirement in 1940 at the age of 68 (he was born on the 28th September 1872) he moved to Surbiton to continue his own private research and towards the end of his life lived in Holmer Park, Hereford where he died on the 30th June 1955. He is buried in Holmer Burial Grounds.

AMATEUR AND TOY GYROSCOPIC MONORAIL MODELS

Publicity surrounding the gyroscopic monorails encouraged many amateurs to try to make working models. Many of these were copies of the prototypes seen in journals.

An example was that made by A. L. Franklin who mounted two double flanged wheels on the underside of a wooden board measuring 10in. square. On the top he mounted two gyroscopes of the type sold as toys powered by pulling a string that had previously been tightly wrapped around its spindle. The design was a simplified version of Brennan's second model with the gyroscopes

Whilst the model by Franklin was simple, it operated in exactly the same was as Brennan's electric version.
Model Engineer and Electrician *Vol. 22, 19 May 1910*

The most complex version of the gyroscopic monorail by Johnson resembled that designed by Schilovsky with its single electrically driven gyroscope wheel. The power source was external through the wires seen to the top of this picture. The control mechanism was the same as Brennan's. The 'contact planes' that touched the extended gyroscope spindle were metal strips mounted above the gyroscope cage.
The Gyroscope *by V. E. Johnson, 1915*

linked by a connecting rod, rather than gear teeth, so that they turned in synchronisation. Four wooden blocks at each corner of the board supported arms or what Brennan called contact planes. The spindles of the gyroscopes were extended so that they touched these contact planes to generate the needed acceleration in a similar manner to that in Brennan's model[22]. Franklin reported that he had run the car about 100ft on a rope and around curves in both directions with considerable success. He found that if the gyroscopes were started at nearly equal rates, their rates of diminution were practically equal and enabled curves to be taken without disaster.

Others were more inclined to experiment. In particular V. E. Johnson, MA, contributed a series of articles to the *Model Engineer and Electrician*[23] which subsequently formed the basis of his book *The Gyroscope*[24]. Starting from very simple experiments with a single gyroscope he progressively encouraged the reader to make quite complex working models of monorails.

The toy industry also cashed in on the gyroscope. An unknown maker in the UK made a toy consisting of a gyroscope with a painted cut out of a gymnast on the frame. At the bottom of the frame was a grooved roller to fit the spiral track. One flange of the roller, however, was of slightly larger diameter than the other and this projecting flange touched the shaft of the gyroscope. Owing to the eccentricity of the contact, the shaft drove the roller at a greatly reduced rate of rotation compared to the gyroscope wheel which was started in the usual way of wrapping a string around the shaft and pulling it off quickly. When placed on the track, the gymnast travelled steadily uphill or downhill.

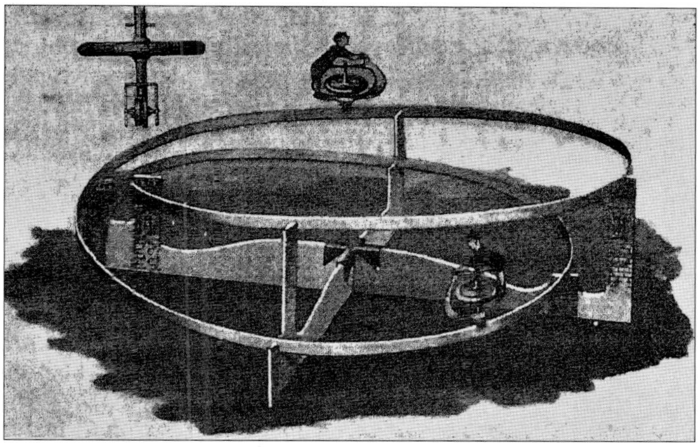

Right: The toy monorail pictured in *Scientific American* Vol. 104, 25 February 1911.

References

1 UK Monorail Patents in the name of August Scherl:

Patent No.	Date of Application	Date of Grant
11129	22 May 1908	27 August 1908
11221	23 May 1908	10 September 1908
13741	29 June 1908	Not accepted

UK Monorail Patents in the name of Richard Scherl:

Patent No.	Date of Application	Date of Grant
21843	15 October 1908	20 May 1909
27590	26 November 1909	9 June 1910
27687	27 November 1909	29 September 1910
27688	27 November 1909	28 November 1910
27838	29 November 1909	29 November 1910
27839	29 November 1909	29 November 1910
27840	29 November 1909	11 August 1910

US Monorail Patents in the name of Richard Scherl:

Patent No.	Date of Application	Date of Grant
897558	21 May 1908	1 September 1908
959077	19 June 1908	24 May 1910

US Monorail Patents in the name of Emil Falcke:

Patent No.	Date of Application	Date of Grant
1048816	26 October 1910	31 December 1912
1048817	26 October 1910	31 December 1912

2 *Scientific American* Vol. 102, 22 January 1910, pp82, 84-85.

3 *New York Times* 5 December 1909, pC4.

4 *New York Times* 9 January 1910, pX14, *Electrical World* Vol. 55, 13 January 1910, p98, *Railway Age Gazette* Vol. 48, 15 January 1910, p104.

5 *Engineering News* Vol. 63, 27 January 1910, pp99, 101.

6 *New York Times* 19 April 1921, p16.

7 *Railway Age Gazette* Vol. 48, 21 January 1910, p138 & *Railway Gazette* Vol. 12, 4 February 1910, p136.

8 *Engineering* Vol. 39, 6 May 1910, p577.

9 *Railway Magazine* Vol. 27, June 1910, p472.

10 *Model Engineer and Electrician* Vol. 22, 16 June 1910, pp563-565.

11 UK Monorail Patents:

Patent No	Date of Application	Date of Grant
12021	21 May 1909	21 June 1910
2503	1 February 1910	1 March 1911
29892	1 February 1910	3 April 1911
940	13 January 1914	13 January 1915
941	13 January 1914	13 January 1915

US Monorail Patents:

Patent No.	Date of Application	Date of Grant
1041680	30 January 1911	15 October 1912
1137234	1 March 1910	27 April 1915

12 *Engineering* Vol. 89, 13 May 1910, p609.

13 *Scientific American* Vol. 104, 28 January 1911, p94.

14 *Engineer* Vol. 117, 23 January 1914, pp106-7.

15 *Engineering* Vol. 97, 23 January 1914, pp127-128.

16 *Engineering* Vol. 97, 1 May 1914, p592, *Scientific American* Vol. 110, 30 May 1914, pp442, 453-454 & *New York Times* 17 May 1914, pX10.

17 *Engineering* Vol. 97, 15 May 1914, p678.

18 *Scientific American Supplement* Vol. 78, 11 July 1914, p28.

19 *Proceedings of the Physical Society* Vol. 35, 1922, pp125-126.

20 *The Gyroscope: its Practical Construction and Application* by P. P. Schilovsky, 1924.

21 *The Gyroscopic Stabilization of Land Vehicles* by J. F. S. Ross, 1933. Thesis approved for the degree of Doctor of Philosophy in the University of London.

22 *Model Engineer and Electrician* Vol. 22, 19 May 1910, p472.

23 *Model Engineer and Electrician*, a series of six articles commencing in Vol. 21, 14 October 1909 with further articles and correspondence in Vol. 22, 1910.

24 *The Gyroscope* by V. E. Johnson, 1915.

A Pelham Park and City Island Railroad carriage. This is probably carriage No. 2 but both carriages were to the same design. *Library of Congress LC-B2-2062-15*

CHAPTER 3
THE TUNIS MONORAILS

"Be it known that I, Howard H. Tunis, a citizen of the United States, residing in Windsor Hills, in the county of Baltimore and State of Maryland, have invented certain new and useful Improvements in Single-Track Railways..." began Patent Number 690,539 filed on the 31st October 1901 and granted on the 7th January 1902. This was to be the first of eight US patents that Tunis would take out for his bicycle monorail system[1].

By 1901 the bicycle monorail was not a new idea. Charles Goulding had proposed such a monorail, in which the carriages run on one rail with balance maintained by an upper rail, to run along Broadway in New York as early as 1854 and many variants had been patented in the UK and Europe based on similar ideas. The "bicycle effect" - that is the train requiring only minimal use of the balance rail when in motion (as on a bicycle!) - had also been demonstrated by Eben Boynton on his experimental lines. The unique features introduced by Tunis related to the upper balancing system.

Baltimore trial

Following the grant of his first patent, Tunis set about constructing a monorail for experimental purposes on a farm in the western suburbs of Baltimore. The line was completed and fully operational by December 1902. It was built in the shape of an ellipse with a circumference of 1,800ft. and included several 2% grades.

The track consisted of a single ground level steel rail weighing 30lb per yard which was spiked to ordinary wooden ties. At regular intervals triangular shaped wooden frames were placed either side of the ground rail which were connected at the top by a wooden beam. Simple cross bracing between these frames prevented them from collapsing like a pack of cards.

The unusual feature of this bicycle railway was that instead of fixing a balancing rail to the frame and mounting balancing wheels on the carriage, Tunis opted to place two balancing rails on the carriage roof and sprung blocks, rubbing against these rails, on the support frame. (The patent showed balancing wheels mounted on the frame. The sprung wooden blocks were probably an economy measure.) This bizarre arrangement, however, would cause the rails to get hooked between the blocks (or balancing wheels) when rounding curved track. Tunis recognised this problem and in his patent he proposed that the roof rails were curved to form a bullet shape when viewed from above. This was incorporated in the Baltimore carriages as two bent strips meeting in the form

The steam carriage or railcar built by Tunis for the trial track outside Baltimore. The wood frames supported greased guide blocks which guided rails mounted on the roof of the railcar. Scientific American *Vol. 87, 6 December 1902*

of a 'V' on the roof. Both the wooden rails and blocks were greased to reduce friction and wear. To ensure stability at least two pairs of spring blocks were always in contact with the roof rails.

Two steam powered carriages were built to run on the line. These were unique in being the only steam powered carriages ever built for a monorail. They had seven compartments, the front compartment containing the engine and boiler. The rear six compartments had bench seats fixed either side of the door which each seated four passengers thus providing room for a total of twenty-four passengers. The carriages weighed three tons empty and about four to five tons when filled with adult passengers.

The carriage had two double flanged wheels. The forward wheel was steam driven using a system similar to that used in the then novel steam powered cars being developed by the Stanley Brothers and others. Steam was raised at high pressure (typically around 500psi in comparable steam powered cars) in a small vertical boiler using kerosene as fuel. The steam was then fed to a cylinder (possibly cylinders) to drive a pair of sprocket wheels. One of these sprockets was connected by a chain to a large heavily constructed sprocket wheel mounted on the wheel axle. The other sprocket was connected to water and air pumps to maintain the supply of water to the boiler and provide braking. The driving wheel axle and possibly the engine crankshaft used ball bearings to reduce friction. The engine generated about 4 horse power, of which ½ horse power was utilised by the pumps leaving 3½ horse power to power the carriage. *Scientific American*[2] reported that speeds of up to 9 miles per hour were attained with no passengers and up to 8 miles per hour with every seat occupied.

By the end of 1902 a company had been formed to build a sixteen mile long railroad on this system in Virginia. Nothing came of this proposal but the experimental line had enabled Howard Hansel Tunis, to give him his full name, to develop his system. Experience with the trial line indicated that reversion to the more conventional approach of mounting the support wheels on the carriage roof, but with (unusually) two rails on the support frame, was more satisfactory. In the Tunis system the support wheels were mounted in a pivoting bogie or truck and for this idea he was granted a patent on the 9th June 1903.

Tunis displayed a small model of his perfected system in Baltimore during late spring 1903 and sufficient interest was generated for another company to be formed to promote the invention. In particular an experimental line was proposed to be built between Washington and Baltimore which it was estimated would be profitable with a fare of five cents for a single journey between these cities. Again nothing came of the proposal[3].

The small vertical boiler and water gauge is visible behind the double flanged wheel. The brake cylinder is on the left and the chain drive on the right.

Scientific American *Vol. 87, 6 December 1902*

Another view of the boiler and the bicycle chain drive of the steam railcar. Scientific American *Vol. 87, 6 December 1902*

Whilst a rather poor picture, this end view shows the blocks on the top of the frame which pressed against the two rails seen on the top of Tunis's Baltimore monorail carriage.
Scientific American *Vol. 87, 6 December 1902*

Jamestown Exposition line

Not daunted, Tunis's next patent, granted in 1905, addressed the problems arising from imperfections in the positioning of the overhead balancing rails. This he solved by arranging that the distance between the balancing wheels in the trucks could expand or contract using a form of scissor action.

By 1907 he was determined to exhibit an electrically powered version and the opportunity arose at the Jamestown Exposition. This was held at Sewell's Point on Hampton Roads near Norfolk, Virginia between the 26th April 1907 and the end of November that year and celebrated the 300th anniversary of the founding of that town. Tunis was granted permission to build a half mile long line on his system and it proved to be a very popular feature for those attending.

At the Exposition the single ground rail was spiked to what appears to have been cut logs used as ties and at regular intervals a longer sawn timber tie was used. To this were secured iron or steel uprights and diagonal supports with bracing. An upper wooden beam connected these frames as on the Baltimore line, but two rails 30in. apart with insulated cross struts, were fixed to these cross beams. These two upper rails were made from angle iron with the horizontal flanges facing inwards which provided not only balance but also electric current for the carriage.

The Tunis monorail at the Jamestown Exposition in 1907. The carriage appears to have been painted in two colours. The lighter shade was probably yellow. Scientific American *Vol. 98, 15 February 1908*

Only one carriage was constructed. The cigar shaped carriage was quoted as being 47ft long and 6ft wide[4] but subsequently quoted as being 50ft long and 6ft 6in. wide[5]. It had two bogies or trucks each with two double flanged wheels. All four wheels were driven and two electric motors were provided for each wheel (making eight motors in total). The reason for so many motors is not clear. On the top of the carriage were two 'X' shaped trucks with wheels running on ball bearings at the four extremities. These balance wheels were double flanged, 1½in. deep. The trucks could rotate in a horizontal plane about the centre of the X. In addition the trucks were mounted on short arms hinged to the carriage roof to allow for vertical displacement of the upper rails in relation to the ground level rail or movement due to flexure of the carriage springs. These arms had a wide base to ensure only vertical movement could occur and to prevent the carriage moving laterally. A coil spring pushed upwards under the truck to offset the weight of the arm and truck[6].

The dismantled motor and axle on the Jamestown carriage, which was designed to allow the motor to removed for maintenance, a key feature of the Tunis design. Scientific American *Vol. 98, 15 February 1908*

Pelham Park and City Island Railroad

Coincident with the Exposition three members of New York's Rapid Transit Commission, who were due to leave office on the 1st July 1907, became interested in the Tunis monorail. These were John H. Starin, the Vice President and members Charles Stewart Smith and Woodbury Langdon. On the 26th June, simultaneously with the announcement of the successful conclusion of the trials of the system at Jamestown, they announced a project to build a Tunis monorail between New Jersey, Newark and New York. The fare was to be five cents from New York to Newark and eight cents from New York to Jersey City and the promoters hoped to use the tunnel under the Hudson being built by William Gibbs McAdoo which was then nearing completion. A construction cost of $75,000 per mile was anticipated which compared well with the cost of the then recent extension of the Subway to the Bronx which had cost $750,000 per mile.

By 1908 the project had obtained financial interest from an influential group. In addition to Starin and Smith, these included:

C. C. Cuyler, of Cuyler, Morgan & Co.
Robert H. McCarter, Attorney General of New Jersey
Samuel McMillan, Congressman
Charles F. Holm, Hudson Trust Company
Henry W. Williams of Baltimore
Bion L. Burrows, former Secretary of the Rapid Transit Commission

Together they formed the Monoroad Construction Company, capitalized at $1.5m, and Bion Burrows was elected President. This company acquired the exclusive rights to adopt the Tunis system in New York, New Jersey and Long Island from the American Monorail Company, which Tunis had used to promote his system. Confident of success, on the 20th October 1908 the company applied to the Public Service Commission for the construction of a monorail line, the Pelham Park and City Island Railroad[7].

In parallel with this application, the company was near to completing arrangements to purchase the so called City Island Line from the Interborough Rapid Transit Company. This consisted of two lines. One was owned by the Pelham Park Railroad Company, which operated a line from Bartow Station on the New York, New Haven and Hartford Railroad in Pelham Park, to Marshall's Corner near the City Island Bridge. The other was owned and operated by the City Island Railroad Company whose line ran from Marshall's Corner across a bridge to City Island and on to Belden's Point at the southern end of the island. Both these companies were controlled by the Interborough Rapid Transit Company but had been kept separate in order that two fares could be charged. They both operated a few antiquated 3ft 6in. gauge horse tram cars which had come in for a lot of humorous adverse comment. The intention was to convert these to an electric monorail described by Bion Burrows as "comparatively noiseless and capable of an express speed of 80 to 100 miles an hour." The company also had the intention that this would form part of the Newark, New Jersey and New York proposals announced earlier.

The application was considered and granted at the meeting of the Public Service Commission on the 17th November 1908 but not without a political fight.

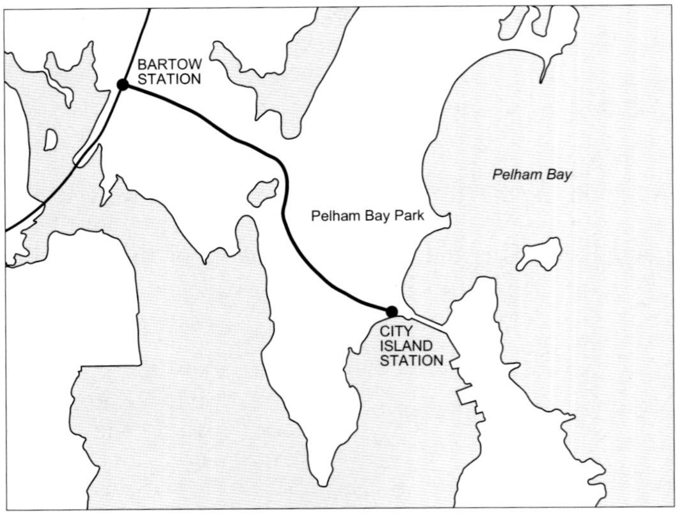

Map of the Pelham Park and City Island Railroad.

A favourable report on the Jamestown line had been prepared by Chief Engineer Rice but this had only been seen by some Commissioners. Commissioner Maltbie refused to vote because he had not seen the report whilst Commissioner Eustis became indignant that Maltbie doubted his word in describing the report[8].

By January 1909 the Monoroad Construction Company was ready to commence building subject to finalising the finance and the granting of the necessary permits from the Bronx Borough President, the Park Commissioner of the Bronx and the Commissioners of the Water Supply, Gas and Electricity. These matters were expected to be resolved shortly, after which construction would commence within a week to ten days. A construction time of three months was envisaged by Bion Burrows[9]. Administrative delays combined with delays in raising finance, however, prevented progress and by September 1909 little had happened except a further announcement that construction would commence in the autumn[10].

Still no progress was made and there was a real risk that construction would not be completed and passengers carried by the 4th July 1910, the deadline provided under the franchise granted to the company. Eventually the financing was resolved by investment into the project by August Belmont, a wealthy and well known financier, who also had a financial interest in the Interborough Rapid Transit Company. To meet the deadline, the construction had to be carried out hastily over just two months. The short monorail line joining Bartow Station to City Island Bridge was finally completed by early July 1910. A ten day extension to the franchise deadline was granted by the City authorities and on Wednesday the 6th July 1910 August Belmont visited the line. Two days later, under the headline "Monorail Car fails in its first test", the *New York Times* reported that Bion Burrows denied that August Belmont had been disappointed when the carriage had failed to make the expected trip from City

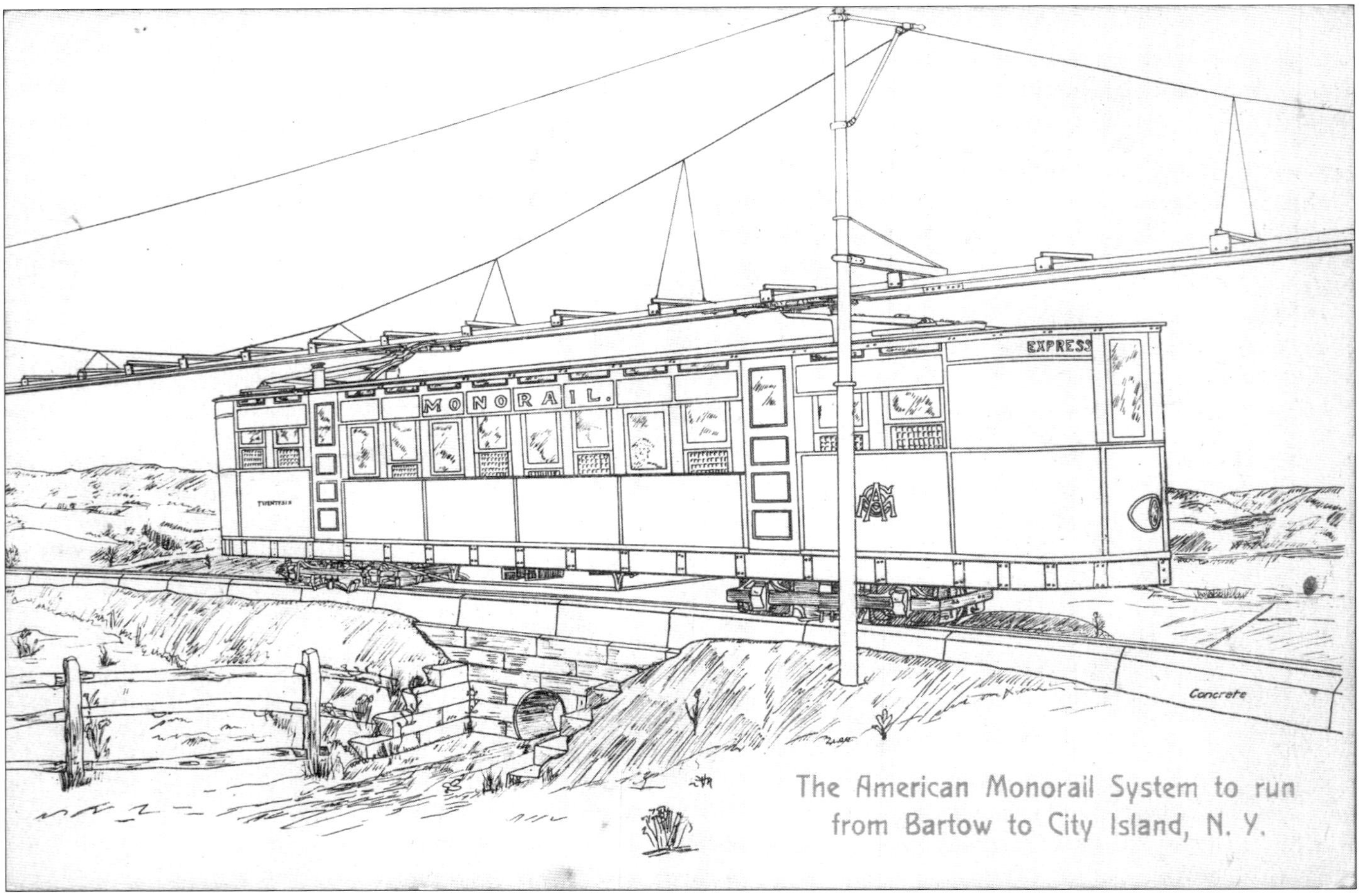

This artist's illustration was published as a post card and also reproduced in the *Electric Railway Journal* 9th January 1909. The suspended upper rails would have provided minimal support for the vehicle and it seems likely the artist based the illustration on the overhead wire systems of street tramways rather than the Tunis design. *Author's collection*

Island Bridge to Bartow Station. Mr Belmont, he said, had just come to look over the system and had known all along that the carriage would not start.

The *New York Times* went on to state that Belmont's party had been required to use the City Island Horse cars, some of which were more than fifty years old, to reach the far end of the line. Bion Burrows, interviewed by the paper at the temporary generating station for the line on the Thursday, said it would be another three days before the line could operate and the cause of the delay was the incorrect position of the motors in the carriage. On that same Thursday afternoon the reporter observed[11]:

> "…the engines in the power house were going full blast and there was every indication, again, that a start was to be made. The electricians were busy under the car with the mechanism and about 4 pm they crawled out and one of them ran to the power house. Then another electrician went through the car and made a dozen little boys and girls who had been sitting inside get out. Then the electricians closed the doors, and a moment later one of them turned the controller of the motor, but the car did not move so much as an inch."

"All this was to be expected," said one of the electricians. "You must remember that it takes time to get the motors in proper shape. It may be a day or it may be three before we are ready, and then we will make several experimental trips before taking any passengers. This identical car ran five months at the Jamestown Exposition, and there is absolutely nothing the matter with it. As soon as we have the motors properly swung we will notify the newspapers…".

The first carriage for the Pelham Park and City Island Monorail was therefore the one used at Jamestown. The electrician went on to say that a further carriage was expected for delivery in a few weeks.

Opening catastrophe

As soon as the teething problems were resolved the company began running the carriage with a few local passengers. This met the requirements of the deadline of the franchise and the line was ceremonially opened on Saturday the 16th July 1910. The carriage, with Tunis at the controls, met the train arriving at 2.16 pm from New York at Bartow Station. The doors of the monorail carriage were opened and passengers poured in to the carriage which they saw as a novelty. Tunis shouted to Supt. A. Fred Atkins, who was acting as conductor, "Cut them off, Cut them off" as more than 100 passengers packed into the carriage which was so full that they could hardly move.

Tunis then started the carriage on its journey to City Island where the passengers from Manhattan and the Bronx were intending to swim and enjoy the day. The heavily laden carriage took the first curve before reaching Shore Boulevard at a slow rate and without trouble. After passing the boulevard it went faster and took the second curve at a speed of twenty miles per hour. It then travelled on straight track through a grove of small trees for another fifty yards, but as soon as it reached the third curve it began to sway. Tunis reported he could see the swaying of the overhead structure and cut the current reducing the speed to fifteen miles per hour but it was too late. Under the heavy load the wooden ties on the ground sank an inch or two into the uncemented dust on

Catastrophe! Taken around 3.00pm on Saturday 16th July 1910, the passengers wearing their best weekend clothes including boaters disembark from the carriage as it rests precariously on one of the bents. Electric Railway Journal *Vol. 36, 23 July 1910*

Most of the passengers were able to walk back to Bartow Station but one lady stayed and looked on indignantly! Perhaps this was Tunis's wife? Electric Railway Journal *Vol. 36, 23 July 1910*

which they were laid and the structure supporting the upper balance rails gave way causing the carriage to fall on its side.

The accident occurred within 100 yards of the power house which enabled Engineer Scott, who was in charge of the generators, to shut off the power immediately. The passengers were also lucky that one of the uprights remained in place and prevented the carriage rolling down a 4ft embankment, which would probably have killed or badly injured them. All the passengers survived and, although most suffered only bruises, fourteen had more serious injuries including Tunis who had a broken rib.

Lying in his bed Tunis said[12]:

"The weight of the heavy laden car depressed these ties and they sank, causing the car to lean too far. We had intended to put concrete under the ties, if we had had more money and time. I know that the ties were not solidly set. The proper lean of the car on that curve should have been 6 degrees. The actual lean of the car at the time of the accident this afternoon was 8 degrees."

On Sunday the 17th July, Coroner Jacob Shongut spent three hours at the scene of the accident. Immediately after he said he would appeal to the Public Service Commission to forbid all operation until the roadbed and superstructure was in better shape. He commented[13]:

"The earthen roadbed on which the ties supporting the rail are laid appeared to me to be so loose that merely a good rainstorm would wash it away. The uprights supporting the superstructure looked to me as though they were fastened to the ties, not with solid rivets, but merely with spikes, which would easily pull out. The cause of the accident, as the newspapers said, was that the ties lay on loose dirt and let the rail sink down when the overloaded car passed over it."

The franchise to operate was immediately revoked and the company set about reconstruction to the standards which had originally been designed, but not adhered to during the hasty construction to meet the deadline. In particular the failures included[14]:

- the ties had been laid on bare earth rather than set in concrete.
- the designed bents (upright frames) to support the upper rail had not arrived in time so the much lighter weight bents which had been used at the Jamestown Exposition had been reused.
- the bents had been bolted to wooden beams laid on the earth instead of being set in concrete as intended.

During closure the company also took the opportunity to erect a handsome station alongside the New Haven Railroad station at Bartow and another at City Island.

Subsequent operation

On the 2nd October 1910 the company announced that the line had been re-granted its franchise following tests by the Public Service Commission and would reopen on Wednesday the 5th October 1910. During the week before, trials had taken place with free rides for passengers (no fare could be charged as the franchise was still awaited) and the trip along the two mile line was taking about three to five minutes by comparison to the twenty to thirty minutes by horse car[15].

The announcement, however, was a little premature as a carriage carrying officials of the Public Service Commission to judge the workings of the line crashed into an automobile on the 11th October 1910. The sharp point of the cigar shaped monorail carriage pierced the tonneau of the automobile which was about two thirds of the way across the track. Two of the occupants had time to jump to safety but one person in the car was injured. Despite this set back, the franchise was re-granted subject to some minor changes in the construction work and a maximum speed limit of fifteen miles per hour[16].

The changes needed were completed and the line finally reopened on the 14th November 1910. The carriages then shuttled back and forth uneventfully for four years. The monorail was never extended on to City Island and passengers had to continue their journey on the horse trams. On the 10th May 1913, the monorail and horse tram companies were merged into the Pelham Park and City Island Railroad Company and in March 1914 the monorail franchise was revoked with the service ending on the 16th March 1914. It was replaced by a gasoline bus leased by the company[17]. The merged company was in turn purchased by the Third Avenue Railway Company from the Interborough Rapid Transit Company in 1914 and the last vestiges of the monorail and horse trams disappeared[18].

Technical description

On the 19th September 1908, about one month before the application to the Public Service Commission for the construction of the Pelham Park and City Island Railroad, Tunis filed for patent No. 982,315 which showed that he intended standard cross section 'T' rail to be used at ground level and for this to be bolted to short concrete ties embedded in ballast. This was to be rubble or crushed

Taken from the same position as the view on page 48, the sheet metal body construction of the carriage can be seen.
Library of Congress LC-B2-2064-2

stone, and according to his patent, a resilient binder, such as pitch, coal tar, asphalt, or the equivalent, was to be melted and poured on the ballast. The intention was to make the ballast a continuous body which was sufficiently elastic but with a secure foundation. As described above, the hasty construction ignored this requirement and the track had to be subsequently strengthened, probably by relaying the wooden sleepers in ballast and concrete.

The original plan in 1909 was for the guide rails to be carried from brackets on steel poles spaced at 75ft to 100ft intervals except in Pelham Park, where the guide rails were to be suspended from wooden beams carried on steel bents set in concrete[19]. Due to the delays, the designed bents and poles did not arrive in time for the construction and instead light weight bents were used spaced at about 20ft intervals. The 'gauge' of the upper guide rails was 30in. After the catastrophe of the opening it is likely that the light weight bents (many of which had come from Jamestown) were just reinforced and set in concrete.

Tunis patented designs for both switches and crossings. The track layout of the Pelham Park and City Island Railroad was a simple end to end but, every quarter of a mile or so, switches provided loops to enable carriages to pass each other. At ground level a stub switch was easily provided. The two guidance rails, however, caused complication in the form of a suspended two rail switch. Because the wheels ran on the insides of the rails, a system of horizontal plates forming channels for the guide wheels to negotiate was provided.

It was planned that three monorail carriages would be built. These were to be constructed of steel, 50ft long and 6ft 6in. wide and weigh fifteen tons when carrying fifty seated passengers. As indicated above, the regulatory and financial delays compressed the construction period to two months necessitating the initial use of the Jamestown carriage. This carriage suffered only modest damage in the catastrophe of the opening day and was repaired. Only one further carriage was built which was delivered during the temporary closure after the catastrophe. This was to the same design[15].

The vehicles were described in the *Electric Railway Journal*[19]. To provide a low centre of gravity, gearless shaft mounted motors were used. Each of the two axles of both trucks carried a pair of 550 volt, 25 (nominal) horse power, four pole motors operated at 800 rpm., connected in series for starting and slow running, but in parallel for full speed. The motors were supplied by the Sterling Electric Company of Dayton, Ohio. The controller was of the General Electric type with an auxiliary multiple unit contactor (motor man's cabs and controllers were provided at both ends of the carriage).

A family photograph taken inside of one of the two Pelham Park and City Island Railroad carriages. The tram type controls, including the hand brake with floor mounted ratchet, are visible at the far end. Also note the ornate lighting and supports for the curved beams on the ceiling. The overhead track can just be seen through the front windows.

Library of Congress LC-B2-2064-1

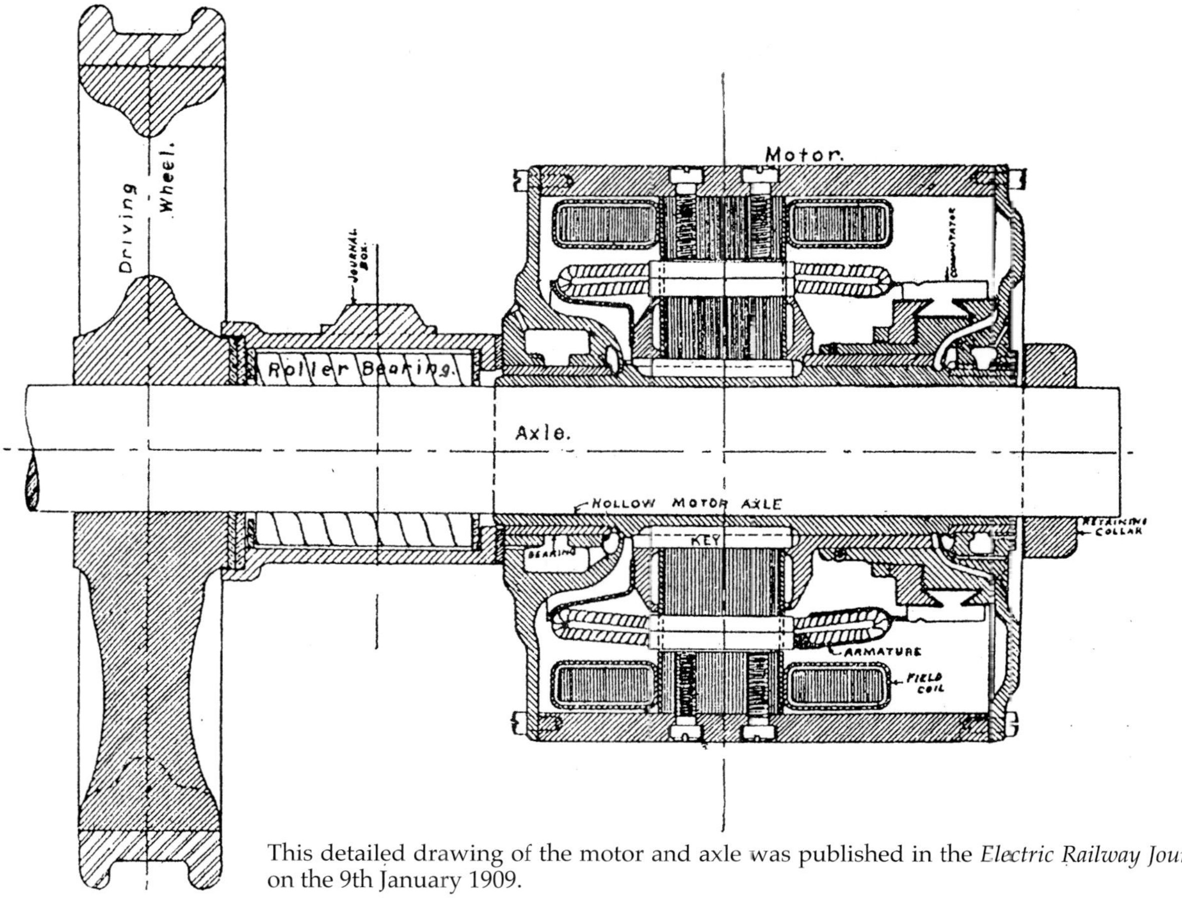

This detailed drawing of the motor and axle was published in the *Electric Railway Journal* on the 9th January 1909.

Unusually the motor armature was clamped on a hollow axle which slid over the carriage axle so that it was possible to remove the complete motor from the truck simply by taking off a retaining collar which held the motor on the carriage axle. This eased maintenance of the brush holders but it may have led to the motor alignment problems that prevented the demonstration to August Belmont in July 1910.

The Jamestown carriage was initially painted yellow[11] and Arcara[17] states that 'Pelham Park & City Island' was lettered in green above the windows and 'Monoroad' below. This carriage would almost certainly have been repainted after repair and the remaining black and white photographs suggest a darker colour than yellow was subsequently used on both carriages.

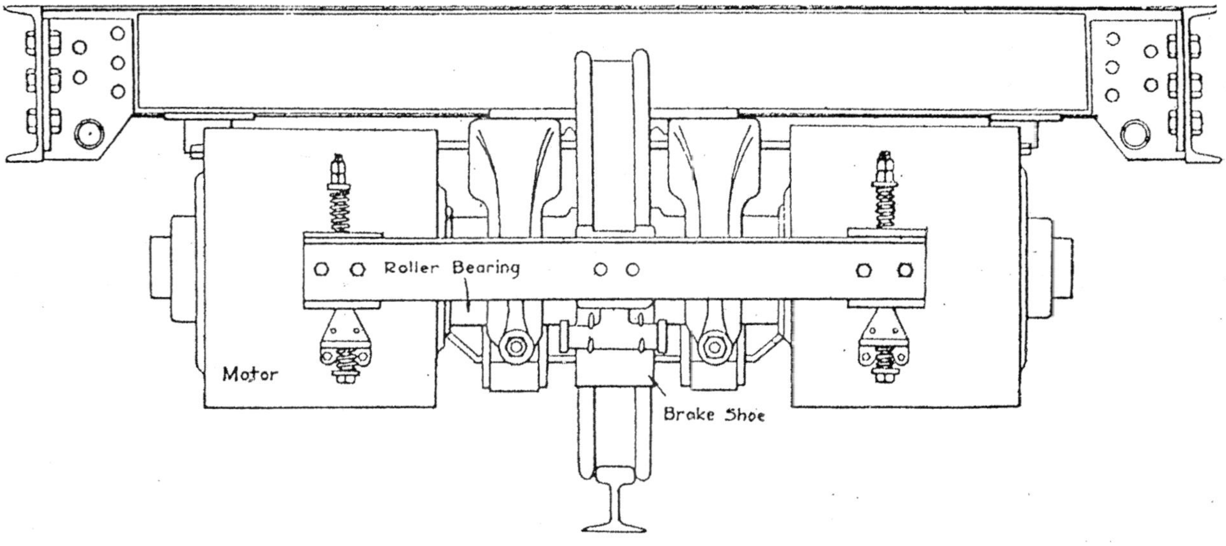

Also from the *Electric Railway Journal* on the 9th January 1909, the end elevation of the drive mechanism.

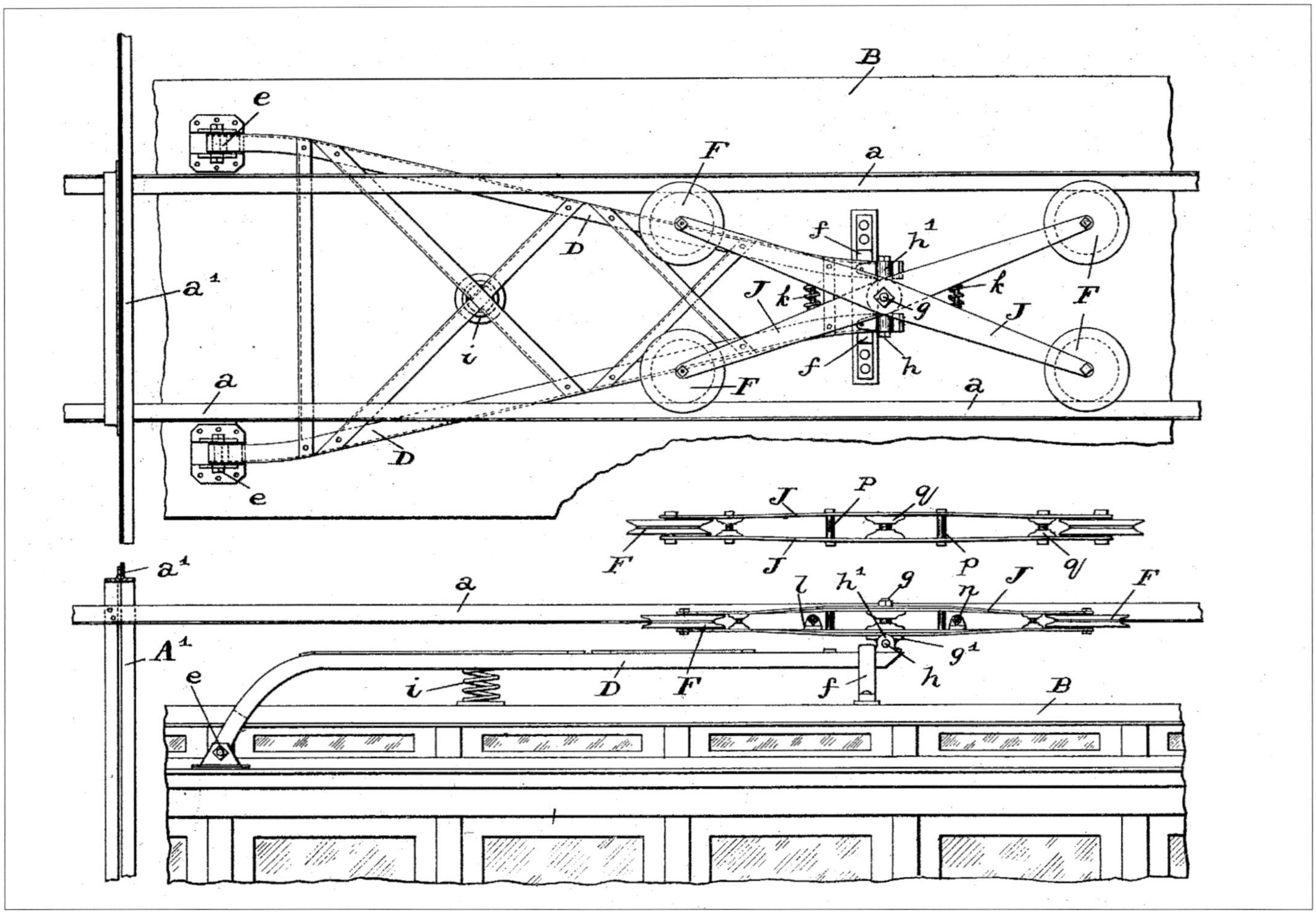

US Patent No. 783,986 shows Tunis's design of the upper balancing truck used on the Pelham Park and City Island Railroad.

References:

1 UK monorail Patents:

Patent No.	Date of Application	Date of Grant
18381	26 August 1903	21 July 1904

US monorail Patents

Patent No.	Date of Application	Date of Grant
690539	31 October 1901	7 January 1902
730586	31 December 1902	9 June 1903
783986	15 December 1904	28 February 1905
955226	19 September 1908	19 April 1910
955227	19 September 1908	19 April 1910
955228	11 January 1909	19 April 1910
962179	19 September 1908	21 June 1910
982315	19 September 1908	24 January 1911

2 *Scientific American* Vol. 87, 6 December 1902, p380.

3 *Scientific American* Vol. 88, 13 June 1903, p454.

4 *New York Times* 27 June 1907, p16.

5 *New York Times* 26 October 1908, p16.

6 *Scientific American* Vol. 98, 15 February 1908, p108.

7 *New York Times* 21 October 1908, p16

8 *New York Times* 18 November 1908, p6.

9 *New York Times* 4 January 1909, p5.

10 *Engineer* Vol. 108, 17 September 1909, p295.

11 *New York Times* 8 July 1910, p16.

12 *New York Times* 17 July 1910, pp1-2.

13 *New York Times* 18 July 1910, p14.

14 *Electric Railway Journal* Vol. 36, 23 July 1910, p145. See also *Engineer* Vol. 110, 5 August 1910, p143.

15 *New York Times* 3 October 1910, p1.

16 *New York Times* 12 October 1910, p1.

17 The Pelham Park Monorail by Roger Arcara, *Bronx County Historical Society Journal*, Vol. 4, No. 1, January 1967, pp24-33.

18 *New York Times* 10 July 1914.

19 *Electric Railway Journal* Vol. 33, 9 January 1909, p75.

The Pelham Park and City Island Railroad carriage. Note, only half of the carriage has been drawn, the other half was a mirror image.

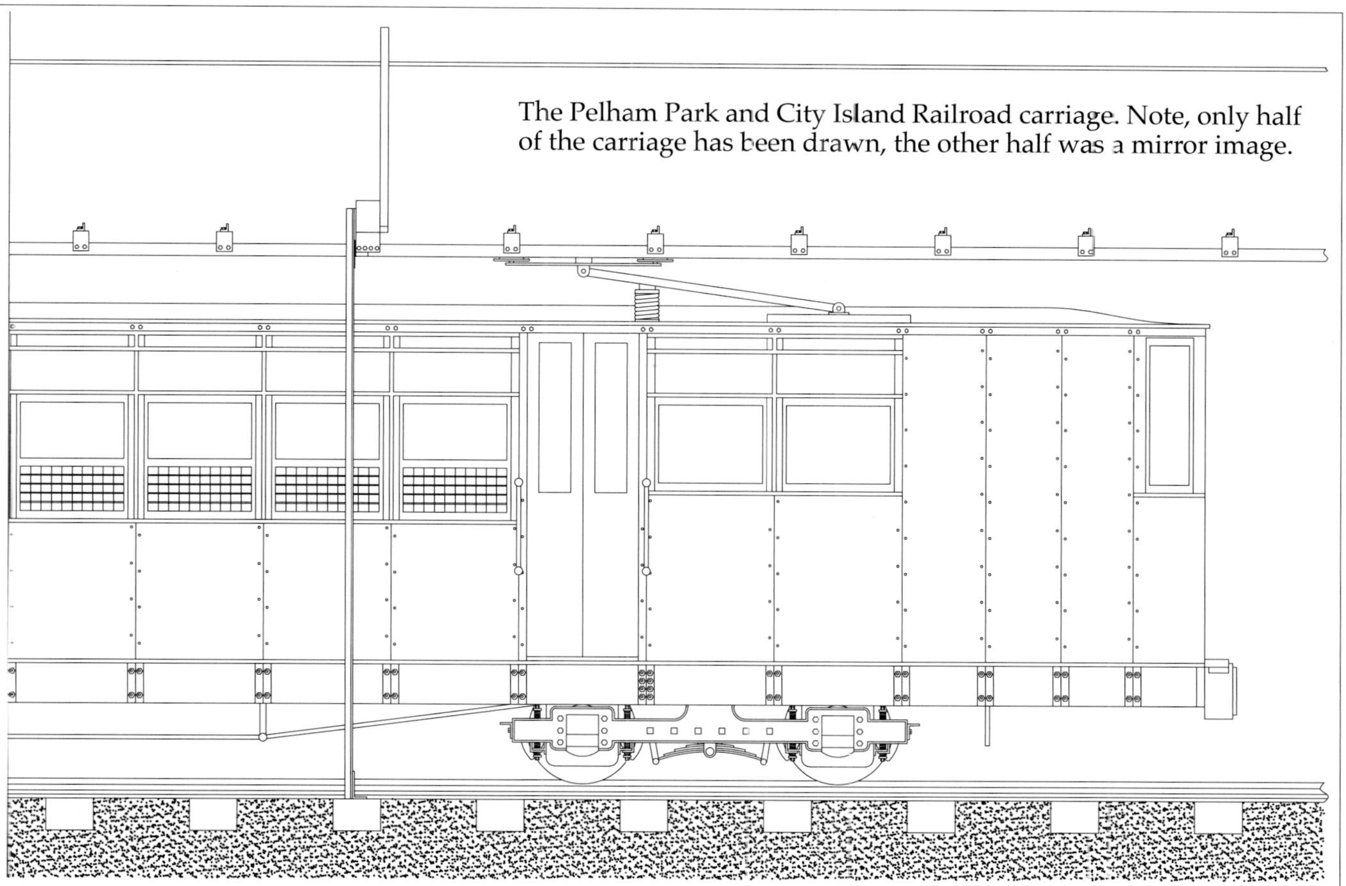

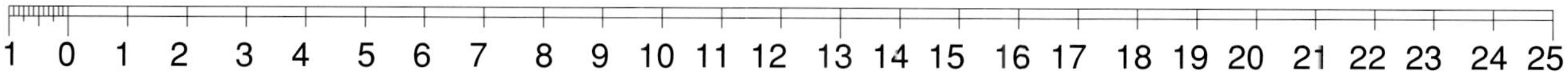

Scale: ¼inch – 1ft

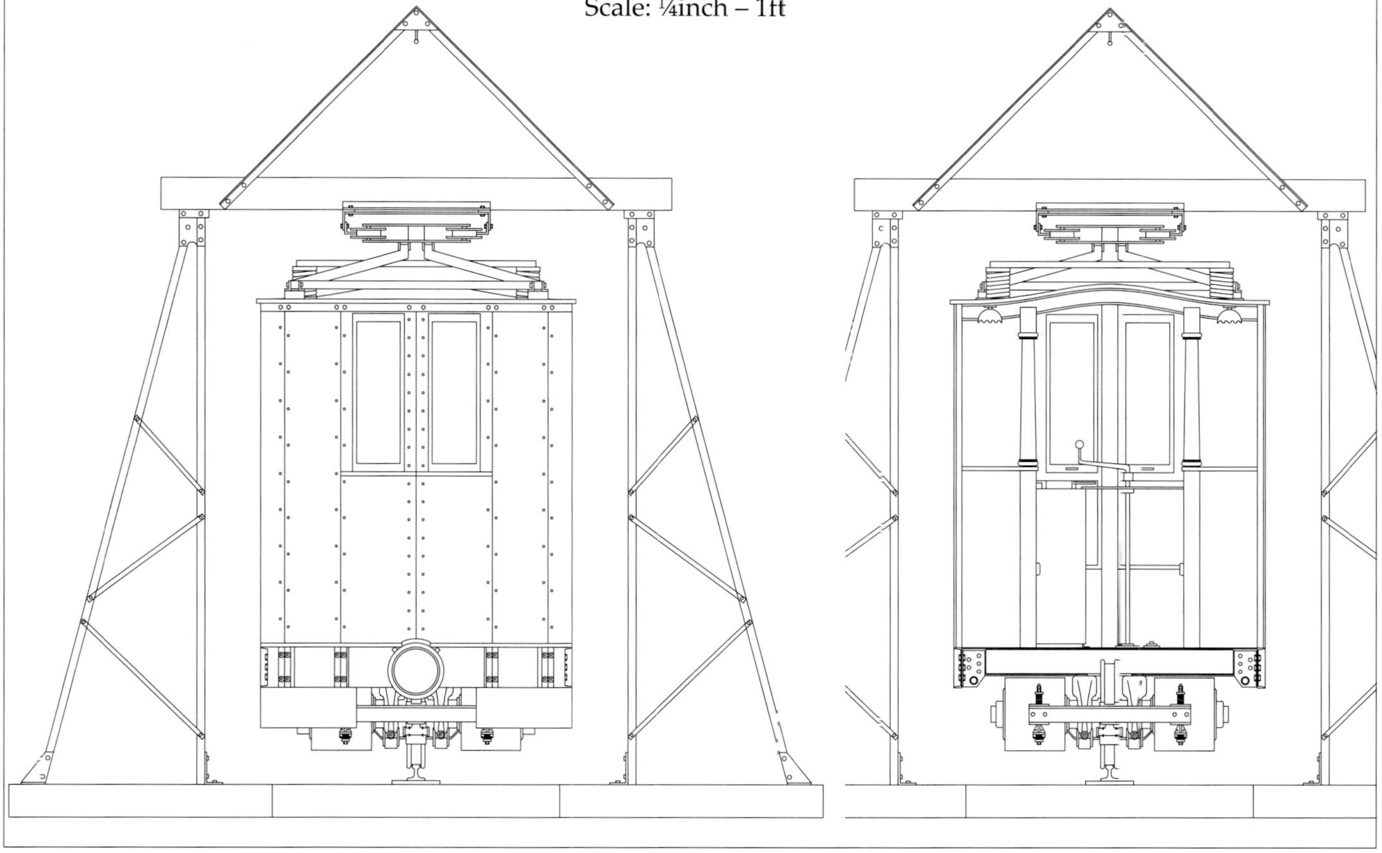

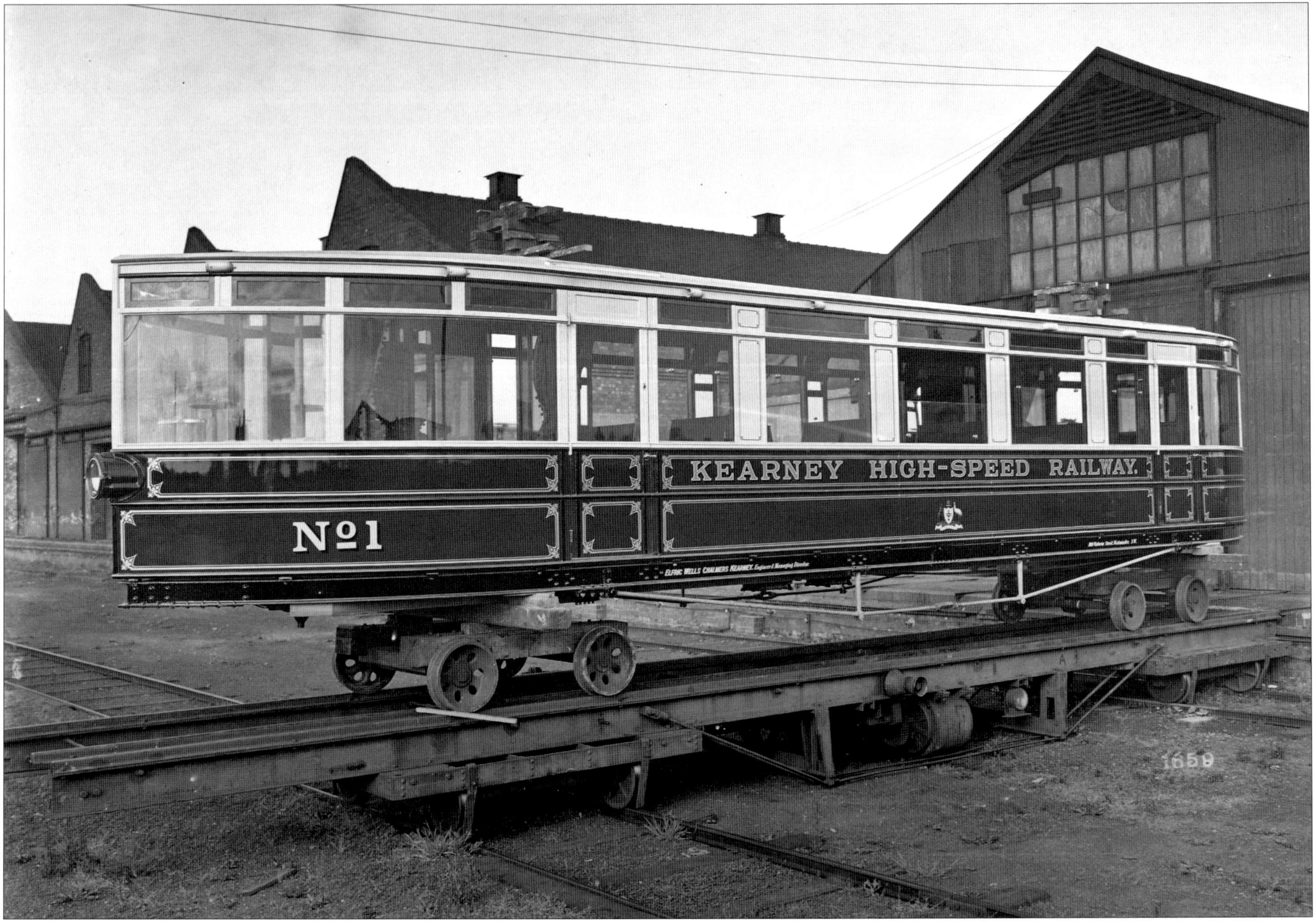

The works photograph of the full size Kearney car at the Loughborough factory of the Brush Electrical Engineering Company around 1912. Only the body was completed.
Courtesy Record Office of Leicestershire, Leicester and Rutland

CHAPTER 4
THE KEARNEY–THOM BICYCLE

News of the Eben Moody Boynton and Howard H. Tunis bicycle monorail trials in the USA would have been known in the UK. Those with imaginative minds thought that the system would revolutionise transport. First off the block was the Reverend R. R. Thom.

Thom's 'Marvo Railway'

In 1902 Robert Riach Thom, a Minister of the United Free Church of Scotland living at 139 Dalkeith Road, Edinburgh took out a patent for a 'new' type of bicycle monorail[1]. This was not his first patent, it was his twenty-second. His earlier patents ranged from ambulance stretchers to wheelbarrows via cycle handlebars and tobacco pipes. Unlike Boynton, however, who had successfully invented various saws before moving on to his bicycle monorail, none of Thom's earlier ideas seem to have been commercially successful. Indeed his first monorail patent was only just novel. In Thom's bicycle monorail, instead of using double flanged wheels both below and above the vehicle to engage with the rails, he replaced the upper wheel with a disc which ran in a rail with a groove.

During 1903 his interest had returned to patenting beds, couches and a camera before applying on the 8th December 1903 for a patent for a recreational monorail. By this time he had moved to Troon and he suggested his railway could carry passengers for the purpose of amusement at shows, exhibitions, pleasure gardens and the like. The patent showed a simple vehicle running on a figure-of-eight track and reflected a model he had commissioned from Messrs. T. McCall & Sons of Kilmarnock. The model was driven by an electric motor.

From the press report in 1904[2], Thom had named his invention the 'Marvo Railway' and the article went on to record that H. MacIndoe, who was a 'well known and enterprising caterer for the entertainment and recreation of the public', had ordered a full size version again adopting the figure-of-eight track work with a total run around the circuit of 220ft. The figure-of-eight was contained in an area measuring 77ft by 33ft and included a switchback element. The carriages for this line would normally have been quite tall, requiring wheels on both the top and bottom of the carriage, but as the line was to be transported on conventional railway trucks to various sites, the height was restricted so that they could pass under bridges. The attraction was initially displayed in Kilmarnock but its subsequent displays have not been traced.

Like so many monorail inventors Thom believed that his system would transform railways and on the 19th February 1904 Thom applied for a patent for a high speed version of his Marvo Railway. An additional novel feature of this patent was that the upper and lower wheels were mounted on a telescopic column which could take up variations in the height of the upper rail.

He subsequently applied for and then abandoned several patents for his monorail system during 1904 before applying for his last patents in 1906 and 1908 for

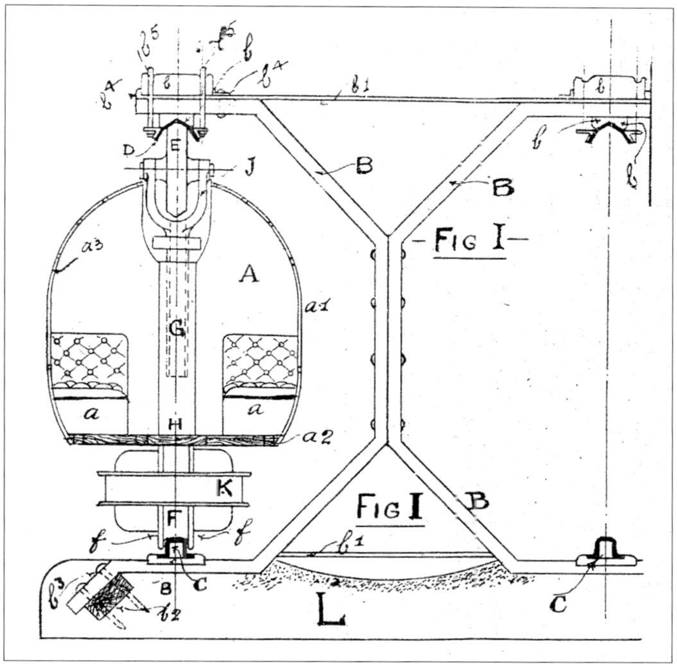

Above: Thom's final development of his monorail design was shown in his UK patent No. 4153. This included both an upper disc wheel rolling in a grooved guide rail with a telescopic column between the lower bogies and the upper guide wheels.

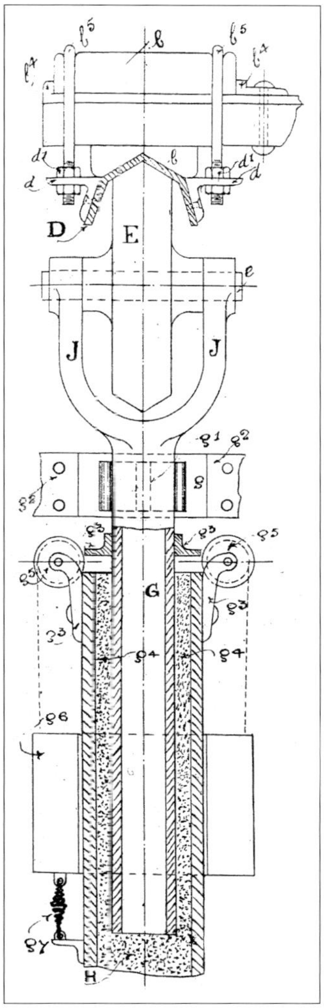

Right: The telescopic column in Thom's high speed monorail connecting the lower wheel bogie and the upper guiding wheel was unique. This detail section shows the weight and pulleys designed to raise the inner tube. The weight was to be a heavy outer ring encircling the lower tube so that it would not swing. In his patent Thom also envisaged using springs. It is doubted whether either or both would have provided a secure mount for the upper guide wheel. A further complication was that the upper and lower tube sections were to be insulated from each other so that the upper and lower wheels could also be used for current collection.

UK Patent No. 4153, 1904

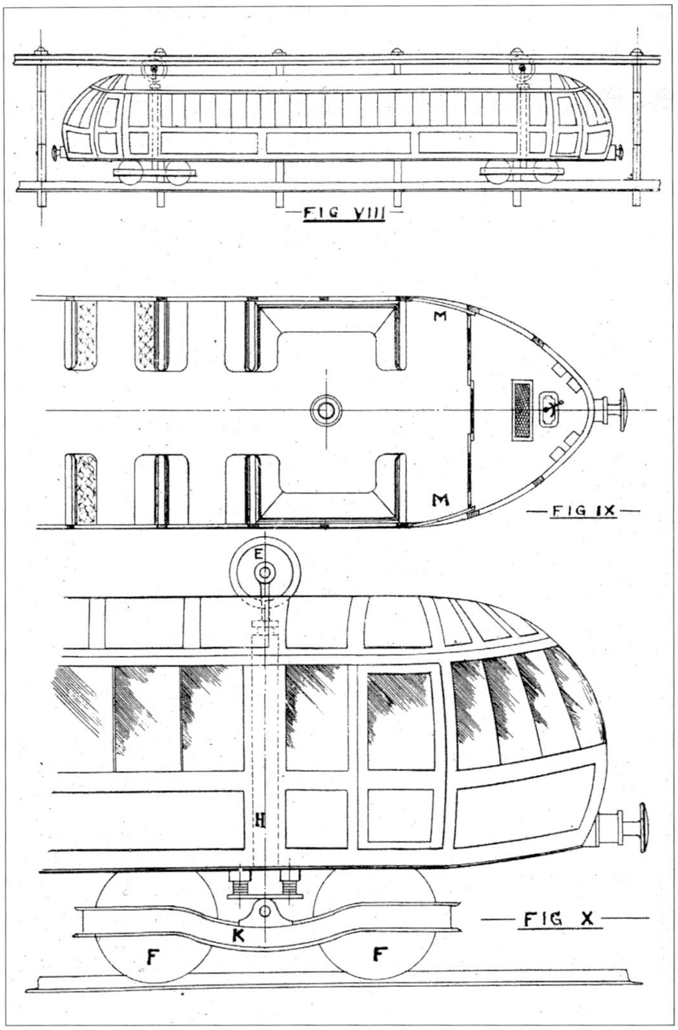

With the exception of the telescopic column, Thom's ideas for his high speed bicycle monorail were not so different from others of that period. *UK Patent No. 4153, 1904*

Elfric Wells Chalmers Kearney.
The Kearney High Speed Railway: *Souvenir of First Exhibition in Australia of the Working Model on Fourth Floor, David Jones 1930*

smoke consuming grates and folding perambulators. Quite what members of his parish thought of their inventive Minister is not recorded.

Kearney's model monorail

In July 1905 The Railway News reported (3):

> "For some time past a young Australian inventor, Mr. E. W. Chalmers Kearney, has been engaged in the promotion of a scheme for a high-speed railway on a new and approved monorail system, which has attracted considerable attention in engineering circles. This system, the invention of the Rev. R. Riach Thom, has been developed and improved by Mr. Kearney, and the result is the Kearney-Thom monorail."

How long Kearney and Thom had been cooperating is not known but they arranged to display a model of a single car occupying one side of a double track on this system which could be seen by appointment at 9 St. Helen's Place in London.

The features promoted for this system were the extreme simplicity of points and crossings and its adaptability to

The model of the Kearney-Thom bicycle monorail displayed in London in 1905. The illustration is extremely poor but the outline of the body is remarkably similar to the design in the patent No. 4153 taken out by Thom in 1904 and is probably the model built for him by Messrs. T. McCall & Sons of Kilmarnock. The Railway News *8 July 1905*

use very light cars. The former was moot as whilst the ground level track was simple having only one rail, the arrangements needed to switch a rail above the cars was more complex.

Above & below: These pictures of Kearney's model demonstrated in Aldwych were published on the 2nd July 1908 in the *Model Engineer and Electrician*. The model included the characteristic bullet shaped nose of the Kearney design intended to minimize air resistance.

Kearney also expressed the opinion to *The Railway News* that the cost of 'his' system (interestingly not saying 'their' system) would not exceed that required for the construction of an ordinary two rail track with electrical equipment but would use considerably less width of land. He was of the view that it would be peculiarly adaptable for tube railways. He claimed that the speed of trains on this system would only be limited by atmospheric resistance and 150 miles an hour was a reasonable estimate of its capabilities.

It then appears that either Thom lost interest or Kearney bought out his rights as all further work was by Kearney and the joint Kearney-Thom name for the bicycle monorail was dropped. During the years 1907 and 1908 Kearney improved the wheel design and patented a variant of his system for use in tube railways[4] and on the 15th June 1908 he launched 'The Kearney High Speed Railway Company Ltd'. The press and prospective investors were invited to 51 Aldwych, London where he displayed a new model, including his improvements. Copies of the share prospectus were also available. The prospectus stated that:

> "...[it is] the result of six years' experiment following upon an exhaustive research into the numerous systems of railway which have been introduced for the purpose of reducing the cost or increasing the speed, as compared with the ordinary twin-rail road."

The *Model Engineer and Electrician* published a detailed description of the model[5]:

> "The body is made of sheet metal, and is to a scale of 1-16th the size proposed for the actual cars. Length over the ends is 40ins; width, 7½in.; height, 7in.; weight of car complete, about 60lbs, each motor weighing 11 lbs. Two motors are fitted – one to drive each set of wheels. They are of ironclad Lahmeyer pattern, designed and

made by Mr. A. H. Avery, of Tunbridge Wells, 1-10th, n. h.-p. The armatures (2½ins diameter by 1½ins length of core) are of toothed-drum pattern, with twelve coils and twelve-section commutators. Each drives its gear independently of the other. The drive is through a hardened steel bevel wheel and pinion having a reduction of 8 to 1. On the bevel wheel are two 'V' pulleys, which drive the track wheels by round leather belts 3-16ths in diameter. One pulley drives the leading wheel and the other the trailing wheel, the pulleys being arranged to speed up in proportion of about 4 to 3. Those on the bevel wheel shaft are 2ins diameter, and those on the track wheel shaft 1½in. diameter. Track wheels are 3⅜ins diameter over all, and about 3ins. diameter at bottom of groove…

…The guide wheels are 1½ins outside diameter and 1 in. diameter at the bottom of the groove…

The model track was 106ft in length, with gradients at the ends rising at a maximum inclination of 1 in 3. The rails were carried in circular supports, the distance between the running surfaces of the top and bottom rails being 11ins; inside diameter supporting rings, 12½ins; distance between each ring and the next 19ins. The field coils of the two motors were connected in series and in shunt to the brushes. The armatures were connected in series with each other. Continuous current at a pressure of 200 volts was obtained from the street mains, the motors taking 2½ to 3½ amps. occasionally rising to 5 amps., at the gradients. The maximum speed was stated to be 23 miles per hour."

Unfortunately for Kearney considerable trouble was experienced in running the car due to changes in temperature distorting the brass flat bottom rail, which was bonded with copper wire at the joints. It was also reported that whilst the track and supports were to scale, they were not stiff enough to withstand the weight of the model.

In addition to the monorail bicycle concept, Kearney promoted its application to tube railways where he proposed to abolish lifts and build tubes on the switchback principle. The stations would be just below ground level, the passengers descending by a short flight of stairs. Leaving the station, the line would dip to a depth of about 90ft by a gradient of 1 in 7 and rise by a similar gradient to the next station after running the local distance on the level between gradients. Kearney's view was that the gradients would be nearly imperceptible to passengers as the effect of the gradient would be counterbalanced by the acceleration and retardation of the car.

Kearney continued to promote his system and in early March 1910 he demonstrated a revised version of his model at the Crystal Palace[6] which was accompanied by plans for a tube railway from Cricklewood to the Oval and from the Strand to the Crystal Place. The lines were to operate with only one tube with loops at passing stations. The revised model was reported to have also been made at the works of Alfred H. Avery but may well have been a rebuilt version of the model shown at Aldwych.

The proposals were detailed in the booklet Rapid Transit in the Future[7] which Kearney launched at the same time. Rather cleverly he quoted from the report

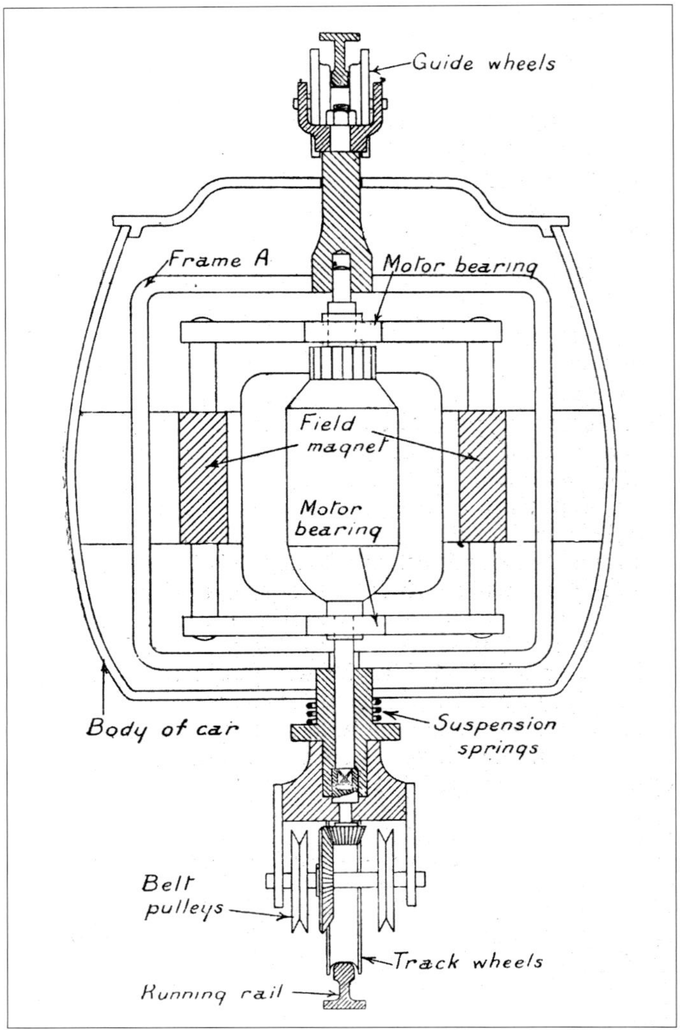

Not to scale, this drawing shows the internal construction of the Kearney model. Unlike the Thom design, the model did not include a sprung telescopic arrangement between the lower and upper wheels. Instead the main structure of the car was rigid with the body of the car resting on springs. This was probably a simplification applied just to the model. The upper guide wheel was also double flanged to mate with a 'normal' model railway rail rather than using a disc wheel to run in a groove in a specially designed rail as proposed by Thom and further developed in Kearney's patents. Again this was probably a simplification applied just to the model.

Model Engineer and Electrician *Vol. 19, 2 July 1908*

of the Royal Commission appointed in 1903 to review transport in London. He named the Commissioners, added comments in italics about how his system would meet their objectives, and the layout of the text nearly implied their support.

A full size prototype

Bolstered by the continued interest in his promotion of the system, The Kearney High-Speed Railway Co. Ltd commissioned the Brush Electrical Engineering Company to construct a full-size car at their works in Loughborough, Leicestershire[8]. The car was 45ft long, 8ft wide and had 7ft 6in. headroom. Air resistance was minimized by tapering the ends which Kearney

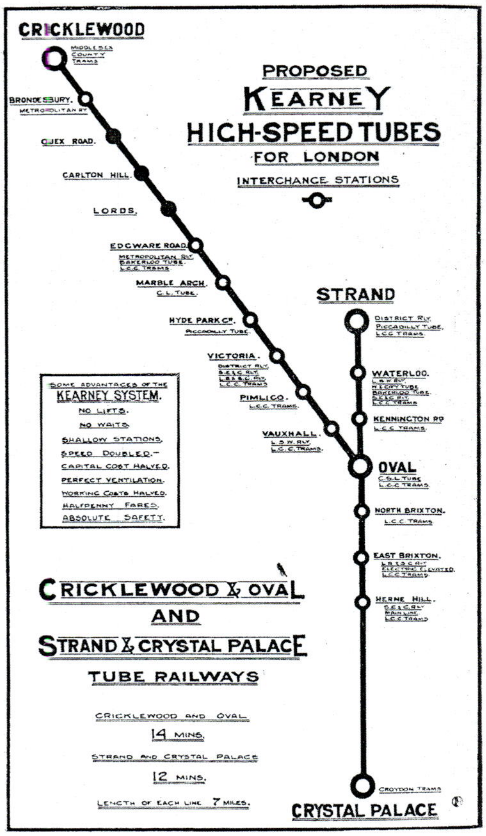

Above: To ease the flow of passengers, which was already heavy on London's tube lines, Kearney's tube system included station designs with a central island platform so that train doors could be opened both sides – one for entrance and one for exit. This was included in the model displayed at Aldwych.

The Kearney High Speed Railway: *Souvenir of First Exhibition in Australia of the Working Model on Fourth Floor, David Jones' 1930*

Left: The route map of the proposed Kearney tube system for London included in the brochure *Rapid Transit in the Future* published in 1910/11.

Below: The switchbacks and passing loops of Kearney's system to be adopted in the lines from Cricklewood and Strand. Rapid Transit in the Future *1910/11*

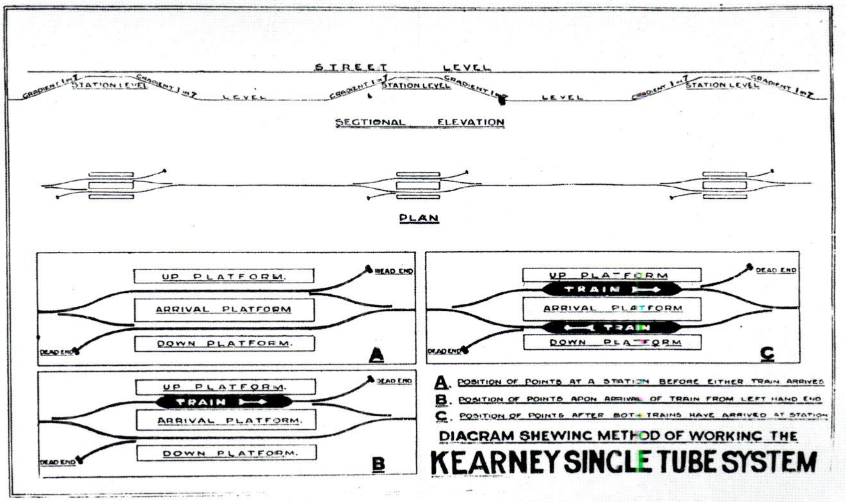

The lounge seating in the Kearney vehicle can be seen behind the central column hiding the telescopic columns connecting the trucks and upper guide wheels. The main compartment can be seen reflected in the mirror mounted on the casing.

Courtesy Record Office of Leicestershire, Leicester and Rutland

estimated would reduce air resistance by about one fifth. The car seated forty-five passengers and at one end was a private compartment with tables, tea cupboard and secret wash basin. At the other end were lounge seats allowing a view out of the curved glass sides. Kearney reported in *The Times Engineering Supplement* that the two telescopic columns to connect the trucks with the guide wheels were handsomely cased in, the principle panels containing mirrors.

The car was to run on two, two-wheeled trucks, each of the four wheels being driven. The wheels were to be 36ins diameter with a flange depth of 2ins. The two guide wheels were to have a rolling diameter of 11in. with a flange depth of 2½ins. The total weight of the car unloaded was about eighteen tons.

The car was to be powered by DC current motors at 1,200 volts. The pick up was to be from two rails mounted on Doulton insulators each side of the main running rail.

Kearney also set out costings of his proposed tube lines in *The Times*[8 & 9]. Based on tenders for the work, Kearney estimated a mono-tube including equipment would not exceed £250,000 per mile whilst a bi-tube would cost about £350,000 per mile. These, he suggested, compared very favourably with the average cost of £638,000 per mile for the existing tube lines. He estimated the cost of the seven and a half mile long Strand and Penge mono-tube line to be two million pounds which was in excess of the £250,000 average due to the necessity for a deep level station and the provision of six escalators at Crystal Palace as well as an unusually ample margin for contingencies.

The promotion of his system in the UK and abroad did bring in some income for The Kearney High-Speed Railway Co. Ltd. At a demonstration of the model at the London Louvre, Oxford Street, on the 12th June 1912 it was announced that a concession had been granted for building a railway between Nice and Monte Carlo, France. This would start at Place de Masséna opposite the Casino and be a tube gravity railway for 1¼ miles and then continue as a surface railway for nine miles through to Villefranche and Beaulieu and terminate as a tube railway in the Place du Casino, Monte Carlo, a total distance of eleven miles. The line would have two tracks and the surface portion would follow the contours of the country. It was reported that the cost would be about 30% less than the cost of a single track of a normal two rail railway. It was expected that the surface section would be ready for traffic by the end of 1913[10].

Whilst the line from Nice to Monte Carlo progressed no further, the Engineer reported in November 1913 that good progress was being made with the survey of the proposed Kearney Railway from the Strand to the Crystal Palace[11]. Kearney needed, however, to obtain local government clearance for his railway and he therefore approached the London County Council for their agreement to occupy temporarily a portion of an island site between the Stand and Aldwych to demonstrate his railway. His application was to be considered on the 5th May 1914 and requested the use of the site until the end of October 1914. He planned to lay a circular track with scenery, laying out the ground as a rustic garden[12].

The timing was unfortunate as the First World War delayed any further development of Kearney's railway. Immediately it finished, however, Kearney resurrected his proposals for the Strand to Crystal Palace and Oval to Cricklewood lines[13]. A short line just three quarters of a mile long under the Thames from Beresford Square, Woolwich to the existing North Woolwich station of the Great Eastern Railway was also proposed as it then took half an hour to cross the Thames by the Free Ferry or the footway tunnel. This scheme was approved by the Woolwich Borough Council, the Ministry of Munitions and the authorities of the Royal Arsenal which occupied much of the local area and by January 1919 it was before the Light Railway Commissioners unopposed[14]. If built, the line would have incorporated the 1 in 7 gradients at each end characteristic of the Kearney system reaching a depth of 110ft below street level and 42ft below the deepest part of the river bed. The car would have shuttled back and forth in the single tunnel with a journey time estimated at one minute. With mechanically operated doors and platforms on each side, emptying and refilling with passengers was expected to be about thirty seconds; so a three minute service in each direction was anticipated.

Coordinating agreement from the various authorities and obtaining finance was becoming increasingly difficult. In July 1919 Kearney again demonstrated his model, this time at Battersea to Mr Kennedy Jones, MP, Chairman of the Select Committee of the House of Commons, which was enquiring into the London traffic problem, and Lieutenant-Colonel Sir Frederick Hall, MP, a member of that Committee. After the demonstration Kearney said "that it would be possible to build a tube on his system as a commercial undertaking, although it was not possible to build an ordinary tube to-day unless it was aided by public money."[15] The problem for Kearney was obtaining that commercial backing without certainty of backing by the authorities.

The main compartment of the Kearney car. The private compartment was at the far end.

Courtesy Record Office of Leicestershire, Leicester and Rutland

By the summer of 1920 a conference had been held between the heads of the various departments of the Ministry of Transport and Kearney at which it was arranged that a section of his high speed railway be built as a demonstration. The site at Aldwych was no longer available and in order to replicate the gradients approaching each station, a site was selected between Brighton and Rottingdean where the natural formation of the ground provided the necessary conditions. The Brighton Corporation (the local authority) had agreed to support the proposal at their last meeting and to loan the land on the East Sussex Estate to The Kearney High-Speed Railway Co. Ltd. The car built by the Brush Electrical Engineering Company was to be used[16].

By January 1925 no progress had been made. The transport infrastructure in London was not coping with the increased traffic and a variety of interested bodies had aligned themselves with the proposals by Kearney to form the Kearney Society which organized a deputation received by Colonel Moore-Brabazon, MP, Parliamentary Secretary to the Ministry of Transport, on the 7th January 1925. Lord Headley, acting as President of the Kearney Society, which included several county councils and London local authorities, said their objective was to call the attention of Government to the urgent need of additional means of transit between the central districts of London and the various areas represented by the deputation. As illustration of the problem Mr A. H. Webb, secretary of the Becontree Tenants Association, said the London County Council had formed a large town at Becontree which was ultimately intended to accommodate 200,000 people without having made provision to enable residents to reach their places of business in the City. Mr E Radford, of the Woolwich Chamber of Commerce, also pointed to the proposed tube line between Woolwich and North Woolwich which was still urgently needed

Colonel Moore-Brabazon responded that the Government was most anxious to solve the tube railway problem and the Trade Facilities Committee would probably arrange to guarantee the interest on the necessary capital but that no more money could be found by Government for extension of the London tube system[17].

The frustration continued. A meeting was held in Becontree on the 2nd July 1925 of the local authorities that had attended the deputation with Colonel Moore-Brabazon. These authorities, representing nearly five million people, passed a resolution that an immediate trial should be made of the Kearney system with a view to its widespread adoption to solve the London traffic problem[18]. The response of the Ministry of Transport was to grant powers for the construction of a trial line under the River Tyne which had also been proposed by Kearney. The grant was made under the Light Railways Acts to save delay and expense of Parliamentary promotions. The formal notice for the application by Kearney was published in the *London Gazette*[19] and described the trial tube line as follows:

> "A railway of 47.12 chains or thereabouts in length commencing in the County Borough of Tynemouth at a point twenty five feet or thereabouts below the surface of Howard Street, 250 feet or thereabouts northward of the North side of Saville Street and passing thence in a South Easterly direction as an underground tube railway beneath Howard Street under private land and Liddell Street under the River Tyne to South Shields, under private lands crossing Wapping Street, Wellington Street, coming to the surface under or near Ladies Walk and terminating as a surface railway upon private land on the West side of Winston Street and North side of Palatine Street at a point eighteen feet or thereabouts North of Palatine Street and twenty feet or thereabouts west of Winston Street in the County Borough of South Shields. Lands for the general purposes of the railway adjoin the line of railway in the County Borough of South Shields."

Kearney's model tube line with its 1 in 7 gradients was displayed in the historic Westminster Hall of the Houses of Parliament against a backdrop of the River Tyne as promotion for this trial line. British Australian and New Zealander *4 October 1928*

This picture appeared in *The Kearney High Speed Railway*: A Souvenir of First Exhibition in Australia of the Working Model on Fourth Floor David Jones' and is a manipulated picture combining a photograph of the full size Brush car mounted on bogies made for the model. The bogies and associated electrics were never completed for the full size Kearney car.

The objective was to avoid the need to use the ferry route which took about half an hour with a gap of fifteen minutes between boats. The tube railway journey time was estimated at about one minute and the tube fare to be two pence based on the cost of installing the tube line at £300,000 and a 10% return on capital.

The cover of the souvenir booklet sold at David Jones' store in Sydney, Australia. This exhibition was opened on 28th July 1930 by His Excellency Sir Philip Game, G.B.E., K.C.B., D.S.O., Governor of New South Wales.

A damning report about the delay was subsequently published in the *British Australian and New Zealander* in October 1928[20]. The Minister, whilst approving the scheme but probably not wishing to take responsibility for it, arranged an exhaustive enquiry and then decided to refer the matter to Parliament for confirmation. The case did not come before a Parliamentary Committee until June 1928. The paper also reported that the committee had a curious beginning. At the last moment three of the four members were replaced; the chairman was replaced by a doctor and none of the other members of the committee were either engineers or had knowledge of the locality of Tyneside.

The case for the promoters was presented by Hon. R. S. Cripps, K.C., Mr H. H. Dalrymple-Hay, M. Inst. C. E, an eminent civil engineer, and Mr Pakenham-Walsh, Fellow of Coopers Hill, and late Chief Engineer of the Indian State Railways, gave evidence in favour of the proposed line. Local support was overwhelming with six out of the seven local authorities sending their mayors and chairman to provide unanimous support. Only Tynemouth Council opposed despite a petition signed by their rate payers expressing their opposition to their council's view. The only other opponent was the Tyne Improvement Commission which owned the ferries and was seeking compensation rather than opposing the scheme. Despite this strength of feeling the Parliamentary Committee rejected the plan.

Without success in the UK, Kearney returned to Australia with the model which he then displayed in 1930 at David Jones, a major department store in Sydney[21].

A monorail air raid shelter?

His ideas re-emerged, however, in 1939. The Second World War did not formally commence until the 1st September 1939 but during the run up many municipal authorities were concerned with the adequate provision of air raid shelters. In this environment Kearney proposed that the construction of his system of tube railway could be fitted to serve as an air raid shelter at little additional cost. He stated that his system would have the advantage of the cut and cover approach at stations combined with the advantage of deep tunnels at the ends of the 1 in 7 gradients. These gradients could easily be managed on foot without the need for escalators or lifts. The internal fittings of the tunnel could also be modified to include seats for use as an air raid shelter and with the live rail at the top of the tunnel there would be reduced risk to pedestrians[22].

In this revised design, Kearney suggested that stations would be just below ground level, as in his earlier designs, but protected by a 3ft thick layer of concrete from exploding bombs, the impact of which would be dissipated by a layer of 3ft thick sand followed by a further 4ft 6ins. layer of concrete between the sand and the roof of the tunnel. From the street level to platform level would be 20ft. An estimated 16,000 persons could be seated per route mile in the tunnels with room for 9,000 standing. Kearney estimated the cost to be about £500,000 per mile or about £10 a head for shelter purposes. He compared this with the cost of £1,000 for a deep level shelter for twenty persons quoted by the Home Office lecturers on Air Raid Precautions.

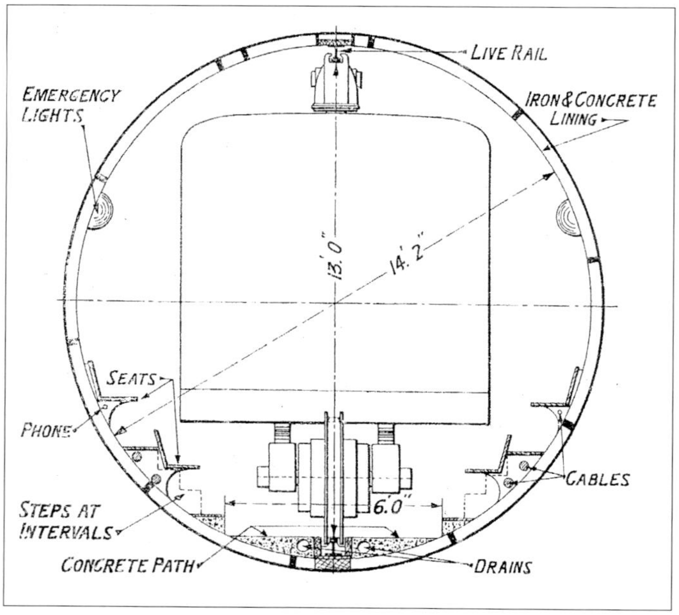

A cross section of Kearney's proposals for his tube railway which could double as an air raid shelter. The lower rail was let into concrete to form a tram track allowing easy pedestrian access to the tunnel. On each side were to be seats which could double as bed bunks. Railway Gazette *14 July 1939*

After promoting the idea, but without success, he wrote an open letter on the 12th September 1940 to the then Prime Minister, Winston Churchill, MP, which was published in the *British Australian and New Zealander*[23]. This letter asked Churchill to put in hand the construction of at least one Kearney tube as the safest and most accessible of large air raid shelters. The proposal was rejected by both the Transport and Home Offices. A subsequent article[24] restated Kearney's case and this was supported by a letter from Mr Arthur Whitley, M. Inst. C.E., lately Chief Engineer of the Civil Engineering Department of Messrs. Sir W. G. Armstrong, Whitworth & Co. Limited, who had been involved with the proposed North and South Shields tube railway scheme. A further letter from William Muirhead, M. Inst. C. E., M. I. Struct. E., was published supporting the plan[25].

The failure of the authorities to take up these ideas ended the Kearney monorail proposals. His last publication was a novel *Erone* published in 1943, a work of science fiction including a monorail tramway not unlike that he had designed.

References

1 UK Patents granted to R. R. Thom:

Patent No.	Date of Application	Patent Title
20344	29 Oct. 1895	Perambulators, invalid carriages, & etc.
23627	10 Dec. 1895	Handcarts, wheelbarrows, & etc.
24671	24 Dec. 1895	Wheelbarrows, hand-carts, & etc.
1435	21 Jan. 1896	Folding barrows
6631	26 Mar. 1896	Perambulators, & etc.
11825	30 May 1896	Folding mail carts & etc.
16381	24 July 1896	Ambulance stretchers & etc.
21817	2 Oct. 1896	Mail carts & etc.
22576	12 Oct. 1896	Road vehicles
5837	5 Mar. 1897	Mailcarts & etc.
9648	15 April 1897	Cycle handle bars
4201	19 Feb. 1898	Cuffs
16932	5 Aug. 1898	Tobacco pipes
18704	1 Sept. 1898	Children's carriages & etc.
20492	28 Sept. 1898	Wheelbarrows
4270	27 Feb. 1899	Carts & etc.
17618	31 Aug. 1899	Traction of vehicles & etc.
2112	2 Feb. 1900	Windows
7815	27 April 1900	Windows
8325	5 May 1900	Window frames & etc.
11813	29 June 1900	Windows
1906	24 Jan. 1902	Improvement in Rails and Carriages for Rapid Transit Date granted 6 Nov. 1902
4021	20 Feb. 1903	Beds & couches
5521	10 Mar. 1903	Spool holders
10892	13 May 1903	Camera view finder & stay
26815	8 Dec. 1903	An Improved Railway for Purposes of Popular Recreation Date granted 25 Aug. 1904
3705	15 Feb. 1904	Railways carriages & rails. Abandoned
4153	19 Feb. 1904	Improvements in and connected with Carriages and Rails of High Speed Railways Date granted 2 Feb. 1905
12294	31 May 1904	Railway & etc. vehicle bogies. Abandoned
15265	8 July 1904	Railway & etc. car wheels & axles. Abandoned
23243	28 Oct. 1904	Railway & etc. wheels & rails. Abandoned
28216	23 Dec. 1904	Shunting cars running on one bearing rail. Abandoned
12103	24 May 1906	Smoke-consuming grates
8667	21 April 1908	Folding perambulators
19865	22 Sept. 1908	Folding perambulators

(Dates granted only shown for monorail patents)

2 *Kilmarnock Standard* 4 June 1904, p5

3 *The Railway News, Finance and Joint Stock Companies* 8 July 1905, p79.

4 UK monorail Patents granted to E. W. C. Kearney:

Patent No.	Date of Application	Patent Title
17583	1 Aug. 1907	Improvements in Grooved Wheels for Mono-railway and Tramway Systems Date granted 6 Feb. 1908

Patent No.	Date of Application	Patent Title
13095	19 June 1908	Improved Tube Railway System Date granted 3 Dec. 1908
14188	3 July 1908	Improvements in Grooved Wheels for Mono-railway and Tramway Systems Date granted 8 Oct. 1908
26739	9 Dec. 1908	Mono-railway & etc. overhead guide-rail. Abandoned
24287	22 Oct 1909	Motor-cars & etc. Abandoned
22987	5 Oct. 1910	Vehicle undercarriages. Abandoned
21042	16 Oct. 1914	Electric switches. v

US monorail Patents granted to E. W. C. Kearney:

Patent No.	Date of Application	Patent Title
921845	19 Jan. 1909	Tube Railway System Date granted 18 May 1909
925106	24 July 1908	Grooved Wheel for Monorailway and Tramway Systems Date granted 15 June 1909

5 *Model Engineer and Electrician* Vol. 19, 2 July 1908, pp18-20.
6 *Model Engineer and Electrician* Vol. 22, 24 March 1910, pp278 & 280.
7 *Rapid Transit in the Future* by E. W. C. Kearney published by The Kearney High-Speed Railway Co. Ltd., 100 Victoria Street, Westminster, S.W. The first edition was published in 1910, the second in 1911.
8 *The Times Engineering Supplement* 21 February 1912, p23.
9 *The Times* 28 February 1912 p24.
10 *The Times* 13 June 1912, p6.
11 *Engineer* Vol. 116, 28 November 1913, p581.
12 *The Times* 4 May 1914, p5.
13 *Railway Magazine* Vol. 44, January 1919, pp56-57.
14 *The Times* 17 January 1919, p10.
15 *The Times* 12 July 1919, p9.
16 *Railway Magazine* Vol. 47, July 1920, p68.
17 *The Times* 8 January 1925, p9.
18 *The Times* 4 July 1925, p11.
19 *London Gazette* 27 November 1925, p7832.
20 *British Australian and New Zealander* 4 October 1928, pp7 & 19.
21 *The Kearney High Speed Railway*: Souvenir of First Exhibition in Australia of the Working Model on Fourth Floor David Jones', (1930)
22 *Railway Gazette* 14 July 1939, pp57-58.
23 *British Australian and New Zealander* 12 September 1940.
24 *British Australian and New Zealander* 6 March 1941, pp10-11.
25 *British Australian and New Zealander* 8 May 1941, p8.

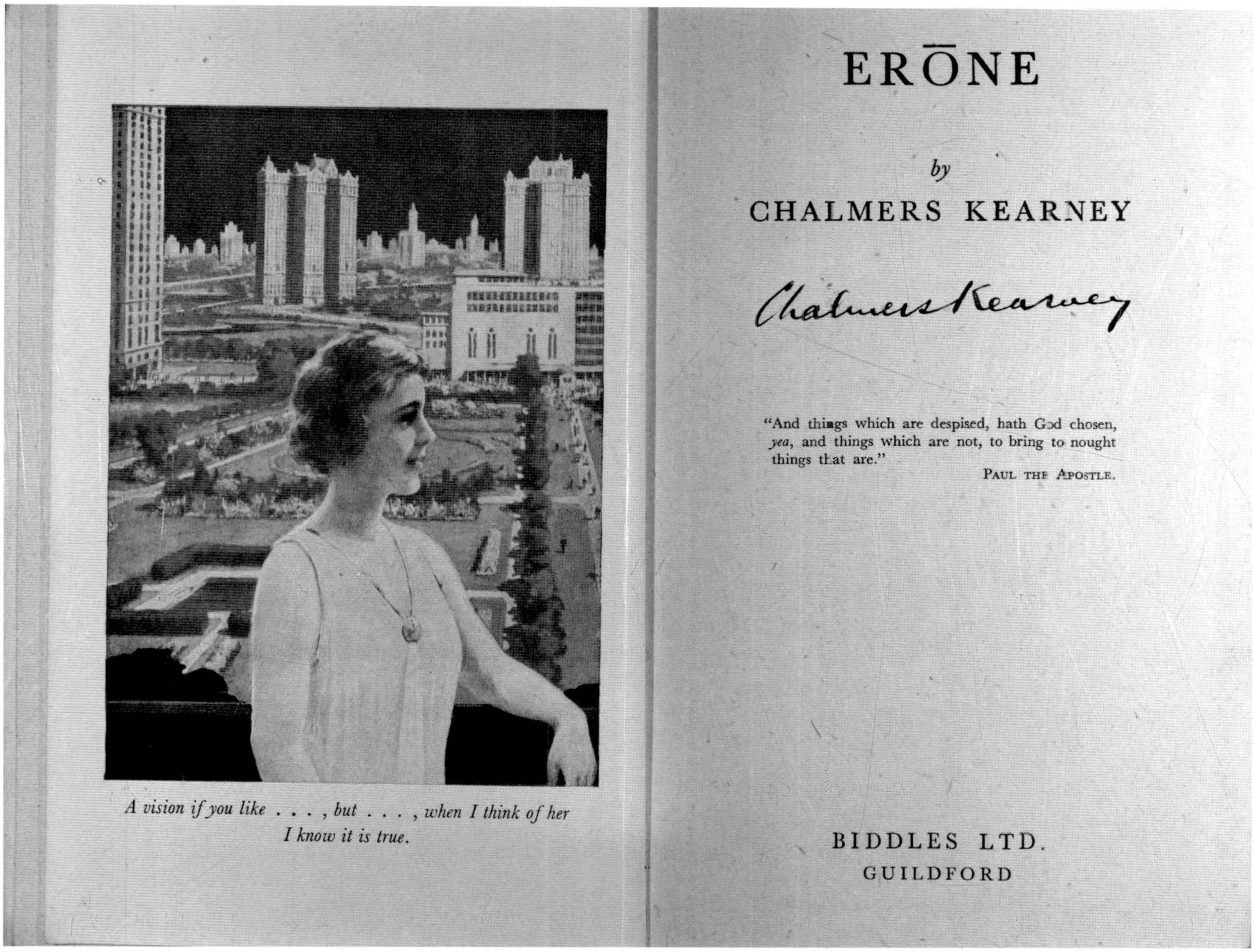

1940s Utopia. The opening pages of a signed copy of Kearney's novel, *Erone* based on the world as he would have liked it to be.
Author's collection

This picture taken in 1916 on the United States Capitol subway system shows the first of the two later vehicles. A vehicle of this type has been preserved and is on display under the Russell Senate House. According to Katy Hopkins[4] a placard near the car claims that up to eighteen passengers could be seated on the car's slim wicker benches. Twelve appears more likely. The preserved car is painted black with red lining and tan coloured seats. *Library of Congress LC-H261-6330*

CHAPTER 5
THE MONORAIL SHORT LINES

From 1900 onwards many short monorails were built as well as experimental lines laid down to try new ideas. The following are set out in approximately chronological order.

ROMANOFF'S MONORAIL AT GATCHINA, RUSSIA

The first suspended electric monorail was designed by John A. Enos and constructed by his company in the USA during 1885-6. By the 1890s the suspended monorail system was being further developed by Carl Eugen Langen in Germany and his system was adopted for the Wuppertal Schwebebahn opened in 1901. At about the same time a Russian named Hippolyte W. Romanoff, who was at that time living in Odessa, Ukraine, was designing a system for the Emperor and in 1896 he took out a UK patent to protect his system[1]. This development was supported by the Russian Minister of the Interior who had appointed a commission to inquire into its adaptability for a line between St. Petersburg and Moscow.

Construction of a demonstration line between the Emperor of Russia's palace at Gatchina to the nearby railway station, a distance of 700 yards, commenced around 1900 and to oversee this Romanoff moved to St. Petersburg. By March 1903 the track was operational and one carriage had been built. The line included a climb of 1 in 55 (1.8%) and a tight radius of 35ft[2]. Power was supplied by an electric feed wire running parallel with the main rail[3].

Like so many monorail inventors, Romanoff was excessively optimistic about the speeds that could be attained suggesting speeds in excess of 120 miles per hour or even 150 miles per hour for light parcel and express letter cars. He must have been fairly persuasive as a report had been made by the Imperial Russian Technical Institute dated the 15th February 1901 that a 345 mile long railway using his monorail system could be built between St. Petersburg and Moscow at a cost of £23,800 per mile. This report was based on:

- Sixty-six trains travelling simultaneously with speeds between 90 and 108 miles per hour.
- Rolling stock for 400 cars each carrying 35 passengers.
- Workshops and carriage sheds.
- Forty generating stations each of 1,500 horse power.
- Eighty high level platform stations.
- Block signalling and related apparatus.
- Cottages for servants (staff)

The Romanoff demonstration line at Gatchina, about 50km. south of St. Petersburg, Russia. Both the main wheels and side wheels that engaged with the upper main rail may be seen at the top of the bogie. The Emperor's palace can also just be seen in the background. Electrical Review *Vol. 52, 13 March 1903 © The British Library Board 1892-1967, LOU.LON TC18*

The suspended car of the Gatchina demonstration line at a simple wooden station platform. Unfortunately not in colour, it is suspected that the carpet on the stairs was red and laid especially for the top hatted dignitaries. These may have included the Emperor as well as ministers of the Russian Government and the inventor Romanoff. The excess of uniform staff reflects the site of the monorail in palace grounds.
Electrical Review *Vol. 52 13 March 1903*
© The British Library Board 1892-1967, LOU.LON TC18

Right: End elevation of the Romanoff system. None of the five wheels bearing on the track had flanges. The upper triangular shaped rail carried the weight and had two side wheels bearing on the rail at an angle which replaced the flanges. A lower structure had two wheels bearing on the outside edge of the girder structure supporting the main rail. These prevented the bogie from swinging. *US Patent No. 843,418*

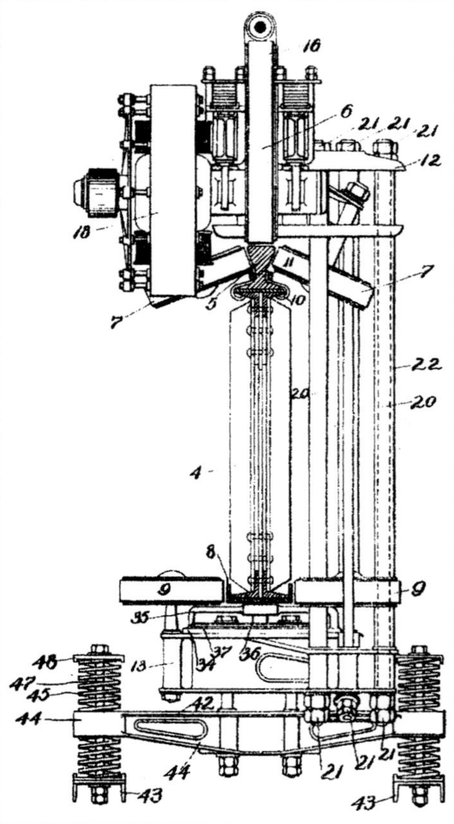

Whilst no construction beyond the demonstration line was undertaken in Russia, Romanoff applied for a US patent in 1905[1]. This showed a large passenger car but the underlying design corresponded to the photographs of the demonstration line. The system was complex and the patent put great emphasis on the impossibility of derailment, except when there was a major structural fault in the track. It did not, however, have the simple elegance of the Langen solution to this issue which used stops to prevent the double flanged wheels from being displaced from the rail. It also reverted to the Enos arrangement whereby the bogies could not swing out on curves ('schwebebahn') although the sprung suspension below the bogies would have allowed some movement of the body of the car. The proposed long line from St.

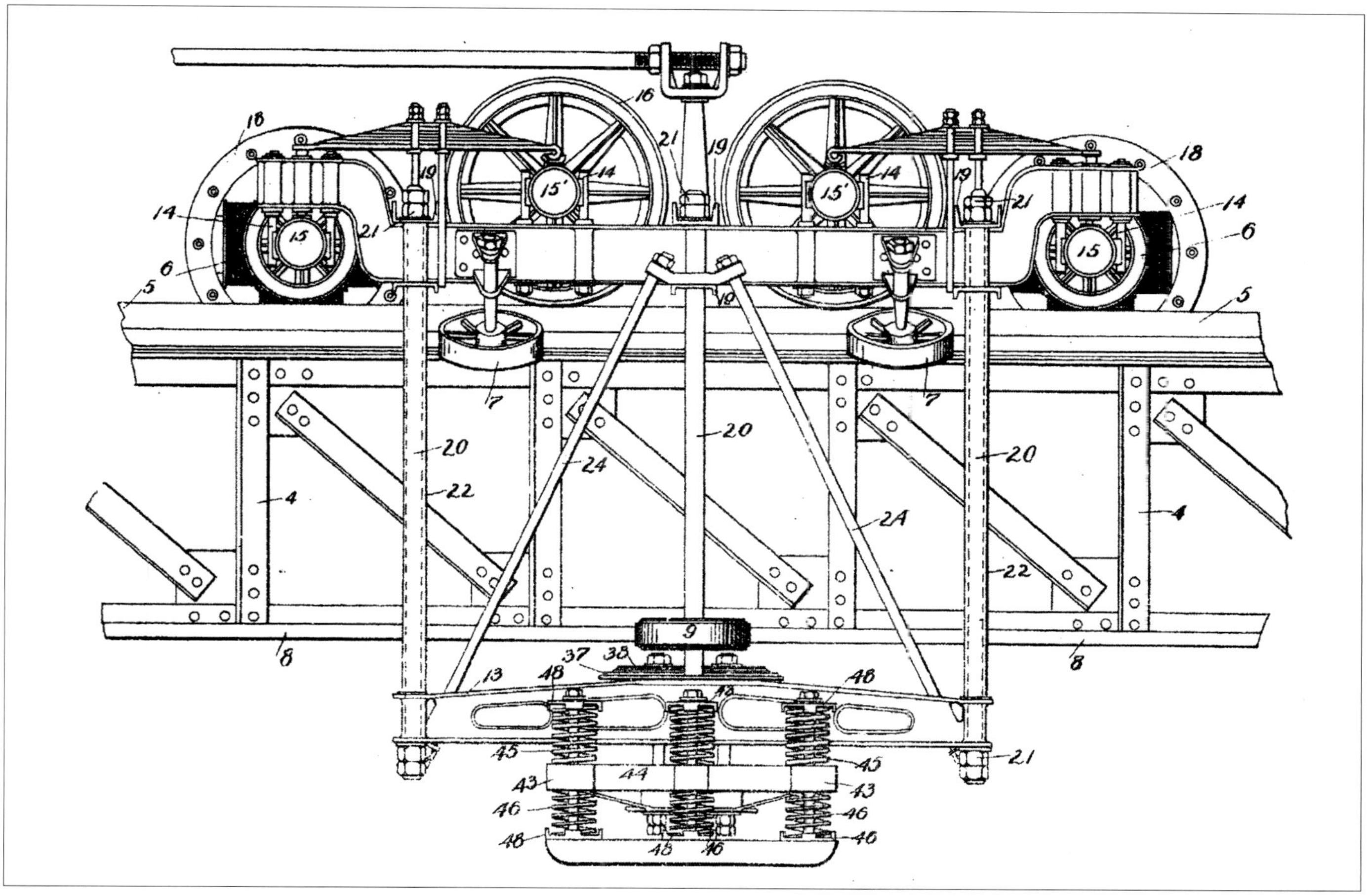

The car shown in US Patent No. 843,418 was to be supported by two bogies which retained many of the features of the demonstration car at Gatchina, including the sprung suspension of the car from the bogies. A few items were changed, in particular the rods connecting the upper and lower structures are spaced more widely and diagonal cross brace rods were added. This design necessitated bringing the upper wheels bearing on the sides of the rail from the ends of the bogies to within the main structure.

Petersburg to Moscow would have to have been straight given the speeds envisaged unless the structure had been excessively strong and the passengers prepared to put up with much discomfort.

The lack of success with the monorail and the effects of the First World War and subsequent revolution in Russia led Romanoff to leave Russia but he continued to be a prolific inventor. On the 25th January 1918 he filed for a US patent for a wire cutter whilst he was living at 200 West 59th Street, New York (Patent No. 1298403, Date of Grant the 25th March 1919). He took up US citizenship and subsequently moved to France where he filed for a variety of patents, none, however, for monorails.

BOYES' MONORAIL IN SEATTLE, USA

On the 23rd July 1900 William H. Boyes and Erwin F. von Wilmowsky, both of the city of New York, filed for a US patent. They claimed to have invented a new and useful 'System of Railroads and Appliances Pertaining Thereto'. After a seven year delay, probably due to the need to prove their ideas were original, they were granted a patent on the 24th September 1907[4].

At first glance the system they patented does not look original and appears to be just another minor variation on the A frame structure that had existed for most of the nineteenth century i.e. the weight of the vehicles was supported by a single rail with side wheels acting on side rails to maintain balance. There were, however, key differences. The first related to the main wheels, the upper rail and balancing wheels as explained in their patent:

> "Our system accomplishes a balancing on principles which are fundamental to two rail systems. The supporting wheel, in the new system, has a broad, concave, soft face, preferably, and a convex track of greater width, and permits lateral play of said wheel and said track, and also permits different inclinations of said wheel.
>
> The above peculiar shape of wheel face and track provides a centralizing influence, forcing the wheel always to return to the track-center or rather oscillate around the track center line describing a practically sinusoidal curve, as said influence is the stronger, the more the said wheel is away from the said centerline.
>
> ...The above smoothly acting centralizing influence with enough lateral play is a characteristic feature of the new system, and forms a contrast when the jarring effect of climbing wheel-flanges in the known one-rail railroads is considered. And the absence of wheel flanges in the new system is an advantage when compared with two-rail railroads, especially for extra high speeds."

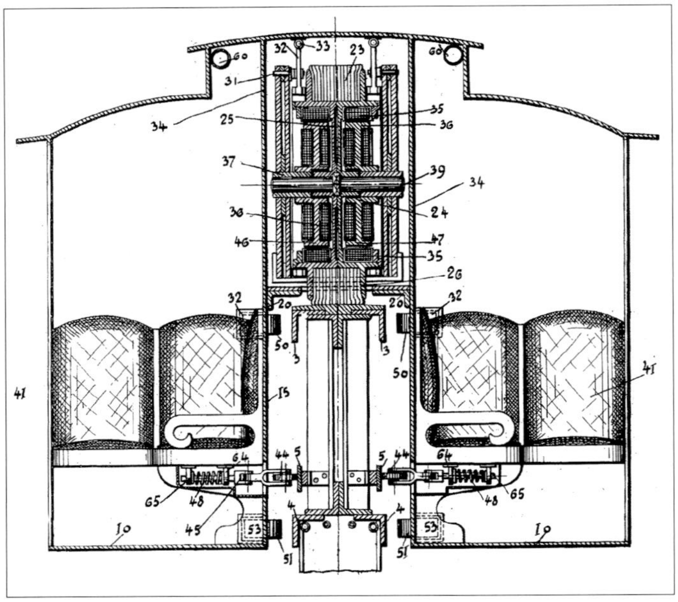

Left: The end elevation from the Boyes-Wilmowsky US Patent No. 867,007 shows the wide main wheel with integral electric motor as well as the upper side wheels labelled '50' bearing against the upper rail '3' and the lower side wheels '44' bearing against the lower rails '5'.
Below: The short so called monocyclic sections were flexibly coupled together "...in such a way that a certain lateral play e.g. up to three inches each way is permitted against elastic lateral pressure."

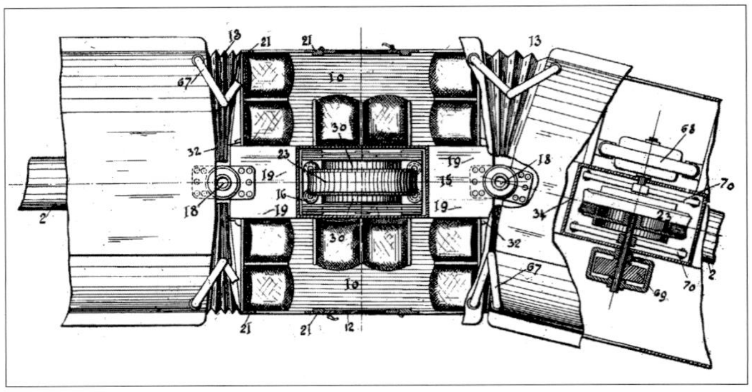

The system did, however, use two pairs of side wheels. The upper pair of side wheels could make contact with the sides of the main rail and were used to maintain direction on curves. The patent indicates that they had a clearance of about 1in from the main rail when not touching.

The lower guide wheels were sprung and according to the patent "In a strong wind and on sharp curves said wheels are used as in systems known, but under ordinary conditions the lower guide-wheels which are essentially further away from the track-structure than the upper ones, remain passive, and therefore are called herein 'safety-wheels'." The patent also envisaged that the lower rails could be used to provide current for the motors.

The other key feature was that the train was made up of a number of 'monocyclic' sections each, according to the patent, being 9ft long. Each monocyclic section had only one main wheel and two pairs of side wheels. Whilst a single section would have been unstable, the sections

The trial line of the Boyes monorail near the Tacoma Tideflats with what appears to be William H. Boyes in the driving seat. The train consisted of four separate sections. The upper rail of the track appears to be wood, wide as described in the patent and deep enough to allow the upper side wheels to bear on it. The lower wooden rails are for the lower side wheels to bear on when necessary for safety. Between these there appears to have been two steel rails mounted on each side of the uprights to provide electric current.
Library of Congress LC-USZ62-60260

were to be flexibly permanently coupled together to form a stable snake like structure.

Wilmowsky died in 1907, the year the patent was granted, and thereafter Boyes took credit for the invention. It is likely, however, that Wilmowsky who had been born in Germany in 1853 and became a naturalized US citizen in 1894, had provided much of the expertise in the design. He had worked very closely with Thomas Edison in the late 1880s and subsequently invented a number of patented processes (e.g. an improvement to electric furnaces, US Patent No. 1,094,354 filed 1896).

To promote the system Boyes signed papers in 1910 incorporating the Seattle-Tacoma Monorail Company with the objective of connecting these two cities with a high speed monorail service[5]. Two further companies also came into existence, the Pacific Railway Company (Monorail) and the Boyes Monorail Edmonds Company. The links between these companies has not been traced.

Using monies raised from the sale of shares a trial line was constructed near the Tacoma Tideflats. Subsequently in the spring of 1911 G. E. Boyes, the president of the Boyes Monorail Edmonds Company, obtained a twenty-five year franchise from the Edmonds City Council to provide a ten minute monorail service between Edmonds and Seattle. The first support post for the monorail track was put in place on the 2nd May 1911 but the timber and steel for the remaining track together with the electric cars never materialized.

On the 21st October 1911 Judge Tallman ordered William H. Boyes to allow stockholders to inspect the Pacific Railway Company (Monorail) books which showed US$15,000 worth of stock had been sold but that Boyes had used US$10,000 for his personal requirements.

The monorail companies went into receivership with loss to the shareholders.

UNITED STATES CAPITOL SUBWAY SYSTEM

Washington D.C. was founded in 1791 and its layout as the national capitol was intentionally designed in the grand baroque style with the US government buildings spaciously laid out. Whilst it is possible to walk between buildings the distances are inconveniently large especially in winter snow or summer heat. This was recognized by the architects of the Russell Senate House which opened in 1909 by arranging for the construction of an underground concrete passage, about one fifth of

This picture was taken during the construction of the monorail in 1912. The overhead supporting beam had been installed and the floor had been chiseled out for the main rail. The tight circle at each terminus had originally been designed for the Studebaker cars and was no doubt a contributory factor to the decision to adopt a monorail. *Library of Congress LC-H261-1768*

a mile long, connecting this building with the Capitol Building. This formed a narrow road and two four-wheeled electric cars were delivered by Studebaker Brothers Manufacturing Company of Southbend, Indiana, for the purpose of speedily transferring both politicians and civil servants between buildings. Each held up to ten passengers and they were colloquially known as Tommy and Peg.

Unfortunately due to the limited turning circle the cars had to run backwards up the tunnel leading to fears of scrapes and collisions. A guided track was the obvious answer and in 1912 the Studebaker cars were retired and an electric monorail installed[6]. The authorization by the Senate to build the monorail may have been encouraged by their knowledge of the Tunis monorail which was then operating in Pelham Park, New York or possibly direct involvement of individual members of the Senate. It is known that Senator Koehler had introduced a bill some thirteen years earlier in February 1897 which would have supported the introduction of the Boynton monorail system in the Queens and Suffolk counties of New York[7] and other senators may have also lobbied to adopt a monorail.

The construction of the line was awarded to the Columbia Construction Company and the electric cars were built by the Washington Navy Yard. The cars delivered in 1912 ran on two, two-wheeled bogies only one of which was powered. The overhead supporting bogie was sprung to take up any variation in the distance between the upper lattice beam and lower rail and had four wheels running against wooden boards fixed to the lattice beam. Current was collected from two wires running parallel with the upper wooden boards. It could seat twelve passengers at a squeeze.

These vehicles proved to be not powerful enough to whisk senators between buildings at the speeds they desired so two further vehicles were built by the Washington Navy Yard and delivered in 1915 and 1920 to replace those supplied in 1912. These larger vehicles had both bogies powered and had more a substantial frame work supporting the upper bogie. Unlike the smaller vehicles they were driven from a central position.

The monorail was a success with each car making an average of 225 trips each day with a short journey time of forty-five seconds for a one way trip. The monorail ran for forty nine years until its replacement in 1961 by a more modern electric guided trolley system. During the monorail period a custom built up that the front seats were reserved for senators, a custom that continues.

Whilst no longer a monorail, this non-public underground system still operates and has been extended and modernised with new lines connecting the Capitol Building with the Dirksen Senate Office, the Hart Senate Office and the Rayburn House Office[8, 9 & 10].

The first type of vehicle, shown here after delivery in 1912, was underpowered and required the driver to sit precariously on a raised rear seat. *Library of Congress LC-H261-6669*

A MARINE MONORAIL FOR CANAL BARGE TOWING, GERMANY

Köttgen's electrically powered monorail for towing canal barges was described in the first volume. Improvements to this system were sought, however, as German industrialization progressed and the United States Consul George Eugene Eager who was based in Barmen reported trials of a new monorail system in 1914[11].

The new system, unfortunately not illustrated, was a marine monorail guidance system using a single rail mounted on pivoted arms secured to the canal bed. The rail could therefore be lifted or lowered from the bed.

The trial tug boat, which Eager described as a water trolley car, was 33ft long by 10ft wide. At the bottom of the boat was an opening surrounded by a vertical tube of sheet iron. This tube was open at both ends and extended well above the water line. Into this tube was placed a pair of rollers mounted on vertical shafts which could rotate on bearings in a frame. In use, the shafts projected down the tube to about 2ft above the bottom of the canal where the rollers grasped the monorail. Power to the operating shafts was transmitted at the top end by conical gears causing them and the rollers to rotate and thus move the boat along. To protect the mechanism from the ingress of sand etc. the frame and shafts were surrounded by sheet iron plates to form a pocket and each roller was partly surrounded by a cast iron shoe.

The shafts were arranged so that they could be opened or closed to grasp or free the rail. To operate the boat, the rollers needed to be lowered to grasp the rail from the canal bed. They were then raised, with the rail on its pivoted arms, to the operating position about 2ft above the canal bed.

Ordinarily the two rollers would be adjusted by a hand wheel to press just hard enough against the rail to generate friction for no load travel of the boat. When tugging, however, the tow rope was linked to an intermediate gear that added additional shear force to the rollers increasing their grasp proportionately to the load being pulled. The intention of this mechanism was to prevent waste of power and unnecessary wear on the mechanism.

The drive motor was electric and power was collected from a wire overhead of the canal. The tests carried out on the Dortmund – Ems canal were reasonably successful using a street car motor but improvement was expected to be obtained with a specially designed motor.

The tug boat also had a normal screw propeller to allow it to manoeuvre away from the rail but the advantage claimed for this monorail system was that did minimal damage to the canal bed through erosion compared with a conventional tug boat using a powered screw.

It is moot whether this was a true monorail. The single rail certainly both guided and provided a basis for propulsion. It did not, however, bear the weight of the floating vehicle. In any event the system does not seem to have been developed any further.

THE GENOA EXHIBITION MONORAIL, ITALY

The monorail at the 'Genova – Esposizione Igiene, Marina e Colonie' was built specially for the exhibition which was opened on the 18th June 1914, just a month before the beginning of the First World War on the 28th

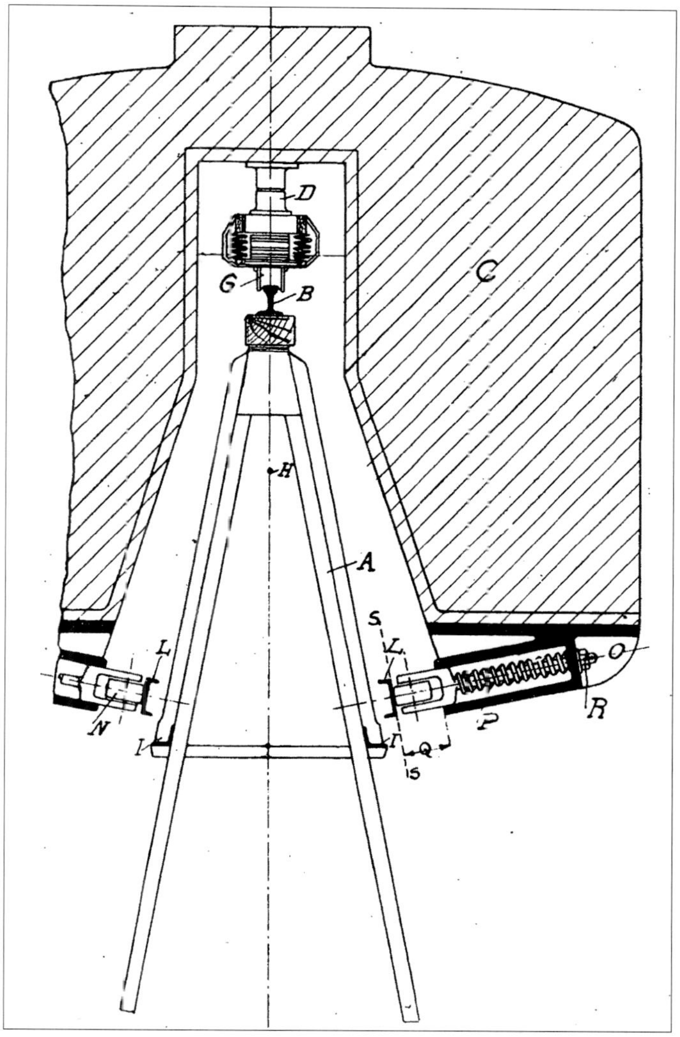

The end elevation of the Bellani and Bonazzoli system shows both the upper bogies and the plain side wheels. The latter allowed the carriage to rotate or tilt about the upper rail when running around curves. They were angled to aid return to the upright position. *French Patent No. 428764*

July 1914. This unfortunate timing could hardly have been predicted by the designers Bellani, Bonazzoli & C. or the constructors, Società anonima Antonio Badoni. Nonetheless it remained open for the duration of the exhibition and provided a half hourly passenger service. Following closure of the exhibition it was adapted to carry general freight and coal to and from the Port until the end of the war. It was operated by Società Unione Italiana Tramways Elettrici and was dismantled in 1918.

The firm of Bellani, Bonazzoli & C. had been set up by M. M. Luigi Bellani and Mario Benazzoli, both civil engineers based in Milan. Three years before the exhibition, in 1911, they applied for patents for a monorail system[12] probably following an approach to provide transport through the crowded city of Genoa. Their design was for a typical 'A' frame monorail but the patents addressed a particular concern about the side forces involved when running at reasonable speed around curves. In the Lartigue type systems the carriages were held upright by the double flanged side wheels. The Bellani and Bonazzoli system allowed the carriages to oscillate freely about the upper

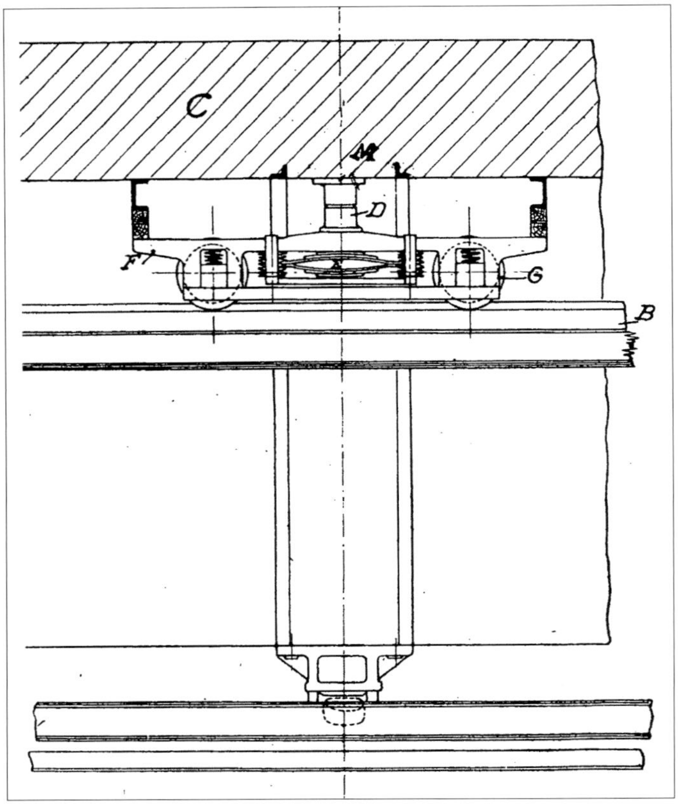

The sprung bogie of the Bellani and Bonazzoli system seen from the side. The isosceles triangle of the A frame structure was narrow allowing both the side wheels and a significant amount of the carriage weight to be mounted well below the upper rail thus keeping the centre of gravity low. *French Patent No. 428764*

rail. This was achieved by having two pivoted sprung bogies carrying the weight of the carriage on double flanged wheels running on the upper rail but with flangeless balancing wheels sprung against flat side rails.

The other feature in the patents was to lower the centre of gravity so that it was well below the upper running rail. This resulted in the carriages naturally remaining upright when static or moving on straight track. When running around curves, however, the low centre of gravity would tend to cause the passenger compartment of the carriage, which was above the upper rail, to lean in offsetting the forces involved on the passengers.

The patents envisaged the 'A' frames would be trestles and indeed a short part of the line in Genoa was constructed using wooden 'A' frames similar to those used by Lartigue and others in the nineteenth century. The majority of the line, however, was constructed using ferro-concrete beams on which the cars rode on a rail secured to the top with balance wheels resting on side rails. The floor of the compartments for the passengers was near to the top rail. This form of construction has become common place for post 1950 monorails.

Rather than use an 'I' section, the concrete beams were shaped like an inverted 'T' with holes cast into the upright section of the beam in order to reduce its weight. The width of the lower cross section was 0.85m and the height was 1.90m. These beams were supported so that the rail was about 8m above sea level by concrete stands with four legs each at 60m intervals. Between these were three, two legged stands. The intervals between these stands were not the same, the outer gaps being 16.75m whilst the inner gaps were 13.25m.

The concrete beam forming the rail support is clearly seen in this picture. To the left is a four legged concrete support to provide track stability. The three following two legged supports are also visible. The train was a novelty and an audience can be seen watching from the pavement. *Author's collection*

The train is just about to turn away from the shore towards the Port terminus seen in the distance on the right. This was the only section of track constructed of wooden trestle A frames. Note the heavy iron work of the carriages chassis and light weight upper bodies to keep the carriages centres of gravity low. *Author's collection*

There were no points or other complications as there was only one train constructed by Carminati & Toselli, Milan. This consisted of four carriages with the electric locomotive permanently coupled in the centre of the train. The locomotive was 6.5m long and weighed 17.4 tons[13]. It collected power at 500V from two rails to power the four AEG 40 horse power motors driving the four 700mm diameter double flanged driving wheels. Conventional tram type controls were installed in the locomotive for the driver. Due to the drivers restricted vision from this central position additional safety devices were provided to ensure the train stopped safely at each terminus. It is not clear why controls were not provided at each end of the train.

The train has just left the show grounds terminus at Piazza della Vittoria and is heading towards the bridge over the main road Aurelio Saffia. The local tram company, whose tracks can be seen to the left of the picture, also operated the monorail. *Author's collection*

The train trundles over the section running along the shoreline with the Port terminus seen in the distance. The simple but solid construction of the carriage frames carrying the side wheels made for a robust and reliable monorail. The lights on the rear carriage were needed as the monorail ran from 9.00am until midnight during the exhibition. *Author's collection*

The carriages were 7.4m long with three side doors which may have opened on one side only. In addition the outer carriages had a door at the end for what was probably a guard's compartment. The carriages had longitudinal seating backing the covers of the central wheels. Each seated thirty-eight people (nineteen each side in two rows) with room for a further twelve people to stand. The seats could be raised in which case each carriage could carry about eighty people.

The line ran from a terminus at the exhibition grounds at Piazza della Vittoria and soon crossed a 28m long bridge over the main road Aurelio Saffia. It continued towards the coast where it turned right to head along the shore with the supporting pillars on concrete sleepers on the sea bed. On reaching the Port it turned left and ran along the only section of wooden 'A' frames before reaching the end terminus. The total journey of 2.23km took about six minutes at a speed of about 25km per hour.

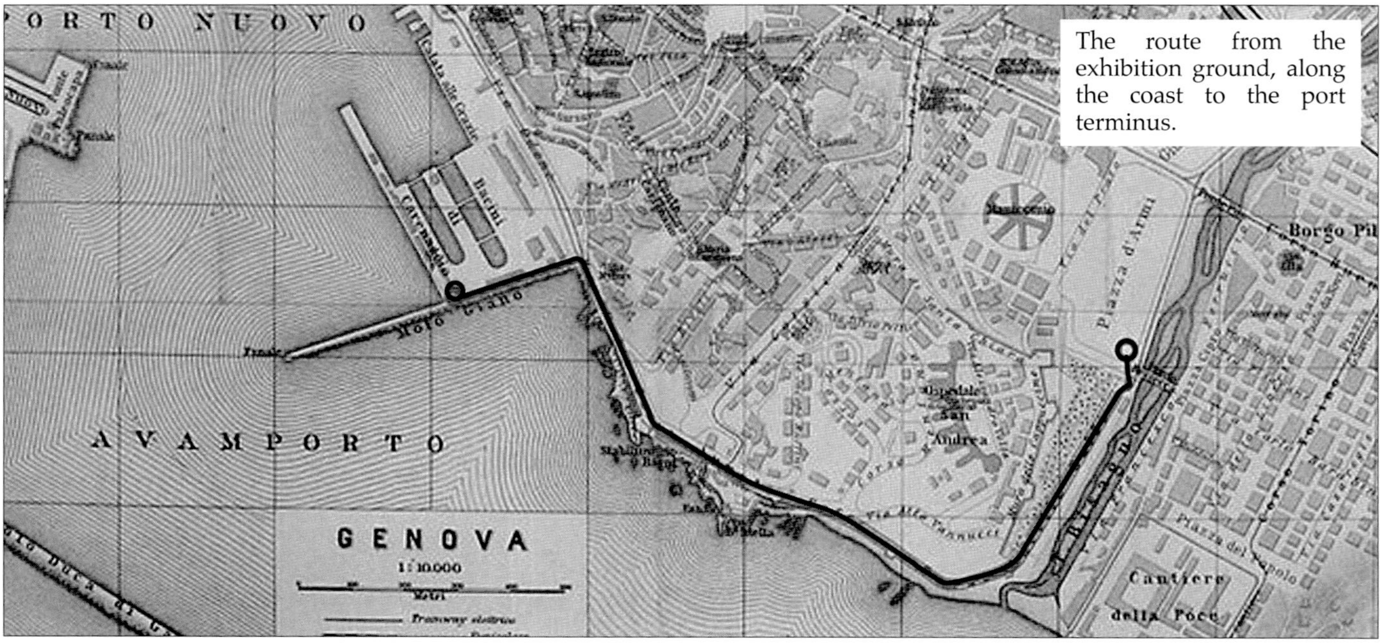

The route from the exhibition ground, along the coast to the port terminus.

THE FAIRGROUND MONORAIL AT TIBIDABO, BARCELONA, SPAIN

The theme park on the small mountain, Tibidabo (~1,700ft) just outside Barcelona was built alongside the Sagrat Cor Church and can still be reached by the funicular railway built in 1901. A suspended monorail ride was added to this popular attraction in 1915 which provided an impressive view of the city and continues to operate (2015).

Intended only as a fairground attraction, the railway was built as and remains a loop supported on tall lattice iron columns which were built in pairs and cross braced to support the 'I' section girder on which the railway runs. The objective was to provide visitors with a view and sensation of height and to this end it was built out over the funicular. Speed was not an objective and the original carriage was lightly constructed with open grill sides and suspended from two, two-wheeled, bogies.

Whilst no new technology was involved in its design, and despite modernization since its construction, this monorail is a rare survivor from a past era.

Right: A postcard from the 1920s showing the monorail carriage at the Tibidabo, Barcelona, passing over the funicular connecting the theme park with the city. The original iron finials at the tops of the columns have been removed and by 2015 the trees below have grown blocking much of this view. *Author's collection*

Below: This enlargement of the postcard shows the original carriage which carried eight passengers in four rows with a peak capped guard at the rear. The electric motor in the rear bogie together with the gearing to the axle can just be seen. This carriage been replaced by a brightly coloured garish gondola vehicle losing the charm of this earlier era. *Author's collection*

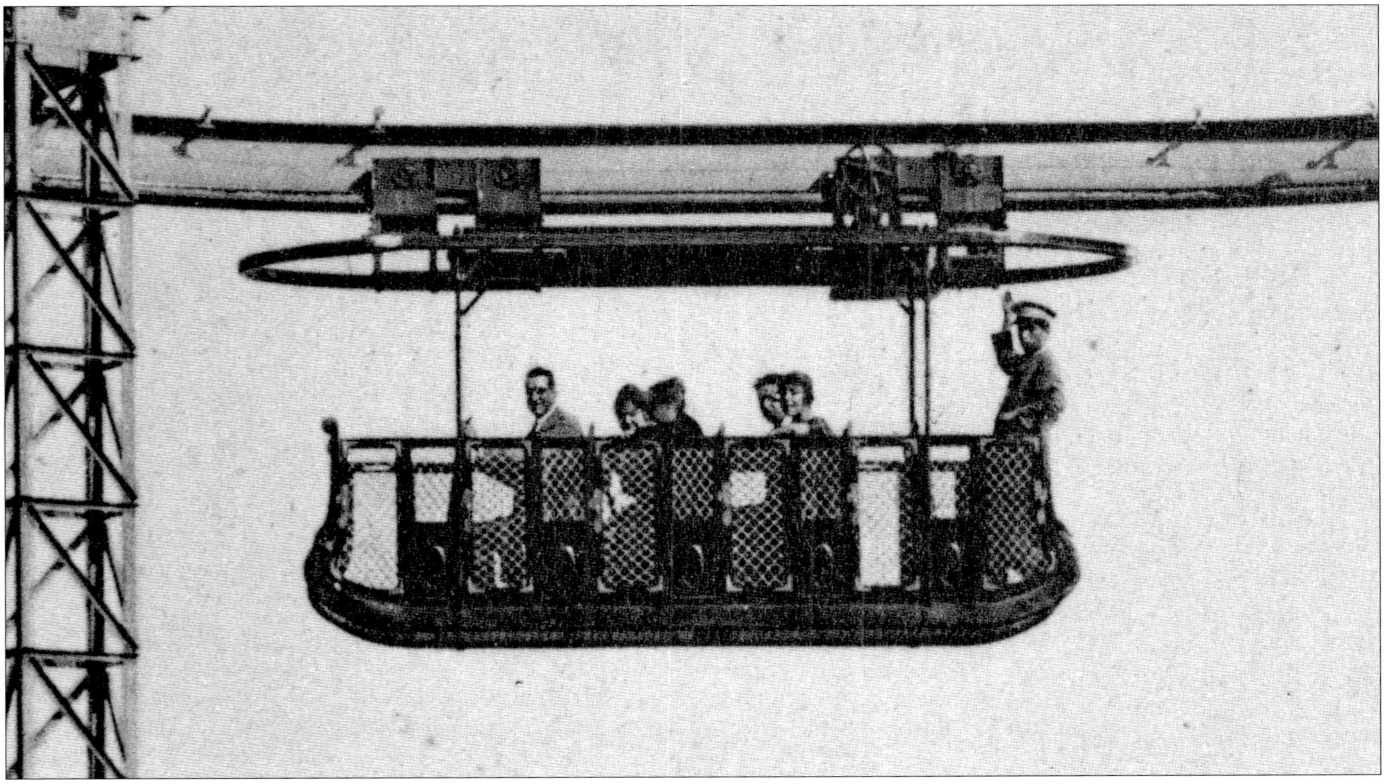

BAKER'S GROUND LEVEL MONORAIL, BALTIMORE, USA

Charles Whiting Baker was born in 1865 and graduated from the University of Vermont with a degree in engineering in 1886 before joining the journal *Engineering News* as an associate editor in 1887. He had strong political views, especially about the railways, and in 1889 he published his book *Monopolies and the People*[14].

He was a prolific inventor and he first worked on his ideas for a light, cheap railway around 1903 when he applied for his first patent for a 'System of Railway Transportation'[15]. His system was not dissimilar to that first proposed and built by M. Jean Larmanjat in 1868 in that vehicles balanced on a single rail secured to the ground and had outrigger wheels on each side to prevent them from toppling over. There were, however, two key differences. First, in the Larmanjat system only these balancing wheels were powered by the steam engine. In the Baker system, the outrigger balancing wheels were free to rotate and instead the power was directly to the double flanged wheel resting on the ground level monorail. Second, the drive to the rail adopted the ideas of John Barraclough Fell in having the wheels grip the side of the central rail.

At the same time as taking out his patent Baker designed a steel freight car with the assistance of George R. Henderson who went on to become a consulting engineer of the Baldwin Locomotive Works[16]. This was exhibited in Washington D.C. in connection with the International Railway Congress in May 1905 by which time he had named his system the 'Economic' monorail.

In 1905 provision of suitable motive power for his design frustrated further development. When combined with the lack of paved or concrete roads, he considered that it was not possible to further proceed with its commercial introduction.

By 1915, however, the petrol engine had developed to the point where it could be used as motive power and in April of that year a Mr. E. S. Tunis built a model line using the Baker system on his grounds at Windsor Hills, Baltimore. E. S. Tunis is reported by Baker to have had a lifelong interest in monorail transportation and it is possible that he was related to H. H. Tunis (ref. Chapter 3) but their same surnames may be just coincidence.

The line in Baltimore was 300ft in length and was laid with 12lb rail on short sleepers with boards nailed on the ends to make paths for the balancing wheels. The car was a narrow wooden frame affair with a comparatively high center of gravity and with seats for twelve people. The car was built without using bogies and ran on just two wheels with two pairs of very small diameter balancing wheels. It was propelled by a small petrol engine through a friction drive mechanism.

Despite the roughly laid track with relatively poor alignment and the simple construction of the car, it was reported that speeds of up to 25mph could be attained. At this speed the ride was said to be steady and there was no swaying or lurching. Essentially the car rode on the central rail, the bicycle effect.

The booklet published by Baker in 1915 did not claim high speed as had so many other monorail inventors.

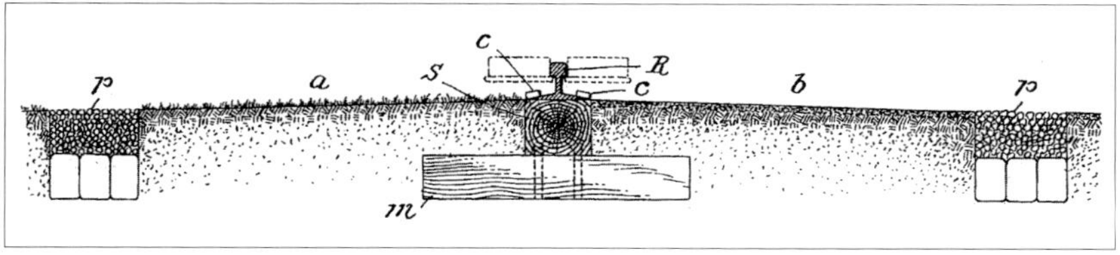

The cross section of the Baker road bed shown in US Patent No. 781988. A mixture of the ideas of both Larmanjat and Fell.

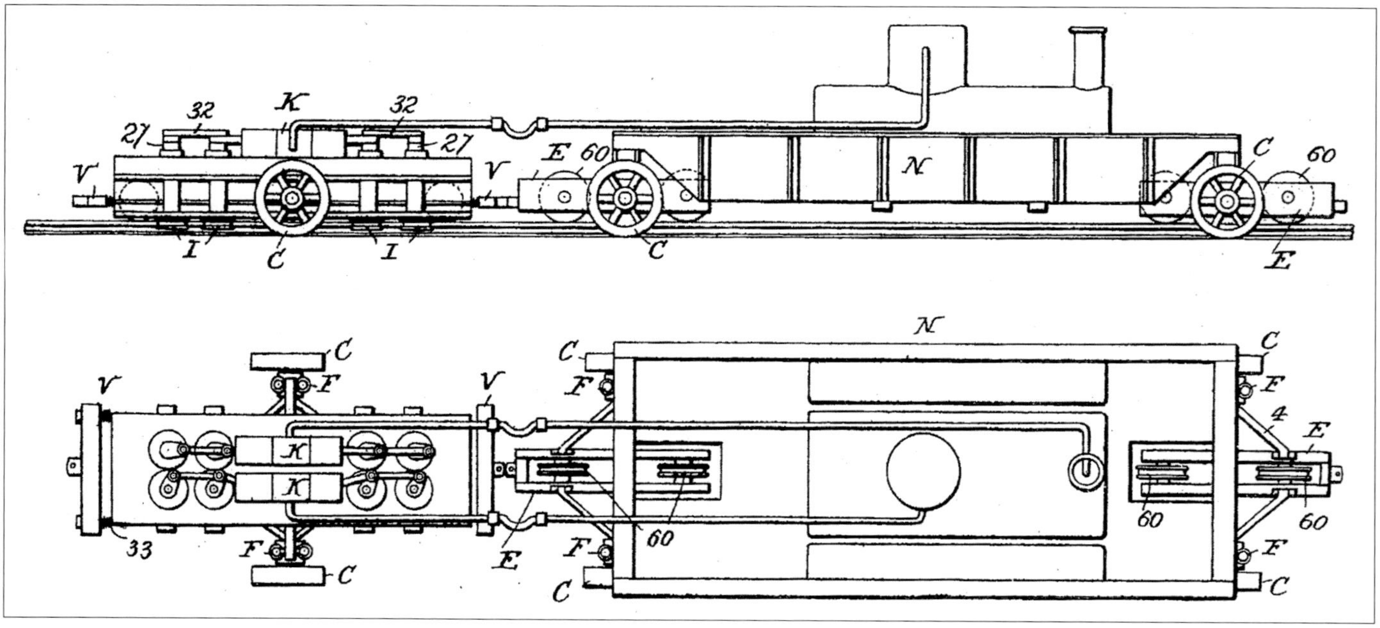

Baker's locomotive design for his railroad in 1904 required a flexible steam coupling to the cylinders to drive vertical shafts on which the wheels gripping the central rail were to be mounted. Baker correctly decided that this was not likely to be a commercial success.

US Patent 766802

The 8-ton steel freight car designed by Baker for his 'Economic' monorail system at the exhibition in Washington D.C.
Low cost transport for lines of light transport *by Charles Whiting Baker, 1915*

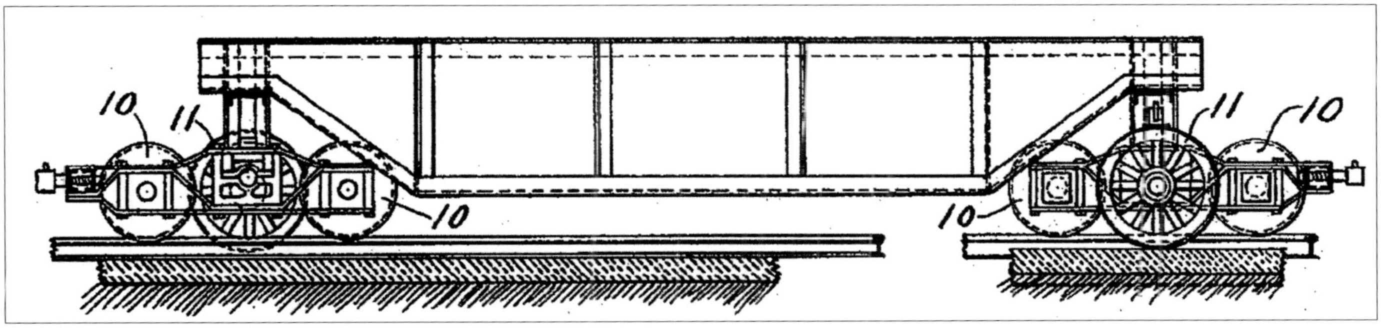

Baker subsequently included the design of the freight car in his application for a US Patent in 1915 (No. 1199751).

His objective was reduced costs and he stated 'It is probable that the street railway field affords the easiest opportunity for rapid profitable introduction of the system.' To this end he illustrated his booklet with a simple side view of a street tram. Despite his enthusiasm and the patents no further development occurred of such arrangements until 2006 when, as illustrated in the first volume, Translor opened a tram system in Padua using not dissimilar ideas.

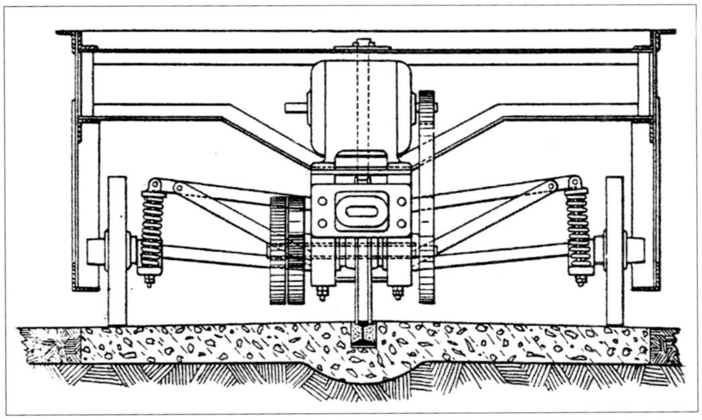

A cross section of Baker's revised vehicle and monorail roadway. The roadway was to be of concrete with a groove moulded along the centre for the rail which was to be secured in the groove by surrounding it with an elastic bituminous compound. The vehicle was to be supported by double flanged wheels resting on this rail with outer wheels sprung just sufficiently to maintain the balance of the vehicle. In this drawing, Baker showed an electric drive to the double flanged central wheel as would have been adopted in a tramcar.
Low cost transport for lines of light transport
by Charles Whiting Baker, 1915

Right: The experimental car used for the Baker system at Baltimore.
Low cost transport for lines of light transport
by Charles Whiting Baker, 1915

TWO CALIFORNIAN TRIALS

MR BROWN'S INVENTION

In August 1916 *Illustrated World* announced that a Mr Brown of San Francisco was carrying out experiments with a monorail car with a view to its adoption as a high speed rail link across the US[17]. Mr. Brown claimed (as was often the case with monorail inventors) that when fully developed his vehicle "will draw a train at a speed of two hundred miles an hour, and can be depended on to cover the distance between New York and the Pacific coast well short of twenty-four hours."

Harry W. Brown had been granted a patent for his monorail in 1914[18]. He made two claims in his patent application as being new and that he desired to protect, notably:

1. The combination with the car, track and its supporting structure, of a monorail system, of a single convexed faced traction wheel for the car, and a rail having a single point of contact with the face of the said wheel and at each side of the vertical center thereof.

2. The combination with the car and track supporting structure of a monorail system, of a laminated track upon the said structure, a rail secured to the said track, the said rail being of substantially U shape in cross section, and a single convex faced traction wheel for the car.

Brown made a large scale prototype model of his electrically powered vehicle and a short run of track. He promoted the monorail as a city transit system and suggested that in San Francisco it could run on heavy cables twenty feet above the street level.

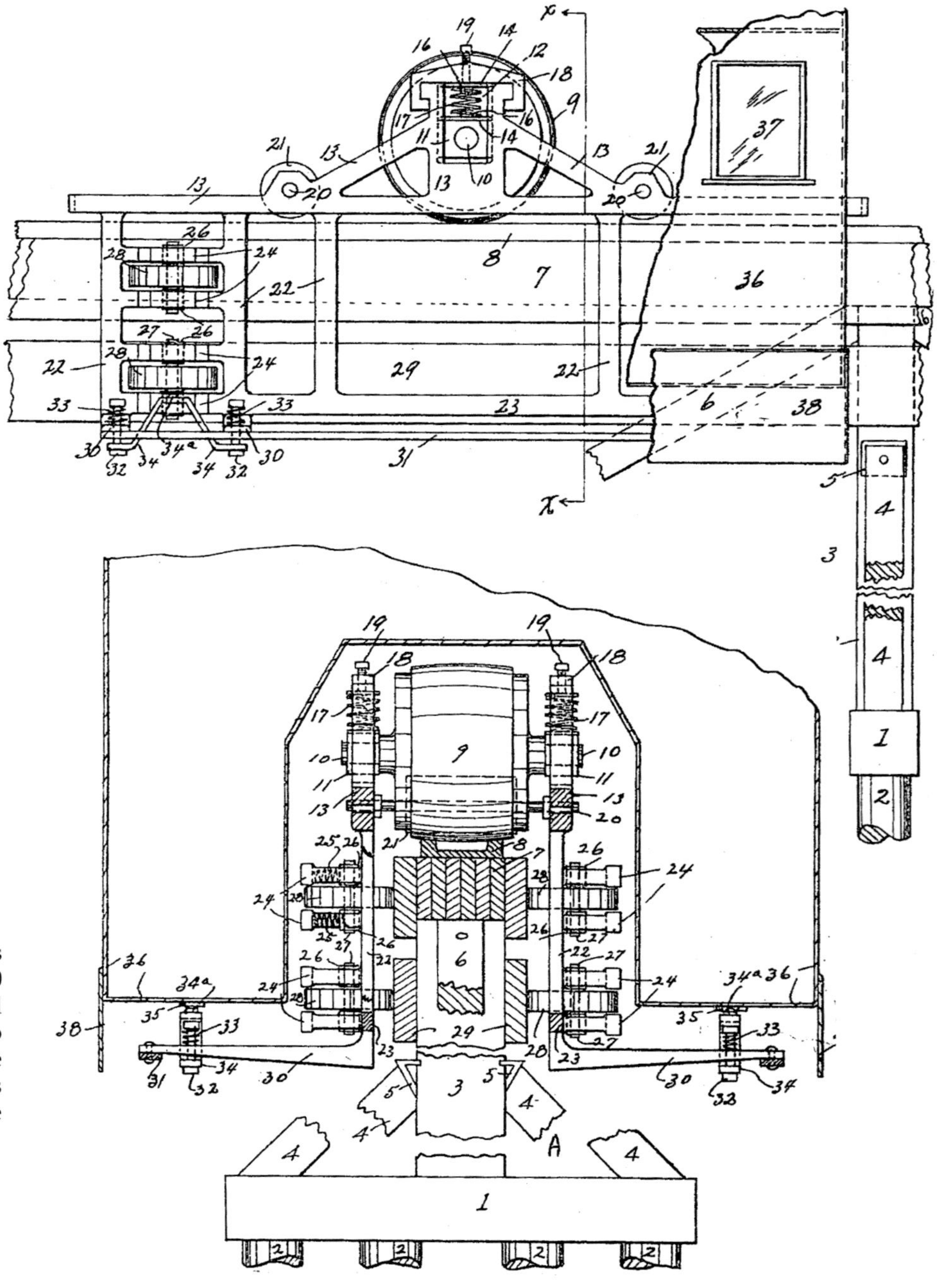

The drawings attached to Brown's application for US Patent No. 1086890 show the broad convex main wheel and supporting side wheels which also collected electric current. The carriage body was to be supported on springs fixed to arms outstretching from the chassis of the carriage.

Mr Brown proudly displays the chassis of his prototype monorail. Illustrated World *Vol. 25, August 1916*

A young passenger takes a ride on Mr Brown's test track in San Francisco.
Illustrated World
Vol. 25, August 1916

THE FIRST PROPELLER DRIVEN MONORAIL

In the same month, August 1916, *Popular Mechanics* published an article entitled 'Novel Aerial Trolley Car built in California' describing a suspended monorail[19]. By this time hanging a vehicle from a single rail was not novel; E. Langen had already invented the successful system which had been adopted for the suspended monorail in the Wuppertal region of Germany. The unusual feature of this Californian monorail was the use of a gasoline engine driving a propeller on the front of the vehicle to provide power. This appears to be the first time that such a system was implemented in practice albeit the idea of using a propeller to obtain motion on a monorail had been patented in 1892 by Anders Anderson[20]. Indeed Anderson's vehicle was very similar to that built in California.

Popular Mechanics coyly described the designer of the system as a western inventor, without giving a name, and stated that it was proposed to adopt the system for a rapid transit line between Burbank and Glendale, California. The inventor may, however, have been Louis E. Fischer who was granted a patent for a propeller driven suspended monorail in 1915[21] albeit the patent states that Fischer was at that time residing in St. Louis, Missouri.

The body of the prototype vehicle was built largely from steel and aluminium and seated more than 50 passengers. Given the vehicle's length and the four sets of suspension wheels it seems likely that only very wide curves could have been negotiated. On the experimental line, which was about 400ft long and probably straight, the single rail was fixed to gallows-like wooden structures at regular intervals. Whilst the main purpose of the line was for trials, it was also used to provide a unique recreational ride.

For the short experimental line the vehicle's propeller was powered by a 24 horse power gasoline engine. Presumably a gearbox was included to allow the rotation of the propeller to be reversed to enable the vehicle to return back up the track. The reverse thrust of the propeller may, perhaps, even have been used as a brake. It was envisaged that a more powerful engine would be adopted if a full length line was built. Like Mr. W. Brown, the inventor believed high speeds would be obtained – in this case a mere one hundred miles per hour. At this speed, the inventor proposed that planes or wings beneath the car would be moved out so that the weight on the overhead rail was reduced leaving no strain upon the overhead track. Presumably that is why the picture shows wheels both below and above the overhead rail, without these the vehicle might have taken off.

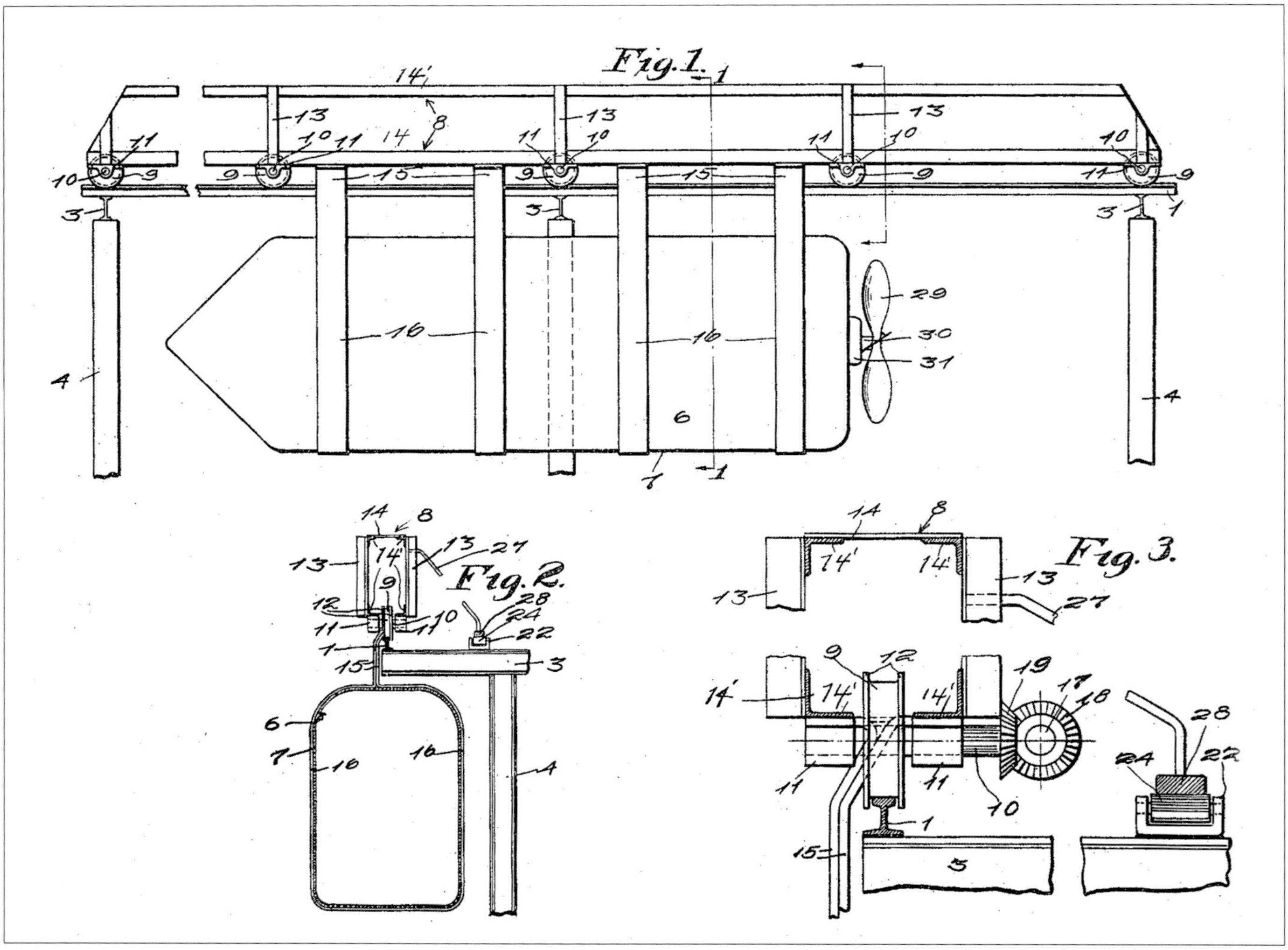

Louis E. Fischer proposed a monorail driven by a propeller in his 1915 US Patent No. 1125284. Anders Anderson had first proposed a similar idea in his US Patent No. 470534 in 1892.

The propeller powered suspended monorail in action. The engineer (pilot?) is wearing a hat, indicating that at least the front windows must have been glazed. Popular Mechanics *Vol. 26, August 1916*

MONORAILS IN THE TRENCHES

Unlike modern warfare which takes place in the air or using mobile vehicles and ships on land and sea, much of the First World War was fought from relatively immobile trenches. The logistics of getting supplies and troops to the front and the wounded to safety were paramount. The shell damage to roads, the weather in northern France and Belgium and the churning of the mud by troops and vehicles led all countries involved to adopt rail transport.

Typically a standard gauge main line brought supplies to within three or four miles of the front line. Conventional 60cm. steam hauled narrow gauge trains then transported the supplies from this rail head to about a mile from the trenches. From there, very light railways, often 60cm. gauge but not hauled by steam locomotives which displayed their position in the form of smoke and steam, hauled supplies to within about 300 yards of the trenches. These railways, built by both the USA and Britain as well as other allies, have been excellently described by Richard Dunn and Roy C. Link in their respective books [22 & 23].

The last few yards to the trenches were handled with ropeways, trolleys and man power. None were perfect. A report by Lieut.-Colonel Arthur A. Crookshank of the Royal Engineers in July 1917[24] set out the problems experienced by UK troops:

"The 60cm Decauville light railway, if laid on the surface in the usual manner, soon disappears into the mud when man power is used. The man power also has been known to disappear into the mud. If heavy trollies are used necessitating animal power, then the track must be stone ballasted or given some form of hard roadway; and stone ballast, owing to the demands of roads, is often not procurable. If procurable it is expensive to maintain both in men and materials owing to the damage done to the animals' hoofs."

Adding to the problems, he recorded that if machine power (petrol or steam) was needed it necessitated scrapping the advantage of the light and easily laid Decauville sleepers and re-sleepering with long wooden sleepers placed very close together or with the use of stone ballast in addition. He stated that laying a 3ft. wide flat formation over ground which consisted almost entirely of shell holes with narrow knife edges required a lot of work.

It was in this most dangerous area that at least three and possibly four types of monorails were in use.

CAILLET SYSTEM

This system was invented in 1893 and, as described in the earlier volume (20), included military vehicles for supplies as well as ambulance cars. The track was light, being based on 4 ½, 7, 9 ½ and 12 kg. 'Vignoles' rail and could easily be moved and repositioned as the line of trenches changed or bombardment caused damage. No direct evidence of the use of this system during the First World War by the British Army has been traced. Given the UK supplier, The Monorail Portable Railway Company based in London, continued to operate throughout the war, it is, however, difficult to imagine that this system was not at least tried. (The Monorail Portable Railway Company ceased trading around 1922 and was struck off the Register of Companies and dissolved on the 11th November 1924[25]).

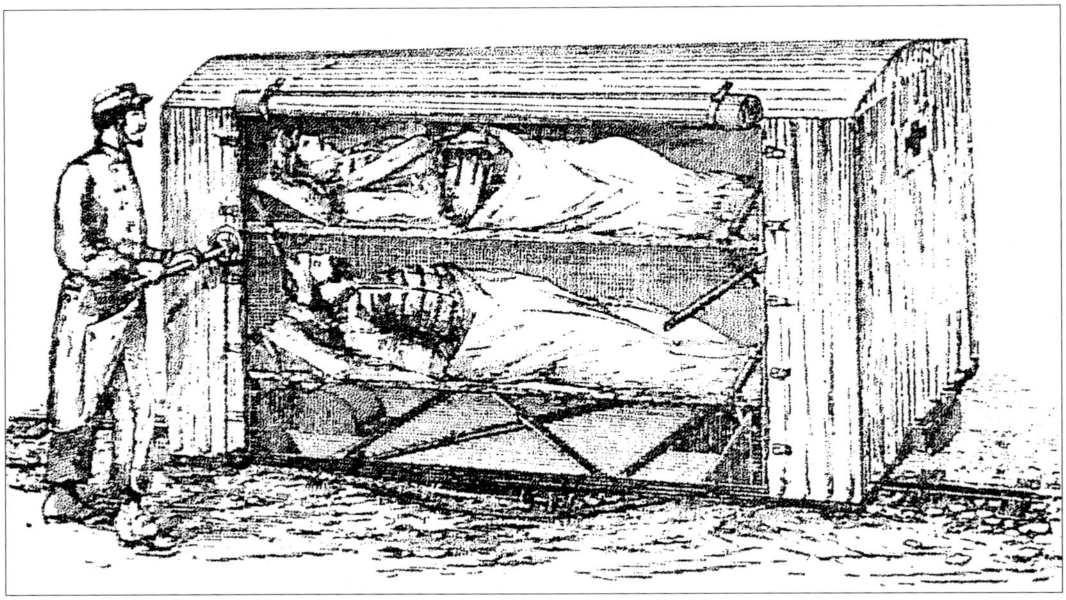

Caillet designed a variety of military ambulances for both human and horse power.
Scientific American Supplement
Vol. 39, 8 June 1895

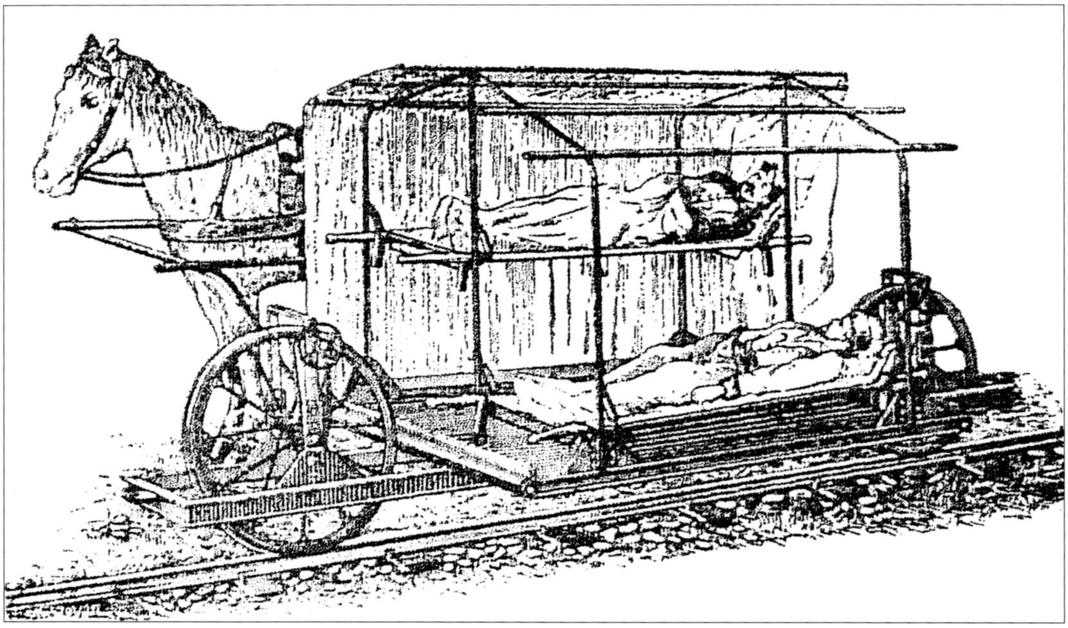

THE TYPE 'M' TRUCK

Whilst no record of the use of the Caillet system has been traced, the Gloucester Railway Carriage & Wagon Company Limited delivered to the War Office so called class 'M' monorail trucks which were only marginally different from the Caillet design. The latter had an extended pole on one side that was gripped so that the vehicle could be raised to the horizontal and pushed along, the loading of the vehicle being intentionally biased so that it rested on an underside support when not being moved. On the Gloucester vehicle, a removable pole extended out both sides and correspondingly had supports underneath the vehicle on both sides. This design may have been developed from experience of the Caillet system. It would have been easier to use by two men for heavy loads such as shells and related equipment, or by one man where one side of the monorail was impassable due to shell craters.

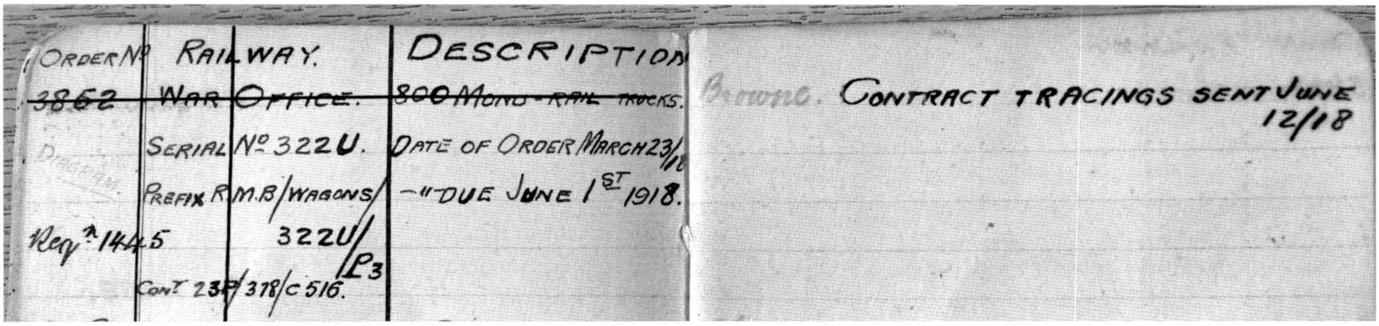
ORDER No | RAILWAY. | DESCRIPTION
3852 | WAR OFFICE. | 800 MONO-RAIL TRUCKS.
SERIAL No 322U. | DATE OF ORDER MARCH 23/18
PREFIX R M.B/WAGONS/ | -"-DUE JUNE 1ST 1918.
Regn. 1445 | 322U/ L3
CONT 23P/378/C 516.
Browne. CONTRACT TRACINGS SENT JUNE 12/18

The entry in the Gloucester Railway Carriage & Wagon Company Limited Order Book shows that 800 class 'M' wagons were ordered on 21st March for delivery by 1st June 1918. (Orders were crossed out once delivery was made.)

GRC&WCo., Gloucestershire Archives

The Gloucester class 'M' monorail wagon was probably derived from the Caillet design. This works photograph taken in May 1918 was taken only six months before the end of the war.

GRC&WCo., Gloucestershire Archives

FINNIMORE'S POST AND RAIL MONORAIL

In the July 1917 report by Crookshank he described the system designed by Major A. C. Finnimore of the Royal Engineers in December 1916. Similar to the system patented by Henry Palmer nearly one hundred years before, it consisted of posts supporting a steel Decauville 9lb rail. The cars were able to carry loads of up to 400lbs and the system was purported to have clear advantages. In particular it did not require the ground to be levelled (an often quoted advantage of monorails but in this case very relevant), it was silent which was rather important if you are being shot at, and camouflaged, showing up in aerial photographs at that time as just an infantry track of wooden gratings.

The rails were fixed to the pickets by nails and the height was set so that the bottom of the cars was usually only about 1ft above the ground. The rail height was therefore not much over 2ft or 3ft higher than the pathway except where gulleys were crossed. Construction was kept simple with the rails only needing two holes to be drilled or punched in the flange at each end and one at 6ft intervals along the rail.

The cars consisted of a light wooden frame with sufficient strength to carry men on stretchers in the trays below the rail level. The trays were made low enough so that the center of gravity of the car when empty was below rail level and thus stable. When loaded the center of gravity was lowered further. Crookshank comments that if one side is heavier than the other balance was achieved by moving a rifle or other goods to the other side. A difference of a few pounds did not materially affect the car.

Crookshank reported that a fully loaded car could be pushed by one man on the level or for short distances up slopes not exceeding 1 in 20. For steeper slopes two men were needed either pushing from the rear or with a rope towing at the front. For curves less than 25ft radius or high speeds on long downgrades side buffers of flat iron needed to be fitted to reduce the risk of collision with a post if the car swung too much. Apparently there was little tendency to swing except on curves. Side or guard rails were also fixed to the posts to limit swing where needed and also to act as a brake.

WILSON'S SUSPENDED MONORAIL

In September 1917 Crookshank reported on another monorail system[26]. This had been developed by Major Wilson of the Royal Engineers and consisted of wooden beams placed across the top of communication trenches at 6ft. intervals with straps of square iron wrapped around which suspended a hook with a split end on which a flat iron rail measuring 2¾in. by ¼in. was mounted. A light wooden car or trolley with a tray big enough to take a stretcher or carry 200lbs was suspended by continuous wire from two pairs of double flanged wheels by means of iron hooks.

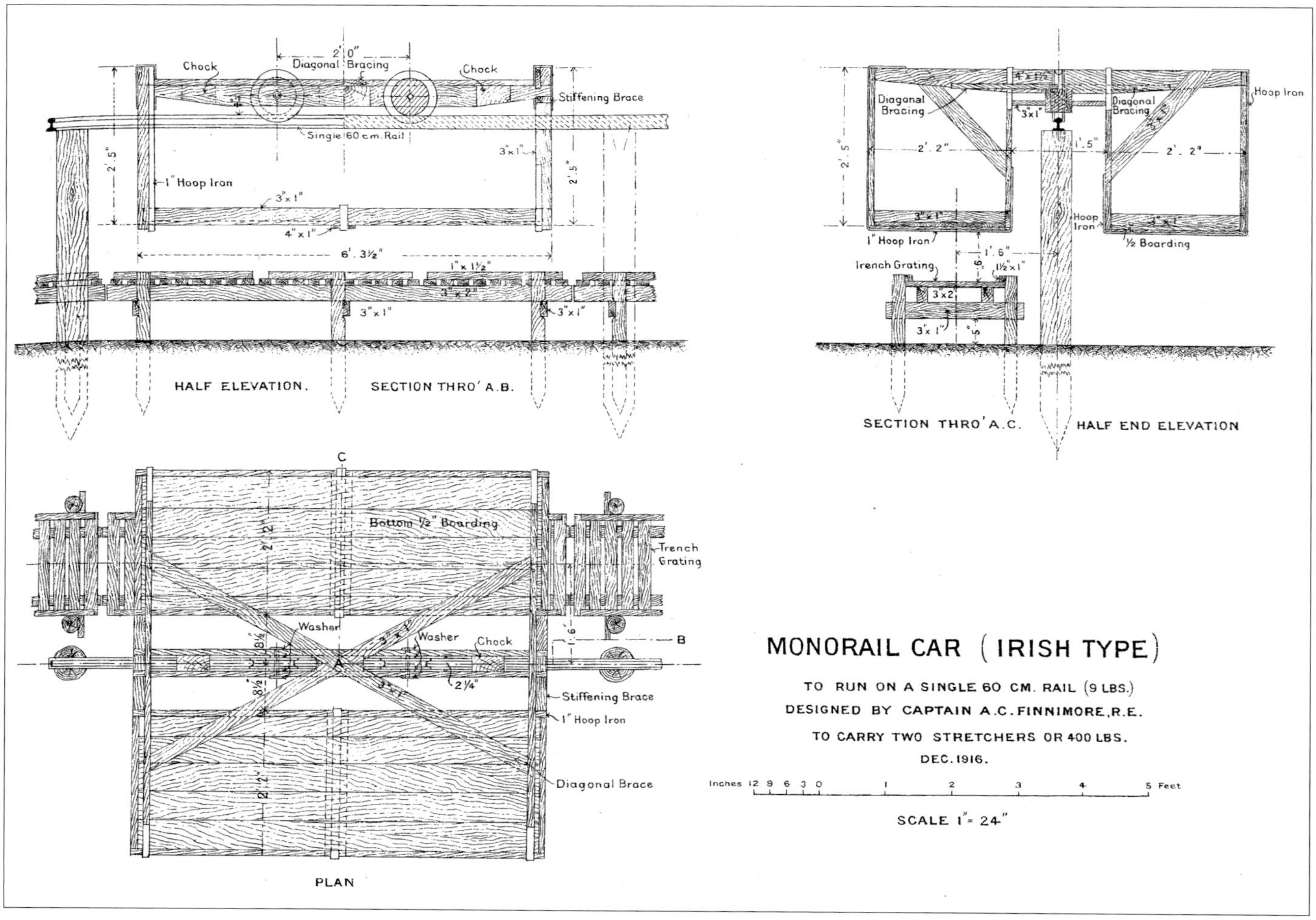

The 'Irish Type' monorail car designed by Captain A. A. Finnimore. Royal Engineers Journal *Vol. 26, July 1917*

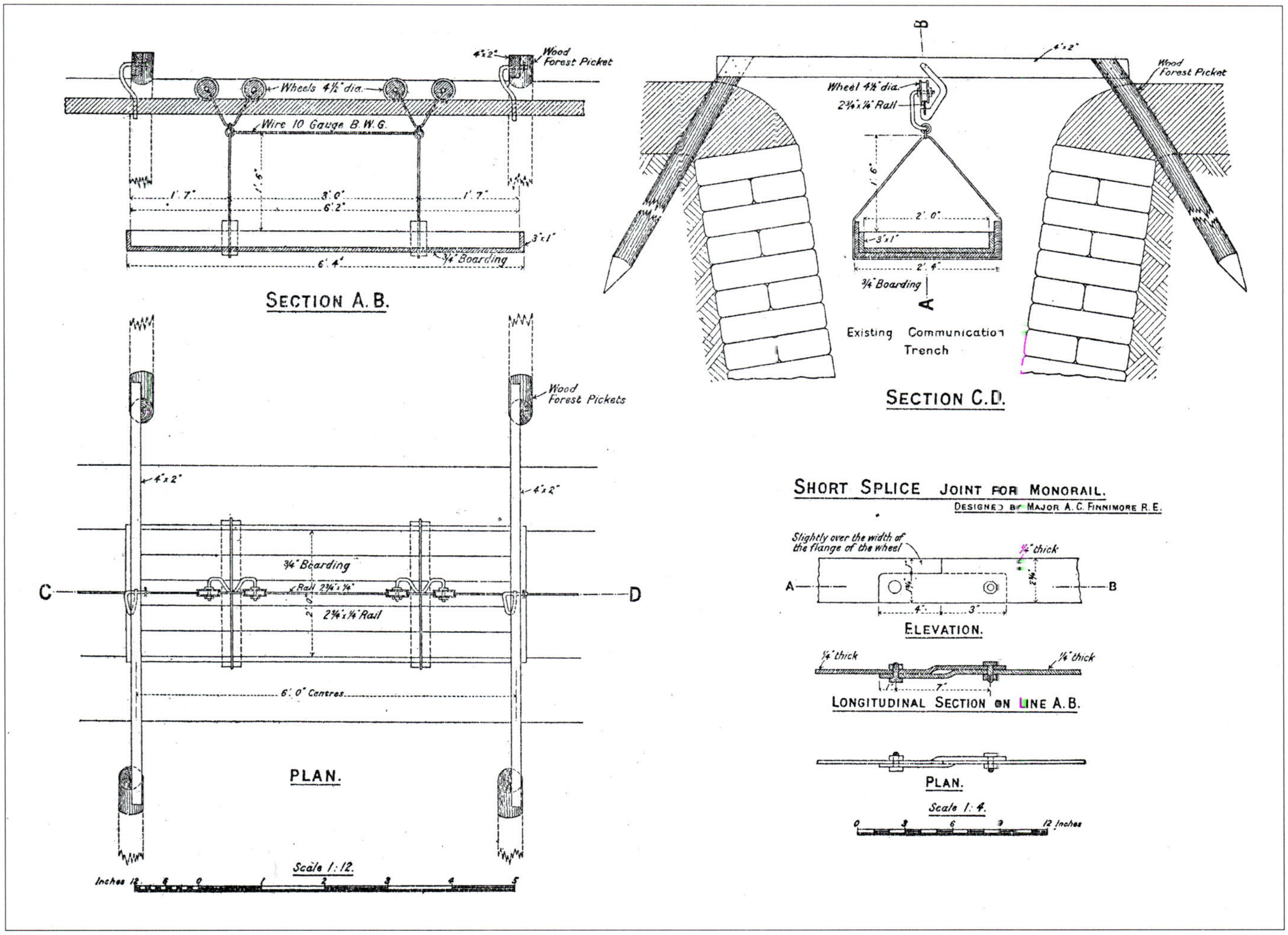

The suspended monorail for use in trenches designed by Major Wilson with improvements by Major Finnimore.
Royal Engineers Journal *Vol. 26, September 1917*

The system had been installed in one portion of the trenches in France but Crookshank, reporting on the arrangement, said that it had little use as the divisions experience had been confined to the 60cm. or 2ft. gauge light railways and they were frightened of it. The system had its drawbacks. Crookshank noted that the iron strap from which the rail was hung was liable to get displaced and needed frequent attention. This was a polite way of saying that the rail came off the hook and fell down on those below. No wonder the troops were frightened of it. As important, if the rails were not flush, it jarred the cars making a noise as did the flanges striking the bolt heads of the rail joint fastenings. Crookshank rightly stated that 'Metallic sounds are very objectionable, especially at night' as it disclosed the position of the troops.

Finnimore, who had designed the post and rail system, was called upon to redesign the system to eliminate the problems. His solutions included shearing rails longitudinally for slightly more than the overlap of about 4in. at joints and also to shear off the upper tongue for about 4in.. The rail supports were also improved and simplified with the strap round the beam being replaced by a hook through the beam.

Whilst designed for use in supplying underground forward bases, further back both the Finnimore and Wilson monorails rose from the trenches to the surface and connected with lorry, 60cm or broad gauge rail heads.

These monorails were claimed to have many advantages. They were invisible to the enemy being mostly in the trenches, they made little noise and such noise that was made could not be located. They were also cheap and easy to maintain.

EPITAPH

The nature of the First World War is reflected in both the Finnimore and Wilson monorail drawings illustrating their use for carrying stretchers. The extent of the use of these lines is lost in history but the following is recorded in the *London Gazette* in relation to a distinguished service award [27]:

> "Lt. Walter Darley Staveley,
> For conspicuous gallantry and devotion to duty. This officer was in charge of a party laying a mono-rail every night being subjected to heavy shelling of high explosive and gas, and the line was hit over and over again. He kept his men at work for an average of six hours each night, walking from group to group, helping and encouraging them. Despite many difficulties and prolonged strain he accomplished his task."

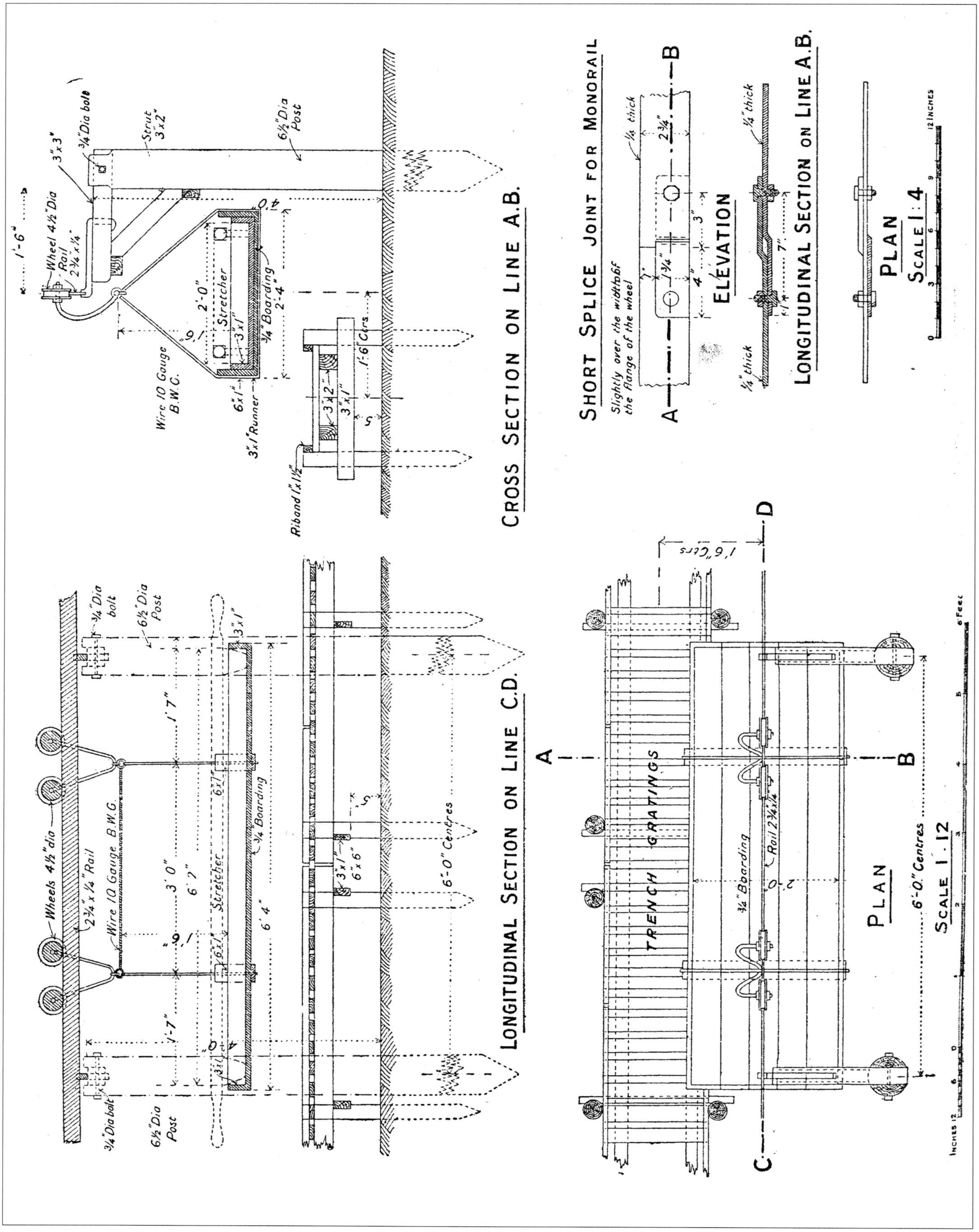

Where appropriate the Wilson suspended monorail could surface from the trenches. It was then supported on 6 1/2in. diameter telegraph type posts. Small platforms were also constructed where trans-shipment to the 60cm. gauge railways took place.

Royal Engineers Journal *Vol. 26, September 1917*

THE E-Z OPENER BAG COMPANY MONORAIL, LOUISIANA, USA

In 1884 Herbert Eugene Westervelt founded a company to operate a small paper mill in Marseilles, Illinois to make wrapping paper from wheat straw. The company grew rapidly and in 1903 the E-Z Opener Bag Company was created to run operations in Fulton, New York and South Bend, Indiana. By 1916 this company had leased a plant in Braithwaite, Louisiana to manufacture high quality paper bags made from southern pine trees. These were conveyed down the Mississippi river in barges and additional pulp wood arrived by rail to the pulp mill. This area of Louisana, however, was near to a bend on the Mississippi river and had experienced a number of floods[28]. Disaster struck in April 1922 when all rail communications were destroyed after the river rose and broke the levees at the nearby town of Poydras.

Acting rapidly to the loss of supply of wood pulp the company designed and installed a 2000ft. long suspended type monorail made of 104,000ft. of creosoted pine and cyprus with a carrying capacity of 3½ tons. The General Manager Hartman and W. E. Penfield of the E-Z Opener Bag Company gave the following detailed description to *Wood Preserving News*[29]:

"The pine was treated by the Rueping process with a final retention of 6lbs of creosote oil per cubic foot.

The bents or supports of the monorail, spaced 15ft apart consist of 8in. by 8in. by 28ft uprights, 8in. by 12in. by 10ft caps, 2in. by 10in. by 7ft sway braces, and 8in. by 8in. by 22ft mud sills; 2in. by 8in. by 2ft cleats for fastening the caps to the uprights; 2in. by 8in. by 1ft cleats for attaching the uprights to the mud sills, and 4in. by 14in. by 2ft 7in. foundation pieces upon which rest the mud sills. A Shepherd hoist runs on a 15in. 'I' beam."

The 'Shephard' hoist was probably a spelling error and most likely referred to a hoist made by Shepard Niles, a firm founded in 1878 who by 1922 were a major manufacturer of cranes and electric powered hoists.

The height of the track structure of the E-Z Opener Bag Company monorail reflected the need to collect the logs for wood pulp from stacks near the accessible railhead. By the time this picture was taken it appears that the flooding had subsided.

Wood Preserving News *July 1923*

The Shephard hoist in action. Normally hoists run short distances across factory floors with electric supply via a suspended cable. The E-Z Opener Bag Company engineers were novel in using the hoist mechanism as an electric powered railcar by suspending a small platform for seating the driver. Power collection appears to have been from wires/rails insulated and supported above the I beam.
Wood Preserving News *July 1923*

RUSSIAN LINES OF THE TWENTIES AND THIRTIES

TICHOTSKY'S EXPERIMENTAL LINES

During the 1920s Vyacheslav Petrovich Tichotsky led a team to build experimental industrial monorails. Russian websites indicate that possibly four lines were built[30]. Whilst little information is easily available, it appears that one of the later lines, opened on the 7th November 1934 in the region of Nizhny Novgorod in mid-west Russia, had a length of about 50km and connected the villages of Bakaldy Maza and Yaloksha. It remained in operation until 1949.

The system was a throw back to the nineteenth century. In an area where wood was in easy supply, wooden uprights were used to support a wooden beam on which the steel main rail was mounted about 5m above ground level. The system relied on balancing the carriages and locomotive by adopting a low centre of gravity as envisaged in Palmer's patent for a monorail in 1821 and subsequently by Lartigue in the 1880s in Algeria.

The four combined locomotive and passenger vehicles were also constructed of wood and had two floors. The two lower pannier sections suspended on each side of the track were for passengers and had central entrances, possibly with a door, resembling carriages on Lartigue's Feurs to Panissières line. On each side of the entrance were closed compartments with a single side window, but with a window at the end, each seating five people (twenty passengers in total). Above the roof of these compartments was a central cabin for the driver and mounted at one end was the petrol motor that powered the double flanged driving wheels. A hand-rail surrounded the upper deck and there were platform extensions to allow access to other vehicles.

Left: The simple structure of the track on the line near Nizhny Novgorod. There do, however, appear to have been major earthworks.

Above: Trains consisted of a railcar plus pannier freight vehicles, probably with two main wheels. These were essentially larger versions of those designed in the 1880s by Lartigue. The main freight traffic appears to have been wood.

Below: It is probably overstating the elegance of this vehicle to call it a railcar but it combined the duty of both locomotive and passenger vehicle on the Russian line near Nizhny Novgorod.

Waldner's model 'air train' on its track in Gorky Park, Moscow.

WALDNER'S SUPERFAST MONORAIL MODEL

In June 1933 *Modern Transport* reported[31] that the Commissariat for Railways of the USSR had decided to build an experimental monorail overhead railway about thirteen miles long in order to test a high speed passenger 'air train' designed by S. Waldner, an engineer attached to the Institute of Railway Construction. The car was described to be in the form of two Zeppelin-like cars linked together by a rigid steel frame and overhanging both sides of the single track. It was claimed that it would be capable of reaching 186 miles per hour.

The 'air train' was to be driven by aeroplane propellers connected to two diesel engines capable of a combined 1,060 horse power. Each of the two cars was to seat forty passengers but Waldner envisaged the air train eventually being capable of carrying up to about 300 seated passengers. Stability was to be maintained by the fitment of runners between the inside of each car and the concrete framework supporting the rail.

Later that year, in October 1933, Waldner demonstrated a model monorail in Gorky Park, Moscow[30]. The track consisted of a central rail with two symmetric but widely placed outer rails. The 2.5m long pannier type vehicle rode on the central rail and had balancing wheels under each of the model passenger carrying panniers. Each of the panniers was bullet shaped with an electrically powered propeller at the rear. Current collection was from two conductor rails. Unusually the panniers were connected by an aerofoil type structure.

The experimental track was about 500m in length and speeds of up to 120km were reported. It was also stated that it was very stable when in motion probably due to the aerodynamic effect of the aerofoil.

Despite support from a number of academics a full size prototype was never built. This did not, however, stop extravagant claims being reported in the US magazine *Popular Science*[32] which published an article in 1934 stating that the Soviet Government planned to tap the mineral wealth of Turkestan using three monorail lines. These were to be 332 miles in total length and air propelled cars were to reach 180 miles per hour 'according to calculations based on tests of models at Moscow.' On the longest of the projected routes the monorail was to cross the river Amu-Daria, 1¼ miles wide, using amphibian cars. These were to leave the monorail and cross the river as a boat. The article reported that Soviet engineers were already surveying the route.

References

1 UK monorail Patent No. 20419. Date of Application 15 September 1896, Date of Grant 31 July 1897.
US monorail Patent No. 843418, Date of Application 1 June 1905, Date of Grant 5 February 1907.

2 *Electrical Review*, Vol. 52, 13 March 1903, pp448-449.

3 *The Americana: A Universal Reference* 1912, Vol. 17.

4 US Patent No. 867007. Date of Application 28 July 1900, Date of Grant 24 September 1907.

5 *The News Tribune* 7 September 1995 p15. Article by Murray C. Morgan.

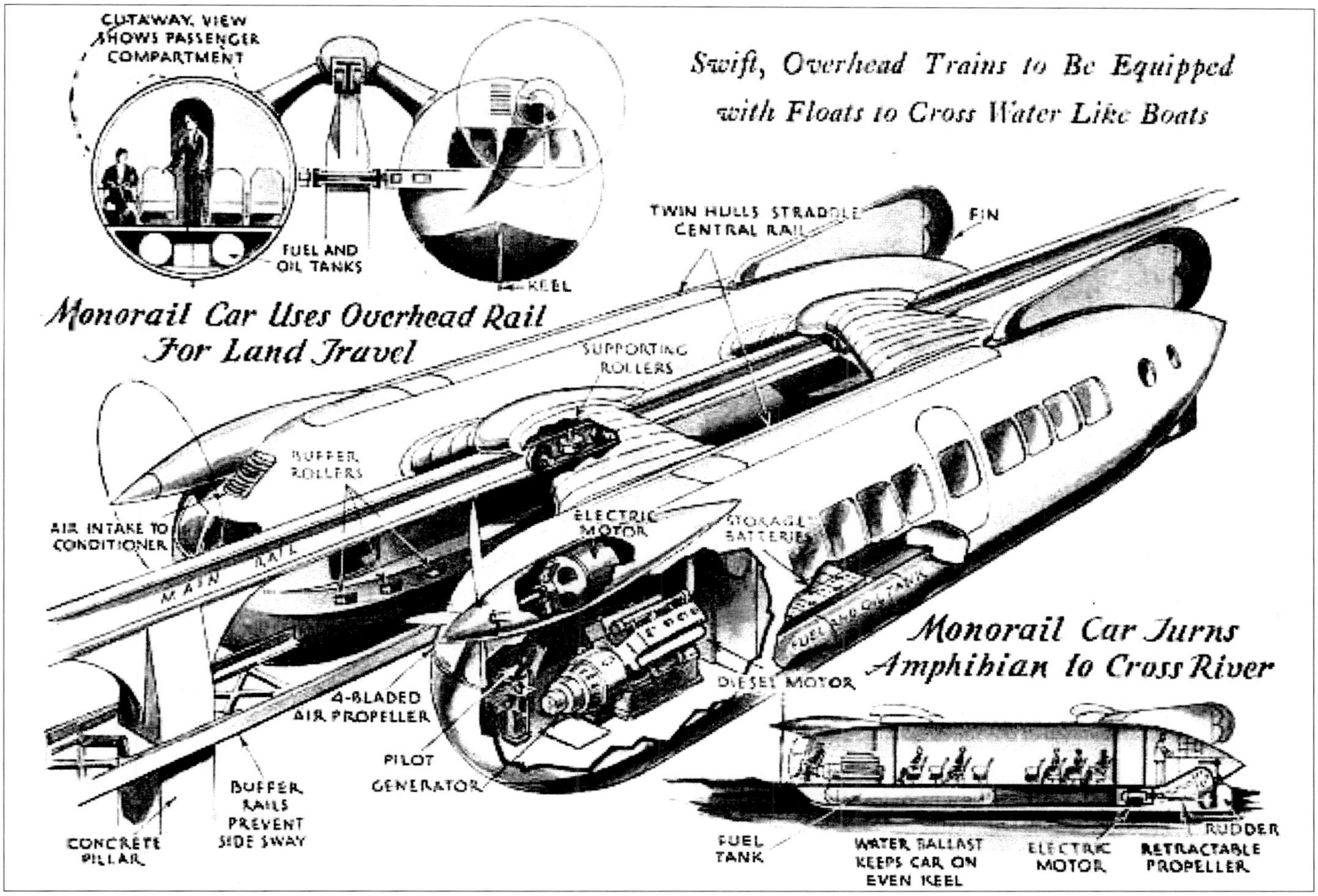

This illustration published in *Popular Science* July 1934, showed the suggested development of the Waldner monorail. The magazine cover had a coloured illustration of the monorail speeding its way across a desert. It was probably based on Soviet propaganda plus the liberal imagination of the magazine's artist.

6 *Russell Senate Office Building: The first century* prepared by the Senate Historical Office under the direction of Nancy Erikson, Secretary of State.

7 *Brooklyn Eagle* 3 February 1897, p1, 16 February 1897, p5.

8 *Inside Congress: The Shocking Scandals, Corruption, and Abuse of Power behind the Scenes on Capitol Hill* by Ronald Kessler, 1998.

9 *The Hill* 1 December 2009, article by Katy Hopkins.

10 *The Hill* 31 May 2006, article by Ariel Alexovich.

11 *United States Daily Consular and Trade Reports* 21 May 1914, No. 119.

12 French monorail Patent No. 428764, Date of Application 28 April 1910, Date of Grant 29 June 1911 & UK monorail Patent No.10157, Date of Application 28 April 1911, Date of Grant 25 January 1912.

13 *Engineering*, Vol. 100, 17 December 1915, p615.

14 *Monopolies and the People* by Charles Whiting Baker, C. E., published by G. P. Putnam's Sons, 1889.

15 UK monorail Patent:

Patent No.	Date of Application	Date of Grant
15236	7 July 1904	11 August 1904

US monorail Patents:

Patent No.	Date of Application	Date of Grant
766802	18 November 1903	9 August 1904
731988	17 February 1904	7 February 1905
1199751	23 April 1915	3 October 1916
1199752	3 July 1915	3 October 1916

16 *Low cost transport for lines of light transport* by Charles Whiting Baker, 1915.

17 *Illustrated World*, Vol. 25, August 1916, pp808-809.

18 US Patent No.1086890, Date of Application 17 March 1913, Date of Grant 10 February 1914.

19 *Popular Mechanics*, Vol. 26, August 1916, p273.

20 *Monorails of the 19th Century* by Adrian S. Garner.

21 US Patent No. 1125284, Date of Application 24 January 1914, Date of Grant 19 January 1915.

22 *Narrow Gauge to No Man's Land* by Richard Dunn, 2009.

23 *WDLR Album* by Roy C. Link, 2014.

24 *Royal Engineers Journal* Vol. 26, July 1917, pp7-10.

25 *London Gazette* 11 November 1924, p8176.

26 *Royal Engineers Journal* Vol. 26, September 1917, pp108-112.

27 Supplement to the London Gazette 11 January 1919, p644.

28 *The Evolution of Competitive Strategies in Global Forestry Industries* edited by Juha-Antti Lamberg, Juha Näsi, Jari Ojala and Pasi Sajasalo. Chapter 8 by Patrick M. Kreiser.

29 *Wood Preserving News* July 1923, p115-116.

30 No contemporary western references have been traced. The above history of the Russian rural lines is based on Russian websites. These sites include including summaries of a monograph by V. P. Tichotsky and B. Kozlov published in 1933 in the Moscow 'Goslesizdate' plan (All Union Scientific Research Institute of Industrial Transport).

31 *Modern Transport* 3 June 1933, p8.

32 *Popular Science* July 1934, cover and p33.

The magnesium company's monorail climbed precariously up Layton Canyon. The umbrella was a much needed feature to protect from the direct sun. *National Park Service DEVA 38675 'Epsom Salts Monorail East of Layton Pass in Slate Range 1924 or 1925'*

CHAPTER 6
THE AMERICAN MAGNESIUM COMPANY MONORAIL

The American Magnesium Company was the creation of Thomas H. Wright, a Los Angeles florist and enthusiastic prospector. The company's objective was to extract magnesium salts from a mineral deposit in the Crystal Hills near the Panamint Range in north western San Bernardino County, California[1].

The deposit had been known about since before the First World War having been discovered by a prospector, Joe Ward. Whilst the deposit was extractable, the high cost of transporting the ore was the limiting economic factor to the development of a mine. There were no roads other than desert sand tracks across the low ridges and ravines surrounding the area and summer temperatures often reach over 40 degrees Centigrade (104 degrees Fahrenheit). The area was rightly named Death Valley and Ward decided not to proceed further[2].

Despite the inhospitable terrain and climate, Wright independently carried out prospecting of this area and rediscovered the deposit in 1917. He made preparation for mining with a temporary camp and in 1919, following analysis of the deposit, he applied for a patent[3] for the process of making potash alum. The patent disclosed that the deposit in San Bernardino County was 'magnesium sulphate 60 to 76%, sodium sulphate 6 to 10%, potassium sulphate 8 to 18%, and lesser amounts of sodium chloride, silica, calcium sulphate, etc.' He then formed the American Magnesium Company, which was incorporated on 18th September 1919 with a share capital of US$1m. In addition to Wright being appointed President, Jasper Stanley was appointed Vice President, M. K. Mahany was appointed Secretary & Treasurer and H. C. Galloupe and E. M. Wright were appointed fellow directors. All were from Los Angeles[4].

The output of the Company was to be Glauber's salt (magnesium carbonate) and pharmaceutical grade Epsom salts (named after the town in Surrey UK where they were first discovered) which was commonly available for sale at high street pharmacies as well as chemicals for industry. In the US alone the demand for magnesium sulphate was estimated in 1921 to be about 50,000 tons a year.

In 1920 the Company made claim to the deposits over an area of 1,440 acres at an average elevation of 2,400ft. The initial proposal was to use water from Anvil Springs and Hidden Springs, which were about 1,000ft above the deposits, to provide water to form a solution of Epsom

The flat bed of Searles Lake rarely sees water with temperatures often exceeding 40C. A train on the Trona Railroad can just be seen on the horizon in the middle of this picture. *Author*

From 1873 to 1895 virtually the only human movement through the mountains and across Searles Lake (previously known as Borax Lake) was the twenty mule train operated by John and Dennis Searles to carry borax to a rail head at Mojave. In 2013 the scene was re-enacted. *Betty Peters*

Salts. This would be piped to a mill to be constructed near the Trona Railroad. It was hoped that the heat of the desert would be sufficient to warm the water at the mine site to allow the salts to dissolve in settling tanks. The three tons of earth to every one ton of salts in the ore would be left in the settling tanks for deposit at the mine site.

Possibly due to the inconsistent supply of water, concerns over pipe blockage or the power needed to pump the solution over the Panamint Range of mountains, the Company eventually decided to install a railroad and reviewed two routes. The first was down Wingate Wash to the floor of Death Valley and then along the banks of the Amargosa River to a junction with the Tonapah and Tidewater Railroad. This was a relatively easy route but one directly through the intense heat of Death Valley. The other was from a junction with the Trona Railroad south of Trona. Neither was attractive as an investment to the respective railroads and the American Magnesium Company could not raise sufficient funds to build either route using standard or three foot gauge track.

It was, however, essential to have transport from the mine site to a railroad as the Company had decided to construct a small processing plant at Wilmington, south of Los Angeles, rather than near Trona as originally envisaged. Despite this change, Wright opted for a rail route to Trona and he made this decision with R. V. Leeson, the consulting engineer Wright had appointed at the time the Company was set up. He also instructed Leeson to design a monorail railroad on the grounds that it would avoid the need for substantial hard rock blasting as the system would allow curves to be tighter, gradients to be steeper and, by varying the length of the A frame legs, the need to level the ground would be reduced. There were probably additional factors; the 'A' frame design lifted the rail and vehicles above the abrasive sand and a monorail permitted the use of wood for the side rails saving the cost of steel rail. Wood also expands less than steel when exposed to high temperatures.

Before construction could begin, the Company filed, on the 9th June 1922, for a right of way from the federal government. This was contested by local prospectors who objected that Layton Canyon was too narrow for both the monorail and the 'burros' – mules – used by prospectors. Wright argued that the success of the Company would bring substantial money to the local county and won the day. Approval was given on 2nd October 1922 and construction began in May the following year. The cost of construction varied from US$7000 to US$8000 a mile and total cost of the line including rolling stock etc. was reported

This picture of a prospector and mule near Searles Lake in the 1920s captures the loneliness of the territory.
Railway Wonders of the World *Vol. 1 circa 1930*

to have been about US $350,000. Investors anticipated that one ton of ore could be hauled over the line for less than US$1. By the summer of 1923 some sixteen miles of the twenty-eight mile line had been constructed[5].

The monorail was fully operational during 1924[6] and on the 24th May 1924 the Company increased its share capital from US$1m to US$3m, the stock being purchased by some 264 shareholders. This additional capital offset costs and was no doubt issued on the back of the completion of the monorail. The success, however, was short lived and mine production slowed from mid 1925. The amount of material shipped from the mine was not sufficient to maintain efficient use of the Company's processing plant based in Wilmington and, problematically, the ore mined had increasing amounts of impurity. Further, the monorail track was deteriorating due to its light construction (the flip side of the low cost) and the effect of the extreme heat. Unluckily for the American Magnesium Company, Searles Lake, which was and is normally totally dry, became nearly one foot or so deep in water during the storms of 1924 and 1925 causing uneven settlement and washouts on sections of track on both sides of Layton Canyon. This combination of events led to serious problems of maintenance.

The monorail under construction looking west out of Layton Canyon towards Searles Lake. The grade at this point was 7.5%. Whilst the picture quality is poor it shows that the legs of the 'A' frames were extended to avoid major earthworks.
Engineering & Mining Journal Press *21 July 1923*

To increase shipments Wright requested A. W. Harrison, an automotive engineer from Los Angeles, to design a new locomotive. With some disregard to the condition and strength of the track he designed a new petrol electric locomotive consisting of an engine and a generator to supply electric power for motors on both the locomotive and large ore wagons. Far too heavy for the deteriorating track, the new train got no further than three miles across Searles Lake before the track gave way.

Added to these problems, there was severe competition from other companies extracting salts from natural and artificial brines and a number of legal disputes drained the Company's resources. The mineral claims by the Company had extended over a large area, 1,440 acres, and the Company now received counter claims. The Wilmington process plant also had problems. After the salts had been removed, the remaining earth and debris was piling up around the plant. The city authorities had objected to the accumulation of the waste within city limits[7].

On the 28th February 1927 the *Los Angeles Times* reported that the Company had updated its Wilmington process plant by adding further dissolving pits with a capacity of eight car loads each. A month later, on 28th March 1927, the paper reported that Wright had stated that the additions to the Wilmington Plant would be completed by 15th April 1927 and that the tracks of the monorail had been reconditioned[8]. It went on to state:

The wooden track of the American Magnesium Company monorail snaked its way through the narrow passes lined with loose boulders.
Engineering & Mining Journal Press *21 July 1923*

"The new equipment for this little [rail] road includes three light locomotives to be used on the level stretches and down-grade traffic, the heavy engines being used as helpers on the steep grades of the line."

The reality, however, was that the operation was on its last legs but the date of final operation is uncertain. Jahns writing in 1951 stated that the mine was put onto stand-by basis in June 1926 and the last train line was then eased down the line[1]. Chalfant, however, writing in 1930, stated that the line was used again in 1927 but closed after hauling in total only about 900 tons of ore[9].

On the 28th April 1928 the property was put up for sale. With no buyer it was left to rust and rot and Wright turned his interests over to the Company. The steel rail was finally taken up and sold in the late 1930s along with most of the longitudinal timbers. By the early 1950s only a few stone foundations, part of the loading table at the mine site and rotting timber A frames survived.

A few of the directors kept the taxes paid for the Company in the hope that the Government might become interested in the ore deposit. This never occurred and with the exception of Searles Lake, the rest of the route of the line and the mine site now form part of the South Range of the US Naval Air Weapons Station.

Description of line

The base of the line was alongside the railroad to Trona, about six miles to the south of the town and on the south western edge of Searles Lake. This site became known as Magnesium Siding. The track layout included a raised section of monorail to allow transfer of the ore to the standard gauge wagons for shipping to Wilmington, as well as loading of supplies. The workshop of the line was also based at this end.

From Trona, the line headed due east in virtually a straight line for eight miles across the flat sand bed of Searles Lake.

On reaching the eastern side of the lake the line then climbed some 1,850ft in five miles through the precipitous Layton Canyon with an average grade of around 7%. Here was the one intermediate station, if that is not being too generous in its description, at Layton Spring. It had one of the few supplies of water.

There then followed a steep descent into the Panamint Valley where the monorail met the only road in the area. This was little more than a sand track heading north from Barstow to Ballarat. Road crossings have been an Achilles' heal of monorails since their invention. Palmer's solution in 1823 had been to incorporate a removable section of track (essentially a section pivoted to swing open) to allow carts etc. to pass on the road. On the Listowel & Ballybunion monorail in Ireland, Lartigue had included such sections for small roads but had also built up the roads to allow drawbridges to be lowered across the track. Milus G. Robinson, the Chief Construction Engineer of the American Magnesium Company decided instead to lower the road through a modest cutting whilst raising the 'A' frames of the monorail in a form of hump back. This compromise required no dangerous removable sections of track but added an element of fair ground to the journey if the hump back was taken at speed.

The line then climbed out of Panamint Valley at nearly 10 to 12% up through Wingate Pass. It is not surprising that the first monorail patent filed by Wright envisaged a toothed wheel alongside the main wheel engaging with a rack rail[10]. This, however, was never incorporated in to the construction. The naming of this pass is moot. It could have been by Lieutenant Bendire after his 1867 expedition

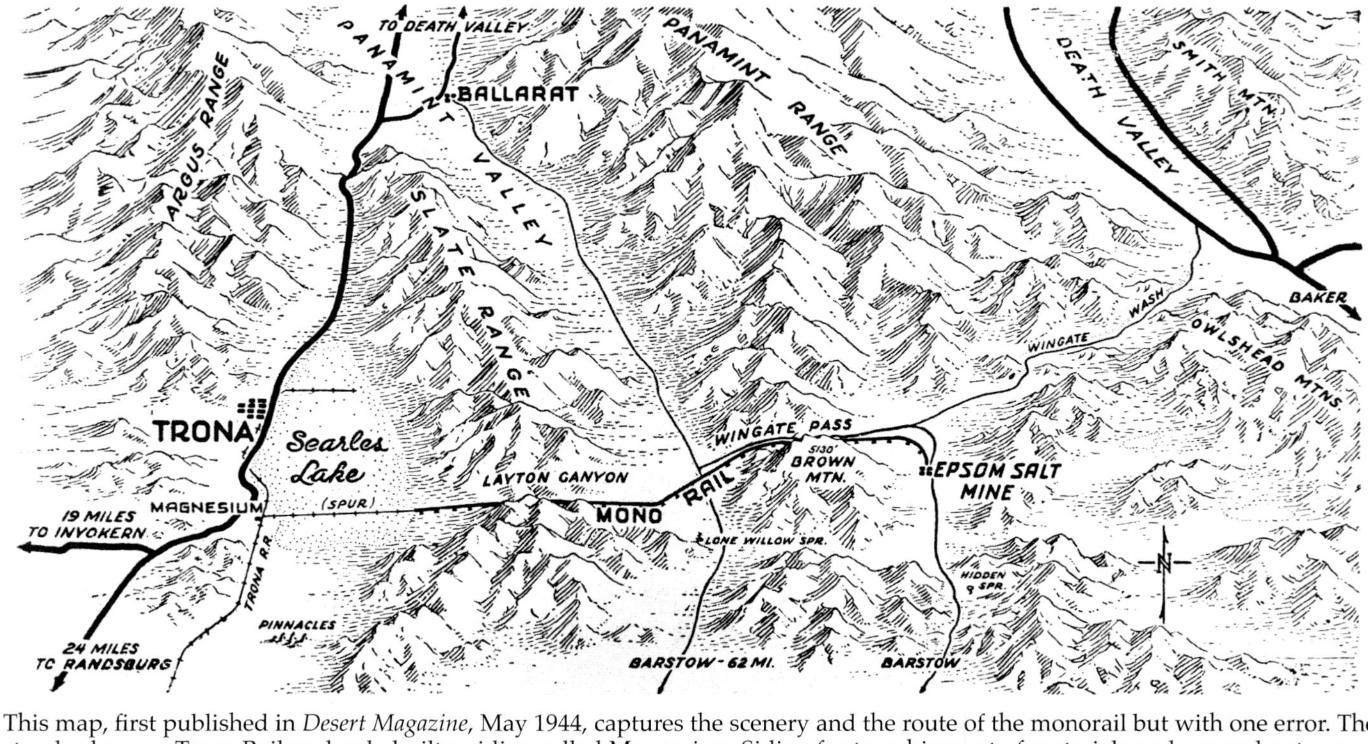

This map, first published in *Desert Magazine*, May 1944, captures the scenery and the route of the monorail but with one error. The standard gauge Trona Railroad only built a siding called Magnesium Siding for transhipment of materials and ore and not a spur as shown on this map. The monorail made most of the journey across Searles Lake.

The railway workshops and the monorail's only shed at Magnesium Siding, Trona. The layout is not recorded but probably consisted of three or four sidings, one of which was raised and ran parallel to the standard gauge to allow the transfer of materials and ore bags. Note the point in the foreground with sections that were slid into position to join the required tracks.
Searles Valley Historical Society

The steeply raised track allowed interchange with the standard gauge at Magnesium Siding, Trona. *Searles Valley Historical Society*

A rare picture of three locomotives and two wagons forming a convoy travelling across Searles Lake with a load of wood. The photograph was probably taken during the construction period. Trains & Travel *October 1951*

Layton Spring. The train takes a short rest for water before continuing the journey. *Searles Valley Historical Society*

The only road crossing was in the form of an overbridge. The car was probably owned by the photographer F. H. Maude of the Pacific Stereopticon Company who took the picture. It would have been a difficult journey on the unmade road in the intense heat. The car was probably positioned under the bridge both for effect and the tiny amount of shade it provided.

Courtesy of the Braun Research Library Collection, Autry National Center, Los Angeles, Photograph LS13399

when he named it in honour of Major Benjamin Wingate who died in 1862. As likely is that it was named 'Wind Gate' or 'Windy Gap' by the twenty mule teams on the 165 mile route from Mojave to mines near Furnace Creek which hauled supplies and returned with borax[11]. Rarely used by the 1920s, the pass was very inhospitable and subject to flash floods when torrents of water would pour down after a cloud burst forming waves twenty feet high.

The line ended at the mine site at Crystal Hills Wash where a cottage for the superintendent and a laboratory had been built. There were few other facilities. No provision was made to turn the engines which just reversed back along the track.

A report by the State of California, Department of Parks and Recreation[12] states that the remains of the two buildings were still extant at the mine site in 1998. One measured 18ft by 17ft, had a dirt floor and sat on a rock rubble and mud foundation. It was 6ft tall with a flat roof and made of 1in. x 6in. and 1in. x 12in. planks nailed together. It appeared to have had one door and three windows. There was evidence of two fire rings.

The remains of the other measured 11ft x 16ft. This was a dry laid rubble and mud chinked cabin, the highest point of the existing walls being 6ft and probably had a hipped roof. There was the remains of a small 12in. x 9in. framed window on the east side made from 2in. x 6in. boards. The door frame measured 2ft x 5ft 4in. and was made of 2in. x 8in. boards. A dry laid rock rubble wall extended from the east side of the cabin for about 22ft. It was 2ft 6in. at its highest point.

The line at Crystal Hills Wash. The picture shows an unusual level of activity with an unusual number of tents. It is likely that this photograph was taken at or near the end of the construction phase.
National Park Service DEVA 25866 'Monorail Construction Camp, Summer 1923'

The mine site in operation. The cottage and laboratory are to the left.
Searles Valley Historical Society

Operation

Trials indicated that loads of between 15 and 20 tons could be hauled by each locomotive at a rate of 8 miles per hour on gradients and from 10 to 15 miles per hour across the flat dry Searles Lake[5]. In practice, each locomotive typically carried a payload of up to 3,400lbs and hauled a single wagon with a maximum payload of about 8,500lbs, a total of about 5 tons. A speed of about 30 miles per hour could be attained on the flat of Searles Lake (a maximum of 35 miles per hour was imposed) but this reduced to a crawl on the steep 10 to 12% gradients. The short trains reflected not only the low power of the Fordson engines, but also the poor braking and the problems of slipping on the steep gradients on the line. Luckily there was a ready supply of sand.

Outbound trains were lightly loaded with supplies for the twelve to fifteen men working at the mine site. The mining operation was simple and consisted of scraping the white epsomite (hydrated magnesium sulphate) from near the surface which was then sacked for transporting on the monorail. Short tunnels and pits were also dug to mine mixtures of magnesium sulphate, magnesium carbonate and clay which was also sacked and shipped.

The monorail had no form of signalling or electric wiring for communication. A formal one train, or convoy, 'in steam' at any one time may have been operated but most likely a general awareness of where the drivers were and a line of sight approach was adopted. There are no known reported accidents, a miracle given the terrain and the nature of the engineering.

A recorded journey

N. M. Thompson of Pittsburgh, Pa., recorded a journey he made on the line on a hot day in August 1924[13]. Thompson and two friends started their day after working the night shift at the American Trona Corporation. They arrived at Magnesium Siding probably an hour or so after their shift, which had finished at 7.00am, ready to join their unofficial passenger train. The monorail train, by then nicknamed the Magnesium Flyer, was delayed, however, due to Fordson engine trouble but it eventually set off with its weekly cargo of a 500lbs block of ice for the mine camp. Thompson reported that the train broke down several more times on route but it finally arrived at the mine site's loading dock late in the afternoon with the ice block reduced to about 75lbs.

After collecting a loaded wagon it set off back. Already hot and now pulling a load it overheated and had to coast down the mountain range to Searles Lake where it stopped unable to haul the load across the flat. Thompson and his friends had to walk the remaining five and a half miles to return for their next night shift. Worse, whilst the day had been hot Searles Lake was not yet dry. Thompson reported:

> "Much of it was a deadening succession of monotonous sounds of 'slurp, slurp, slurp' as we crossed the so called 'dry' lake. With each step, we would sink ankle and even knee deep in the soft, gooey, slimy muck."

Locomotive No. 4 is identifiable by the crudely painted 4 on the front buffer immediately below the drum containing sand to aid adhesion. Loading bags of ore at the mine site was hot work. Note the umbrella for the brakeman. *Searles Valley Historical Society*

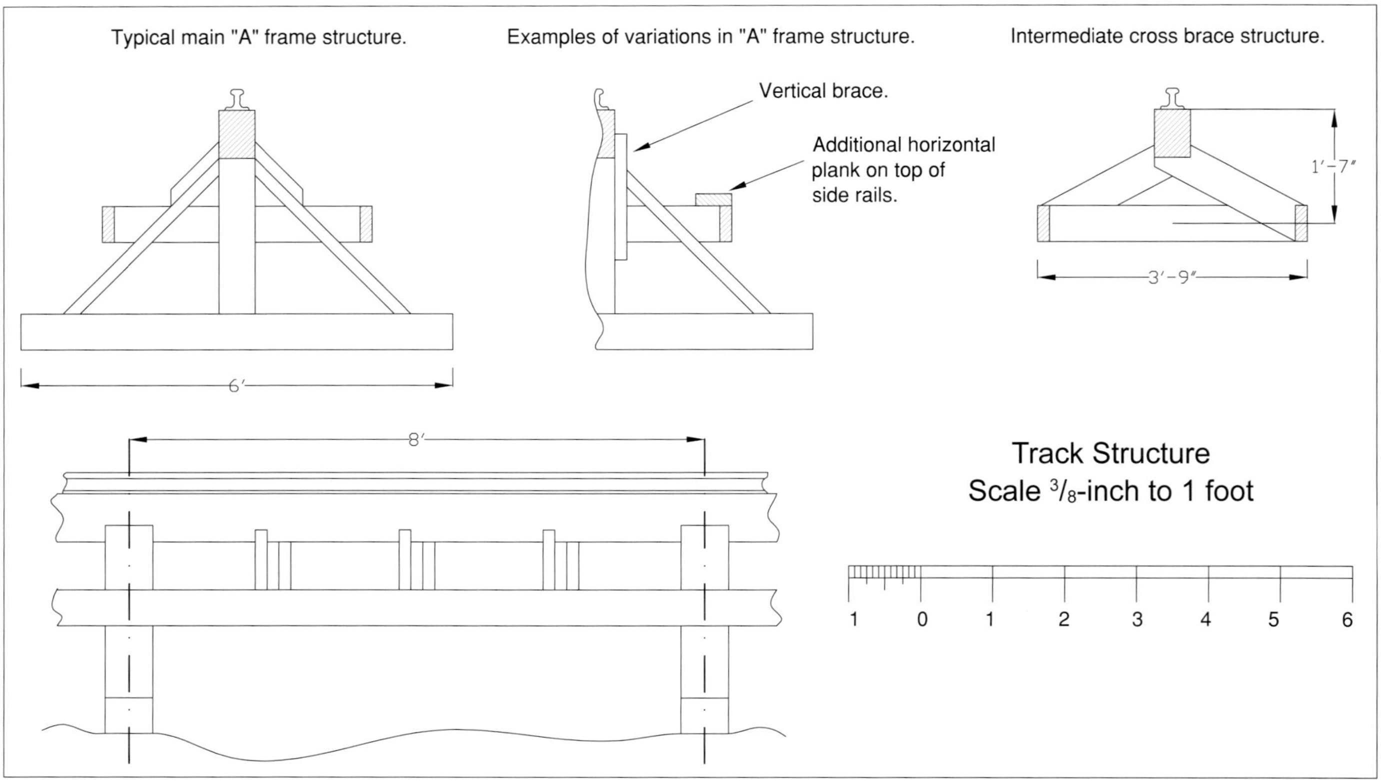

The track

Whilst much of the design work was done by the American Magnesium Company's engineer, Leeson, the patents were taken out in Wright's name. Five applications were made on the 15th September 1922 and the first monorail patent granted in 1923[10] described the basic structure of a rail fixed to a wooden beam mounted on top of an 'A' frame. The patent included the concept of side rollers mounted on the locomotives and wagons bearing on the wooden side rails. It is possible that it was the use of such rollers on wooden side rails that made the concept sufficiently unique to be patentable. As previously indicated, the patent also envisaged an option of mounting a rack beside the rail on the top wooden beam to engage with a pinion on the locomotive wheel to provide traction up high grades – a concept already demonstrated by Lartigue on an experimental monorail at Tothill Fields, London in 1886.

The track was constructed of sawn boards of Douglas Fir which had been shipped by boat to San Pedro and then by rail to Magnesium Siding. The upright posts and main beam measured 6in. x 8in. whilst the rest of the structure, including the side rails, was from 6in. x 2in. boards. Fastening was by bolts and spikes. The flat bottom rail weighed variously between 30lb and 70lb per yard (typically 50lb per yard) and was spiked to the main beam. Leeson, like Lartigue, extended the legs of the A frames, which were spaced at 8ft. intervals, to maintain a level track. This was widely adopted in the canyons.

Wright also took out a patent[14] for both a point and a turntable[15]. The latter does not appear ever to have been built or at least not photographed.

Examination of the photographs indicates that, over the short life of the railway, repairs were carried out in a pragmatic rather than systematic manner. Indeed, around Magnesium Siding the construction varied enormously with 6in. x 2in. boards spiked on to the structure as needed to reinforce and repair.

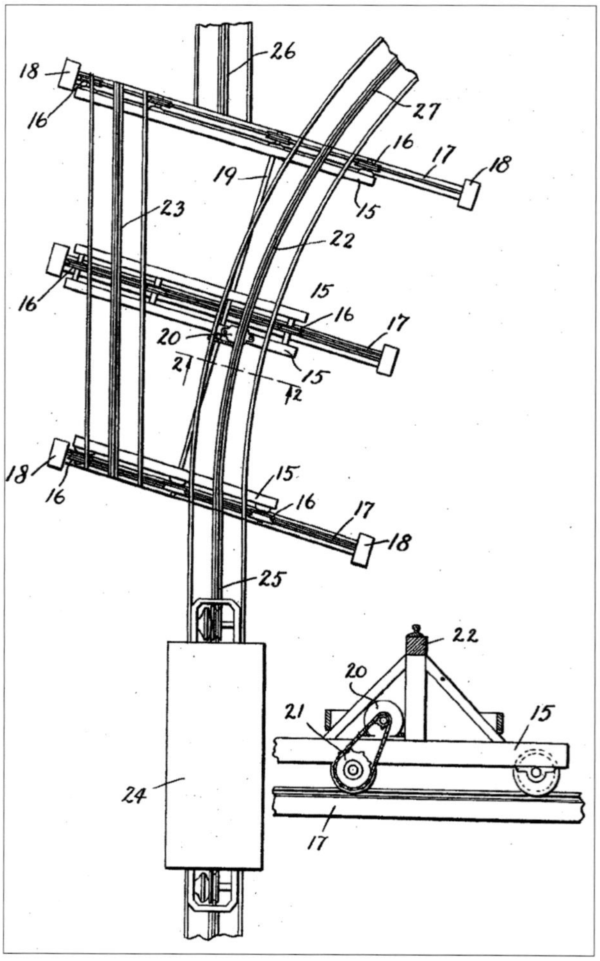

Points consisted of straight and curved sections of track mounted on carriages allowing them to be slid into place to join the relevant tracks. *US Patent No. 1454806*

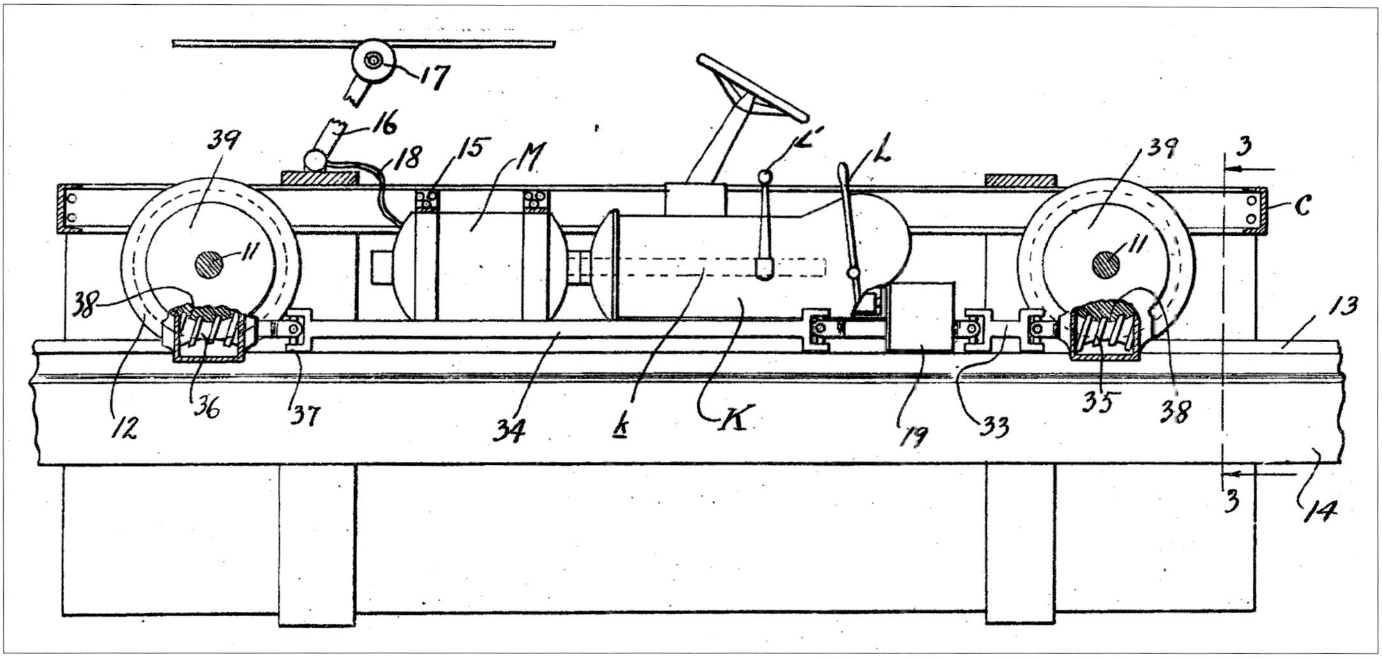

Wright's proposed electric locomotive with overhead power supply and an electric motor connected via worm gears to the two main wheels. *US Patent No. 1590610*

The locomotives

Whilst three of the patent applications made by Wright in 1922 related to the design of the track, two related to the locomotives. Wright's original idea was to adopt electric traction and US Patent No. 1590610[16] showed a design in which an electric motor drove a shaft running the length of the locomotive parallel with, but just above and to one side of, the running rail. At the ends of the shaft worm gears engaged with worm wheels mounted to one side of the main wheels. Electric power for the motor was to be from an overhead wire via a trolley pole.

The other locomotive patent[17] filed at the same time proposed that the main running wheels were mounted on swivel trucks to allow easier negotiation of curves. In this patent each wheel was powered by a separate electric motor mounted on the swivel truck but again using worm and wheel gearing. This no doubt reflected Wright's desire to allow the use of tight curves on the line to minimise the cost of blasting and earthworks.

Jahns[1], Myrick[18] and Keagle[7] state that a battery powered locomotive was initially utilised during construction but failed to produce sufficient power. Unfortunately no photographs exist of this locomotive. Such a locomotive would have been doomed to failure. Even if enough initial power could be developed, the state of battery development in the 1920s together with the intense heat of the desert would have led to its early expiration.

The next seven locomotives used the power unit from the Fordson type 'F' Tractor which Henry Ford had developed between late 1905 and 1916. The tractor was launched in 1916 with mass production commencing in 1917 in Henry Ford's separate tractor company, Henry Ford & Son. The success of this tractor was in part fortuitous in that its launch coincided with the First World War. The Germans were sinking cargo ships heading to Britain at around one a day leading to a loss of imported food and home grown food became a necessity. To this end Britain ordered large numbers of Fordson Tractors – some 7,000 had been shipped by spring 1917[19].

A key design aspect of the Fordson tractor was the rigidity of the engine and gearbox structure which enabled it to support the machine without a separate chassis frame. This enabled efficient manufacture and provided ruggedness in use around farms. The design did, however, have one uncomfortable fault. The driver's seat was a pressed steel plate connected by a sprung steel support to the top of the gearbox. The heat generated by the engine and gearbox was thus conducted up the steel support to the driver's steel seat and thence to the driver's rear end! This was subsequently solved by redesigning the gearbox and its cooling. It does, however, explain why the steel tractor seat was perforated.

A characteristic of the Fordson tractor was the apparently single tank mounted between the steering column and the radiator but with three filler holes. This was actually three separate tanks, the forward section contained water for the radiator whilst the rear two held gasoline, used for starting, and kerosene for use in running.

Whilst production of these tractors ceased in the US in 1928, the design continued to be manufactured in Ireland and the UK until 1939.

The American Magnesium Company adapted this self-contained power unit to be mounted into two types of locomotive. Locomotives were not named but could be identified by a number crudely painted – probably in black paint – on the buffer beam.

Locomotives No's 1, 2 & 3

Photographs show that locomotives No's 1 and 3 were similar and the bold assumption is made that locomotive No. 2 was of the same design. The design integrated both a locomotive and an ore wagon. They were constructed of steel and each side pannier had three lower doors to allow ore to be easily deposited as envisaged in the patent[20].

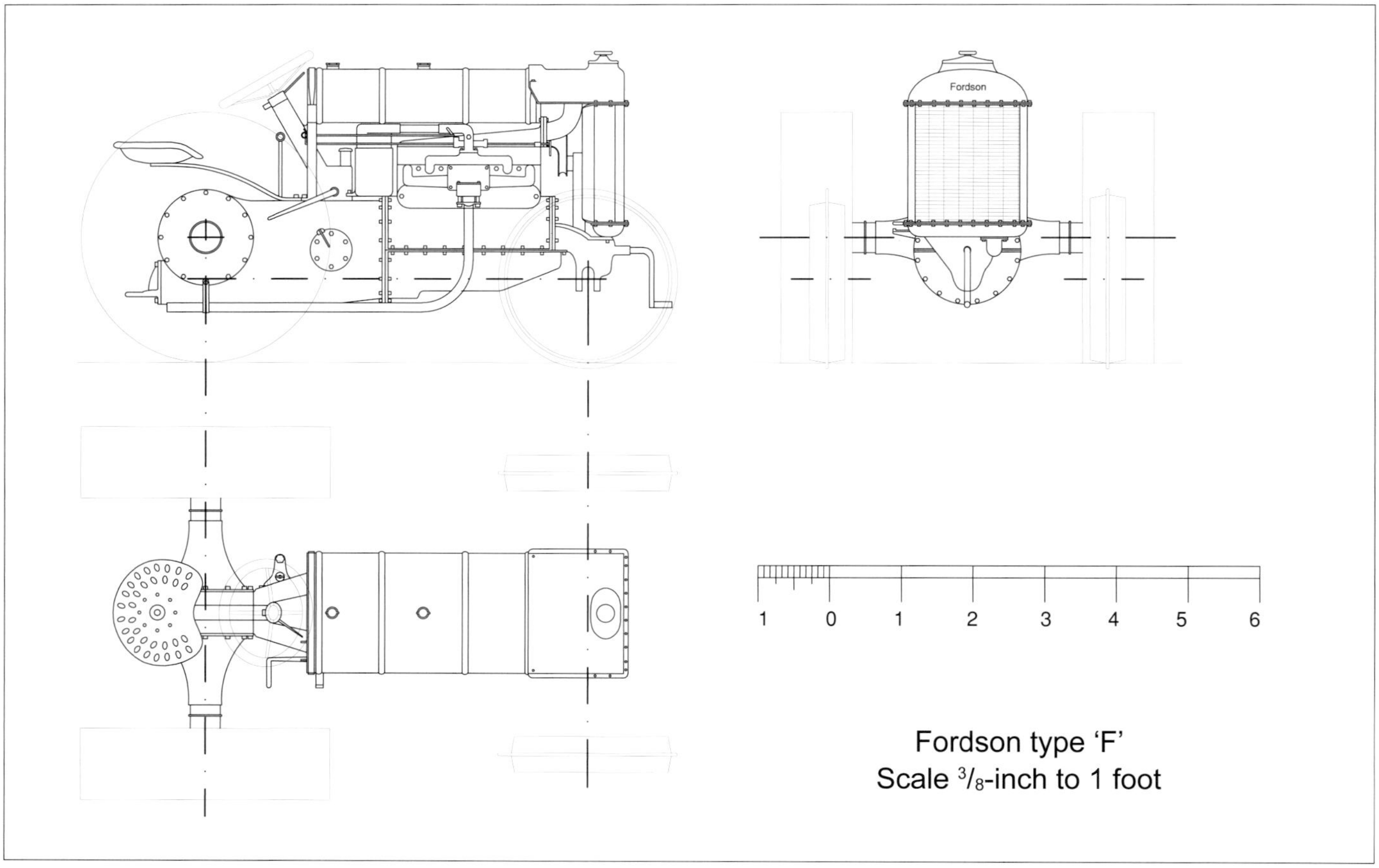

Many examples of the very successful Fordson type 'F' Tractor have been preserved. This one, built in 1923, has been displayed a number of times at the Great Dorset Steam Fair and still runs on the original ignition system of magnets mounted on the flywheel with stationary coils and trembler coils for HT.
Author

The Fordson power unit was mounted amidships. Precise detail of how the power unit was secured is not visible in the photographs. It is probable that the front wheel assembly of the tractor was replaced by a beam mounted between the panniers.

At the rear, after removing the tractor's large wheels, significant engineering was required. The rear axle/gearbox under the driver's seat included a differential which was not needed on the locomotive. The curved conic section castings bolted either side between the gearbox and the large rear wheels on the tractor (and which contained the axle bearings) would also have protruded into the panniers. The photographs indicate that these were removed along with the differential

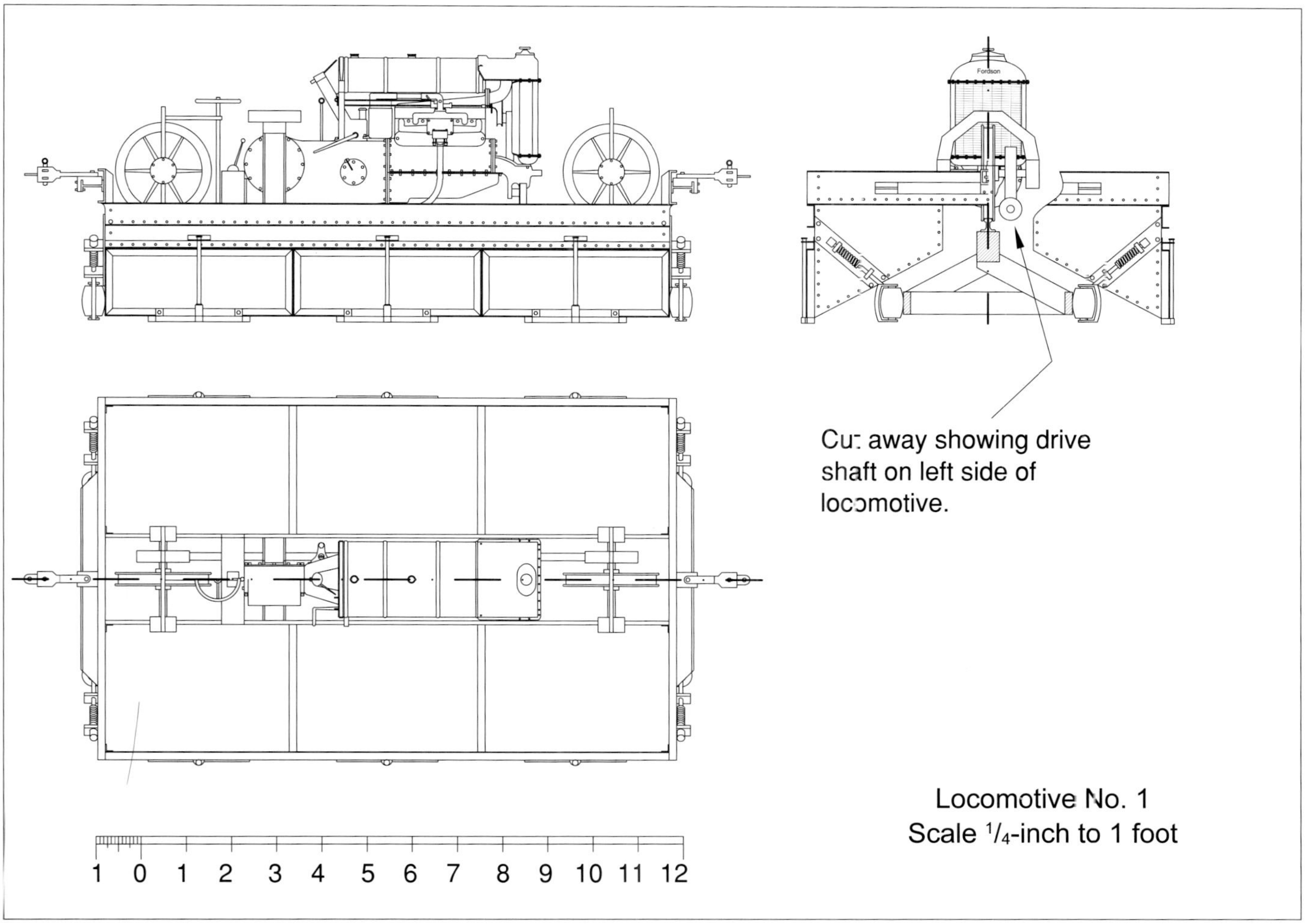

Locomotive No. 1 with either No. 2 or 3 at Magnesium Siding. The ramp up to the interchange can be seen to the left as well as the track of the Trona Railway in the background just above the monorail track to the right. *Searles Valley Historical Society*

The end view of Locomotive No. 3 pictured from the works shed at Magnesium Siding, Trona, shows the rigid nature of the structure which allowed the sprung mounts for the balancing side wheels to be directly secured to the body on these first three locomotives.

Searles Valley Historical Society

contained therein and blanked off. The drive shaft from the Fordson gearbox was then extended out the rear into a smaller gear box mounted behind the driver. This used spur gears to drive a lay shaft running the length of the locomotive, as envisaged in the patents for the electric locomotives. The lay shaft drive had worm gears mounted at each end which engaged with worm wheels mounted on the left side of the wheel axle. This arrangement is almost certain as:

- Such a design would have been consistent with the early patents.
- The photographs indicate some form of relatively thick wheel mounted on the left side of the main wheels of these locomotives. Whilst the pictures are not of sufficient quality to determine whether these wheels were toothed or grooved, their existence, size and position is consistent with the lay shaft/worm/worm wheel design. A photograph also shows of one of the wagons with a worm wheel on the axle, probably from a locomotive that had been rebuilt to chain drive (see below).
- The photographs reveal a box with a protruding lever behind the driver's seat exactly as shown in the patent applications. Examination of the internal workings of a Fordson Tractor confirms that a gear box in this position would have enabled a link between the gearbox drive shaft and the parallel lay shaft.

Unfortunately whilst the Fordson power unit was robust, the structure of the locomotives was not rugged enough to withstand the unevenness of the line and the lay shaft flexed and bent under the strain. This problem with the worm drive shaft was discovered soon after construction commenced as on the 2nd November 1923 Wright applied for a patent for a revised design of locomotive[21]. In this design a chain drive was adopted which took up any flexing of the structure.

No record or photographic evidence has been found by the author indicating whether these three locomotives were modified. In earlier articles[22] the author suggested that they were not modified but that locomotives No's 4 to 7 were subsequently built with the chain drive. Photographs show, however, that locomotives No's 4 to 7 were used during construction and were thus not a subsequent batch.

Locomotives No's 1 to 3 may well have been rebuilt with chain drive but they are infrequently seen in photographs operating outside Magnesium Siding. This could be because they were too heavy when the panniers were loaded with ore or because the other type of locomotive was more adaptable and suitable for the traffic back and forth to the mine.

A wagon on the raised interchange at Magnesia Siding. Note the worm wheel mounted on the axle. Built from parts of an earlier locomotive? *Searles Valley Historical Society*

Locomotives No's 4 to 7

The design of these locomotives appears to have been specifically for carrying lengths of wood for track or mine construction. They did not have rigid steel panniers. Instead they had 'legs' secured to the main chassis which extended down and under the load to be carried. These were supported at their outer end by chains or rods connected to cross beams mounted above the chassis.

As the sprung rollers which acted as balance wheels could no longer be mounted on the end of each (non-existent) pannier, a revised balance arrangement was patented in which the rollers were mounted on cranks[23]. The cranks were connected by a central spring to provide the necessary pressure. This approach is similar to many other monorail designs – for instance the Listowel and Ballybunion Railway in Ireland.

On these locomotives the Fordson motor unit was mounted between the frames rather than balanced on top. This would have lowered their centre of gravity which would have made them more stable. The frames were spaced significantly wide apart making it easier to install a chain drive to the wheels. This might imply that whilst these locomotives were used during track construction, they were built after the lay shaft and worm drive problem had been discovered.

This design required a significant raising of the coupling height, the couplers on all the vehicles having come secondhand from Los Angeles trolley cars. The change in height gave rise to few difficulties, however, as trains rarely consisted of more than two vehicles and long rods – some six feet or so in length – were used as links between the couplings.

Experience also showed that the gradients required the use of a significant amount of sand. Cut down oil drums containing sand were therefore mounted above the couplings.

One problem that had to be addressed was that by mounting the Fordson engine between the frames the hand crank to start the engine which was below the radiator was now out of reach. An uncovered pulley mechanism was therefore welded to the top of the radiator. This connected the crank handle mounted at the top of the radiator with the crank shaft below. Starting this machine would hardly have met modern safety standards.

Regrettably the numbering of locomotives No's 5 to 7 cannot be determined from the photographs. There was significant variation around the basic design. For instance:

- Photographs show that at one time at least two locomotives adopted steel rods from the cross beams to support the loads whilst another picture shows that two of the locomotives used chains to support the structure. (It could, of course, be that the locomotives were rebuilt and thus photographs show them in different phases).
- Whilst the steel seats of the Fordson tractor were initially retained, burnt rear ends from the heat of the gearbox and the scorching sun led to their

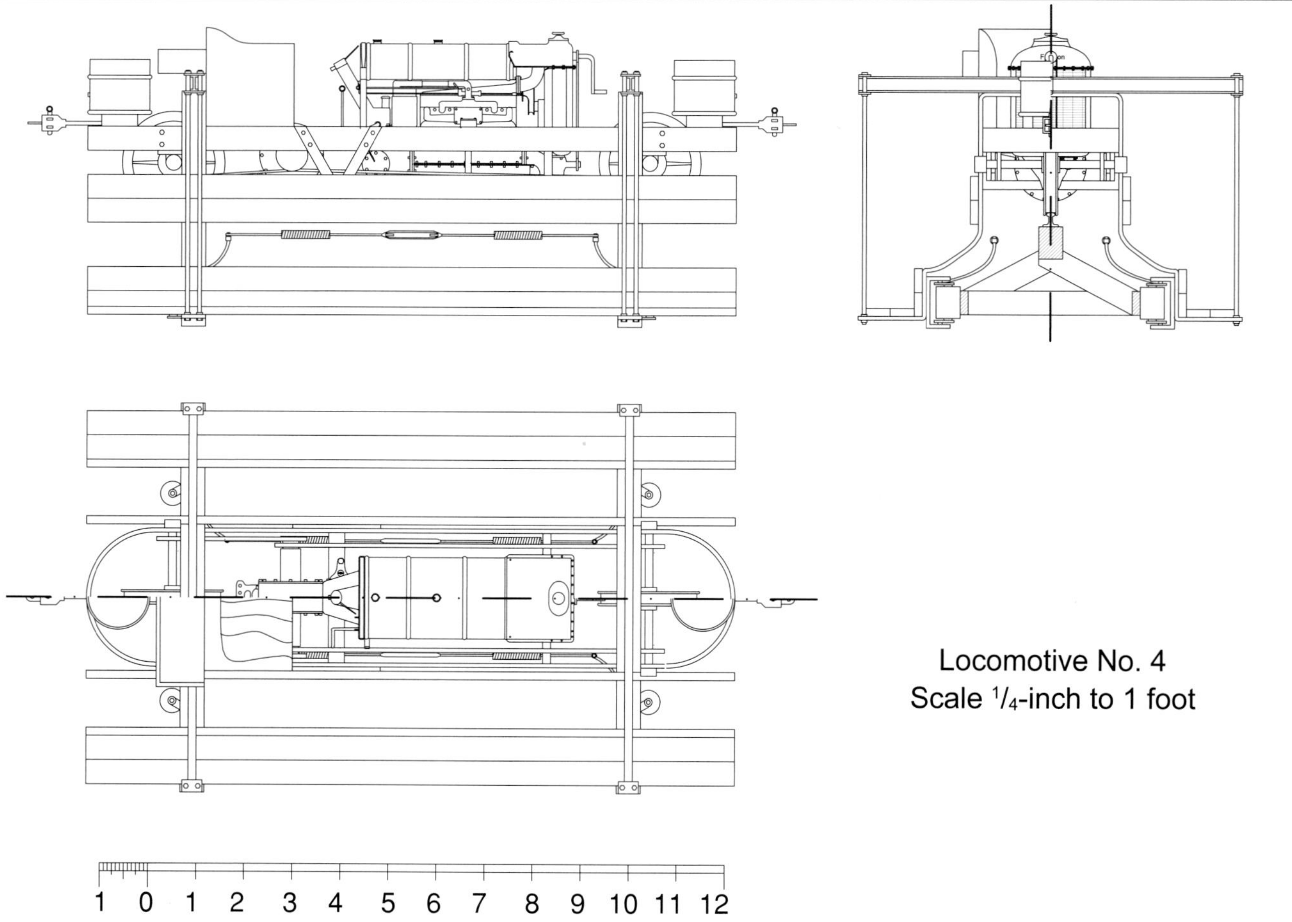

Locomotive No. 4
Scale 1/4-inch to 1 foot

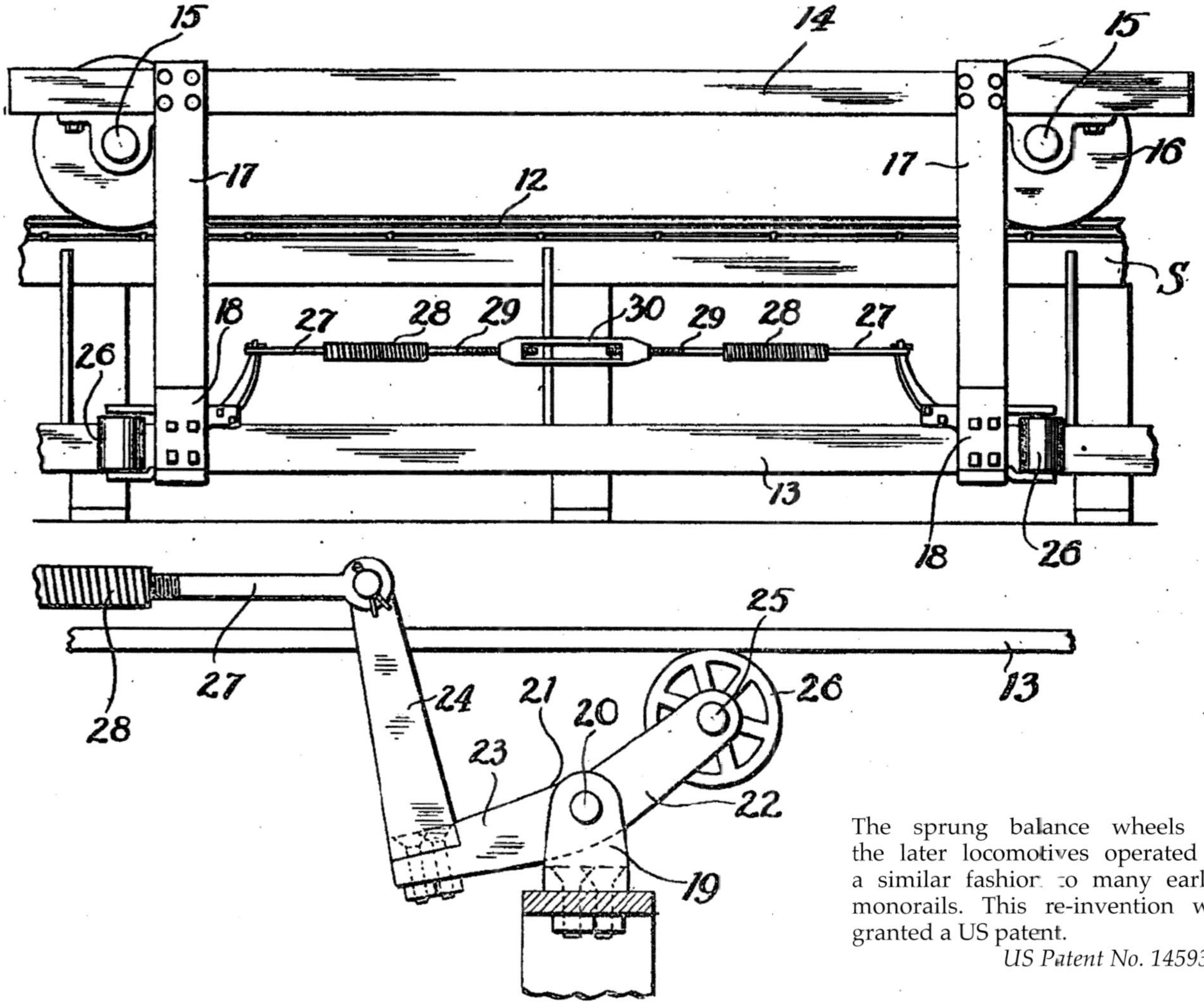

The sprung balance wheels on the later locomotives operated in a similar fashion to many earlier monorails. This re-invention was granted a US patent.

US Patent No. 1459386

The design by Harrison was patented by Wright (US Patent No. 1523335). The driver was to sit in a cab above the upper rail with the generator mounted on the side of the locomotive.

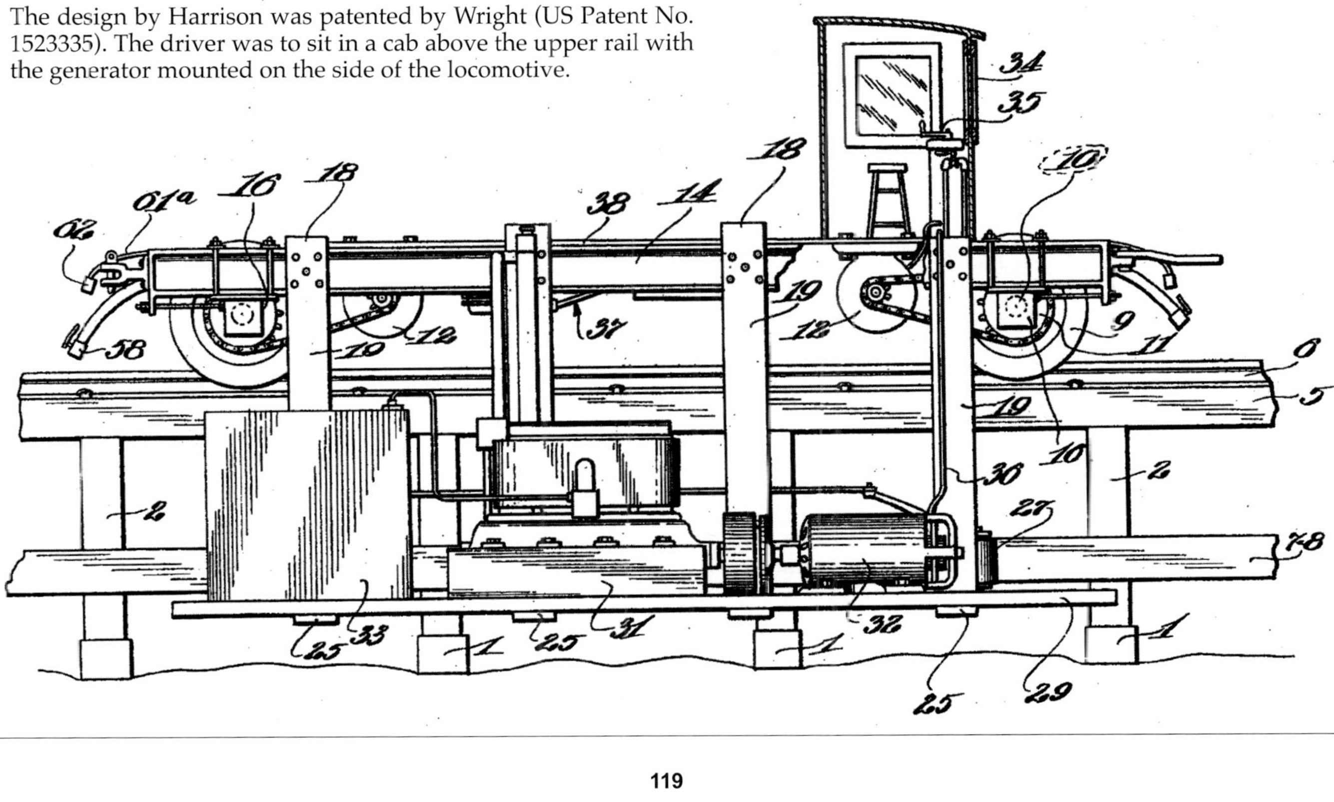

replacement. Some pictures show plain square padded seats. Locomotive No. 4 appears to have had a settee mounted on the chassis.

- A variety of sun shades were adopted to provide some protection from the heat. A wide umbrella was mounted on one locomotive whilst a sort of tent was erected over another.
- Locomotive 4 had rounded ends. Others had a rectangular frame structure.
- The sand boxes on one locomotive appear to be rectangular tanks.

Locomotive No. 8

From the first patents it is clear that Wright wanted to adopt electric traction. As indicated above a battery locomotive was tried during construction but by April 1923 Wright realised that if electric traction was to be used a reliable source of current was necessary and he applied for a patent which included a current collector from a light metal side rail[24]. There were, however, good reasons not to adopt this system, in particular the cost of adding an additional rail to the track and the drop in voltage inevitable over the twenty-eight mile length of the line.

There was also the need for greater hauling power and so Wright worked with Harrison, and probably Leeson, to design a petrol electric train. Wright filed for a patent showing the basis of the design in 1924[25]. This patent envisaged petrol engines mounted in one or both locomotive panniers driving electric generators. These powered individual motors on the two main wheels of the locomotive via a chain drive. Cables were also to be connected to the train of wagons each of which would have further electric motors.

To implement the concept Harrison utilised a Buda petrol engine with a generator to provide electric power to motors connected to the drive wheels on both the locomotive and the ore wagons. Unfortunately by the time the locomotive was built the track had deteriorated to such an extent that many of the side rails were in splinters and the nails and screws loosened so that it could not support the weight.

Wright continued to the end patenting innovations designed by Leeson. In 1925 Wright filed a patent for a double flanged monorail wheel tire which could be easily and quickly removed[26].

Locomotive 8 powered by a Buda engine and generator. The three, possibly four, electric power cables connecting to the ore truck are just visible. The wagon was also unusual in having a covered section between the panniers and was of the same robust steel construction as adopted for the locomotives No's 1 to 3. *Searles Valley Historical Society*

Now derelict, locomotive No. 8 rests under a collapsed shed at Magnesium Siding. The frame of the cab can be seen supporting part of the shed roof. To the left is one of the pannier type locomotives (possibly No. 1). The remains of the frame of dismantled locomotive No. 3 is in the foreground. The 'N' appears to be a mirror image whilst the '3' is written correctly. The reason is not known. *National Parks Service DEVA 48106*

Rolling stock

As most trains consisted of just a locomotive plus one wagon, there were probably around eight to twelve wagons during the line's existence. They do not appear to have been numbered.

The construction was somewhat flimsy. The upper chassis consisted of two steel girders with spacers between which the two main wheels were mounted. Bolted to this structure were four bent steel straps on which the ubiquitous 6in. x 2in. wooden beams were mounted. The structure was hardly rigid and left to its own devices the bent steel straps would have flexed significantly. Some rigidity was obtained by tightly strapping the load with chains between the bottom of the straps and the upper sections as shown in the photograph and drawing. Care would have been needed to balance the loads in each pannier in order to maintain the structures shape.

The braking system on both the locomotives and wagons was again patented by Wright and probably to a design by Leeson[21]. With the steep gradients it was only just sufficient. Keagle[7] reports an engineer writing:

> "I had one ride on the mono rail as far as Wingate Pass and was rather relieved to get back with a safe skin, keeping a watchful eye on the braking arrangements all the time."

No two wagons were exactly the same. On some, the brake system above was doubled up with a brake wheel

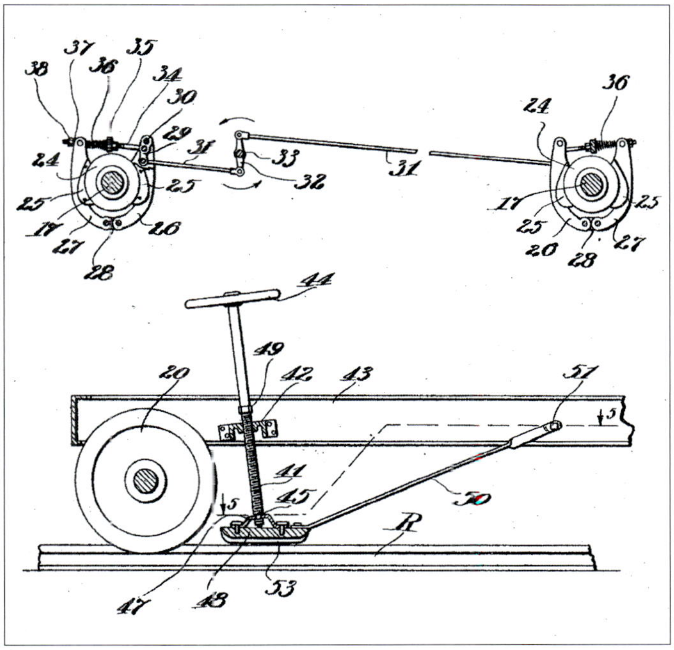

Braking was a major issue given the gradients on the line. Wright was granted US Patent No. 1575304 for the system which gripped both the wheels and axles, and operated a skid on the upper rail. Some care would have been needed not to raise the vehicle so far that the double flanged wheel derailed.

A monorail wagon at Magnesium Siding laden with wood. More supplies can be seen piled up to the right of the picture. The wood could have been destined for the mine site but more likely it was for constructing the track implying that the picture was taken during the construction phase. The Trona Railway siding can be seen to the left of the picture.
Searles Valley Historical Society

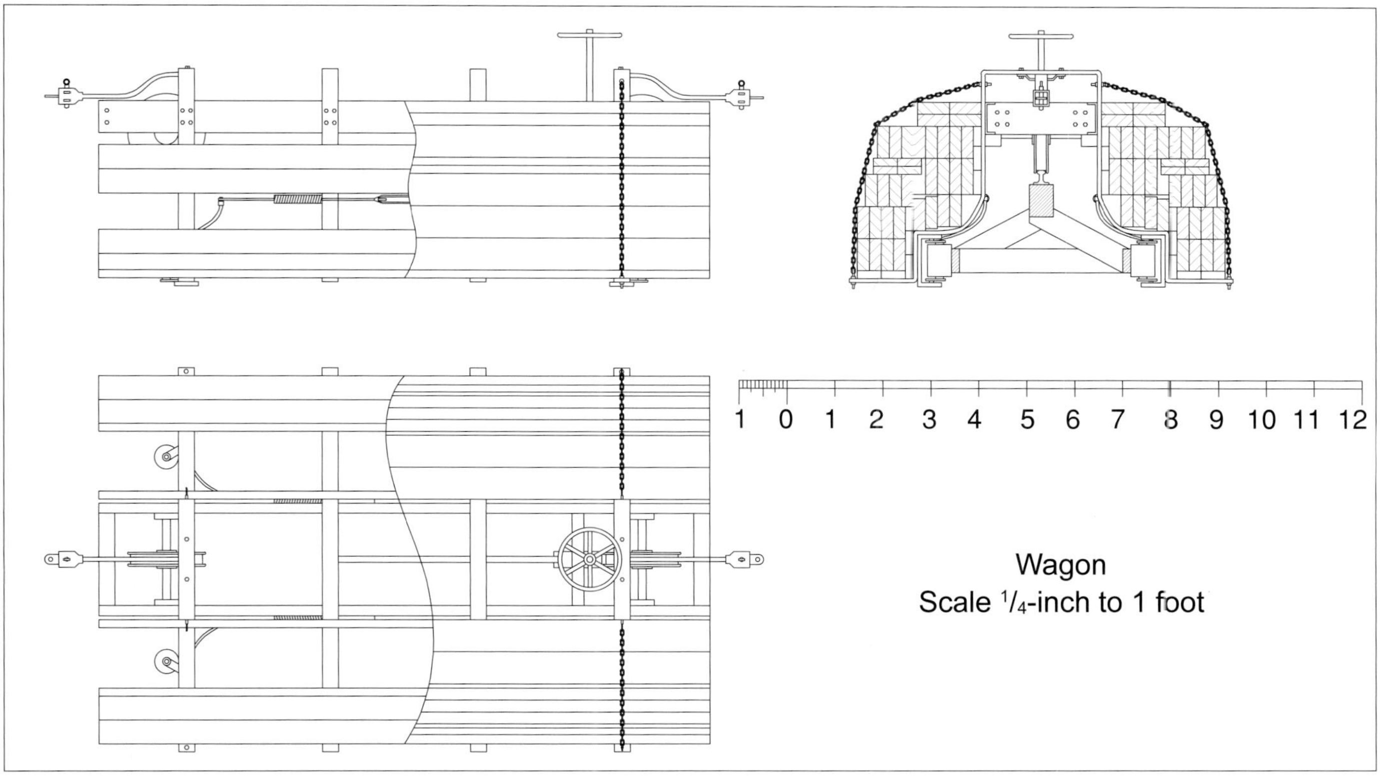

and shoe mounted at each end of the wagon. On others, the chains supporting the panniers were abandoned and instead two 'I' beams were mounted on top of the steel straps at each end of the wagon. In this configuration vertical rods were attached to the 'I' beams to support the panniers as on locomotive No. 4. The wheel diameters also appear to vary between wagons.

References

Readers are strongly recommended to read *The Epsom Salts Monorail* by Alexander K. Rogers, Maturango Museum Publication No. 16, 2014 which includes copies of the relevant patents.

1 *Trains & Travel*, Vol. 11, No. 12, October 1951, pp24-26, (Reprinted from Engineering & Science Monthly. April 1951, Californian Institute of Technology).

2 Historic Resources Report: *American Magnesium Company's Epsom Salts Monorail, Naval Air Weapons Station, China Lake, San Bernardino County, California* submitted to the Department of Navy, Naval Facilities Engineering Command, January 2000

3 US Patent No. 1359011 Application filed 28 May, 1919, granted 16 November 1920. Subsequent patents relating to the chemical process were No. 1396675 granted 8 November 1921 and No. 1457225 granted 29 May 1923. The latter patent was taken out by George Hutchinson who assigned half of the rights to Thomas H. Wright.

4 *Los Angeles Times*, 20 November 1921, Part V, p8.

5 *Engineering and Mining Journal-Press*, Vol. 116, No. 3, 21 July 1923, p100.

6 *The Railway Review*, Vol. 78, 1 March 1924, p388.

7 *Desert Magazine*, Vol. 7, May 1944, pp9-12 (includes reference to Engineering News 27 September 1923).

8 *Los Angeles Times*, 28 February 1927, Part 1, p13 & 28 March 1927, Part 1, p15.

9 *Death Valley: The Facts* by W. A. Chalfant, Stanford University Press, 1930.

10 US Patent No. 1454804 Application filed 15 September 1922, granted 8 May 1923.

11 *Death Valley National Monument: Historic Resource Study. A History of Mining* by Linda W. Greene and John A. Latschar, March 1981, National Park Service, Denver Colorado.

12 State of California Department of Parks and Recreation No. P-36-003806, CA-SBR-3806-H.

13 *Desert*, Magazine of the Southwest, Vol.26, No. 1, January 1963, pp12-15.

14 US Patent No. 1454806 Application filed 15 September 1922, granted 8 May 1923.

15 US Patent No. 1454805 Application filed 15 September 1922, granted 8 May 1923.

16 US Patent No. 1590610 Application filed 15 September 1922, granted 29 June 1923

17 US Patent No. 1454807 Application filed 15 September 1922, granted 8 May 1923.

18 *Railroads of Nevada and Eastern California* Vol. 2 by David F. Myrick, 1963.

19 *Illustrated History of the American Farm Tractor* by Randy Leffingwell, 1995.

20 US Patent No. 1513205 Application filed 15 March 1923, granted 28 October 1924.

21 US Patent No. 1575304 Application filed 2 November 1923, granted 2 March 1926.

22 *Narrow Gauge and Shortline Gazette* January/February 2008, pp32-36 & March/April 2008, 62-67.

23 US Patent No. 1459386 Application filed 15 February 1923, granted 19 June 1923.

24 US Patent No. 1523334 Application filed 23 April 1923, granted 13 January 1925.

25 US Patent No. 1523335 Application filed 11 February 1924, granted 13 January 1925.

26 US Patent No. 1585068 Application filed 1 July 1925, granted 18 May 1926.

The classic publicity photograph of the Railplane above an L&NER goods train. Locomotive No. 4740 was built by the North British Locomotive Company, Glasgow to Gresley's N2 type 0-6-2T design and entered service on 28th February 1921. Originally built with condensers for use in the London area, these were removed and Westinghouse brakes added in 1928 on its transfer to the north before this picture was taken. It was withdrawn on 31st October 1957 and scrapped.

The Bennie Railplane System of Transport Inter-Counties Ltd., 1935

CHAPTER 7
THE BENNIE RAILPLANE

The Bennie Railplane was the last of the extravagant monorail ventures before the Second World War and included all the attributes needed for failure contained in earlier proposals, such as Behr's Lightning Express, some forty years earlier. These included a belief that this system would provide impractically high speeds given the technology of the time, an over enthusiastic promoter and a complete lack of commercial reality.

Background

George Bennie was born in Auldhouse at the southern edge of Glasgow on 29th August 1891[1] although many recent sources have repeated an error that he was born in 1892.

Whilst he had no formal engineering training he was inventive and at the age of twenty one took out his first patent, a design to support a model ship or boat on a theatre stage and '... permitting rolling and pitching or like movements to be imparted to the ship or boat.'[2]

He continued pursuing his inventive career up until the First World War when he joined the Army Service Corps. In 1916 he transferred to the Royal Flying Corps and when the Royal Air Force was formed on the 1st April 1918 he was recorded as being a Fitter (Aero Engine). After hostilities ended he returned to the family house named 'Normanhurst' in the village of Craigmore, Bute, where his mother, now a widow, and his sister lived. Here he resumed his inventive career and applied his knowledge of aero engineering to civilian transport.

By 1920 the UK railway system was extensive and formed the main form of transport for both passengers and freight. The desire for high speed transport by passengers and the movement of heavy goods were in conflict. The system was congested and Bennie saw the Railplane as the solution.

The idea of a propeller driven suspended high speed monorail was not new. Some thirty years before Bennie set down his ideas Anders Anderson had proposed such a system in the USA and, as described in Chapter 5, a version of a propeller driven suspended monorail had already been operated in California. There had also been many high speed electric suspended monorails proposed without the use of a propeller and the success of a 'slow' electric suspended monorail had been proven in Germany on the Wuppertalbahn.

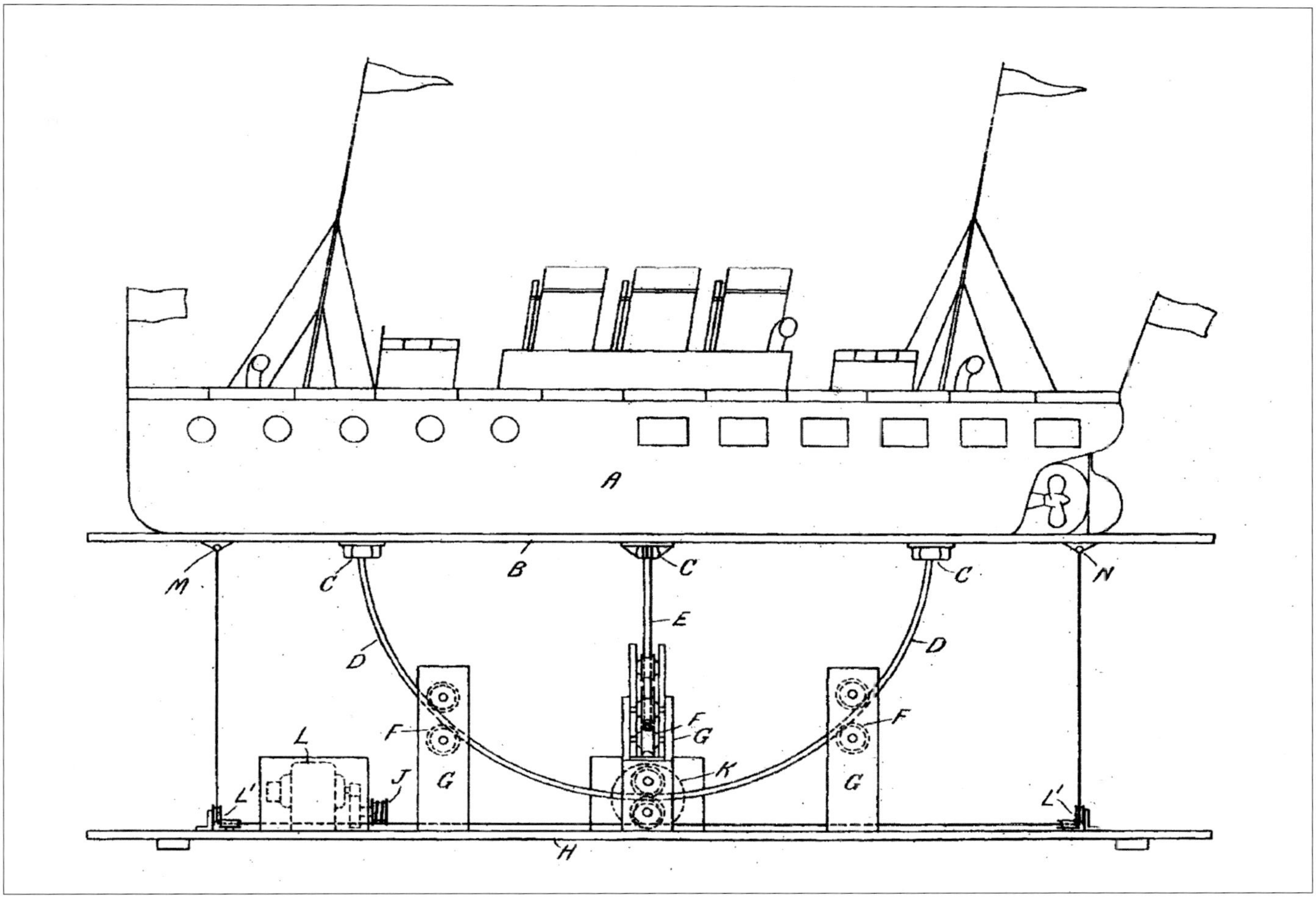

Bennie's first patent; stage machinery for creating motion to a model ship in a theatre. *UK Patent No. 5382, 1912*

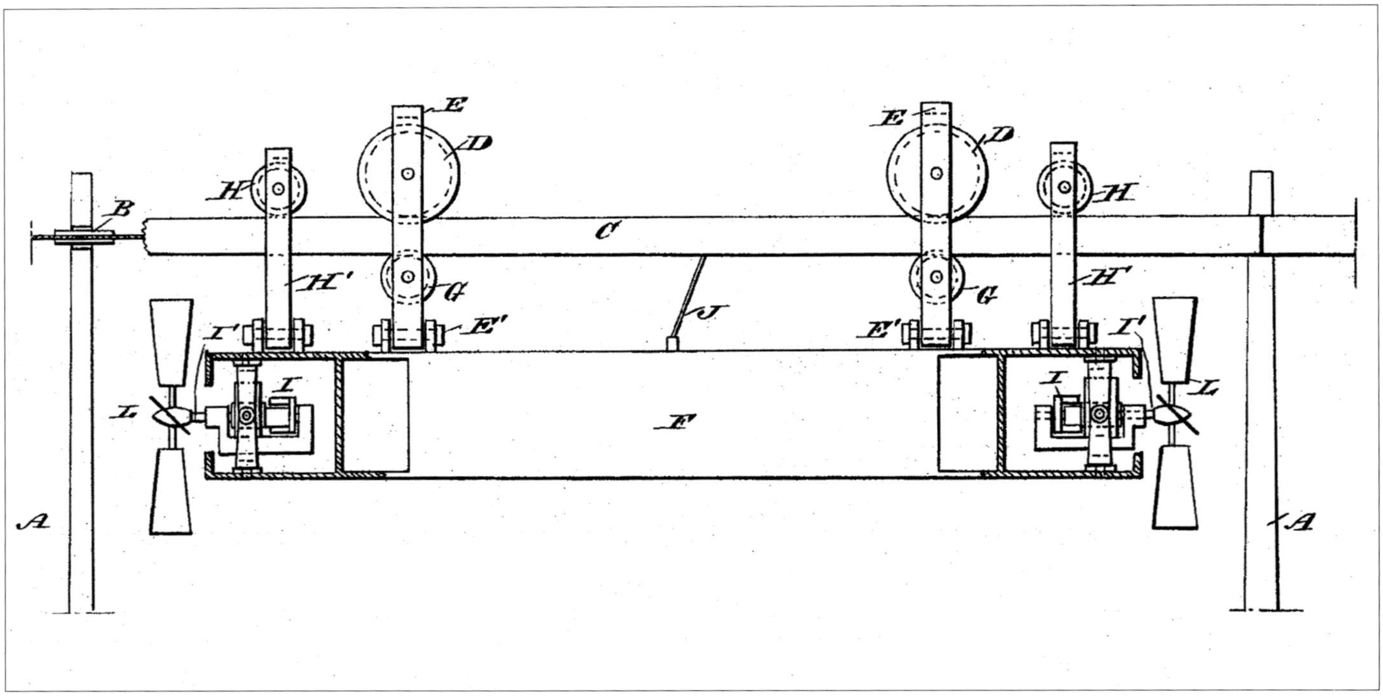

The earliest proposal traced for an air propelled suspended monorail is by Anders Anderson. Based in Blossburg, Montana, USA, Anderson took out a patent for a design in 1892 which had wheels both above and below the upper rail. He suggested that the electric motors and propeller shafts be pivoted so that the forward propeller could be tilted slightly upwards relieving part of the weight on the front wheels and the rear propeller be tilted slightly downwards to relieve part of the weight on the rear wheel. On reversing the carriage, the angles were to correspondingly change. His patent also suggested the use of variable pitch propellers.
US Patent No. 470534

Bennie may have been aware of the Californian propeller driven suspended monorail from reading Popular Mechanics[3] which in theory would have been available in the UK albeit not on the typical newsstand and in limited supply given the hostilities at that time. It has been suggested[1] that Bennie had visited the Wuppertalbahn and this seems a more likely source of his inspiration. There were frequent articles about this railway in the railway and general press.

The impact of technical developments during the First World War was undoubtedly a major influence. Bennie had experience of the use of the propeller and the internal combustion engine but he would also have become familiar with the aerodynamics of wings in terms of lift and drag as well as the development of the airship. This influence was international and seen not only in the shape of the Bennie Railplane but also the contemporary design independently proposed by Rudolf Wagner in Germany (Chapter 9). This influence continued throughout the 1920s (see also Franz Kruckenberg *et al*, Chapter 9).

Wembley Aerial Railway

By the 22nd September 1921 Bennie had developed his ideas sufficiently to apply for a UK patent[4] and he was then able to share them with the press. Whilst it did not immediately get wide press coverage the Glasgow Herald published an artist's impression of his railway system laid out across a hilly countryside in November 1921[5]. In 1922 he presented his ideas to the Edinburgh Industrial Exhibition where he was awarded a medal.

In this first monorail patent the carriage was to be suspended by a bogie from an upper rail and powered at each end by two engines connected through suitable clutches to propellers. The use of clutches indicates that he may have originally envisaged internal combustion engines being used rather than electric motors but the patent allowed for both. Above the roof of the carriage were to be mounted two lifting planes arranged longitudinally. The patent describes that when at rest the entire weight of the Railplane would be borne by the upper rail. As the speed of the Railplane increased, however, Bennie believed that the weight would gradually be transferred from the upper rail to the lifting planes which had an aerofoil cross section. The carriage would be designed so that the entire weight was relieved from the upper rail when it reached maximum speed. Any tendency to rise further once wholly air-borne could be overcome by adjusting the lifting planes.

Whilst the patent stated that friction brakes may be provided to secure the Railplane when at rest, braking when in motion was to be controlled by either reducing or stopping the rate of rotation of the forward propeller or by use of the rear propeller as an air brake.

In order to bring his ideas to fruition Bennie needed additional engineering expertise and after applying for his patent he recruited Hugh Fraser as Chief Engineer in 1922. With this vital engineering help, Bennie, now in his thirties, was very much aware that success required his ideas to be promoted. The British Empire Exhibition to be held in 1924 provided the opportunity. Based at an official address in Austin Friars House, London E.C.2., Bennie proposed a line connecting Stonebridge Park Station of the London, Midland and Scottish Railway with the exhibition grounds at Wembley Park, over a mile away[6].

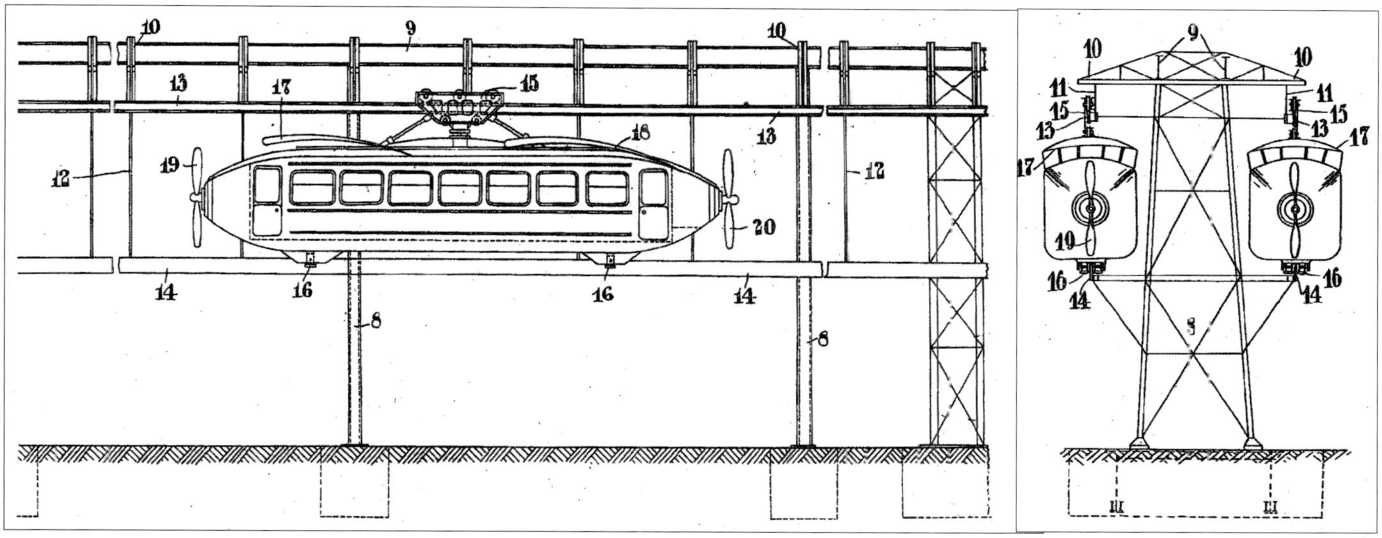

The monorail patents granted to Bennie in the UK and USA in 1923 envisaged a carriage suspended from a single upper bogie but prevented from swinging by a lower rail. The UK Patent was titled 'Aerial Tracks for Guiding Aircraft' whilst the US Patent No. 1459495 more realistically titled the patent 'System of Aerial Transport'. The end elevation of Bennie's 1923 Railplane design showed wings or more precisely aerofoil sections which he described as lifting planes mounted above the carriages. These are labeled 17 in the drawings from the 1923 US patent.

For this temporary line it was not necessary to own the land over which it would travel as under 1920s legislation the aerial structure only required wayleaves similar to those granted for the erection of telegraph poles and radio aerials. These were granted by both the Great Central section of the London and the North Eastern Railway and by the owners of the intervening land. Bennie immediately set to work designing the Railplanes. Given the short length of the proposed line it was not, in his view, necessary for the vehicles to include the use of lifting planes. Instead, he and Fraser designed 50ft long carriages (ignoring propellers), 8ft in diameter with a streamlined shape suspended from two bogies each with a 6ft wheelbase, the centres being 24ft apart. The cast steel wheels were to be 2ft 3in. in diameter with rubber self-aligning bearings, the bogies having rubber springs and ball thrust bearings. The weight of the Railplane when fully loaded was expected to be less than ten tons due to its light construction and the use of aluminium sheeting on the sides. Bennie suggested that when it attained sixty miles per hour, even without lifting planes, it would be partly air-borne due to its light weight, aerodynamic shape and method of propulsion.

The two pairs of guide rollers to be mounted under the body to maintain the carriages attitude were to be provided with rubber tyres and mounted on a sliding

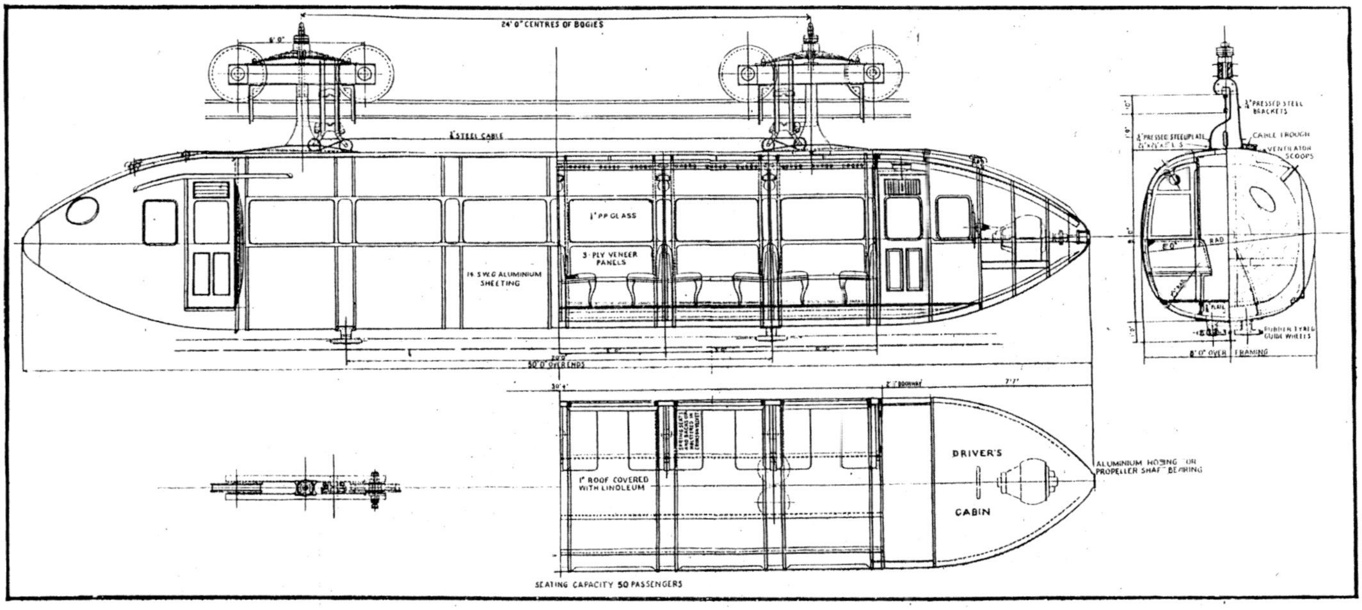

The general arrangement drawing of the Railplane for the Wembley Aerial Railway was published in *Modern Transport* on the 24th November 1923. The four stabilising wheels bearing on the lower rail (two each side) were to be placed at 20ft centres, inside the 24ft upper bogie centres. The steel cable and small pulleys immediately above the body were to work the mechanical brakes on the upper rail.

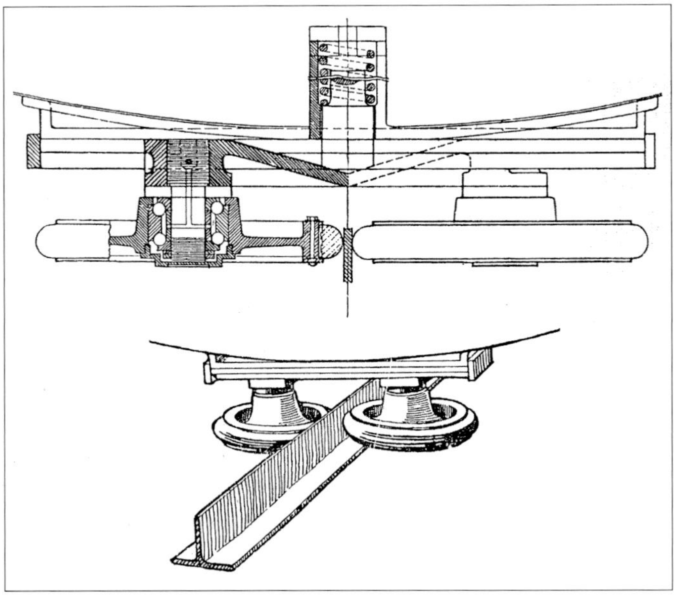

Tramway & Railway World published this drawing on the 16th September 1926 of the stabilising wheels under the proposed Wembley Aerial Railway Railplane. It shows the roller bearings and the rubber faced tyres but failed to include the 1½in. gap between the wheels and the rail which was part of the design.

bracket to give lateral movement. The gap between these wheels was to exceed the lower rail width by a clearance of 1½in.

Bennie hoped to use this line to demonstrate carriages powered by both electricity and internal combustion. For the electric carriages the electric system was to be 500V DC, which was expected to provide 42 horse power, rising to 100 horse power for up to fifteen seconds giving full torque during the starting load. For the internal combustion powered carriage the petrol engines were to be 20 horse power. Each carriage was to accommodate 50 seated passengers and, to reduce station time and congestion, passengers were to enter by one door at the end of the car and leave by the other.

In proposing his system Bennie had approached various suppliers including the British Power Railway Signal Company Ltd of Caxton House, Westminster, London to provide a three aspect colour light system, Alexander Finlay & Company Ltd of Motherwell to provide the steelwork for the rail structure, P. & W. Anderson Ltd of Piccadilly, London, a firm able to provide the foundations for the steelwork and Hurst, Nelson & Company Ltd to build the Railplanes. The electric motors were to be provided by Bruce Peebles & Company Ltd. of Edinburgh.

By November 1923 a company was being formed for the construction of this proposed Wembley Aerial Railway. In promoting the line Bennie claimed that it would demonstrate the system's invaluable use as a feeder line to main line railways and that it would be more economical in initial cost, maintenance and operation than a light railway. However, it was, he said, primarily intended for rapid transport with speeds of up to 150 miles per hour considered possible.

Despite his efforts, this proposal got no further.

On-going promotion

Bennie continued promoting his system and in 1926 he gained further publicity in an article in *Tramway & Railway World* comparing his system with the Wuppertalbahn[7]. Probably based on his work on the Wembley proposal, Bennie estimated the cost of construction of a double line of track on his method at £15,000 to £19,000 per mile,

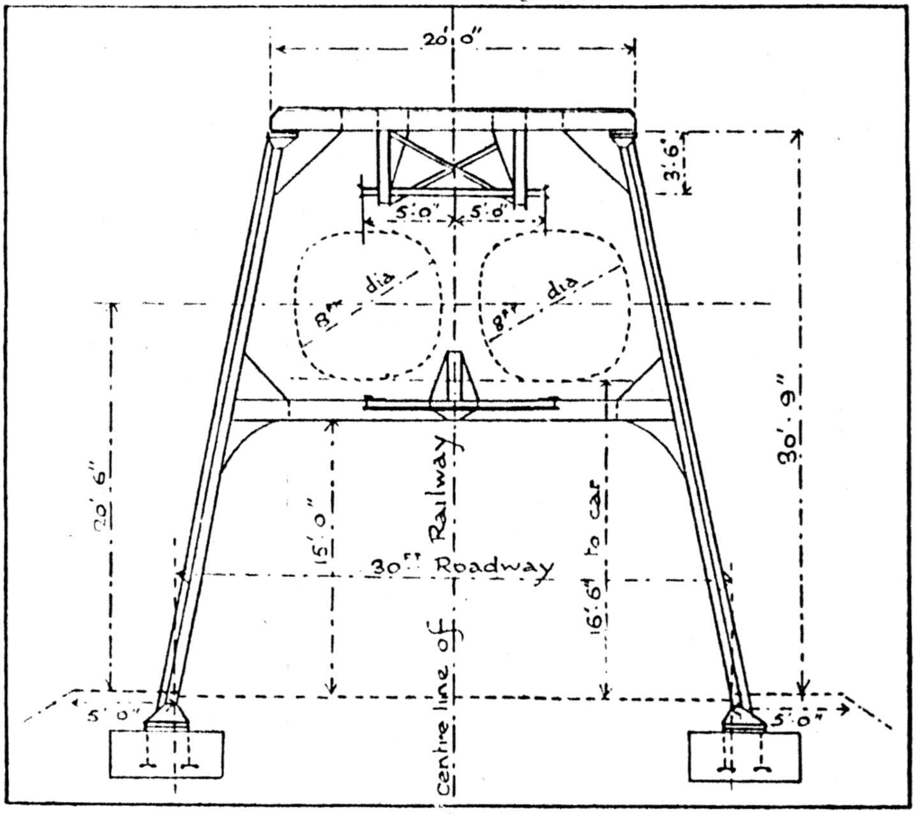

The proposed design of track structure of the Wembley Aerial Railway. The columns to be made from braced channels were to be at 50ft intervals. This corresponded with the length of the Railplane which Bennie believed would ensure an even strain throughout the track.

Modern Transport *Vol. 10, 24 November 1923*

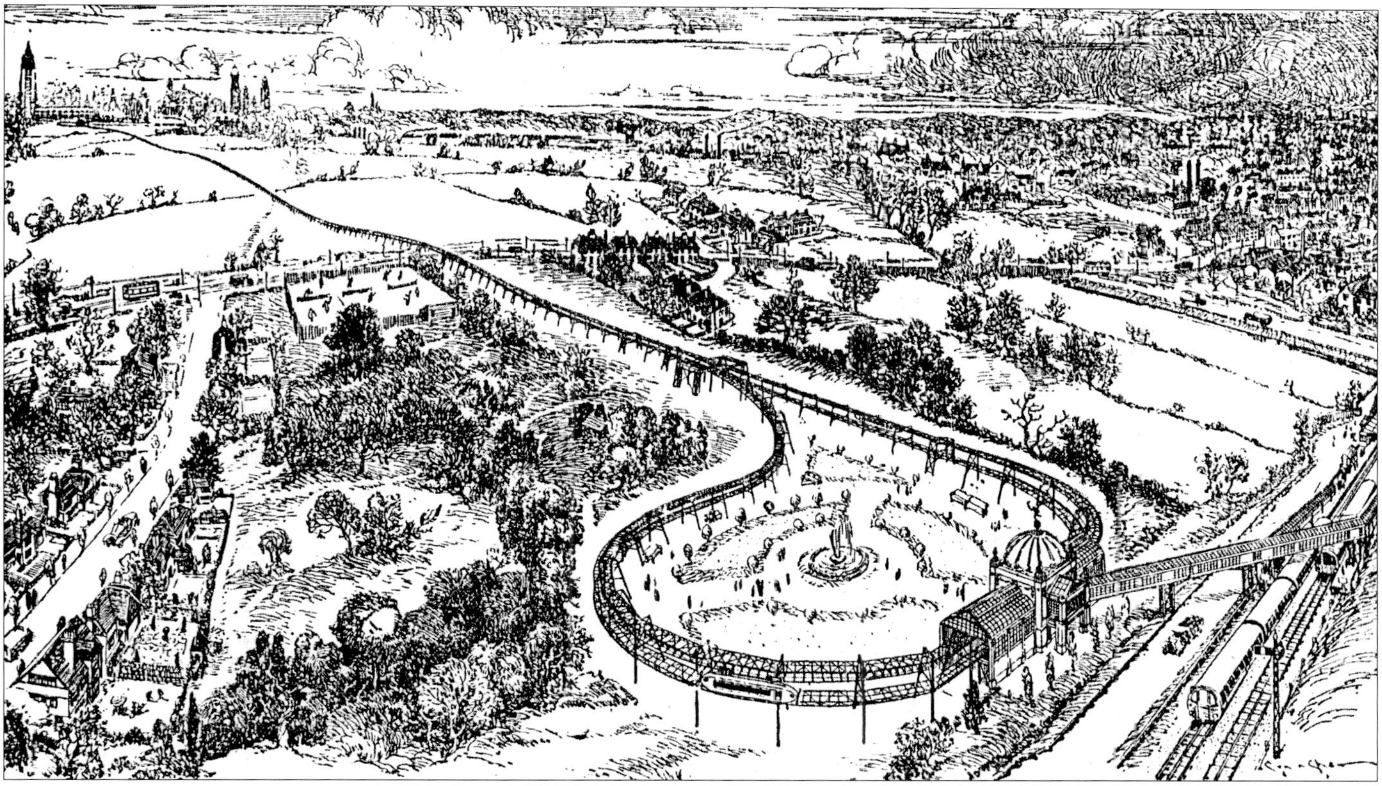

An artist's impression of the proposed Wembley Aerial Railway with Stonebridge Park Station of the then London, Midland and Scottish Railway, also served by the Bakerloo Line, bottom right. The suspended monorail would have been double track except at the termini where 200ft radius loops included a 100ft straight length of track by the station platform. Sidings, not shown, were to be provided to accommodate six carriages at each end of the line. Up to six carriages were expected to be in continuous service with an average speed of between 10 and 12 miles per hour. Modern Transport *Vol. 10, 24 November 1923*

whereas the cost of constructing a double line of tramway track with overhead trolley equipment would amount to between £25,000 and £30,000 and for railways the cost would be between £47,000 and £60,000 per mile. He also considered that the cost of maintenance would be low as although the steel frameworks for the track would need painting he estimated this to be only about £200 per year. When added to the cost of maintaining rails, signaling etc. the total would be about £300 per mile per year. These costs, he suggested, would be offset by the need for only one attendant for each Railplane and minimal station staff as the entrance and exit gates would be automatically controlled thus keeping wage costs to a minimum. As previously, he expressed the opinion that speeds of up to 120 miles per hour could easily be attained.

The need to demonstrate the system was pressing and between 1926 and 1929 Bennie applied for, but was denied, permission to build tracks over the Southern Railway between Brighton and Eastbourne, Waterloo and Brighton and London and Dover[8]. He also forwarded a proposal in 1927 to the Lytham St. Annes Corporation to construct a line from Blackpool to Southport, a distance of over twenty miles. This would have linked areas of the Fylde district by way of Guides House and Hesketh Bank[9] and was to include a bridge across the Ribble River near the Guides House Hotel, Freckleton and Crossens[10]. The Lytham St. Annes Corporation appointed a deputation to confer with the authorities in Blackpool and Southport. Blackpool was enthusiastic and sought Parliamentary powers, but the proposal finally failed to progress due to objections from Preston which had plans to develop a deep water port involving the River Ribble. The discussions on this continued between Bennie and the subsequent company, Inter-Counties Ltd., and the authorities into the late 1930s.

During this period Bennie and Fraser continued their design work. Bennie was particularly keen that the ride should be smooth and to this end he patented "Improvements in and relating to Wheels Running on Rails or other Metal Surfaces" (UK Patent No. 273041)[4]. The wheel consisted of interposing between the hub and the steel or other metal tyre, a rubber member held in position by the flanges, one of which was removable. The object was to provide a wheel that would run silently.

The breakthrough finally came in 1928. During the September meeting of the British Association held in Glasgow, Bennie was able to present to the many engineers and scientists attending his ideas and demonstrate a large scale model installed at his offices at 276 St. Vincent Street[9]. About a month later, on 13th November, G. B. Howden, District Engineer to the London & North Eastern Railway, Edinburgh, presented a paper titled 'High Speed Transport' to the Scottish section of the Institute of Transport relating to transport in Glasgow[11]. He said that:

"After reviewing the various developments which had taken place in recent years, [he] was of the opinion that future developments in regard to problems of fast transport in Glasgow would best proceed overhead, and the existing roads and streets should be reserved exclusively for pedestrian and slow moving vehicular traffic, including local tramways."

He then commented on the speeds of trains on conventional railways being limited by the speed of slow moving goods trains, the future use of railcars on dedicated lines and concluded that the Bennie system fulfilled four conditions he considered vital for high speed lines, notably:

- Absolute safety and comfort of travelling at all speeds
- Freedom from lateral oscillation
- Stability should be independent of any mechanism such as gyroscopes
- The centrifugal and wind forces should not be concentrated on a single line

Shortly thereafter the decision was made by the London & North Eastern Railway Company to allow the construction of a test track over a goods siding at Milngavie, near Glasgow, which had served the former Burnbrae Dye Works. *The Scotsman* reported in January 1929[12] that work had begun on the construction with the rails of the goods siding being straightened or 'slewed' preparatory to the iron frameworks being erected overhead. *The Engineer*[9] confirmed that it had been agreed the test track would be 426ft long and that it expected that the line would be in operation before the end of year.

Bolstered by this progress and continuing his publicity, Bennie was reported by *The Scotsman* to have stated that the Railplane will reduce the journey time from Glasgow to Edinburgh to twenty minutes at a fare of 3s 9d (about 18p).

The George Bennie Railplane Trust Ltd, which had been formed to hold the patents and develop the system in October 1927 with a capital of £10,500, was now insufficient to progress the system further[13]. A new company called Inter-Counties Ltd. was therefore inaugurated in December 1928. This company was formed to build and evaluate the short test railway. Bennie was appointed a director for ten years (on a salary of £4000 per year) supported by Alfred E. Holt, A. F. Simpson and H. J. Dunsmuir as fellow directors. The original but now dormant company 'The George Bennie Railplane Trust Ltd' was struck off from the Register of Companies on the 5th December 1933[14].

Milngavie test track

The year 1929 was a period of intense activity for both Bennie and Fraser, his Chief Engineer in the newly formed company. As the design and construction continued Bennie took out four further patents for details of the system. These included a "turntable" for the Railplane. No test construction of a turntable was made at Milngavie and its purpose was described in the patent as to allow cars to be '...transferred by the turning device from the down track to the up track or vice-versa and in the case of a single line of double track, the device may be used for side tracking.' Essentially it was a rotating point equivalent to that used on the Listowel & Ballybunion Railway, which had been designed by Bocandé in 1888.

Progress was rapid and *Modern Transport*[15] reported in November 1929 that the line was nearly ready for testing. During the construction British Pathé made the first of two silent cinematograph films commissioned by Bennie. This first film recorded the construction and erection of the track as well as the building of the Railplane. The twelve minute long film was for publicity use only, not for general public release, and luckily it is still extant. As at 2015 it is available for viewing on the British Pathé website[16].

In April 1930 *Tramway & Railway World* published photographs of the completed track[17] and also recorded that Bennie was submitting a proposal for a line between Anniesland to Balloch Park to meet Glasgow Corporation's desire to improve links from the city to its property at the park.

Bennie, Fraser and another engineer inspect progress on the construction of the Railplane in 1930. Modern Transport *Vol. 23, 5 July 1930*

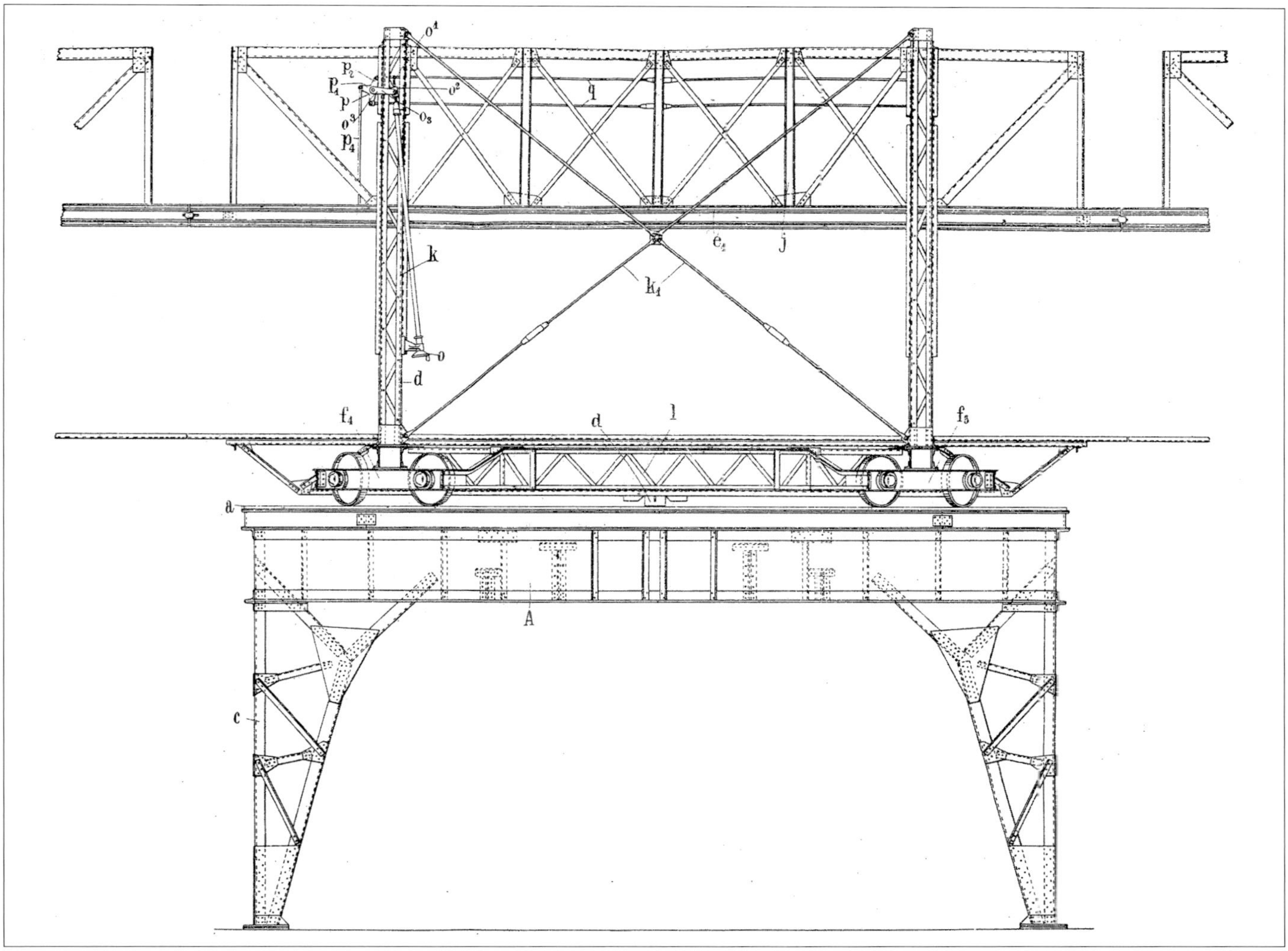

Whilst the Railplane had propellers at both ends Bennie invented and patented a 'turntable' type point (UK Patent No. 323391 granted the 2nd January 1930). The device included locks to stop the carriage coming off the turntable during rotation and was to be combined with a signalling system.

The Railplane was delivered and mounted on the track on Saturday 20th June. Immediately after checking its operation, Bennie invited members of the press to have the first run on this novel system of transport on Thursday the 3rd July 1930[18]. Two days later, on Saturday 5th July, leading officials of the London & North Eastern Railway, which had provided the test site, were received by Bennie for a private inspection of the line[19]. The Southern Railway's London East Engineer, C. A. G. Hinton and W. J. England, Assistant to the Superintendent for train services also inspected the line[8]. They reported that the system was practical but were unable to recommend any portion of the Southern Railway adopting the system due to 'interests of this Company' – code for it not being financially viable.

More positively, on Wednesday 9th July Bennie was able to entertain over 140 delegates attending the annual congress of the Transport Institute in Glasgow. The local press[19] described the event:

"The little station at Burnbrae presented an animated scene on Wednesday afternoon. The delegates, who were conducted by Mr Lachlan Mackinnon, general manager of the Corporation Tramways, and Mr. Robert Killin, general superintendent of the Northern Division, L.M.S. were conveyed thither in eight Corporation 'buses, and in addition to these were many private motors, and cars belonging to film companies, that took up position on the Glasgow Road opposite the railplane. Cinematograph operators were present in force, several taking pictures from underneath the railplane, while others took up position in the turnip field adjoining, and a car bearing the title, 'The Pathé Sound Unit,' filmed the proceedings from the road. A large number of townspeople viewed the scene from outside the railings."

The guests were given a tour of inspection followed by tea and then a run in the Railplane on the short line.

The Pathé Sound Unit made two films. For their newsreel service they made a short film including brief interviews, probably with sound, titled 'Milngavie, Nr. Glasgow. The "George Bennie" railplane! Novel method of high speed transport…claimed to be cheaper, faster and safer…successfully tried out' which was released to cinemas on the 14th July 1930. Separately Bennie had

A general view of the single station on the experimental line. Note the fence part way down the platform. Bennie proposed rapid boarding of passengers through one door whilst those departing would leave by the other door, boarding and departing passengers being separated on the platform. Similarly there were separate stair cases to and from the platform.
The Bennie Railplane System of Transport Inter-Counties Ltd, *1935*

commissioned the second (silent) publicity film with subtitles which recorded the opening of the line. The sub-titles state the opening to have been on the 8th July. The line had certainly been used for demonstrations the previous week so the precise date of filming is uncertain (it may have been over a few days) but it includes a sequence showing Bennie's mother hoisting a flag for the occasion. Again both the newsreel and privately commissioned film still exist (2015) but the sound track of the newsreel, if it existed, has been lost. They are both available for viewing at British Pathé's website.

To generate further publicity, and no doubt to help offset costs and allow testing with passenger loads, the test track was opened to the public from the 12th July 1930 for rides from 1 pm to 9 pm daily, including Sundays which may have upset the local church goers. The admission charges were one shilling (5p) for adults and 6d (2½p) for children under age 16.

Bennie certainly managed to gain publicity with some amusement to the local press. In September the *Milngavie and Bearsden Herald* noted that a recent American publication, somewhat incorrectly referred to 'the Scotch city of Milngavie'[20].

Experience of the construction of the test track caused Bennie to update his ideas about costs of building his system. The July 1930 edition of *Modern Transport*[21] stated that he estimated costs of constructing his system now to be in the range of £18,000 to £19,000 per mile. Bennie was careful to update only the lower figure from that published in 1926.

The increased publicity also enabled Bennie to interest overseas opportunities and in August 1930 a party of Jewish business men inspected the line with the object of reviewing the possibility of adopting the system to connect Jerusalem with Tel Aviv and Jaffa[22].

Public access to the Milngavie test track, however, was short lived probably because local residents had all had a ride and very few other members of the general public wanted to travel far for such a short ride on the Railplane. It closed just two months after it was opened.

By October 1930 Bennie had, however, received enquiries and entertained representatives from Belgium, France, Germany, the Irish Free State, Argentine, Japan and USA[23]. One private company was apparently considering the system for a 30 km long line in the South of France. In the USA he managed to interest officials in New York who considered a proposal to build a Bennie type monorail using 200 horse power cars running at 45 miles per hour in an outlying borough[24].

Not one for understatement, Bennie wildly stated to the press that the Blackpool to Southport proposal has "...been approved by Blackpool Corporation, who

The Railplane waits silently on its short track at Milngavie. *The Bennie Railplane System of Transport Inter-Counties Ltd.*, 1935

have agreed to support the Bill when it comes before Parliament. This will be the first step towards linking up of Fleetwood, Blackpool, Kirkham, Hundredend, Southport, Liverpool and Manchester."

The Blackpool to Southport proposal was certainly still under discussion, but Bennie's extension to Manchester and Liverpool was effectively a repeat of Behr's failed ideas to join these cities by a monorail some thirty years earlier.

None of the proposals came to fruition.

The slow exit of Bennie from Inter-Counties Ltd

The press was not damning of the system. Indeed *Mechanical Engineering* published a review in March 1931[25] recognizing the ever increasing use of cars and the need for 'automobile highways'. Their suggestion was that as the Bennie track structure had the Railplanes hung below the upper surface, the upper surface could be concreted to provide an automobile highway on the toll principle. Further, the sale of gasoline and supplies could form a further source of income for the railway.

With the test track closed to the public and no contracts signed Bennie's financial position deteriorated but he continued to promote the system. In 1931 he hoped to raise capital as a joint venture with the Southern Railway for a line between Holborn Viaduct and Croydon Air Park[8]. This was rebuffed by the Southern as competing with their already existing service but they countered by suggesting a line from London Bridge to Dartford via Blackheath and Bexley Heath.

He also tried to get his system supported by the Ministry of Transport but with no success. On the 18th November 1931 Mr Pybus, MP for Norwich and Minister for Transport, responded to a question raised by Mr Wedderburn, MP for Renfrew, in the House of Commons about whether any investigations had been made by his Ministry into the possibilities of the Bennie Railplane system. *The Times* reported that his somewhat abrupt response was '...[the Ministry] had investigated it. They had pointed out that statutory powers would be necessary to enable the inventor to proceed with his proposals, and that was his business and not that of the Government.'[26]

By 1933 Inter-Counties Ltd had no contracts signed to generate income and was no longer a viable going concern. Bennie had developed and promoted the system and had been Managing Director but like so many monorail promoters before him he had no sense of commercial reality or business skills. The Board of Inter-Counties could have opted to wind up the company but by chance Charles Boot of Messrs. Henry Boot & Sons, Limited, Sheffield, engineers and contractors took an interest in the Railplane. He had become aware of the launch by the London County Council of a slum clearance scheme with a total capital expenditure of £35m which was intended to rehouse about 250,000 people over a period of ten years. This was a major financial opportunity for his company and he set out a proposal to the Ministry of Health to house 50,000 families in two new towns in Essex, one situated east south-east of Waltham Abbey and the other in the vicinity of Dagenham and Becontree. He also published a booklet *A Scheme for the Abolition of Large Slum Areas* promoting his construction plans.

The housing developments needed a corresponding transport system and he proposed adopting the Railplane. He suggested a double line track between the two towns with single line loops within the towns, the total length of single line being 46½ miles. The cost of the Railplane system was estimated at £2.7m[27]. The ticket pricing for the proposed Waltham Abbey to Dagenham line had also been calculated to be not more than 6d (2½p) for a return fare.

The Board of Inter-Counties Ltd, realised this was an opportunity to save the company and restructured the Board appointing Boot as Managing Director, Hugh Fraser, Bennie's engineer, and William Davison Stephenson directors and the share capital was restructured. Bennie effectively lost all control of the company and his shareholding was seriously diminished. Developments of the design no longer continued to be registered in Bennie's name. Instead these were patented by Fraser, who had been recruited by Bennie and was now in charge of all engineering.

Shortly thereafter the company's address was moved to 10 The Boltons, London, S.W.10 but it still advertised their test line at Burnbrae Depot in Milngavie Road, Bearsden. The address in London was the same as that of the firm of consulting engineers, Hitchins, Jervis and Partners, which was also appointed as consultants to Inter-Counties Ltd.

In October 1933 the working model of the Railplane that had been built for Bennie for use as publicity in 1928 was demonstrated in a garage in Kensington, London to both the press and the authorities[28]. It had been made to a scale of 1in.:1ft. The torpedo shaped car was about 4ft 6in. long (scaling up to 54ft) fitted with small electric motors allowing it to accelerate rapidly to about five miles per hour over the 30ft length of track.

Whilst the Waltham Abbey to Dagenham line proposal was being pursued, Inter-Counties Ltd. also encouraged the idea during 1934 of using the Railplane to connect cities and aerodromes in London, Glasgow, Edinburgh, Belfast and Paris[29]. Boot also suggested that the system could operate a service on the Cathcart Circle route without fog curtailing its operation.

A year later, in 1935, Boot and the board of Inter-Counties also became enthused with the possibility of a fast line from London to Folkstone and Dover to connect with ferries to Calais and Boulogne, which would connect with a further Railplane monorail running from Brussels to Paris.

To this end Inter-Counties Ltd published a booklet in 1935 promoting their system[30]. The booklet contained a 'Consulting Engineers' Report' dated the 23rd July 1935 by the firm of Hitchins, Jervis & Partners with an address now shown as Hallam House Westminster. Needless to say, as they were engineering consultants to the Company, their report was very positive.

By 1935 cost for construction of the Railplane system had increased again and the booklet now quoted the cost as £22,000 per double track mile with maintenance at £350 per mile per year. It also contained an interesting table on the anticipated effects of weather:

The working model constructed for Bennie in 1928 was demonstrated in London in 1933. It included a rather crude representation of the standard gauge track below the line at Milngavie. Engineer *Vol. 148, 23 August 1929*

	Railways	Railplane	Aeroplane
GALE	Slight delay	Normal Service	Complete hold up
FOG	Delay and curtailed service	Normal Service	Complete hold up
SNOW	Slight delay with occasional hold up	Normal Service	Partial hold up
RAIN	Slight delay with occasional hold up	Normal Service	Partial hold up
FLOODS	Slight delay with occasional hold up	Normal Service	Normal Service

Henry Boot was not the only developer and architect who found the concept of the Railplane appealing. In the USA, Frank Lloyd Wright, described by the New York Times as one of the originators of the 'modern' movement in architecture, had designed a model to be shown in New York's Industrial Arts Exposition in the Rockefeller Centre. This was a visualization of a self-contained community called by its creator 'Broadacre City'. The arterial rights of way were to have Bennie type monorails speeding along the centre of the main roads[31].

Again none of these proposals moved forward and the relationship between Bennie and the Board of Inter-Counties deteriorated further. On the 1st September 1936 *The Times* published the following[32]:

"**PERSONAL ANNOUNCMENTS**

"Disclaimer – Inter-counties Limited, Railplane Test Line, Milngavie Road, Bearsden, Glasgow announces that Mr. George Bennie is no longer a Director of the Company and that he has assigned his whole rights and interests in and to his Railplane Patents to the Company.""

Just over three months later, Bennie was named on a Receiving Order published on the 18th December 1936 under the Bankruptcy Acts[33]. On the 19th February 1937, he was adjudged bankrupt. Mr Registrar Kean presided at a sitting of the Bankruptcy Court on the 30th June 1937 for a public examination of the financial position of Bennie, who was then residing at the Great Northern Hotel, King's Cross Road[13 & 34].

From the record of this examination it is clear that Bennie's optimism for his system had clouded his financial judgement. When Inter-Counties Ltd had been set up in 1928 Bennie had transferred all his patent rights to it and he had also made commitments to the shareholders of that new company that he could only keep if his system was a success, notably:

- He entered into an agreement with the company that his patent rights would revert to him on payment by him of £20,000 plus 5% interest if a public company (i.e. one with shares on the open market) had not been set up by November 1930. Effectively this required a

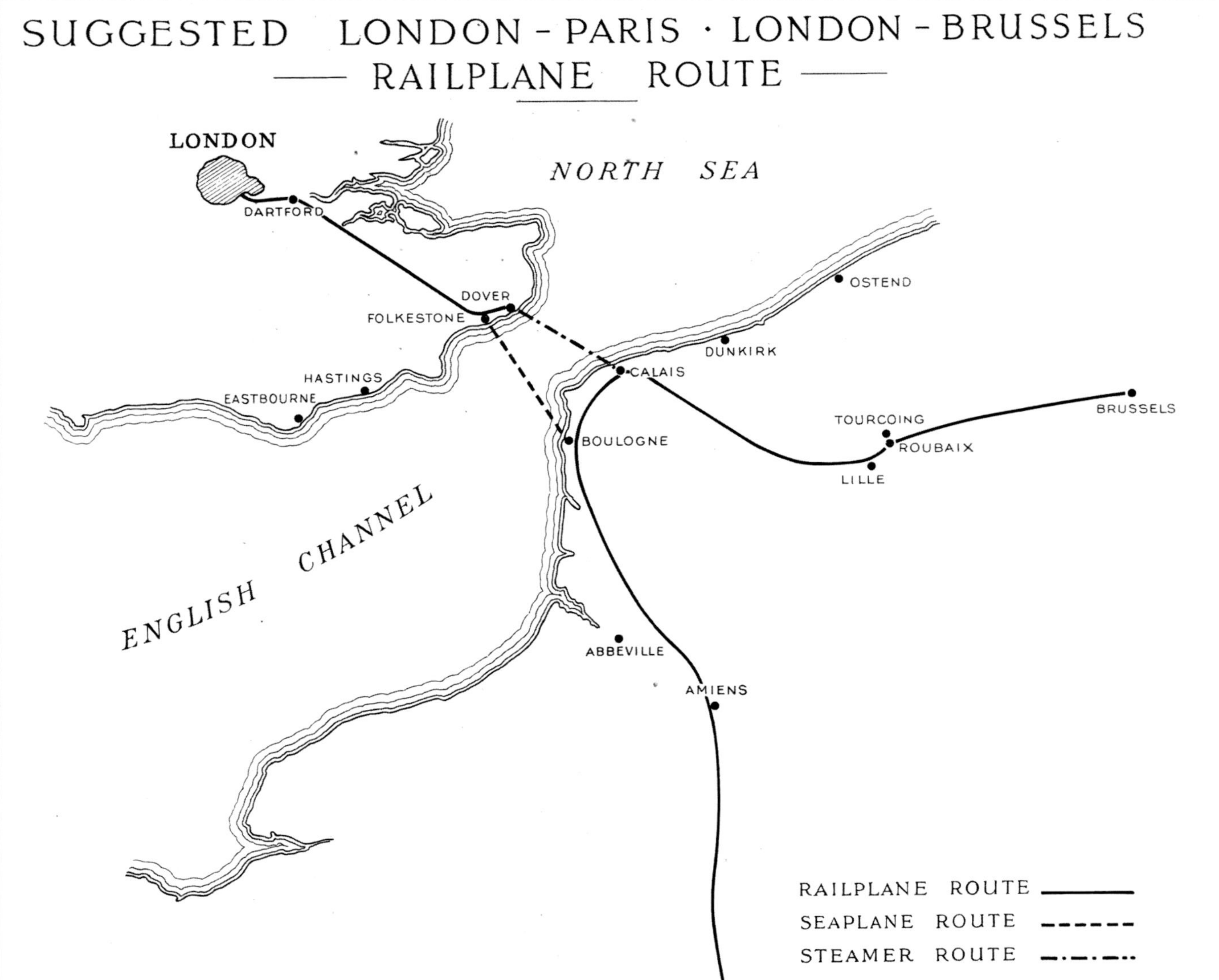

The proposed Railplane routes from London to Folkestone and Dover and the mainland Europe line joining Brussels with Paris. The Bennie Railplane System of Transport Inter-Counties Ltd, *1935*

Railplane line to have been agreed and financed.

- He would pay a cash bonus of £20,000 to shareholders of Inter-Counties Ltd. after that date out of anticipated profits.

The Mr L. A. West, the Senior Official Receiver, said that Bennie's unsecured debts amounted to £5,061 and contingent liabilities of £22,231, but that he had assets valued at £120,000. This was probably illiquid property, but may also have included shares in Inter-Counties Ltd. His bankruptcy arose from lack of liquid cash rather than assets.

Bennie – his remaining years

Despite his exit from Inter-Counties Ltd and his bankruptcy, he remained committed to the Railplane system. Indeed, in early July 1937, shortly after he was summoned to appear at the London Bankruptcy Court, he hosted the projection of the films made at Milngavie to members of the engineering press. As noted above these showed the building and equipping of the Railplane, the construction of the overhead track and the operation of the finished test track. They also showed, important from the view point of publicity, James Calder, formerly General Manager, Scotland, and other officials of the London & North Eastern Railway making an inspection. Bennie made known that the films had already been seen by Sir Charles Bressey and Edwin Lutyens who were engaged in the Highway Development Survey of Greater London. Bennie was again promoting the system and had estimated the capital cost of a line from London to Heston Airport, which then operated in west London (near the site of Heathrow Airport), at £1 million which he forecast would generate a net revenue of £411,000 based on wayleaves rather than land purchase. He again mentioned the ongoing proposal of a line joining Blackpool and Southport, which had continued from 1927, and discussions with the Air Attaché to the French Embassy in London regarding a proposed link between Le Bourget Airport and Paris. He said he was also preparing plans for the erection of a line from Birmingham City to its airport[35].

Up to and including the period of the Second World War Bennie continued to advocate his system as a means of solving the problem of providing speedy transport between the centres of large towns and their airports[36]. Undaunted by the failure to obtain a contract, he continued making detailed design improvements to the Railplane taking out further patents in 1944 and 1945. During this period he also patented ideas for improvements to control rooms at airports and related matters.

After the war, out of bankruptcy, Bennie formed the company George Bennie Airspeed Railway Ltd in 1946 to promote his system. In 1947 the Ministry of Transport gave him permission to erect a four mile long experimental stretch of track on the outskirts of Glasgow[37]. Provost David Bonnar, foreseeing a transport problem for inhabitants living in Airdrie and Coatbridge and working at the new industrial estate being constructed at Newhouse to the east of Glasgow, proposed that Bennie's test line be built to connect these areas. The Council, however, decided that the solution should not be confined to the Bennie Railplane and opted for alternative solutions.

Bennie's reason for setting up the company George Bennie Airspeed Railway Ltd, however, was primarily to build Railplanes connecting UK city centres and airports and in 1948 he proposed a monorail from Victoria, London to the new London Airport, which had opened in 1946 (now called Heathrow). He expected this to take about two and a half years to build at a cost quoted at £3m in the Sunday Empire News and £6m in the Dundee Evening Telegraph[38].

Then, in 1950, Bennie spent three months in Syria and Iraq following which he claimed to have received an enthusiastic response from government officials to the construction of 700 miles of track at a cost of £27m linking several major Arab cities[39]. At the age of sixty in 1951 he formed a further company, George Bennie Airspeed Railway (Iraq) Ltd. to build the line from Damascus to Bagdad. In these ventures Bennie had a number of supporters including Sir Patrick Abercrombie, an influential and eminent town planner and architect, who was appointed, with John Henry Forshaw, to prepare a plan for the post war rebuilding of the County of London. Abercrombie wrote to The Times supporting lines from London to Heathrow and Gatwick as well as a connection between Plymouth to its airport[40].

In 1953 Bennie submitted a proposal to the Isle of Wight Council for Railplane lines to replace two branch lines which had recently been closed[41] but by the middle of the 1950s Bennie gave up the struggle to promote his Railplane. George Bennie Airspeed (Iraq) Railway Ltd was dissolved on the 25th May 1956 followed by George Bennie Airspeed Railway Ltd on the 27th November 1956[42]. Bennie died a year later on the 1st November 1957 aged 66.

In June 1990 a plaque was unveiled by Provost Joan Cameron of the Bearsden and District Council commemorating the site of the test track of the Railplane (unfortunately showing Bennie's year of birth incorrectly as 1892)[43].

Milngavie test track – deferred demolition

Following the flurry of activity on the test track in 1930, its subsequent use was intermittent and by the beginning of the Second World War it was effectively out of use. Shortly after the war started, supplies of steel to make munitions became scarce as these were not being met by the convoys of ships and the public were asked to give up their garden railings to aid supply. The test track nearly suffered the same fate. In July 1940 'The Scrap Heap' in the *Railway Gazette*[36] reported that the experimental Railplane installation at Milngavie, which had formed a landmark in the north-west outskirts of Glasgow, was to be demolished to assist with the Second World War scrap metal campaign. It was estimated that it would contribute about 100 tons of scrap steel.

No action occurred and a letter to the editor of the *Milngavie and Bearden Herald* in June 1942[44] complained that in any event much of the 'scrap'" that had been stockpiled for the war effort would never be used. The same paper reported that 'Man in the Street' had written in *The Evening Times* that some correspondents had asked why the Milngavie test track had not been added to the national smelting pot. He had been informed that a law firm in Edinburgh had told him that the Railplane track was not scheduled for scrap and reported that it was being given a coat of protective paint for use after the war.

It presumably escaped demolition at the request of the owners, Inter-Counties Ltd, but was never used again as the rail systems subsequently developed bore little resemblance to the original Bennie track. The track structure and Railplane was eventually purchased for scrap by John R. Adams & Sons Ltd and was demolished in 1956[45].

Inter-Counties Ltd – a protracted end

Despite the renewed energy after 1936 with Boot at its head, Inter-Counties Ltd had no more success under its new leadership in promoting the system than it had done under Bennie. Early in 1937 the company applied to the Streets and Buildings Committee of the Glasgow Corporation to build a Railplane track from Govan Cross and Bellahouston Park during the period of the forthcoming Empire Exhibition to be held in Glasgow in 1938. This was refused, probably because it would pass over two city streets, Edmiston Drive and Paisley Road West. Inter-Counties Ltd. was, however, able to enthuse the Exhibition Executive and two months later, in April, the company submitted another application with the backing of the exhibition organisers, who thought it would prove an attraction as a novel form of transport. Under 'Standing Orders' at the Committee meeting, re-applications could only be accepted within six months if agreed by two thirds of its members. At a vote this was just missed[46].

In the same year, 1937, the company commenced work on a proposal for a major system in Rio de Janeiro and in 1938 the company opened up negotiations with the Southern Railway about the proposal they had made in 1931 for a London Bridge to Dartford line[8]. Following four patents in 1935 in which Fraser had continued to develop Bennie's ideas[47], Fraser now began to design his own larger carriage which would seat 100 passengers.

He increasingly sought the help of Hitchins, Jervis & Partners, who had already helped in relation to the London to Paris proposal.

In 1942 Inter-Counties Ltd sold all its rights to a new company, Railplanes Ltd, which also had Boot as a Director. Once the war was over, Fraser completed the fundamental redesign of the Railplane and applied for patents which were granted in 1950. This new system was no longer a monorail. The carriage was suspended from a beam on wheels with rubber tyres running either side of an inverted 'T' rail. Fraser named it the F.A.S.T. system (Fraser Airrail System of Transport) to distance it from Bennie's original.

On the 17th July 1953 Railplanes Ltd signed an intercompany agreement with Société Lyonaisse des Eaux et de L'Eclairage to develop the system under the name S.A.F.A.G.E. (Société Anonyme Français de Gestion et d'Entreprises) and also formed the company International Monorail Limited, the name of the latter being a misnomer; it was not a monorail system. A major proposal was then launched to build a rubber tyred two track suspended railway from the Cromwell Road terminal, near Earls Court, London, where it was then possible to check in for flights, direct to London Airport[48]. The consultants Hitchins, Jervis and Partners were again involved.

Eventually involving the UK aeronautical engineering firm of Hawker Siddeley and a consortium of eighteen French companies, a test track was built at Chateuneuf sur Loire, near Orleans, France. Despite being seen by over 3,000 engineers and transport officials from thirty five countries the enterprise failed to reach any contracts[49]. Its patent rights were sold to Misubishi in Japan in 1970.

As neither the later F.A.S.T. nor S.A.F.A.G.E. systems were monorails, and both were developed post Second World War, detailed histories are outside the scope of this book. For more detail the reader is referred to *Modern Transport*[48] and the paper by Malcolm Thwaite[8].

Technical description of the Railplane and Milngavie test track

The steel work for the overhead girders and their supporting trestles for the track was made by Tees Side Bridge & Engineering Works Ltd, of Middlesbrough and assembled on site on prepared foundations[9]. The structures were considerably more rigid than those proposed for the Wembley Aerial Railway and were essentially large 'A' frames with the tracks supported by the 'cross bar' of the "A.

The Railplane had a light weight duralumin frame and plate work body mounted on a steel keel. It was originally reported in the *Engineer* in 1929 that it was to be built by Arrol-Johnston & Aster Engineering Company Ltd, Dumfries, a subsidiary of William Beardmore & Company Ltd, which specialized in car manufacture. Subsequent reports confirmed that it was actually constructed by the parent company, William Beardmore & Company Ltd, at their Dalmuir works near Glasgow. The body was 52ft long and just over 8ft in diameter with sliding doors, overall fractionally larger than the design for the Wembley Aerial Railway. The outside was painted with a border in gold, black and blue. The British Pathé films show that the sliding doors were hand operated rather than powered which is surprising for the 1930s and may have been due to cost. Inside, however, it was lavishly appointed with mahogany lining to the carriage and twenty two upholstered seats and shaded electric lights on tables, all designed and fitted by Waring & Gillow Ltd, London and Liverpool[18 & 21]. The local press[19] stated that 'It looked just like a Pullman tube train with its beautifully upholstered armchairs, and little shaded electric lights on tables ranged along the windows.'

The nose ends and suspension bogies were constructed in Glasgow by Mirrlees Watson Company Ltd. An unusual feature of the bogies was the braking system which was granted a patent in 1930. This was both hand

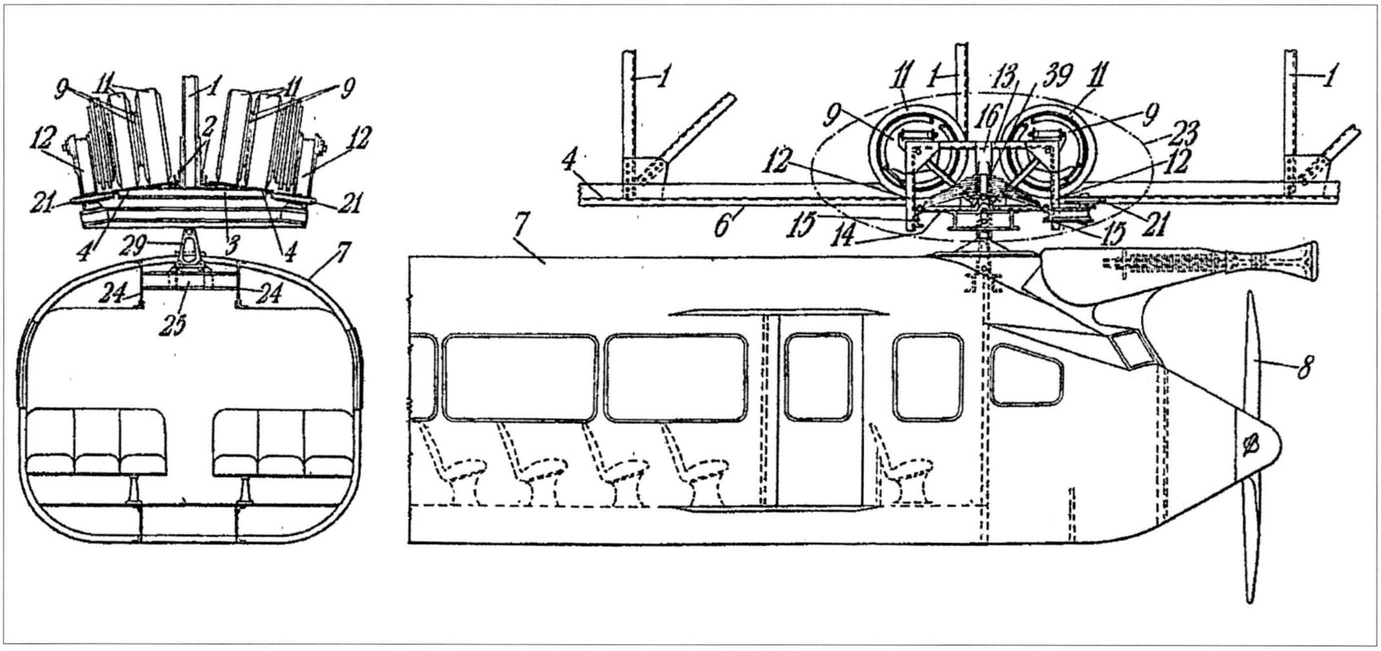

The Railplane patented by Fraser in 1950 (Patent No. 640623) reflected contemporary aircraft design with its rounded nose cone and variable pitch propeller. The end elevation shows the four rubber tyres running either side of an inverted 'T' beam. The lower rail of the original Bennie design has been abandoned.

Abcve: A major deterrent to building a Railplane system was the expensive track structure with its associated maintenance. The structure built at Milngavie was far more substantial than the design published in 1923 and proposed for the Wembley Aerial Railway. Unlike the Wuppertalbahn designed by Langen, no system seems to have been included to allow for expansion and contraction with changes in temperature. This was probably not necessary given the test track was short. Also note its standard box like structure by comparison to the design Rieppel successfully applied, and proved, on the Wuppertabahn.

The Bennie Railplane System of Transport
Inter-Counties Ltd, *1935*

Right: The inside of the Railplane during construction shows the rib like body structure with duralumin plate work.

Modern Transport *Vol. 23, 5 July 1930*

The upper bogies of the model Railplane. Note the cables connecting the brake system with the brake blocks above and below the upper rail.
Engineer *Vol. 148, 23 August 1929*

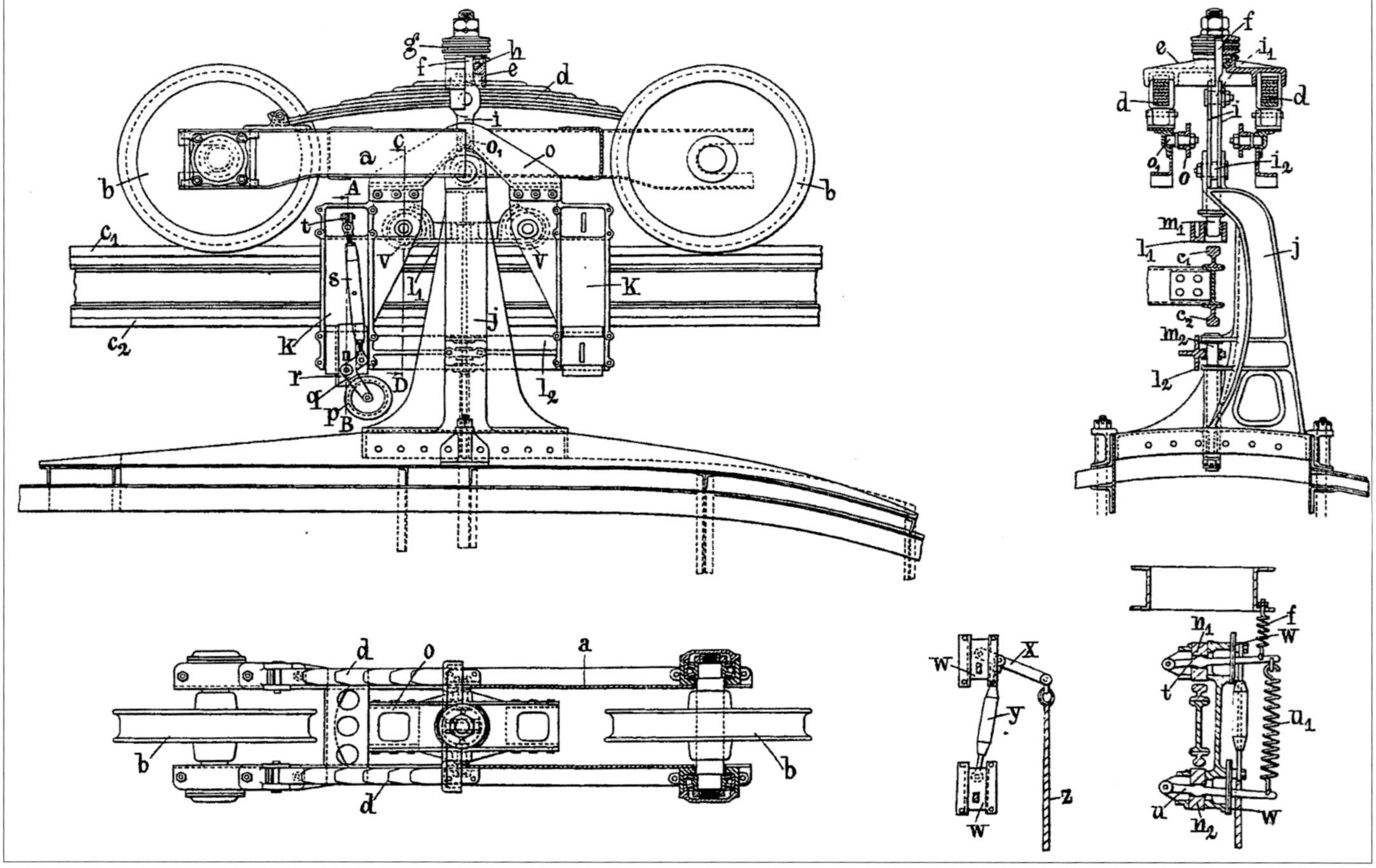

The structure of the final design of the upper bogie included in UK Patent No. 328946 granted on the 5th May 1930 as part of the drawings of the braking system. The steel cable and pulleys operated brakes which gripped the upper rail. Bennie and his chief engineer, Fraser, were keen not to apply brakes to the wheels as any slipping would cause flats to be formed by wear. They feared that these would prevent a smooth ride especially at the high speeds envisaged. Eight shock absorbers were also included to assist in the smooth running with the Bennie patented 'silent' wheels running on roller bearings.

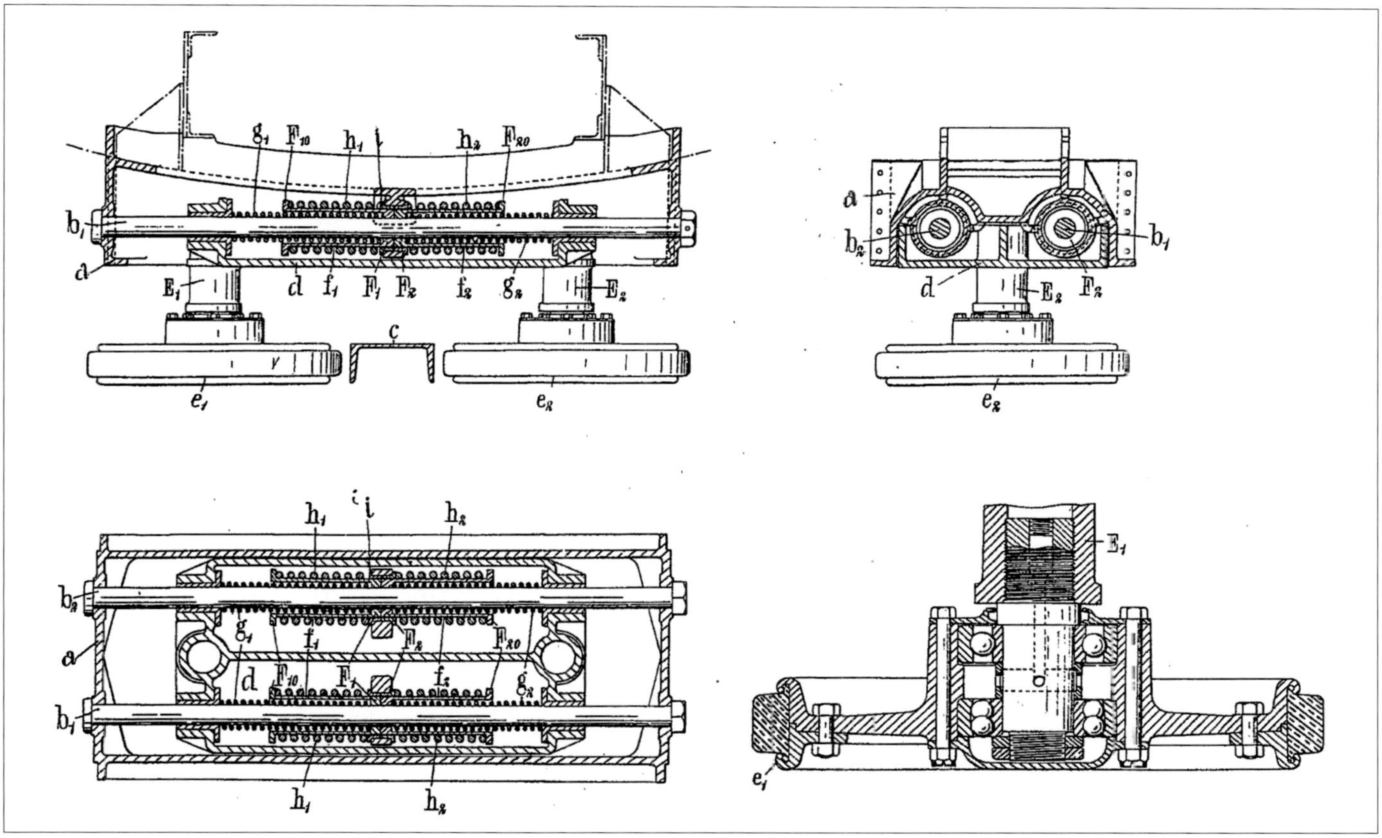

A more advanced system of guiding the carriage was patented by Bennie in his UK Patent No. 328600, granted 30th April 1930, and applied to the full sized Railplane. In this design the rubber faced side wheels running on roller bearings were laterally sprung to allow some smoothing of the motion. The patent drawing also showed the small gap between the wheels and lower rail when the vehicle was upright.

and electrically controlled and arranged to grip both the top and bottom rails so that the wheels ran freely when decelerating. The intention was to avoid the harmful effect of flats on the wheel surfaces and unequal wear arising from friction caused by surface braking.

Bennie and Fraser opted to power the Railplane by electricity probably due to the short length of the test track. To this end they ordered two specially designed electric motors from Laurence, Scott and Electromotors Ltd, of Norwich. These provided an output of 60 horse power at 1,200rpm on a one hour rating, quite sufficient for this short line. As importantly they could provide 240 horse power, at 1,800rpm for up to thirty seconds allowing rapid acceleration and air braking over the short run. Each motor drove a fixed pitch four bladed propeller designed and built by Airscrews Ltd, of Weybridge, Surrey.

The nose of the Railplane consisted of a casting bolted to the longitudinal members of the car with an inwardly extending central housing for the bearings of the propeller shaft. This allowed the propeller, its shaft, bearings and housing to form a self-contained unit which could be removed for maintenance or replacement. *UK Patent No. 328601, 30 April 1930*

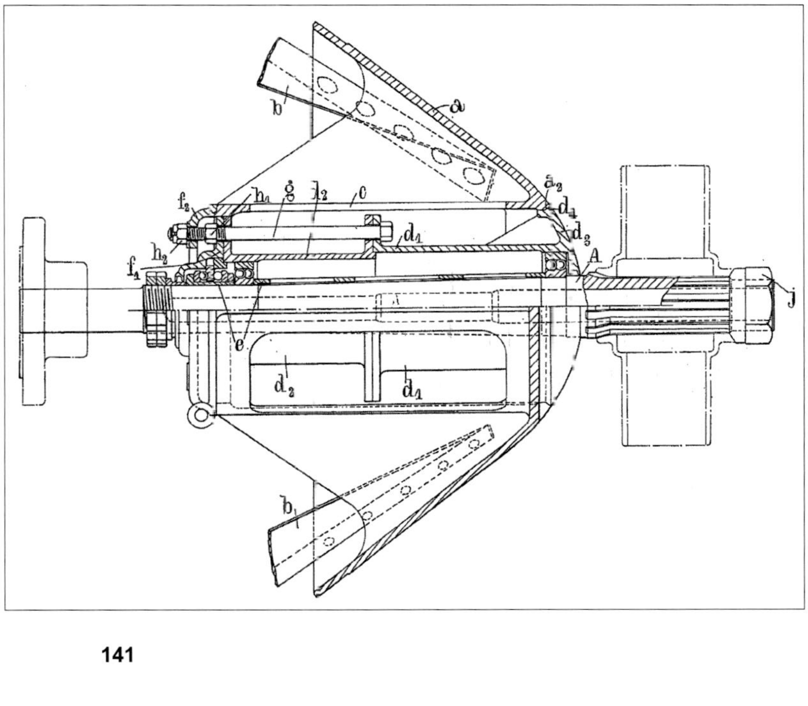

The wooden propeller with its protective leading edge metal strip. Unlike the subsequent Fraser designs, the propeller was of fixed pitch. The wheels embracing the lower rail to provide stability can be seen below the main carriage. At the top left is the colour light signal albeit this short line had only one Railplane.

The Bennie Railplane System of Transport Inter-Counties Ltd, *1935*

From the viewpoint of 2015 it is difficult to understand why Bennie, Kruckenberg and others opted to try propeller propulsion on both monorails and conventional railways. It was certainly the desire for speed, but there was also a mechanical engineering reason detailed in a paper by Otto Steinitz in 1931[50]. Gearboxes, clutches and indirect drives etc. were not fully reliable and the high revolutions needed by the propeller to become efficient permitted direct connection to a high speed electric motor or internal combustion engine.

Power for the Milngavie test railway track was supplied by the Glasgow Corporation Tramways by arrangement with the Clyde Valley Electrical Power Company Ltd, of Glasgow.

Automatic signaling and braking systems were also demonstrated on the line with hardware provided by Tyer & Company Ltd, of Dalston.

References

1 *The Bennie Railplane* by William B. Black, East Dunbartonshire Council, 2004.

2 UK Patent No. 5382 Date of Application 4 March 1912 Date of Grant 17 October 1912.

3 *Popular Mechanics* Vol. 26, August 1916, p273.

4 Bennie monorail patents (excludes non-monorail inventions)

UK Patent No.	Date of Application	Date of Grant
191760	22 September 1921	22 January 1923
273041	13 April 1926	30 June 1927
323391	30 January 1929	2 January 1930
328600	30 January 1929	30 April 1930
328601	30 January 1929	30 April 1930
328946	5 February 1929	5 May 1930
559038	7 November 1942	1 February 1944
560068	7 November 1942	17 March 1944
560919	7 November 1942	26 April 1944
560997	7 November 1942	1 May 1944
565327	29 November 1943	6 November 1944
572660	31 July 1944	17 October 1945

US Patent No. 1459495 Date of Application 9 April 1923 Date of Grant 19 June 1923.

5 *Glasgow Herald* 22 November 1921, p9.

6 *Modern Transport* Vol.10, 24 November 1923, pp10-11 & *The Times* 24 November 1923, p17.

7 *Tramway & Railway World* Vol. 60, 16 September 1926, pp131-134.

8 *Transactions of the Newcomen Society* "The George Bennie Railplane and Hugh Fraser Airrail Systems of Transport" by Malcolm Thwaite, Vol. 75, No.1, 2005, pp37-84.

9 *Engineer* Vol. 148, 23 August 1929, p206.

10 *The Times* 29 September 1927, p14, *The Scotsman* 4 July 1930, p8 & *Lancashire Daily Post* 16 April 1934, p4.

11 *Modern Transport* Vol. 20, 17 November 1928, p6.

12 *The Scotsman* 16 January 1929, p7.

13 *Milngavie and Bearsden* Herald 3 July 1937, p4.

14 *London Gazette* 1 September 1933, p5741 & 5 December 1933, p7871.

15 *Modern Transport* Vol. 21, 9 November 1929, p7.

16 British Pathé www.britishpathe.com

Film ID	Date	Duration
3181.06	Filmed late 1929/early1930	12m 43s B/W Silent
3181.07	Filmed 5th to 9th July 1930	12m 56s B/W Silent
715.09	General release 14/07/1930	2m 27s B/W Sound

17 *Tramway & Railway World* Vol. 67, 17 April 1930, pp186-187.

18 *The Scotsman* 4 July 1930, p7.

19 *Milngavie and Bearsden Herald* 11 July 1930, p1.

20 *Milngavie and Bearsden Herald* 19 September 1930, p2.

21 *Modern Transport* Vol. 23, 5 July 1930, page ix.

22 *Milngavie and Bearsden Herald* 3 August 1940, p2.

23 *The Scotsman* 28 October 1930, p11.

24 *Popular Science Monthly* October 1930, cover & p42.

25 *Mechanical Engineering* Vol. 53, March 1931, cover & pp190-192.

26 *The Times* 19 November 1931, p7.

27 *The Times* 31 August 1933, p7 & *New York Times* 17 September 1933, pRE2.

28 *The Times* 11 October 1933, p9.

29 *Milngavie and Bearsden Herald* 19 October 1934, p6.

30 *The Railplane System of Transport Inter-Counties Ltd*, 1935. See also *Railway Gazette* Vol. 64, 24 January 1936, p139.

31 *New York Times* 27 March 1935, p16.

32 *The Times* 1 September 1936, p1.

33 *Edinburgh Gazette* 18 December 1936, p1066.

34 *The Times* 1 July 1937, p4.

35 *Railway Gazette* Vol. 67, 30 July 1937, p212 & *Engineering* 3 September 1937, p257.

36 *Railway Gazette* Vol. 73, 5 July 1940, pp5 & 18.

37 *Scottish Daily Express* 16 December 1947, p3 & *Milngavie and Bearsden Herald* 24 January 1948, p3.

38 *Sunday Empire News* 4 April 1948, p3, *Dundee Evening Telegraph* 14 May 1948, p2 & *Dundee Courier and Advertiser* 18 January 1949, p4.

39 *Dundee Evening Telegraph* 6 September 1950, p3.

40 *The Times* 3 December 1952, p9.

41 *The Times* 21 October 1953, p4.

42 *Edinburgh Gazette* 24 February 1956, p123, 25 May 1956, p313, 24 August 1956, p502 & 27 November 1956, p693.

43 *Milngavie and Bearsden Herald* 29 June 1990, p9.

44 *Milngavie and Bearsden Herald* 6 June 1942, pp2 & 3.

45 *Glasgow Herald* 24 March 1956, p8.

46 *Glasgow Herald* 6 April 1937, p6.

47 Fraser monorail patents

UK Patent No.	Date of Application	Date of Grant
433726	21 February 1934	20 August 1935
434444	8 March 1934	2 September 1935
434534	8 March 1934	4 September 193
435801	28 February 1934	30 September 1935
640620	11 June 1948	26 July 1950
640623	14 June 1948	26 July 1950

48 *Modern Transport* 4 February 1956, pp3 & 6, 11 February 1956, pp11, 14 & 18 and February 1956, p2.

49 The Times 23 May 1962, p9.

50 *Glasers Annalen* Vol. 108, 15 January 1931, pp13-18. See also *Mechanical Engineering* Vol. 53, April 1931, p299.

CHAPTER 8
FURTHER PROPOSALS PLAIN AND EXOTIC

The volume on 19th century monorails included a chapter describing monorail proposals that appeared never to have got further than the drawing board or a small model. No claim was made that the list was exhaustive but it showed the variety of inventors' ideas. From 1900 onwards designs and ideas proliferated and only a sample can be included in this book. The number of magazines and journals recording these inventions also mushroomed but one research tool has been invaluable. The free internet based database 'Espacenet' now covers some 90 million patents in over ninety countries showing most patents from 1900 and allows very easy access when at least some details are known.

From 1900 to the start of the Second World War most monorail inventions fell into one of four categories:

- Development of the monorail for passenger and freight purposes.
- Use of the monorail as a novelty or amusement.
- Reinvention of past ideas only very thinly describable as novel.
- What can only be described as flights of impractical fantasy.

By 1935, however, a fifth category had emerged, notably the development of the monorail as a crane or hoist. In most cases this was accomplished by suspending a movable carriage with lifting gear below an 'I' beam. Typically these had wheels either side of the main 'I' beam section and were thus strictly two rail but in any event in your author's view these have little interest from a railway perspective and are not included below. Often the companies developing these cranes had 'monorail' in their title, for example the American Monorail Company based in Cleveland Ohio took out multiple patents for their designs from around 1930.

One other trend emerged. Whilst many monorail inventors continued to stress speed of travel, the control of cost and the provision of economic transport were increasingly mentioned.

Two notes apply to this chapter.

1 Many inventors patented their ideas in more than one country. Only UK and US patent details are shown below. Equivalent patents in other countries can be traced through Espacenet.

2 Inventors of monorails often designed and patented other railway and indeed non-railway items. These are not detailed below.

Opposite: An artist's impression of the Mähl monorail system formed the cover of *Scientific American* Vol. 112, 27 March 1915.

1900

Inventor: **Alexander A. Welsh** (USA) & **Adam A. Welsh** (USA)
Type: Unique

US Patent No.	Date of Grant
663525	11 December 1900 (Alexander A. Welsh)
676670	18 June 1901 (Adam A. Welsh)

Alexander A. Welsh, who lived in Allegheny, Pennsylvania, patented a system which he considered particularly adapted to scenic or pleasure railways. His patent envisaged the use of wood to make the track frame which he designed for safety at high speeds.

Under a year later, Adam A. Welsh of Parkersburg, West Virginia, filed a patent for a very similar system. It is possible the two gentlemen were related.

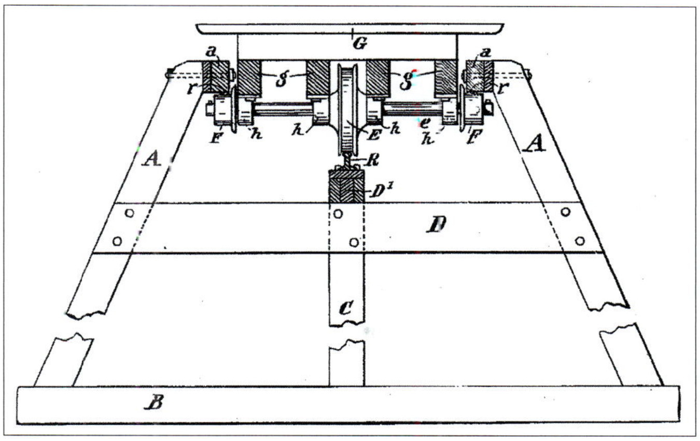

Alexander A. Welsh's design (US Patent No. 663525) for pleasure monorails was to have a strong wooden raised track frame with the weight of the vehicle borne through a central double flanged wheel bearing on a central rail. To maintain balance and provide security rollers mounted on extensions of the main axle were to bear upwards on outer guard rails.

1901

Inventor: **Henry Fisher-Spenser & Howard Brunlees** (UK)
Type: Ground level centre rail
UK Patent No. 13949 Date of Grant 29 June 1901
Railway Engineer Vol. 22, September 1901, p273.

Fisher-Spenser, based in Trafalgar Buildings, London, and Brunlees, a civil engineer based in Lindfield, Kent, invented a design not dissimilar to that invented by Larmanjat some thirty years previously. The vehicle was to balance on a central rail with outer wheels to prevent toppling. They stated the chief object of their invention was to enable the load to be shifted so that the greater part of its weight was borne by the central wheels and for that purpose the whole body of the vehicle was arranged to be movable transversely. This was to be achieved by screws carried by the underframe and nuts mounted on the body.

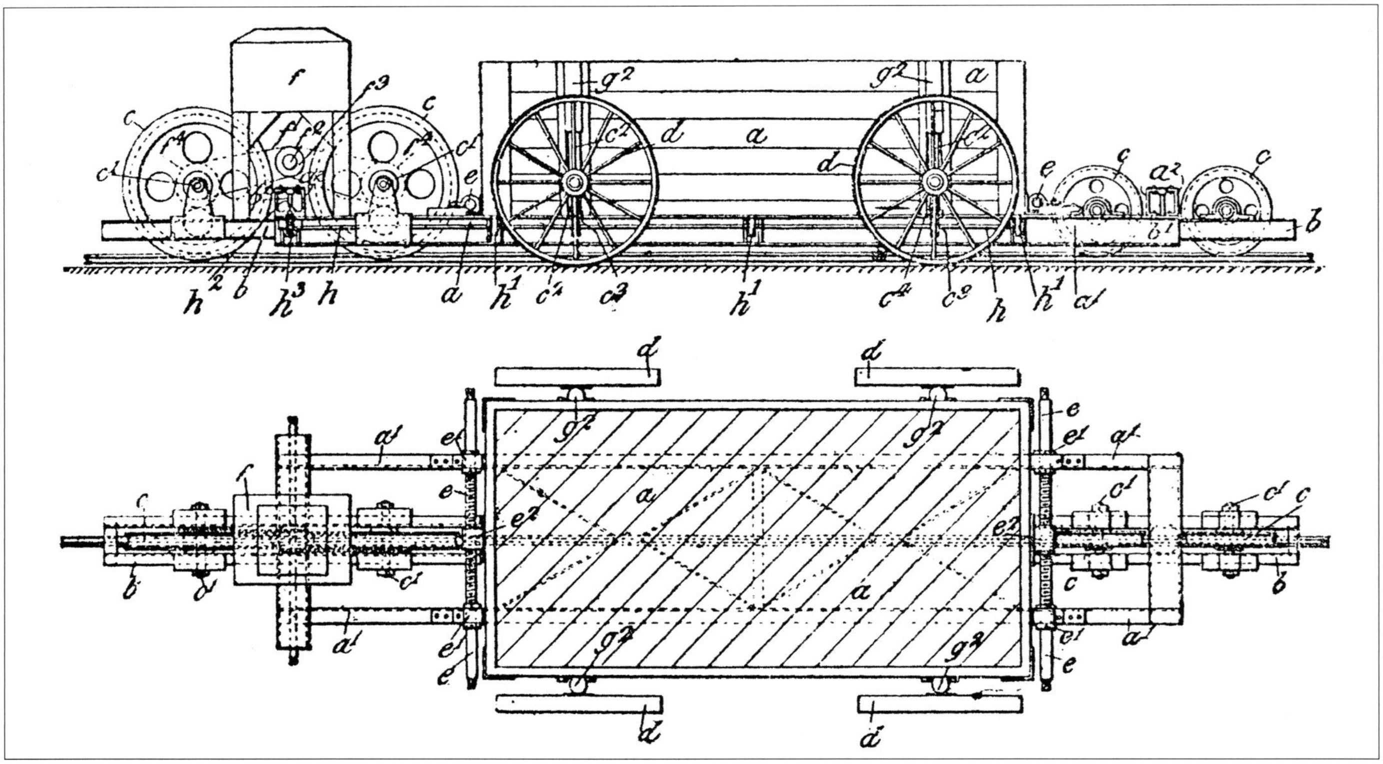

The Fisher-Spenser & Brunlees patent shows their design for a vehicle to balance on a central track. To reduce friction when transversely shifting the fully laden body, it was to be rested on 'anti-friction' rollers eccentrically mounted on rods located beneath the body and adapted to be operated to support the weight during its movement. *Railway Engineer* Vol. 22, September 1901

1902

Inventor: **Albert Lehmann** (Austria)
Type: Ground level rail & Unique
UK Patent No. 9809 Date of Grant 17 April 1902
US Patent No. 737748 Date of Grant 1 September 1903

The UK patent by Lehmann, who was living at 102 Hütteldorfstrasse, Vienna, contained two innovations. The first was to enable 'Caillet' type vehicles to negotiate curves of less than 10ft radius. This was to be achieved by mounting the wheels on vertical pivots so that they could rotate. The second was to enable these vehicles to be connected in parallel so that they could be used on two rail track. Separately, he also included the design of an electric powered bicycle tramcar.

The US patent incorporated only the first of the above inventions, notably, wheels mounted on central pivots on a 'Caillet' type vehicle, but in addition added a metal hoop for securing a horse.

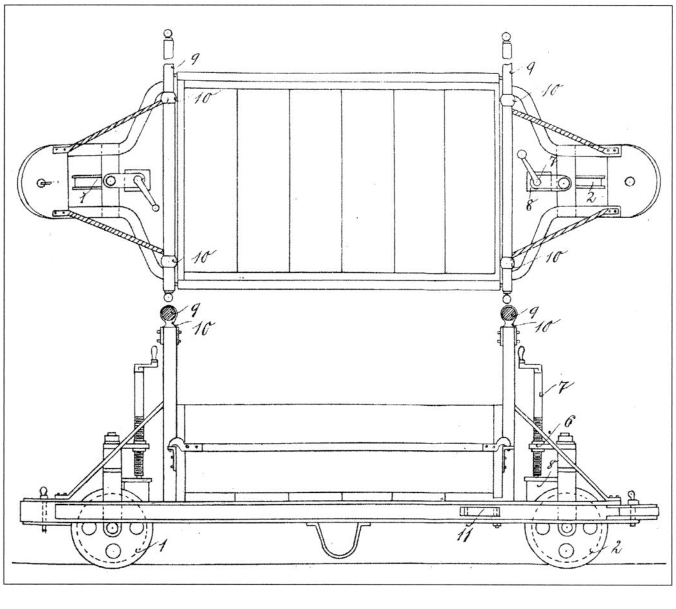

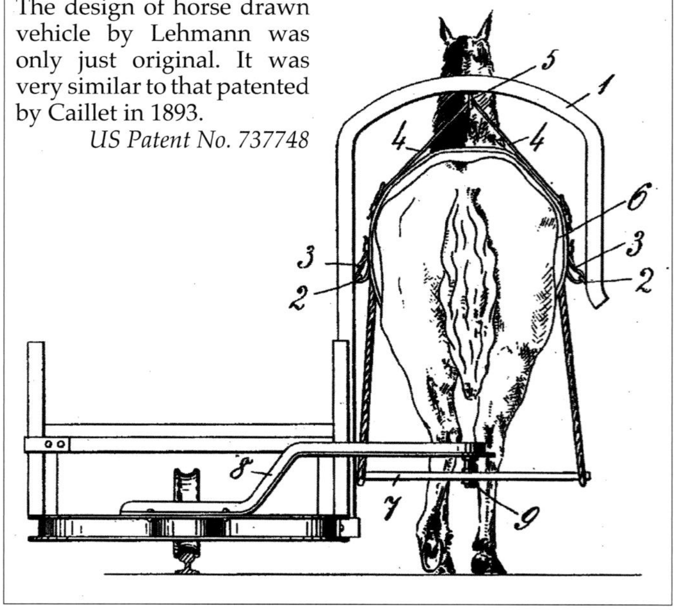

The design of horse drawn vehicle by Lehmann was only just original. It was very similar to that patented by Caillet in 1893.
US Patent No. 737748

Left: Lehmann's single rail vehicle with rotating vertical pivots for the wheels. Lehmann proposed linking two vehicles together for two rail operation by using long poles labelled q on the drawing. *UK Patent No. 9809*

Lehman's electric tramcar. Whilst superficially similar to those developed by Tunis and others in the USA, the method of stabilising the vehicle using the overhead support rails was little more than a vague idea. *UK Patent No. 9809*

Inventor: **Robert Cooke Sayer** (UK)
Type: Suspended/Unique

UK Patent No.	Date of Grant
20690	16 October 1902
19393	8 September 1904

US Patent No. 766392 Date of Grant 2 August 1904

Cooke was a prolific inventor who patented a wide range of ideas in many countries. He worked as a civil engineer in Redland, Bristol, and his monorail design was unique as described in the patent titled 'Improvements in Elevated and Subaqueous Railways and in Motor Vehicles therefor.' The object, he claimed, was to form 'a single rail railway equally applicable for cars to traverse on shore or on waters; to suspend the rail at equal distances apart by single suspension ties or struts, or standards fixed in the ground, or by floats in water; that the rails and cars may pass at a minimum height above traffic of roadways, pathways, or surface of the ground, or below the traffic of rivers or seas, or on their surface, without interfering with their traffic.'

The system was horrendously complicated with designs for water tight cars that were to be made sufficiently buoyant so that they would slightly raise the rails when they pass underwater and if derailed would float to the surface. The floats also had mechanisms to reduce the effects of waves; there were to be underwater electrically operated points etc. A true flight of fantasy.

1903

Inventor: **Louis A. Gross** (USA)
Type: Suspended
US Patent No. 725838 Date of Grant 21 April 1903

Gross lived in San Francisco and invented what he described as an improved aerial railway system. Whilst it looked like a novelty, Gross intended the system to be used for transport. The idea was that passengers would

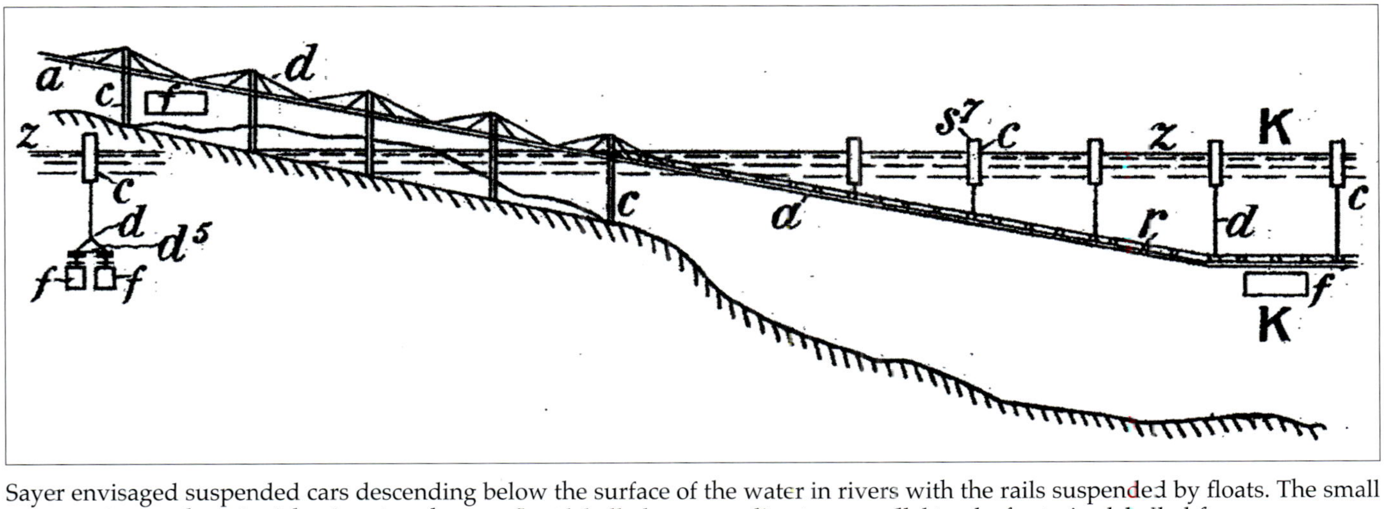

Sayer envisaged suspended cars descending below the surface of the water in rivers with the rails suspended by floats. The small cross section on the left of the drawing shows a float labelled c suspending two parallel tracks for trains labelled *f*.
US Patent No. 766392

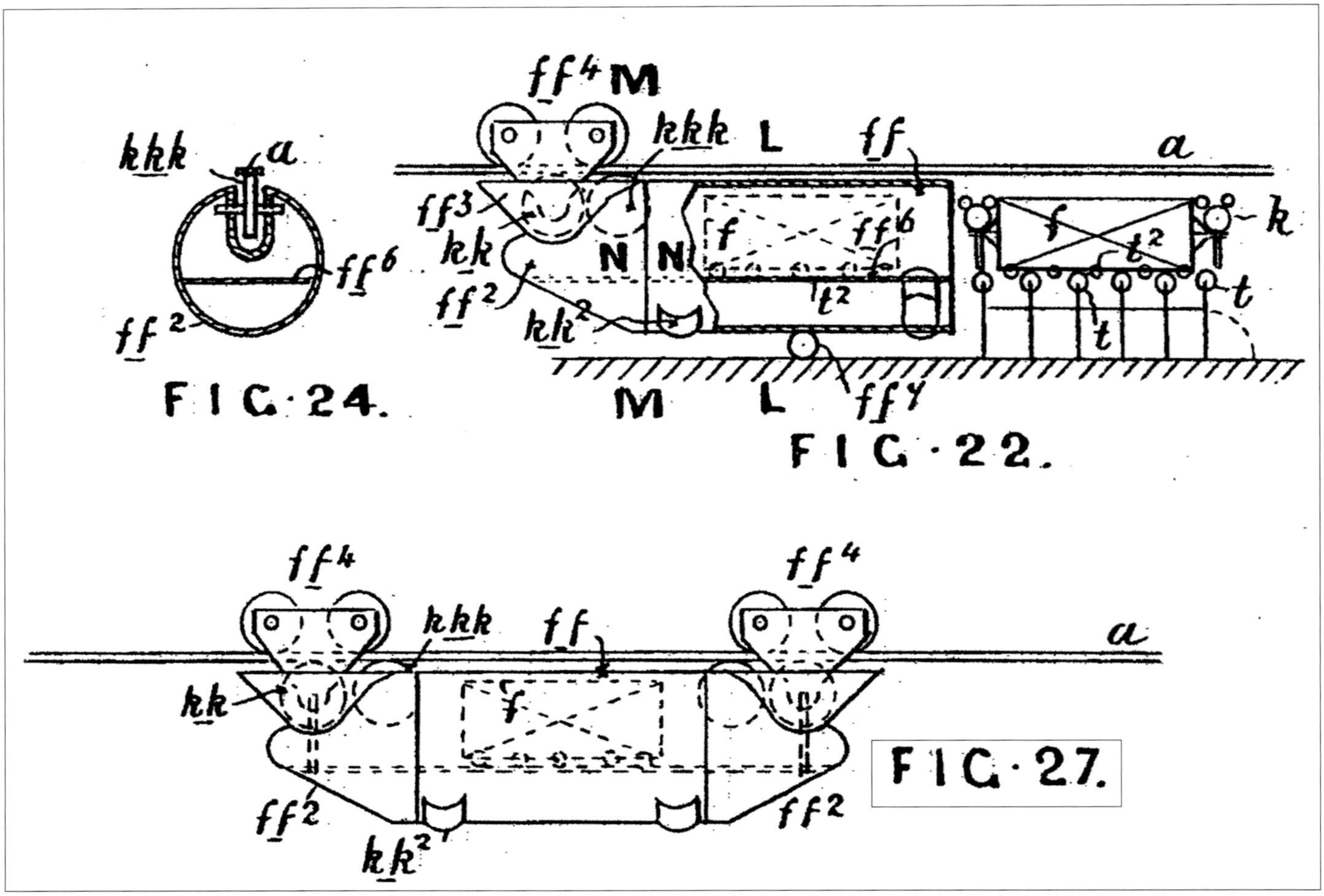

To quote from US Patent No. 766392 'In following a car *f* from traversing land to traversing subaqueously the car upon its arrival near the water is run upon and carried by rollers *t*, Fig. 22.........The car *f* is then run upon the rollers t^2 into a water-transit case or car f f to the position shown dotted and there secured.' Figure 27 shows a subaqueous vehicle en route with car labelled *f_f*. Figure 24 shows a cross section of the front of the subaqueous vehicle.

ride in individual or two person chair cars which could travel uninterrupted until the destination was reached or alternatively stop at way stations without interfering with other cars by the use of side loop lines, the points being controlled by the occupants of each car.

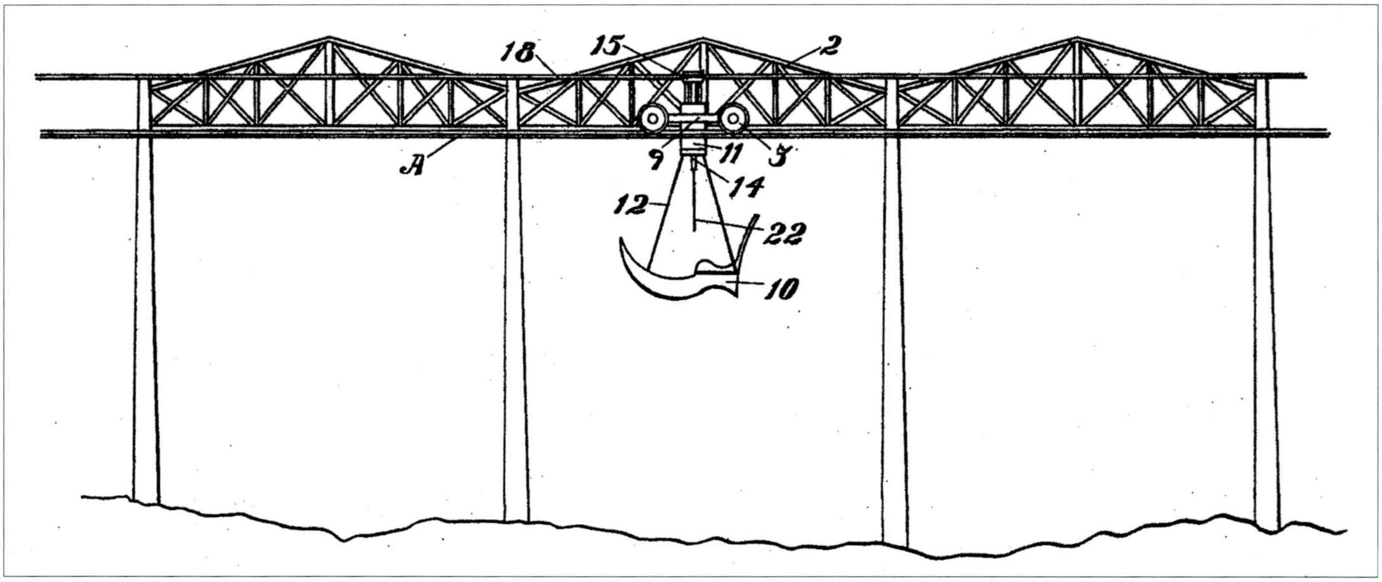

The Gross system was intended to allow individual occupants of suspended monorail cars to control their direction at points by pulling on the cord labelled 22. *US Patent No. 725838*

Ganz Works Company
Inventor: **Fabre** (Hungary)
Type: Ground level rail
Scientific American Vol. 89, 31 October 1903, p303.

Fabre designed a canal barge towing locomotive for the Ganz Works Company, the company which had built the Zipernowsky balancing tram described in the earlier volume. The design appears to owe much to the original Zipernowsky design as it was described as having two inclined pairs of axles instead of the ordinary horizontal axles usually employed with two vertical wheels. In this construction, there was an inclined wheel on every axle and each pair of wheels embraced the single rail head. Another lateral wheel was provided to brace and steady the locomotive, the wheel operating upon the ground or towpath.

It is not clear if locomotives of this form were ever sold. They would have been very similar to the ones built by Siemens and Halske to the Köttgen design in 1898 (see earlier volume) or that described in Chapter 5.

The three phase motor for the locomotive was said to operate at 500 Volts AC (frequency 50Hz) operating through gearing. Power was to be supplied by two overhead copper wires 0.314 in. in diameter located 11.8 in. apart placed 19.6 ft. from the ground. The conductors were to be supported by poles placed 100ft. apart.

Inventor: **M. Devic** (France)
Type: Unknown
Scientific American Vol. 89, 22 August 1903, p134.

The French engineer Devic based in Nemours was reported to have constructed a 1/10th scale electric model monorail which had attained the speed of thirteen miles per hour. The inventor claimed to have designed a rail which would afford the wheels sufficient grip irrespective of the weight they may be supporting. Devic was sanguine of attaining a speed of up to 200 miles per hour.

Inventor: **Cassius I. White** (USA)
Type: Suspended
US Patent No. 743786 Date of Grant 10 November 1903

White of Nottingham, Indiana, claimed as his chief objective 'the provision of a railway system composed of a minimum of mechanical elements adapted to subserve the highest economic ends with a minimum of power applied, and that at a reduced cost of construction and maintenance.' To this end he added to the electric suspended monorail a system of cranks to allow the driver to control the points.

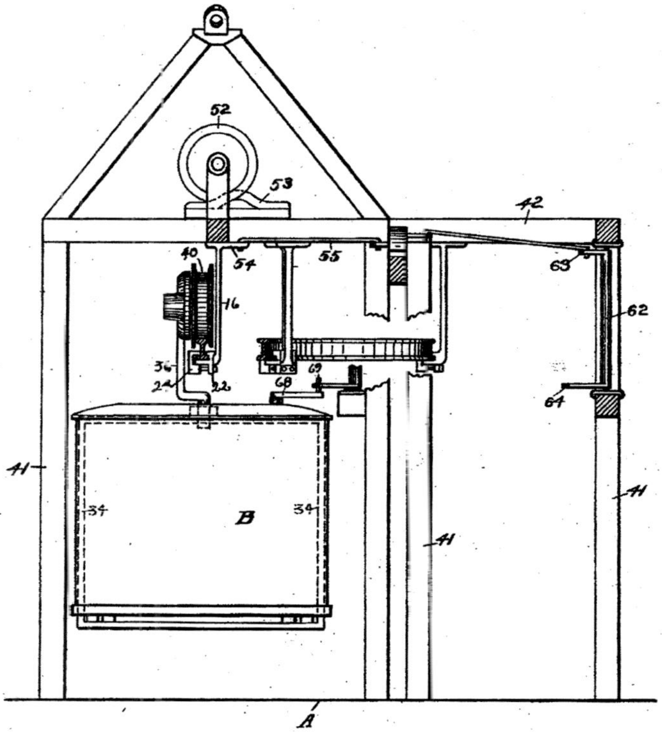

Looked at end on, the White vehicle was to be suspended from a single rail without the safety mechanism employed by Langen. The crank labelled 68 mounted on the top of the vehicle was controlled by the driver and engaged with the crank labelled 69 to rotate a large wheel and thus the upper rail point as shown on the plan. US Patent No. 743786

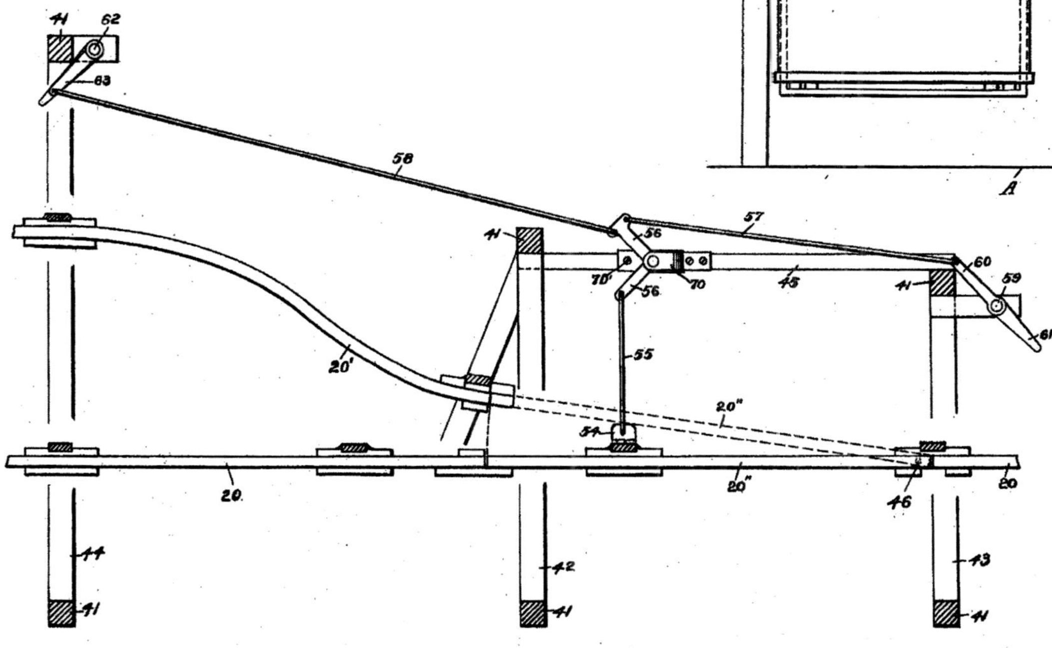

1904

Inventor: **Robert Emett Terry** (USA)
Type: Post and rail
US Patent No. 751960 Date of Grant 9 February 1904

Terry, who lived in Mobile, Alabama, patented a system which was only just novel. The unique feature claimed was to secure the load of logs the vehicle was designed to carry by chains connected to pivoted arms. These allowed some adjustment to the centre of gravity to balance the vehicle.

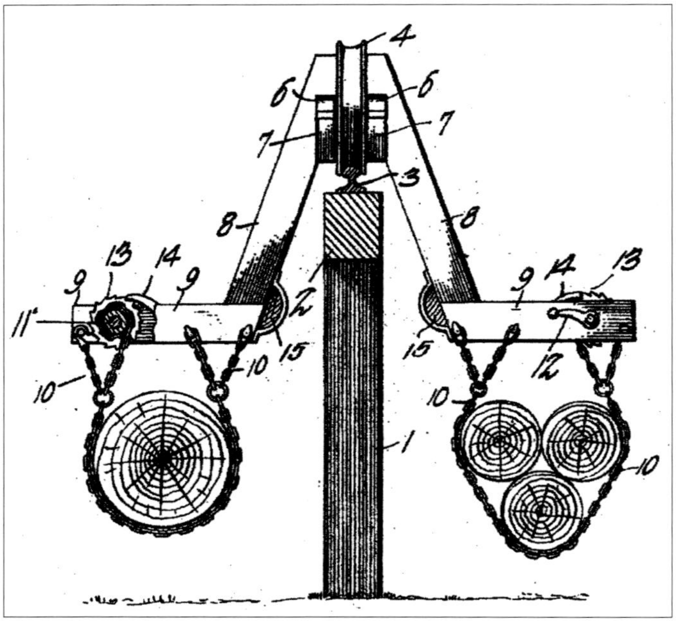

This end view of Terry's monorail (US Patent No. 751960) was hardly different from that taken out by Palmer in 1821. The only unique feature was the ratchet mechanism controlling the chains carrying the logs which, Terry claimed, enabled some movement to help centralise the centre of gravity.

Inventor: **Joseph Oliver Raymond** (USA)
Type: Suspended
US Patent No. 764766 Date of Grant 12 July 1904

Raymond's electric carrier was designed whilst he lived in Concord, New Hampshire and was intended to carry freight or passengers in a suspended vehicle. The carrier, essentially a bogie from which the vehicles were suspended, had features that would be included in the subsequent designs of monorail hoists. In particular it featured an automatic electric stop at each end of travel with braking.

1905

Inventor: **Charles Mehring** (USA)
Type: Bicycle/Unique
US Patent No. 788322 Date of Grant 25 April 1905

According to Mehring's patent, he believed he could simplify and improve railroad systems. A resident of Charlottesville, Virginia, his bicycle system required very heavy weight construction and a unique rail form engaging with rollers rather than wheels. He claimed that this system would prevent derailment and "thus rendered secure for speeds not safe with railroad systems as they have heretofore been constructed."

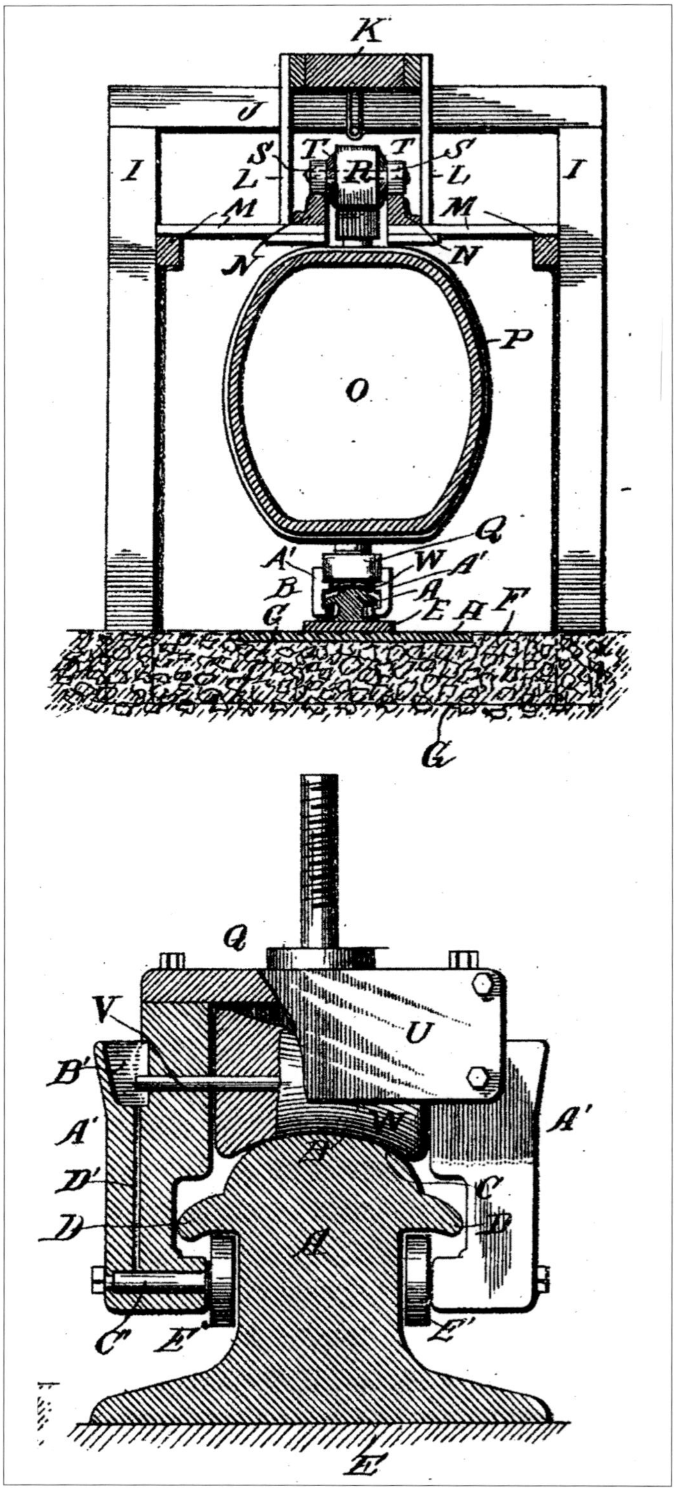

The Mehring bicycle car. The lower illustration shows a cross section of the complex lower rail form. *US Patent No. 788322*

Inventor: **David Humphrey** (USA)
Type: Bicycle

US Patent No.	Date of Grant
799908	19 September 1905
1306225	10 June 1919

Humphrey of Cleveland, Ohio, proposed an overhead bicycle railway track and supporting structure made from varying diameters of tube.

Inventor: **James W. Abernethy** (USA)
Type: 'A' frame
US Patent No. 801832 Date of Grant 17 October 1905
The ideas of Abernethy, from Atlanta, Mississippi, were a throwback to the 19th century. It is difficult to suggest a useful development contained in this patent.

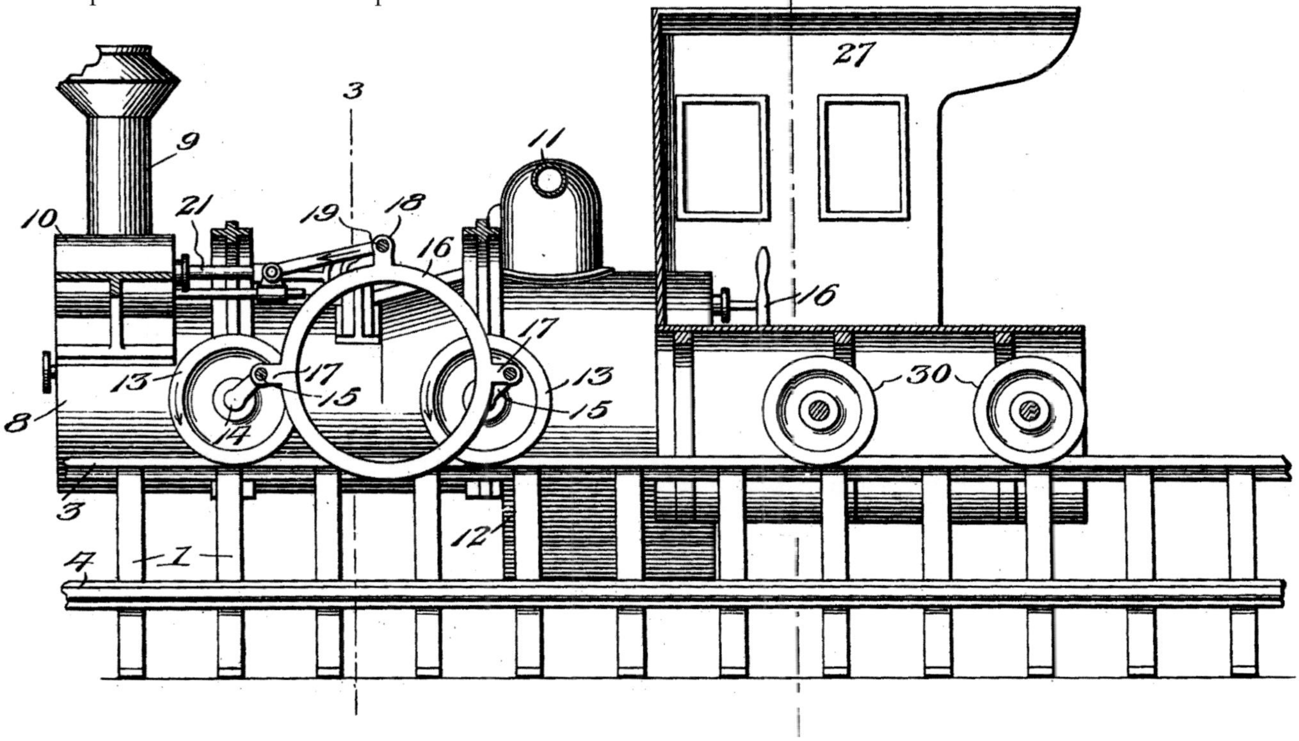

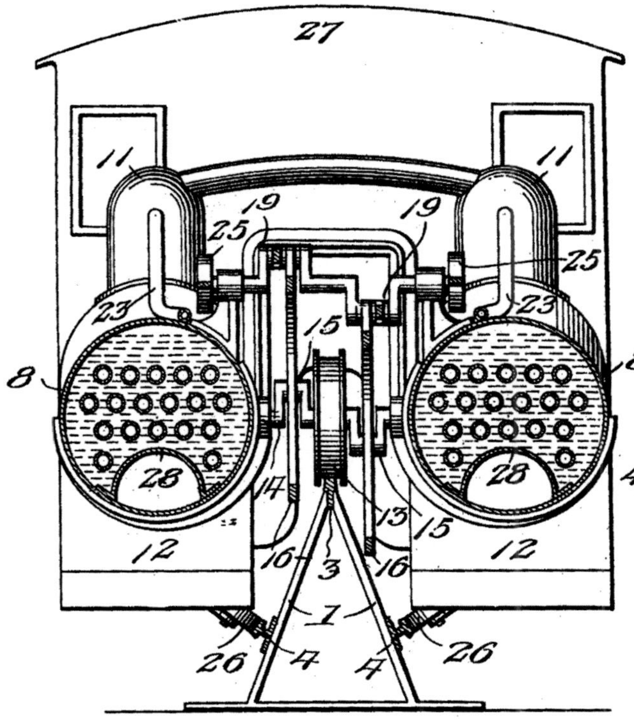

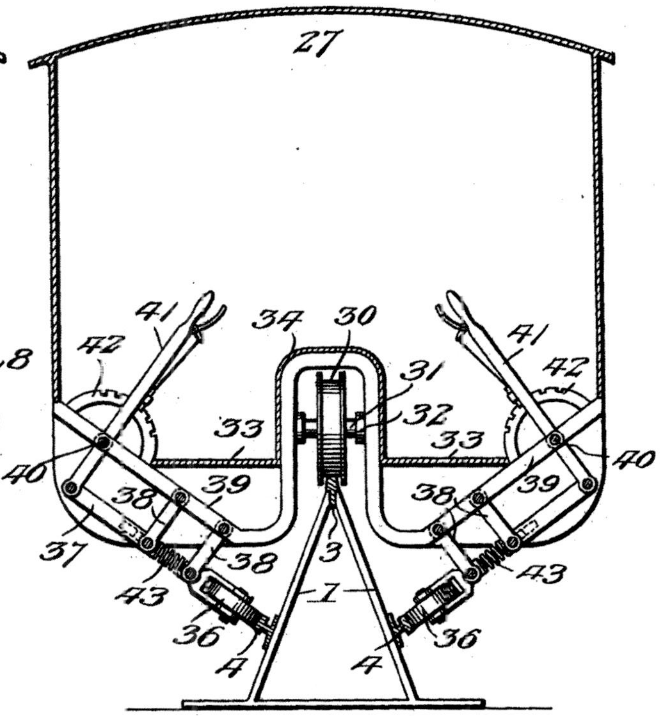

Whilst included in the earlier volume this drawing is worth including again. The linkage from the upper cylinder to the wheels would have been fun to watch and is not dissimilar to that designed by Mallet in UK Patent No. 8705 (Date of Grant 3 May 1887) and illustrated in the earlier volume. The end elevations of Abernethy's design show one unique but unworkable idea. The pressure on the side wheels was to be controlled by levers operated by the locomotive driver. He would have needed to be super human to ensure that when releasing the ratchet mechanism the locomotive did not topple over. *US Patent No. 801832*

1906

Inventor: **George W. Brower** (USA)
Type: Unique
US Patent No. 818608 Date of Grant 24 April 1906

Brower's electric monorail design split the two halves of a typical monorail car in half so that each section ran on opposite sides of the wooden rail structure. Based in Santa Monica, California, he believed his system was very simple and both easily and cheaply operated. Indeed he suggested it could run along the side of telegraph poles.

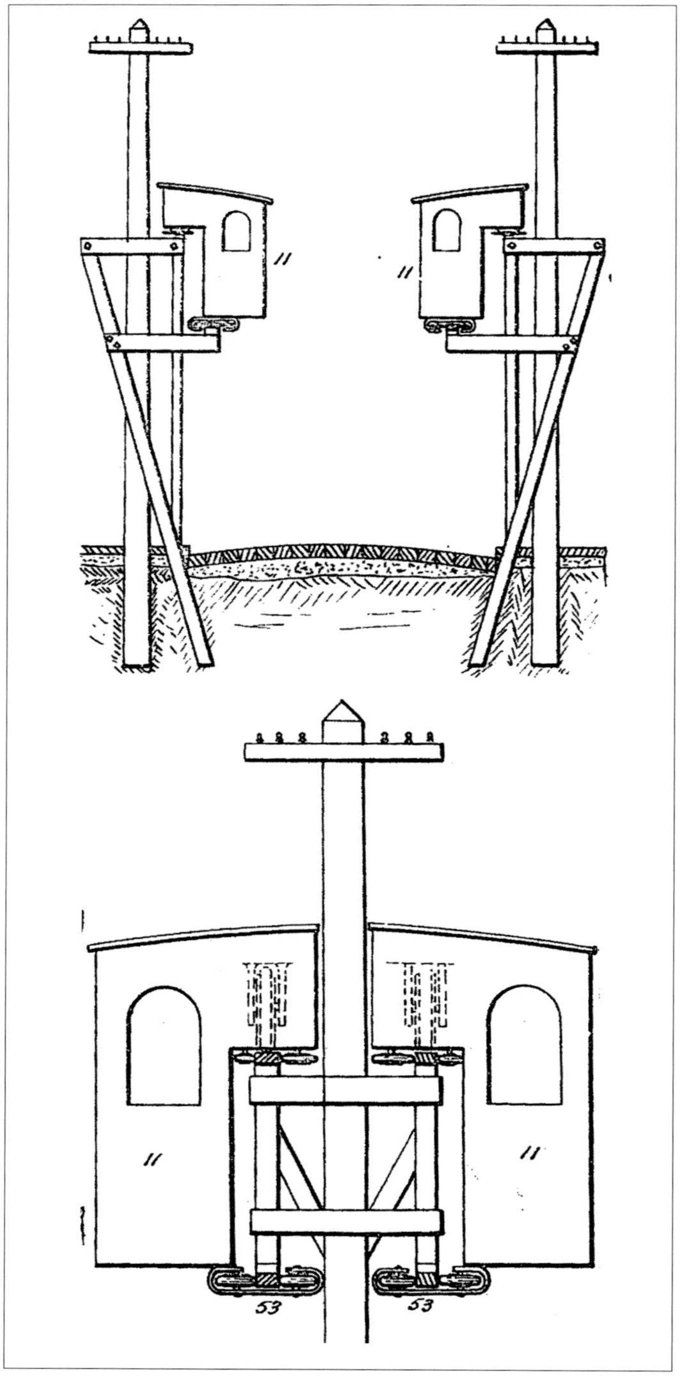

In designing his monorail, Brower gave little thought to the strength needed in the telegraph poles that were to support his track. He also cannot have had much concern about the side forces on the rails which probably would have sheered from the wooden frame. *US Patent No. 818608*

Inventor: **Lycurgus C. Harrison** (USA)
Type: Bicycle
US Patent No. 821799 Date of Grant 29 May 1906

Harrison proposed a miniature monorail system to carry mail to and from the road and residences in rural areas. The idea was presumably based on his experience of living in Stockwell, Indiana.

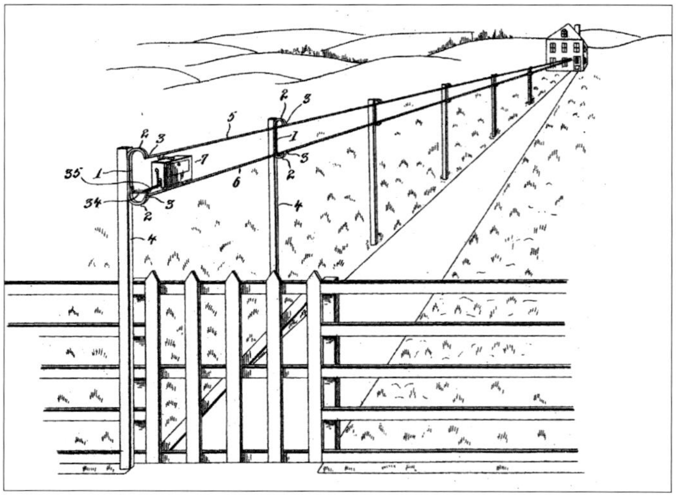

This idyllic image of Harrison's rural postal monorail was shown in US Patent No. 821799. The miniature vehicle was to collect current from the upper and lower rails and the electric motor was to be prevented from accelerating the vehicle to too high speed by gearing the motor to drive a small pneumatic piston to dampen excess motion.

1907

Inventor: **James M. Gilstrap** (USA)
Type: Bicycle
UK Patent No. 17539 Date of Grant 5 March 1908
US Patent No. 845459 Date of Grant 26 February 1907

Gilstrap, a dentist based in Oakland, California, proposed an overhead multi-level network of bicycle monorails 'whereby machine-shops, car-barns, and other properties which ordinarily require additional ground-space may be arranged one above the other at the terminals, thereby greatly economizing on the required acreage.' Combined with other changes he declared in his patent that his ideas would render great speed.

1908

Inventor: **Napoleon B. Dixon** (USA)
Type: 'A' frame variant
US Patent No. 900269 Date of Grant 6 October 1908

Dixon suggested two changes to the usual A frame configuration. First he proposed replacing the conventional upper rail with a form of bent tube shaped rail. To match this shape, the vehicle was to have rollers together with double flanged wheels to run on the sides and flanges of the tube. Second, he proposed replacing the lower guide rails with stretched cables. Separately, he also proposed using '…propellers being preferably of conical form and having spiral flutes or blades….arranged with their axes forwardly and upwardly converged with the result that the developed force resulting when said propellers are in motion, tends to both propel and to lift the car,…' No such line was built in his home town of Dixie, Alabama.

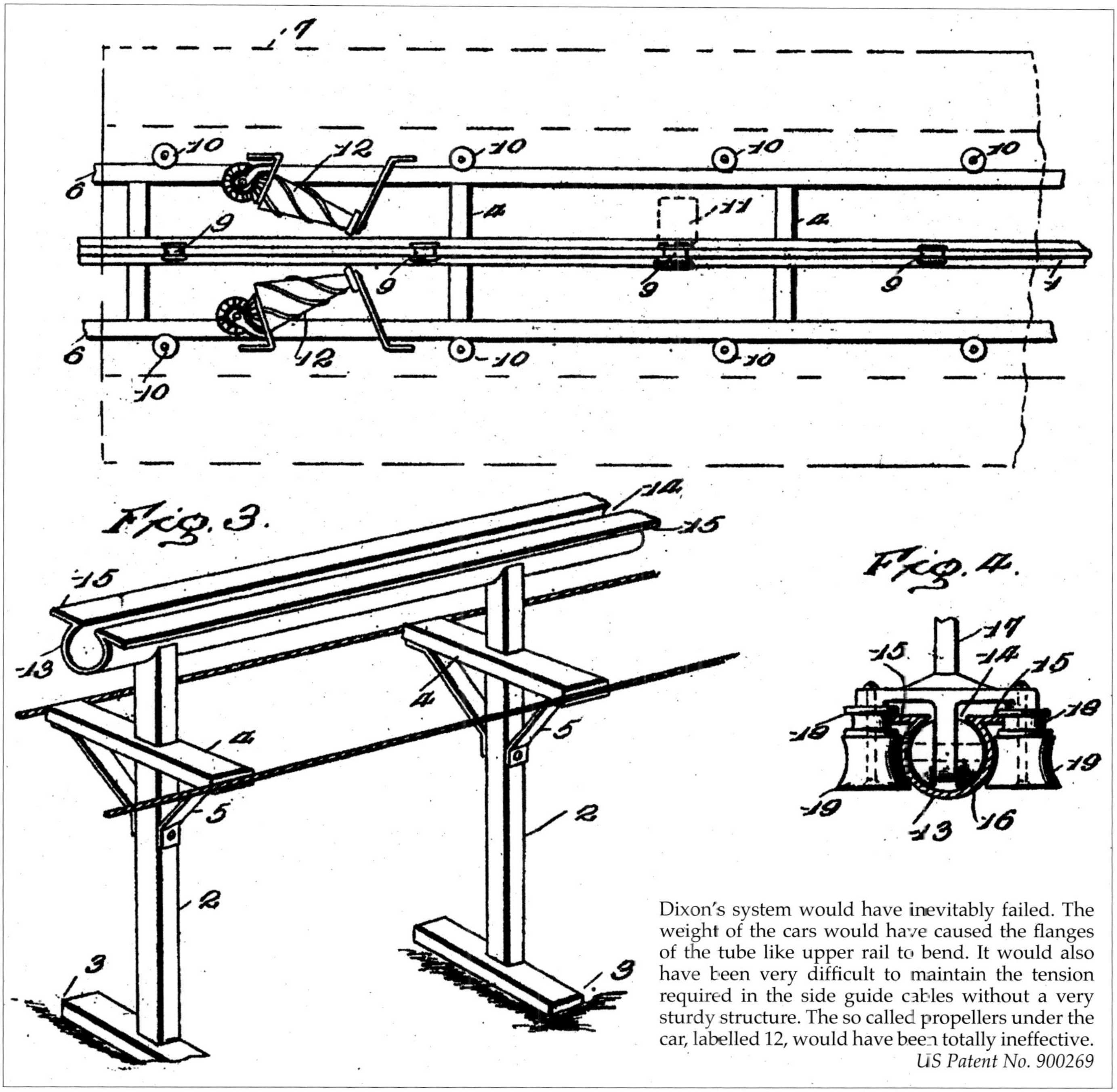

Dixon's system would have inevitably failed. The weight of the cars would have caused the flanges of the tube like upper rail to bend. It would also have been very difficult to maintain the tension required in the side guide cables without a very sturdy structure. The so called propellers under the car, labelled 12, would have been totally ineffective.
US Patent No. 900269

1909

Inventor: **Fletcher E. Felts** (USA)
Type: Suspended
US Patent No. 928435 Date of Grant 20 July 1909
Despite claiming to use a single track, Felts' system was not a true monorail as it involved two I beams bolted together with a complex system of dual support wheels. He was based in Los Angeles, California.

1910

Inventor: **Ernst Mittag** (Germany)
Type: Bicycle
UK Patent No. 28468 Date of Grant 17 August 1911

US Patent No.	Date of Grant
968384	23 August 1910
992025	9 May 1911

The patents by Mittag who lived in Berlin have little that was novel except that he suggested the overhead rail be displaced from being directly above the lower rail on curves so that the vehicle was tilted into the curve to mitigate centrifugal forces.

Inventor: **Unknown** (UK)
Type: 'Mono-rail tramway'
Railway Times Vol. 98, 17 December 1910, p627.
Engineer Vol. 110, 30 December 1910, p695.
Both journals reported that a project was under consideration in the Glossop and Marple district of the High Peak for the revival of a tramway scheme that had been previously proposed, but this time as a monorail. The Glossop terminus was to be located near the Plough Inn, Dinting and the line was to pass through Gamesby,

Charlesworth, Chisworth, Lulworth, Lane Ends and Comstall Road before reaching the terminus at Marple Bridge, just a few minutes walk from Marple Station. The line was to serve the coal and gannister mines at Chisworth as well as carry goods and passengers. The proposed 5½ mile long monorail was never built.

1911

Inventor: **William Maloney** (Canada/UK)
Type: Post and rail/Bicycle

UK Patent No.	Date of Grant
16533	6 February 1911
17075	23 March 1911
14900	13 June 1912
US Patent No.	**Date of Grant**
1019331	5 March 1912

Maloney described himself as a machinist and was a UK national living in Sherbrooke, Quebec. He designed a typical form of vehicle used on A frame monorails but without guide wheels underneath. Instead he proposed adding rollers overhead which were to run in an inverted 'U' shaped rail.

Inventor: **Pierre Barnes** (USA)
Type: 'A' frame

US Patent No.	Date of Grant
1004135	26 September 1911
1043793	12 November 1912
1043794	12 November 1912

The proposals by Barnes of Seattle, Washington, were only marginally novel. He suggested using wheels without flanges on both the main rail and lower guide rails. The main wheel, however, was to be unusually wide. He also included end platforms on his carriages to ease and speed up entry and exit of passengers.

Inventor: **William H. Shepard** (USA)
Type: 'A' frame
US Patent No. 1004210 Date of Grant 26 September 1911
Shepard was also based in Seattle, Washington, and like Barnes his invention was hardly novel. He merely suggested adding bracing to an A frame mounted on posts.

1912

Inventor: **Max Scheftel** (USA)
Type: Inverted 'A'
US Patent No. 1034840 Date of Grant 6 August 1912
Scheftel of Brooklyn, New York, proposed vehicles with side wheels mounted in a variety of positions. These side wheels were to be of gear form and to also act as driving wheels. He stated in his patent that 'It is a well known fact that cars placed on a single line of wheels will run much faster than if placed on a double rail as at present and it follows that if a car or locomotive can be made to run on a single rail in a normal stable upright position it must necessarily travel faster than the ordinary trains, at the same time using an equal amount of fuel or electricity.'

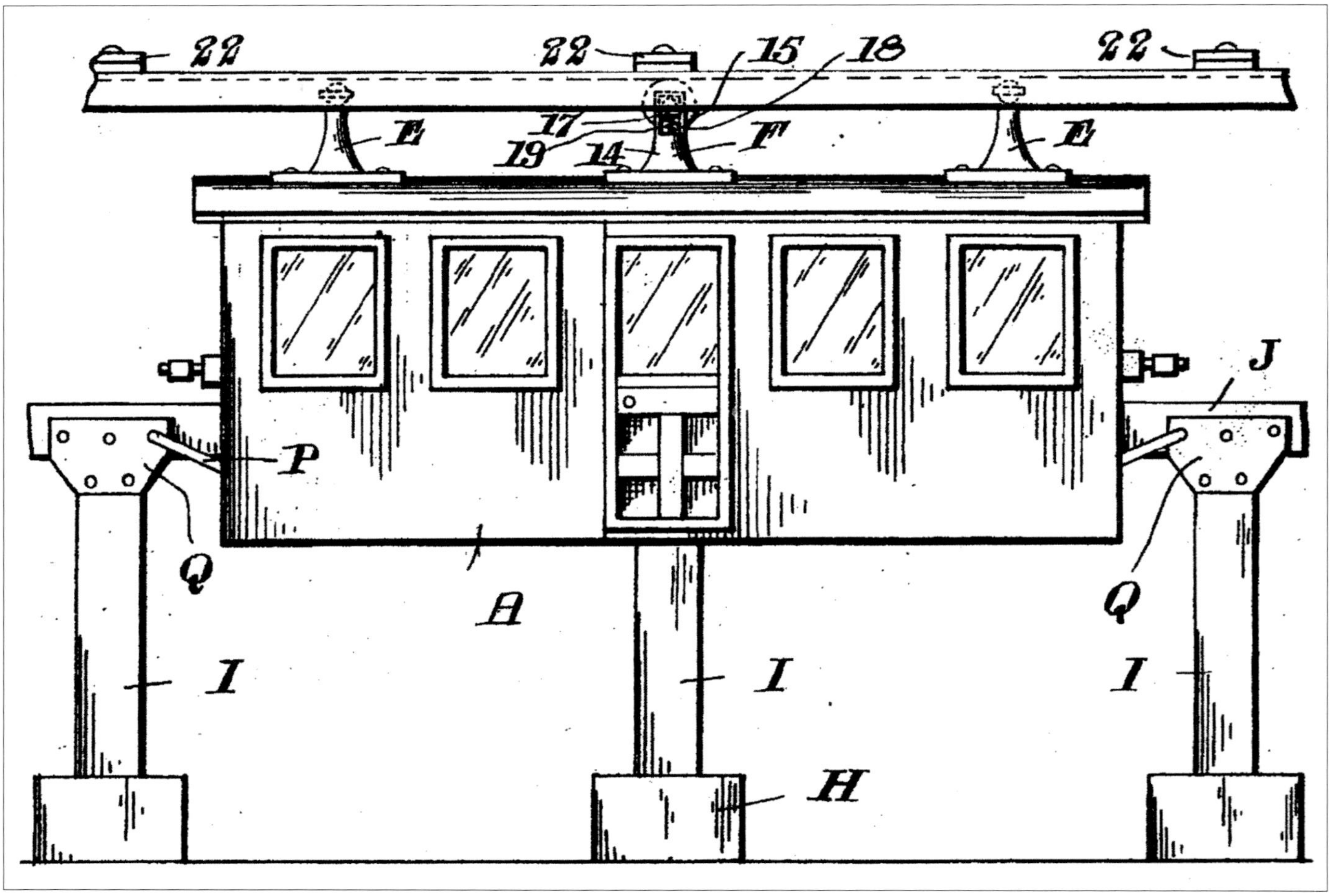

Maloney combined the post and rail structure with the overhead stabilising rail used on bicycle monorails. *US Patent No. 1019331*

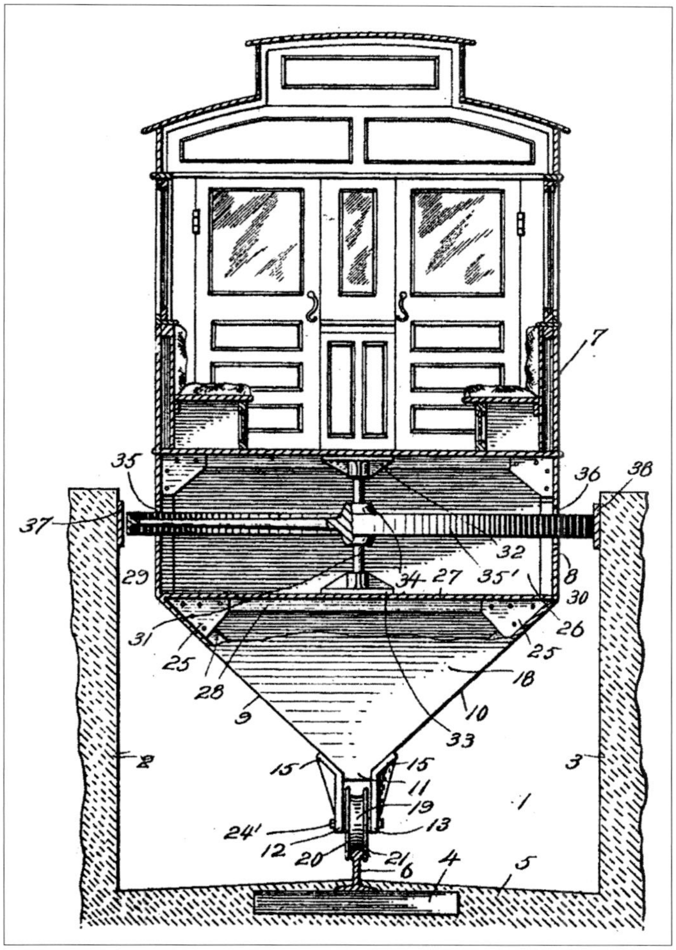

Scheftel proposed running his monorail in an excavated trench with the guide wheels bearing on rails mounted on each side beneath the main compartment of the carriage. These rails were to be of rack form to engage with the toothed guide/driving wheels. US Patent No. 1034840

Inventor: **Steven Zsinko** (Hungary/USA)
Type: Unique

UK Patent No. 21768	Date of Grant 30 January 1913
US Patent No.	Date of Grant
1042066	22 October 1912
1042067	22 October 1912

Zsinko, a Hungarian, lived in Los Angeles, California and took out his patents whilst seeking US citizenship. He stated that his invention could be used for transporting passengers or merchandise but the form shown in his patent described the use of his monorail as an amusement.

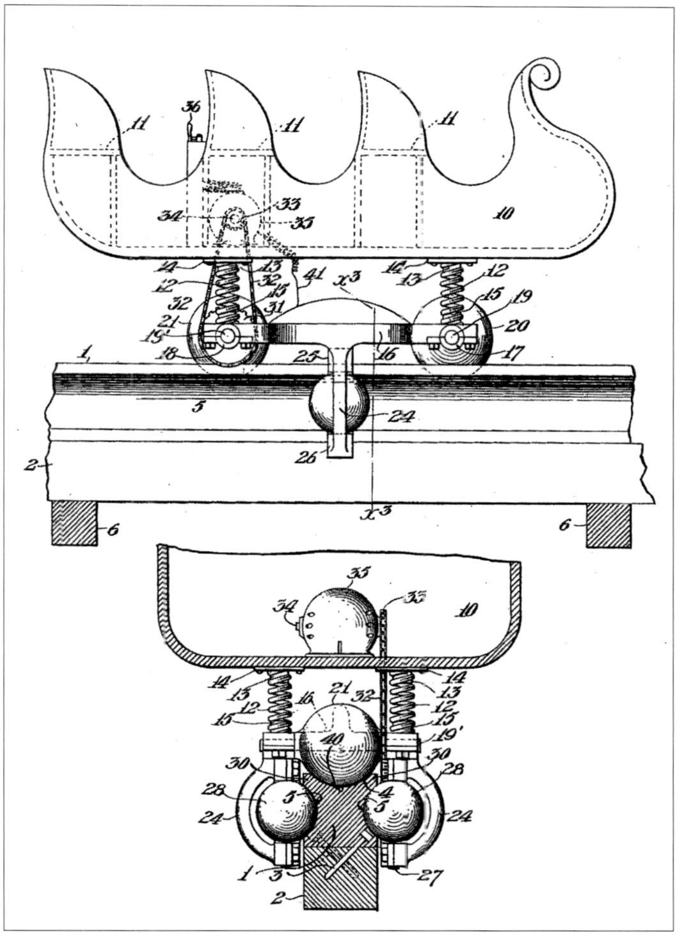

Zsinko's first US Patent No. 1042C66 described a novelty carriage running on a single wooden rail with the top and both sides scalloped to fit the revolving balls of the undercarriage of the car.

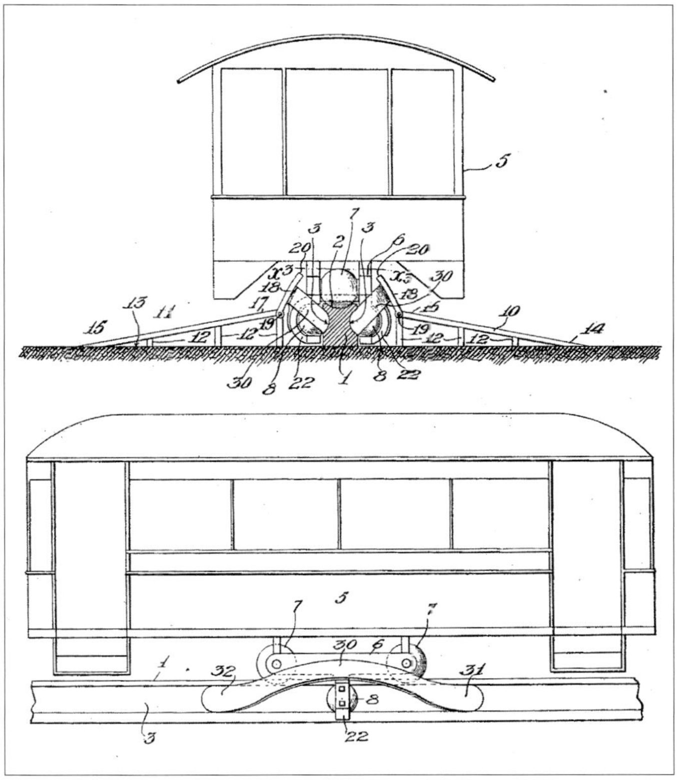

Zsinko's second US Patent (No. 1042067) showed a more conventional carriage but patented a novel form of level crossing. The road crossing the line was to have ramps with flaps that fell by weight on to the track thus allowing road vehicles to pass. To allow the monorail train to pass, curved cam bars mounted on the sides of the carriage lifted the flaps and then lowered them again once the wheels of the carriage had passed.

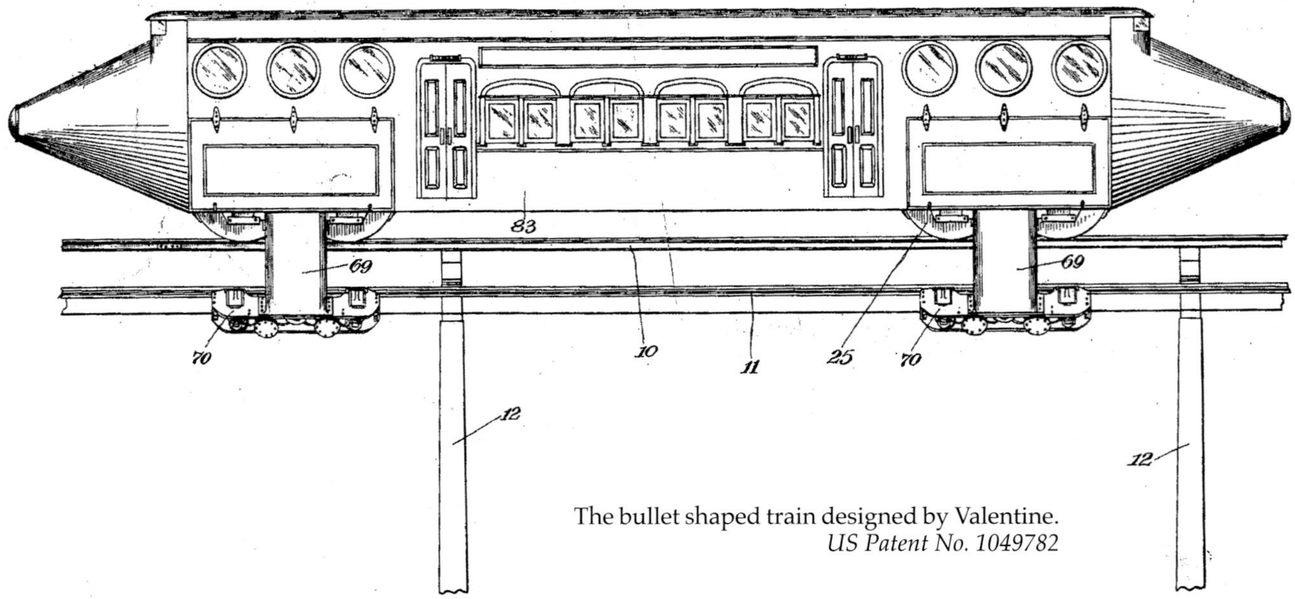

The bullet shaped train designed by Valentine.
US Patent No. 1049782

Right: The end elevation in US Patent No. 1049782 by Valentine showed the electric motor to be integral with the main double flanged wheel. The guide wheels were inverted to ensure safe working.

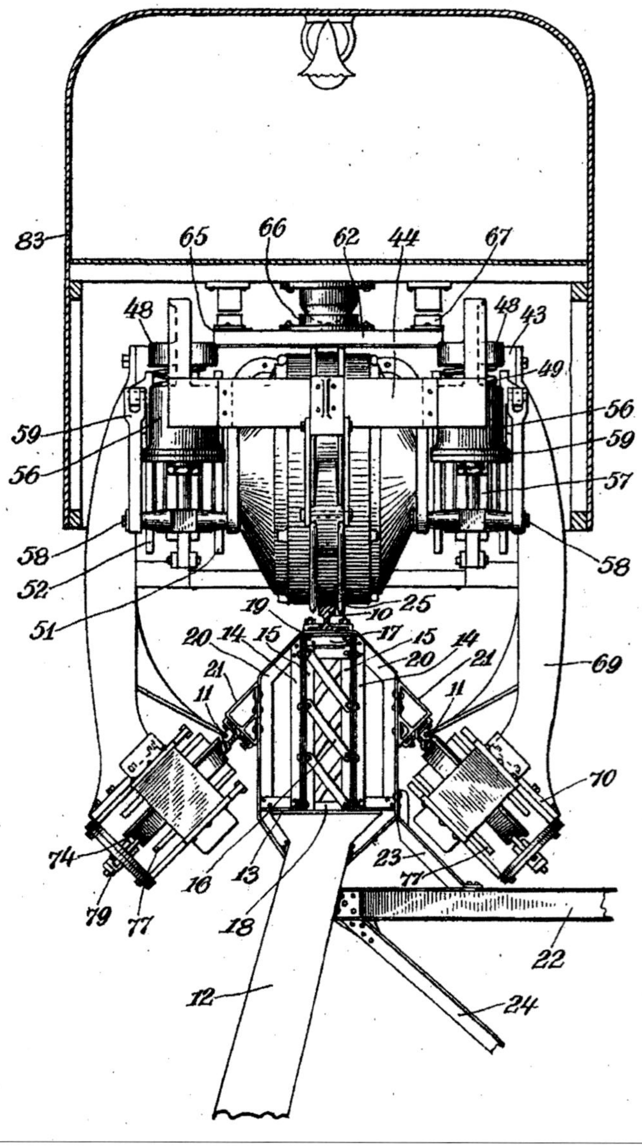

1913

Inventor: **Walter D. Valentine** (USA)
Type: Unique
US Patent No. 1049782 Date of Grant 7 January 1913
Like others, Valentine from East Orange, New Jersey, stated in his patent 'It is well known that much greater speed is possible to a train supported on a single rail…' and to this end he designed in detail an electric monorail carriage. The key feature of his design was that the guide rails were substantially inverted so that the train was effectively threaded on to the track.

Inventor: **Thomas Carl Spelling** (USA)
Type: Inverted 'A' frame

US Patent No.	Date of Grant
1058481	8 April 1913
1105540	28 July 1914
1140412	25 May 1915
1184039	23 May 1916

The Triangular Monorailroad by Thomas Carl Spelling, 1913 and reprinted 1914.
Spelling, based in New York City, was a prolific inventor with patents covering items such as necktie and collar button fasteners, bottle stoppers, fountain pens and toy railroads as well as full size monorails. Whilst he suggested variations to his monorail designs, his main concept was to run trains through a triangular structure with upper guide wheels.

1914

Inventor: **Esson** (South Africa)
Type: Probably bicycle
Engineer Vol. 117, 29 May 1914, p593.
To quote from the *Engineer*: 'An inventor in South

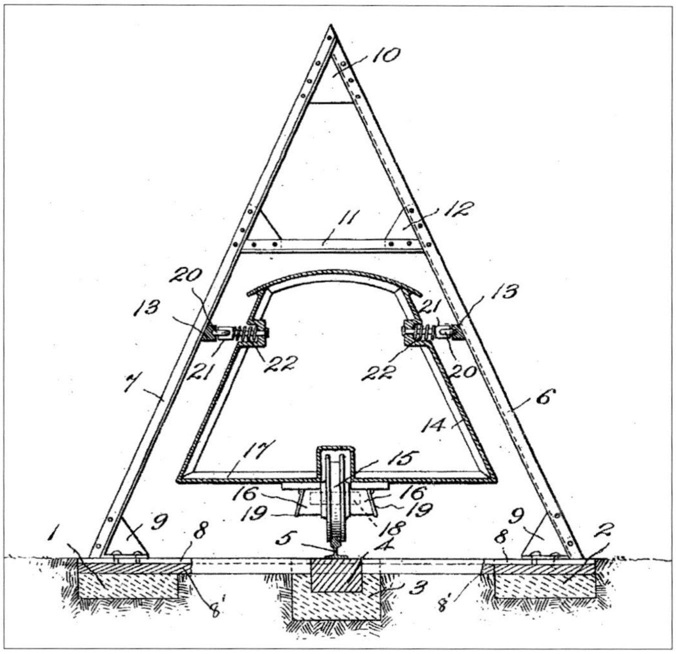

Spelling went to enormous effort to promote his so-called 'Triangular' system both in terms of patents and publications. In fairness to him, the triangular frame would have been relatively strong but the cost of construction and maintenance would have been excessive compared to two rail conventional railways. *US Patent No. 1058481*

Africa – a Mr. Esson – is reported to claim that he has devised a car which can travel at 500 miles an hour. The idea is to use a monorail and an overhead trolley wire; when the car, driven by an air propeller, attains sufficient speed, it will leave the rail and fly. The idea (but not the car), the *Electrical Review* remarks, appears to be in the air.'

Inventor: **Berthold Lindemann** (USA)
Type: Suspended
US Patent No. 1106102 Date of Grant 4 August 1914
Lindemann of Los Angeles, California, proposed that suspended monorails should have many wheels so that the load was evenly spread along the upper carrying rail. To this end he designed coupled bogies to distribute the weight and thus, he suggested, allow a lighter weight structure to support the upper rail.

Inventor: **M. Mähl** (France)
Type: Suspended
Engineer Vol. 118, 31 July 1914, p123.
Scientific American Vol. 111, 29 August 1914, p143 & Vol. 112, 27 March 1915, cover and p292.
During the First World War Mähl submitted to the Minister of Public Works in Paris detailed plans for trains with speeds up to 180 miles per hour. By that time experiments had shown that with electric traction speeds of up to 120 miles per hour could be attained on conventional two rail track (Scientific American 27 March 1915 references Zossen in 1902) but Mähl suggested that such speeds were incompatible with two rails resting on

This cross section of Mähl's design (also seen on page 144) shows the seating arrangements as well as the allowance for cars to swing on curves. Scientific American *Vol. 112, 27 March 1915*

the earth. Instead, Mähl, an engineer well known for his studies in the transmission of power, suggested a track which was to be from 20-25ft. above ground with light articulated cars suspended from the upper rail. The towers to support the rails were to be 150-200ft apart. There were to be no crossings or tunnels and curves were to be at least one kilometre in radius with grades limited to 5%. The track was to be divided into five kilometre sections with two dead sections between trains.

The light cars were to have the seats placed longitudinally in a single row and to have fish shaped ends to reduce aerodynamic friction. Mähl was concerned that the high speeds would unduly heat the bearings and so he proposed to enclose thermostats in every axle bearing which would notify the driver of any undue rise in temperature. There was also to be an elaborate plant for lubricating bearings with a constant flow of oil.

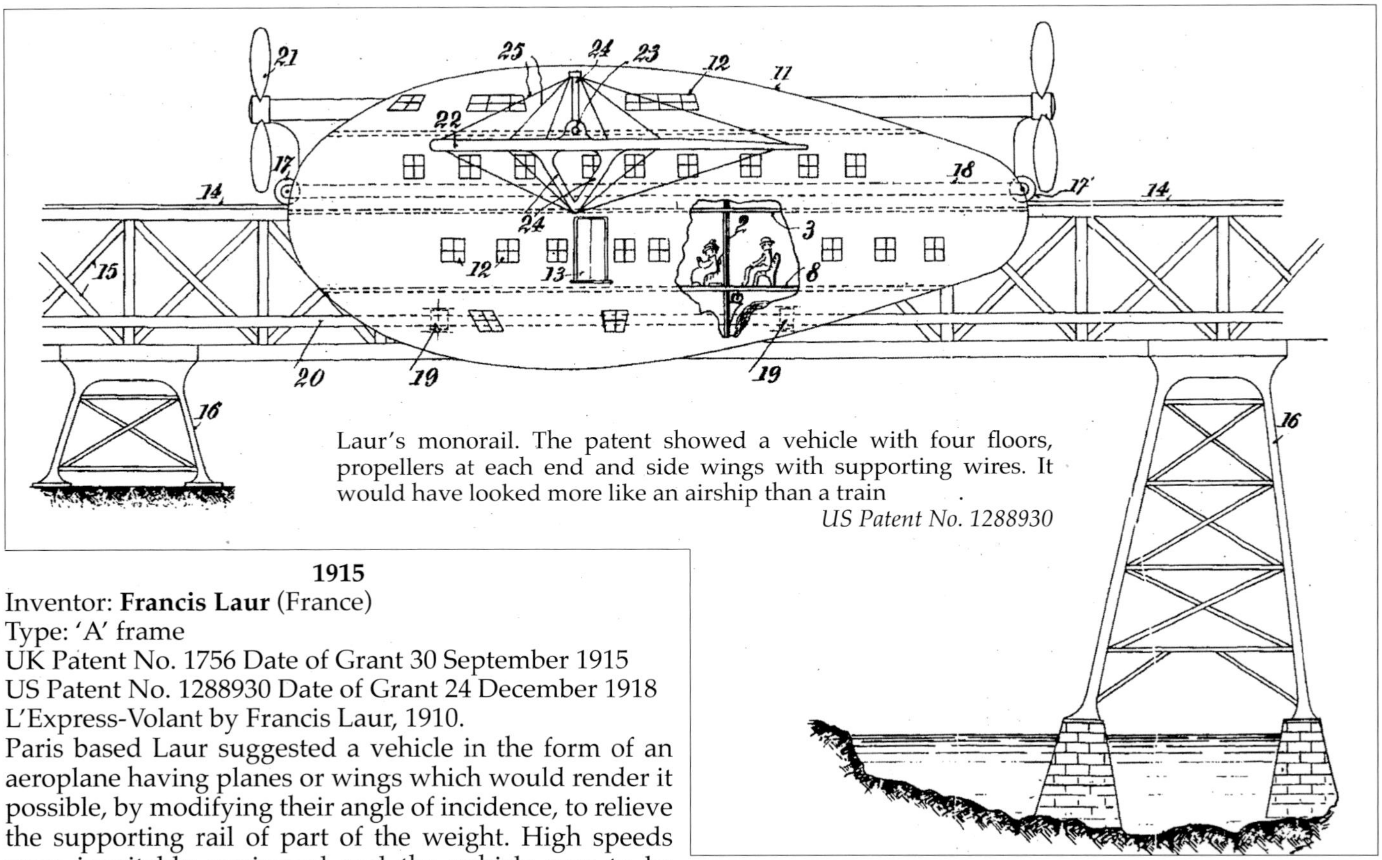

Laur's monorail. The patent showed a vehicle with four floors, propellers at each end and side wings with supporting wires. It would have looked more like an airship than a train

US Patent No. 1288930

1915

Inventor: **Francis Laur** (France)
Type: 'A' frame
UK Patent No. 1756 Date of Grant 30 September 1915
US Patent No. 1288930 Date of Grant 24 December 1918
L'Express-Volant by Francis Laur, 1910.

Paris based Laur suggested a vehicle in the form of an aeroplane having planes or wings which would render it possible, by modifying their angle of incidence, to relieve the supporting rail of part of the weight. High speeds were inevitably envisaged and the vehicle was to be driven by propellers at each end.

1916

Clear Lake Suspended Monorail Company

Inventor: **Unknown** (USA)
Type: Suspended
California Railroads by Alvin A. Fickewirth, 1992, p 30.

This Company was incorporated on the 23rd March 1916. It proposed to purchase the Clear Lake T. R. Company and to build a suspended electric monorail for freight and passengers to run from Lakeport via Kelseyville to Hopland in Mendocino County, California. The proposal was short lived as the line, which would have been 24 miles long, was denied permission by the Railroad Commission of California on 1st June 1916.

Monorail Company of America

Inventor: **Peter English** (USA)
Type: Bicycle

UK Patent No.	Date of Grant
17652	18 December 1916
102811	18 December 1916

US Patent No. 1253800 Date of Grant 15 January 1918

English assigned his US patent to the Monorail Company of America, Detroit, Michigan, which may have been a company set up by him to develop his invention. In any event, his bicycle system never got further than the drawing board. It had two unusual features. The lower wheel was to be wide and without flanges and was to run on the top of an 'I' beam. Guide wheels were to run on the sides of both the lower and upper 'I' beams. The other feature was that the trains were to run overhead of roads etc. with the rails mounted high above the ground on tall unbraced metal posts. A very unstable arrangement.

1917

National Suspended Monorail Company

Inventor: **Richard W. Shoemaker** (USA)
Type: Suspended

US Patent No.	Date of Grant
1355800	12 October 1920
1355801	12 October 1920

Banking Law Journal Vol. 34, October 1917, pp693-694 & 749-756.
Christian Science Monitor 8, 10, 12, 15 & 18 October 1918.
New York Globe 8 May 1920.
Chicago Leader 20 February 1920.

An artist's impression of the monorail promoted by the National Suspended Moncrail Company.
Banking Law Journal *Vol. 34, October 1917*

Chicago Daily News 11 March 1920.
Christian Science Monitor 19 April 1920.
Science and Invention July 1920.
Suspended Monorail System of Railways published by the National Suspended Monorail Company, 1927.

In 1912 studies were made by a group of US entrepreneurs of the Langen monorail system used on the Wuppertalbahn in Germany with the objective of constructing and operating not dissimilar monorails in the USA. The intervention of the First World War delayed progress and it was not until July 1916 that The National Suspended Monorail Company was incorporated with offices in the Michigan Boulevard Building, Chicago. Mr F. D. Flint was appointed President and Shoemaker was the Chief of Staff of the corps of engineers engaged for the research work by the company. Prior to this appointment he had for many years been associated with Westinghouse as a mathematician and designer as well as the engineer in charge of the Southern California engineering offices for Westinghouse. In this role he had been closely involved with the development of the high speed electric locomotive for the Pennsylvania Railway. He had subsequently been associated with the Southern California Edison Company designing high power transmission lines with the related towers.

Shoemaker filed for his first monorail patent whilst residing in Alameda, California in April 1918 and then moved to Seattle, Washington, where he was assisted by F. K. Caswell, formerly Chief Designer and Mathematician for the Schenectady Locomotive Works, where he filed for his second patent in June of that year. He assigned both patents to the National Suspended Monorail Company.

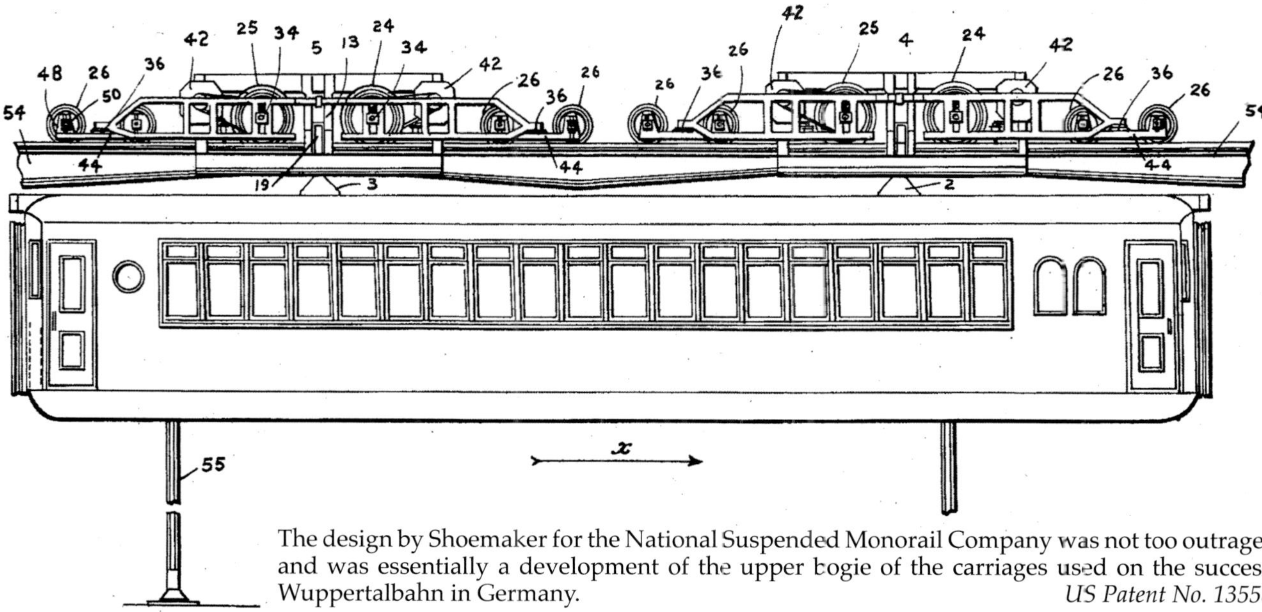

The design by Shoemaker for the National Suspended Monorail Company was not too outrageous and was essentially a development of the upper bogie of the carriages used on the successful Wuppertalbahn in Germany.
US Patent No. 1355801

Like Lindemann's system (above), a key feature was the use of multi-wheeled bogies to distribute the load on the rail in order to reduce the cost of construction of the supporting structure. Shoemaker's past experience in designing both high speed traction and power line towers was thus relevant.

The company built a working model and tried to promote an urban system within Chicago as well as a line from Los Angeles to Pasadena, California, but despite detailed studies no prototype was ever built.

By 1927 Frank S. Lyon had been appointed President, based in New York. (See Atlantic Suspended Monorail Corporation below).

1921

Inventor: **Albert P. Lee** (USA)
Type: Unique
US Patent No. 1376444 Date of Grant 3 May 1921
Based in Chicago, Illinois, Lee stated in his patent that his objectives were to provide a monorail which could be easily and cheaply constructed and which could be moved to other locations in short time. It was probably designed for construction sites or factories as it was intended that it could be mounted on the tops of walls or fences or brackets close to walls. The vehicle shown in his patent included a hopper which could dump material.

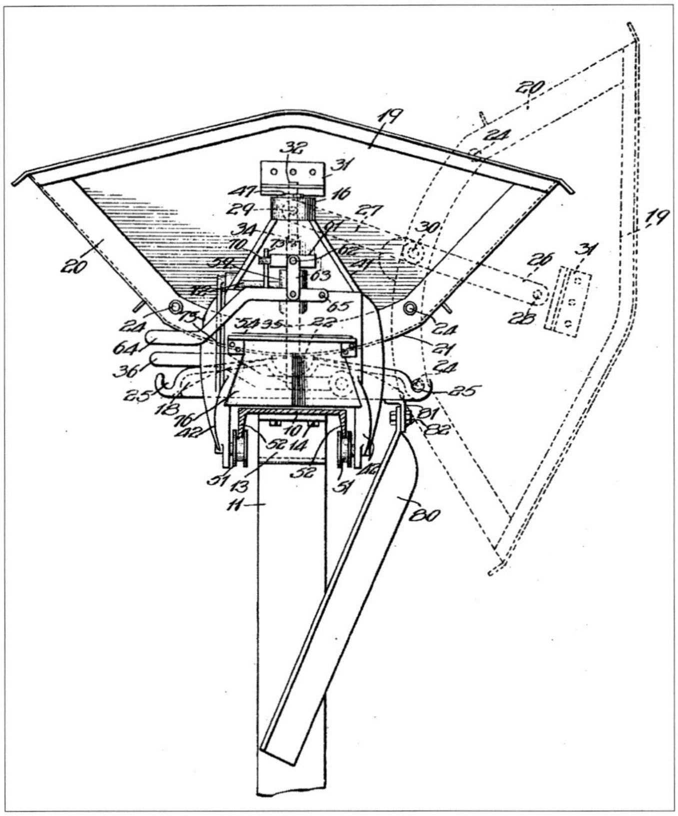

Lee's monorail dumper truck. The wide double flanged main wheel was to run on the upper surface of the inverted U shaped rail, labelled 52, with stabilizing wheels, labelled 51, running underneath. The design would have put considerable stress on the bolts securing the rail to the support beam.
US Patent No. 1376444

Inventor: **Rudolf Wagner** (Germany)
Type: Suspended (not monorail)
UK Patent No. 140095 Date of Grant 7 April 1921
US Patent No. 1422394 Date of Grant 11 July 1922
Wagner described himself in his patent as '...chief engineer, a citizen of the Free State of Bavaria, Germany, residing at Hamburg, 105 Bismarckstrasse...' and claimed that his design of suspended railcar using propeller drive and wings would allow speeds of up to 200 to 300 kilometres per hour. The design was not a monorail as the body of the railcar was to hang from two rail trucks but allowed to swing, the amount of swing being controlled by ailerons on the short wings. This patent is included as it is a forerunner of the design by Bennie (Chapter 7).

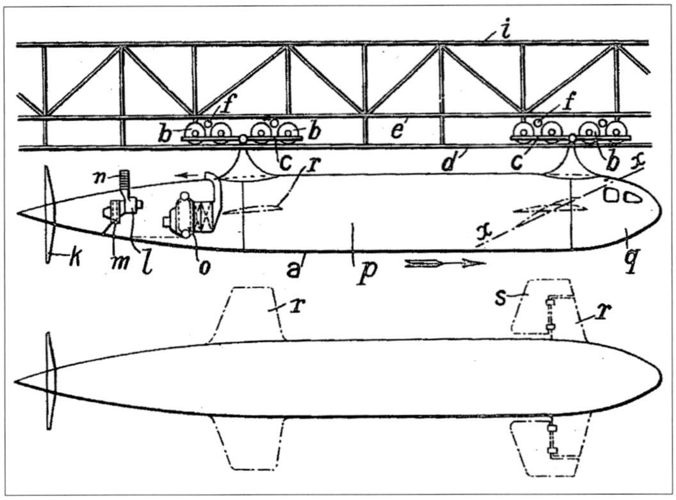

Wagner's suspended high speed (two rail) railway contains many of the features built into the Bennie Railplane.
US Patent No. 1422394

1926

Inventor: **Antonio Chiarelli** (USA)
Type: 'A' frame
US Patent No. 1592821 Date of Grant 20 July 1926
In addition to the usual claims of monorail inventors, Chiarelli stated one of the principal objectives of his design was to allow the transportation of a considerable number of passengers in a limited number of cars. The need for this attribute was no doubt based on the transport conditions surrounding his residence in New York.

1927

Inventor: **Franz Kruckenberg** *et al* (Germany)
Type: Suspended / Unique
US Patent No. 1628595 10 May 1927 etc. (see text).
Transactions of the Newcomen Society, Vol. 75, No. 1 (2005) pp37-84
Prior to the First World War Kruckenberg worked for the Schütte-Lanz airship construction company. When the war ended Germany was forbidden to design or build airships and he applied his knowledge to the design of a high speed airship shaped suspended monorail to run from Berlin to the Rhineland. To this end he founded the Gesellschaft für Verkehrstechnik (Transport Technology Company) in 1924 and applied for a patent for his design of 'Hängeschnellbahn'. Like others before him, his patent envisaged speeds of 200 to 300 miles per hour.

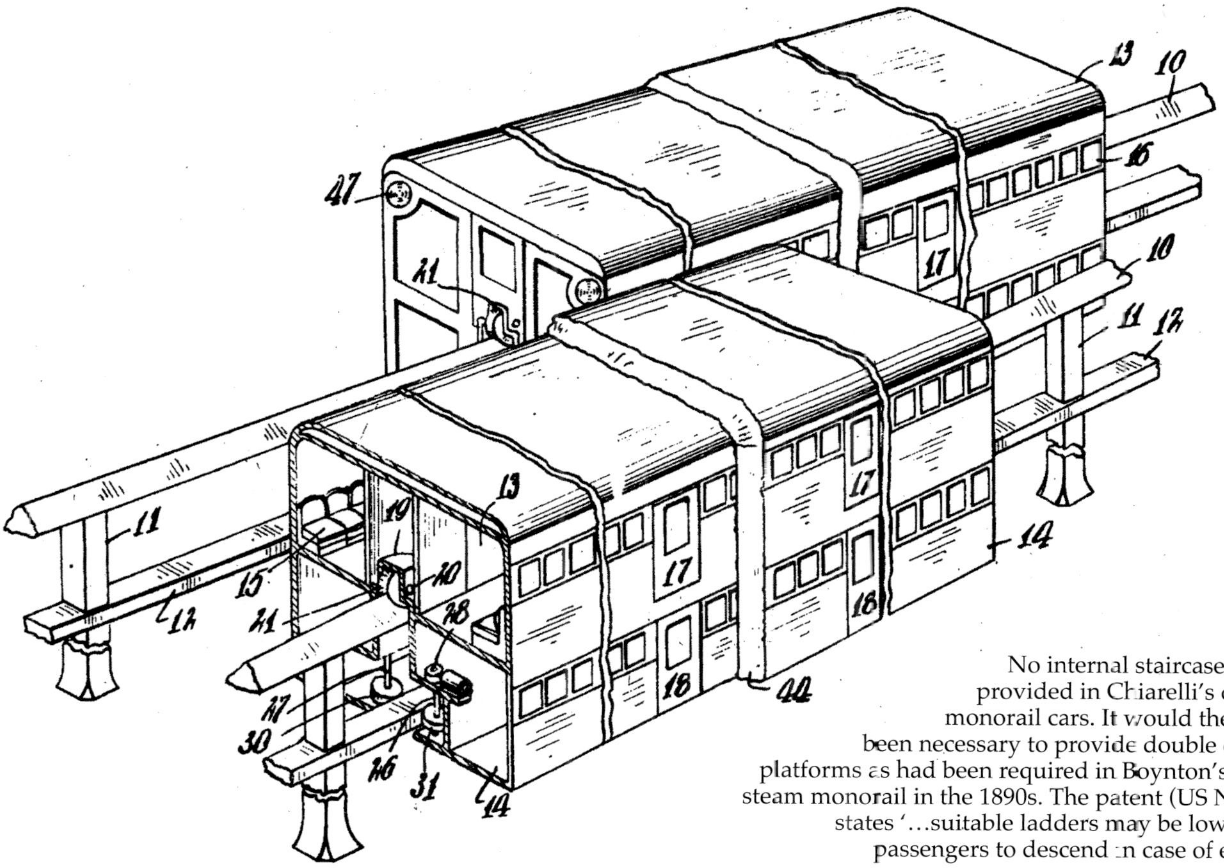

No internal staircases were to be provided in Chiarelli's double deck monorail cars. It would therefore have been necessary to provide double deck station platforms as had been required in Boynton's short-lived steam monorail in the 1890s. The patent (US No. 1592821) states '...suitable ladders may be lowered for the passengers to descend in case of emergency."

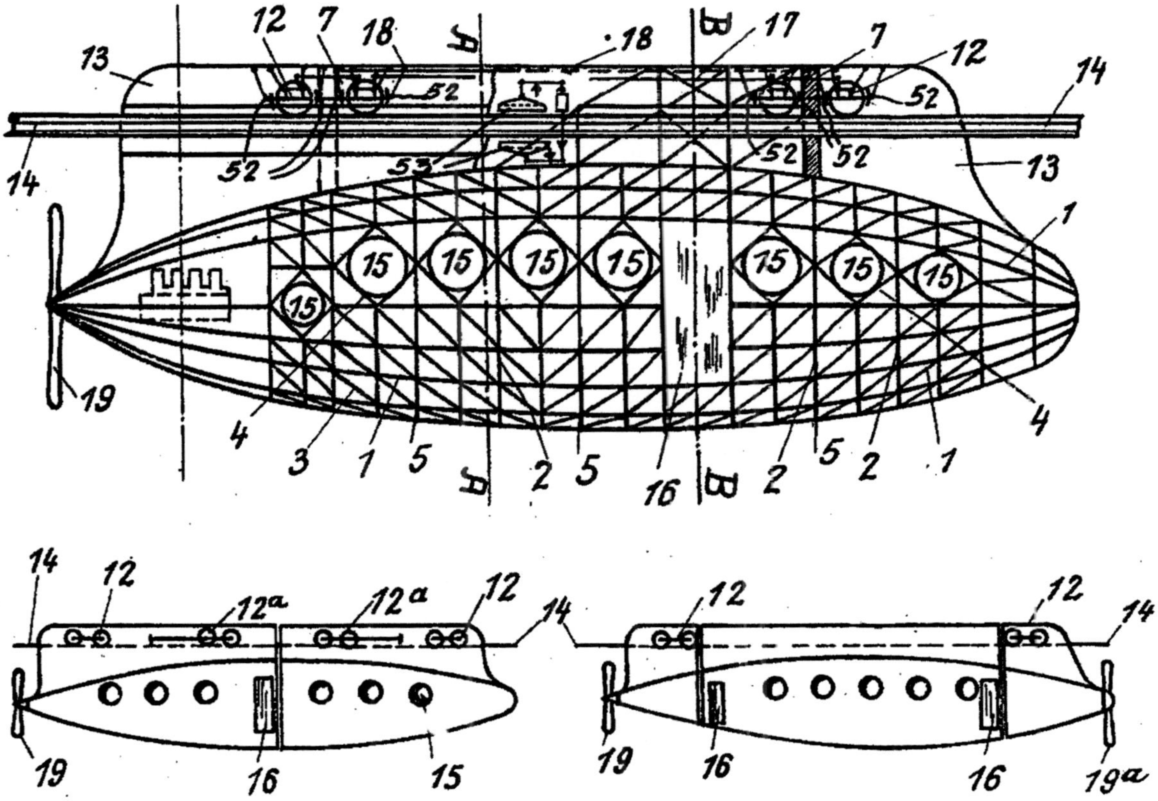

Kruckenberg's design of suspended railcar was essentially a suspended airship form of construction. Like the design by Bennie he envisaged propellers at both ends in some of his designs. *US Patent No. 1628595*

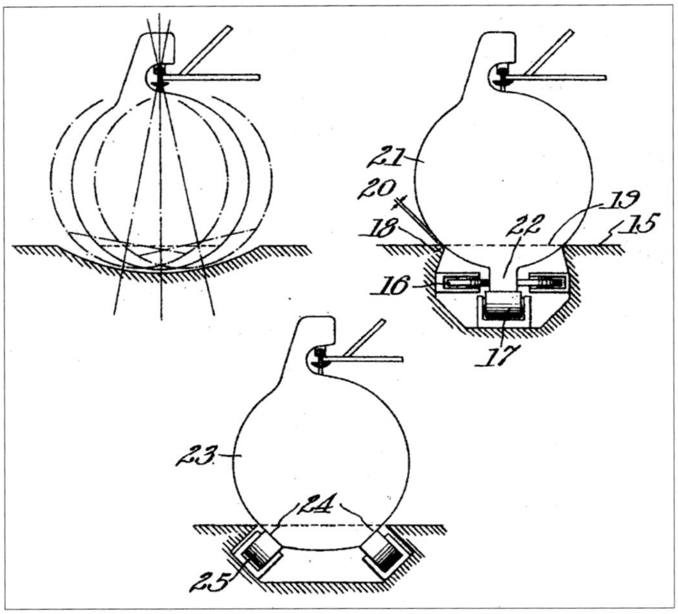

These end elevations show some of the more bizarre ways that Kruckenberg thought it might be possible to stabilize his suspended monorail. *US Patent No. 1789872*

Similar to the ideas of Bennie, Kruckenberg did not intend his system to replace conventional two rail railways. His system was to provide additional high speed access and to be constructed above existing lines. In 1927 his company tried to raise share capital for such a venture but failed to appeal to investors. He subsequently developed and constructed a 'Schienenzeppelin', a bullet shaped two rail standard gauge propeller driven railcar.

Kruckenberg worked with Curt Stedefeld and Willy Black on many of the designs (see below) as well as Fritz Gentzcke, named in US Patent No. 1628595. Together they took out too many patents to be listed in this volume for suspended and conventional two rail designs. None of their ideas came to fruition.

1929

Monorail Engineering Corporation
Inventor: **Presley Stuart Combs** (USA)
Type: Suspended

US Patent No.	Date of Grant
1740415	17 December 1929
1740416	17 December 1929
1740417	17 December 1929
1874907	30 August 1932
2532661	5 December 1950

Combs filed for patents in 1926 whilst based in Chicago, Illinois, and subsequently forfeited the applications and substituted new applications for the first three patents shown above on the 5th October 1929. After grant, he assigned all three patents to the Monorail Engineering Corporation, also based in Chicago. It is possible that this company was connected to the National Suspended Monorail Company (see above) but most likely he was working alone. These three patents related to providing stable but universal movement of the bogies from which the cars were to be suspended and the method of securing the upper rail to an 'I' beam.

By 1930 he had moved to Los Angeles, California, where he applied for, and was granted, a patent for a system of preventing derailment. This was nearly identical to the system invented by Langen for the Wuppertalbahn. He developed this idea and filed for a further patent on 22nd June 1945, granted in 1950, which was assigned, in trust, to P. S. Combs and Anson S. Bilger. Bilger was also working on monorail designs (ref. US Patents No. 2488523, Date of Grant 22 November 1949 & No. 2489740 Date of Grant 29 November 1949).

1930

Atlantic Suspended Monorail Corporation
Type: Suspended
New York Times 7 August 1930, p17.
Presentation to the Saturday Science Luncheon of The American Institute of the City of New York, 13 December 1930
New York Times 14 December 1930, pN20.
Mechanical Engineering Vol. 53, March 1931, pp190-192.
In August 1930 the *New York Times* reported that the Queens Planning Commission will study the possibility of adopting a suspended monorail for transportation projects proposed by Frank. S. Lyon, President of the Atlantic Suspended Monorail Corporation based at 67 Wall Street, New York. This was a spin off from the National Suspended Monorail Company (see above). The design of the cars for the monorail were illustrated in the subsequent talk to The American Institute and were based on those proposed for Chicago with the bodies modified to look more like those of the conventional underground services already in operation. The carriages were to be 64ft long, 9ft wide and provide seats for 80 passengers. The body was to be kept light by the use of aluminium construction, rather than steel, and the bogies were to have twelve wheels to each carriage.

The initial line was to run from Flushing to Whitestone with a later extension to Rockaway, Queens. The cost was estimated at $3m for the four mile long line to Whitestone. The proposal came to nothing.

1931

Inventor: **Theodor Roghmanns** (Germany)
Type: 'A' frame
US Patent No. 1798852 Date of Grant 31 March 1931
The German inventor Roghmanns, who lived in Sonsbeck, Niederrhein, patented a monorail with wings which he thought would provide a smoother and more stable ride at a greater speed. More importantly he proposed using pneumatic tyres to improve the ride.

Inventor: **Curt Stedefeld** and **Willy Black** (Germany)
Type: Suspended
US Patent No. 1825683 Date of Grant 6 October 1931
Stedefeld and Black from Heidelberg noted in their patent that high speed monorails with propeller drive and torpedo shaped bodies cannot run equally well forwards and backwards. They also noted that whilst a turntable can turn a single vehicle, to turn a train required a rail loop taking up much room. Their patented solution was to provide turntable bridges arranged next to each other in series so that all cars of the train could be turned simultaneously.

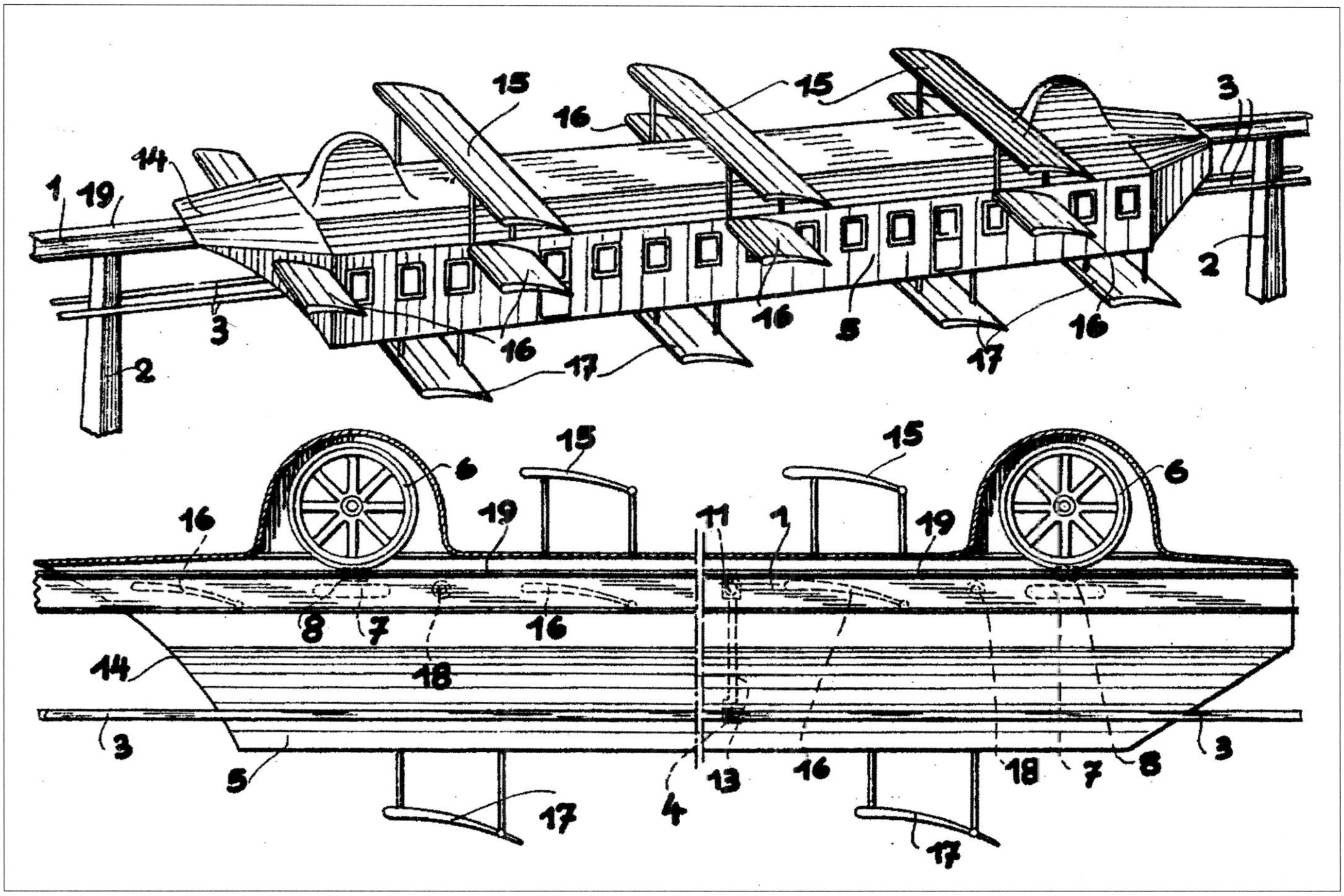

Roghmanns added wings to his design of monorail carriage which, he suggested, would reduce the weight of the carriage on the main rail thus avoiding '…jerks, jars and other irregular movement.' In the text of his patent he also suggested using pneumatic tyres, a now common feature of many monorails.

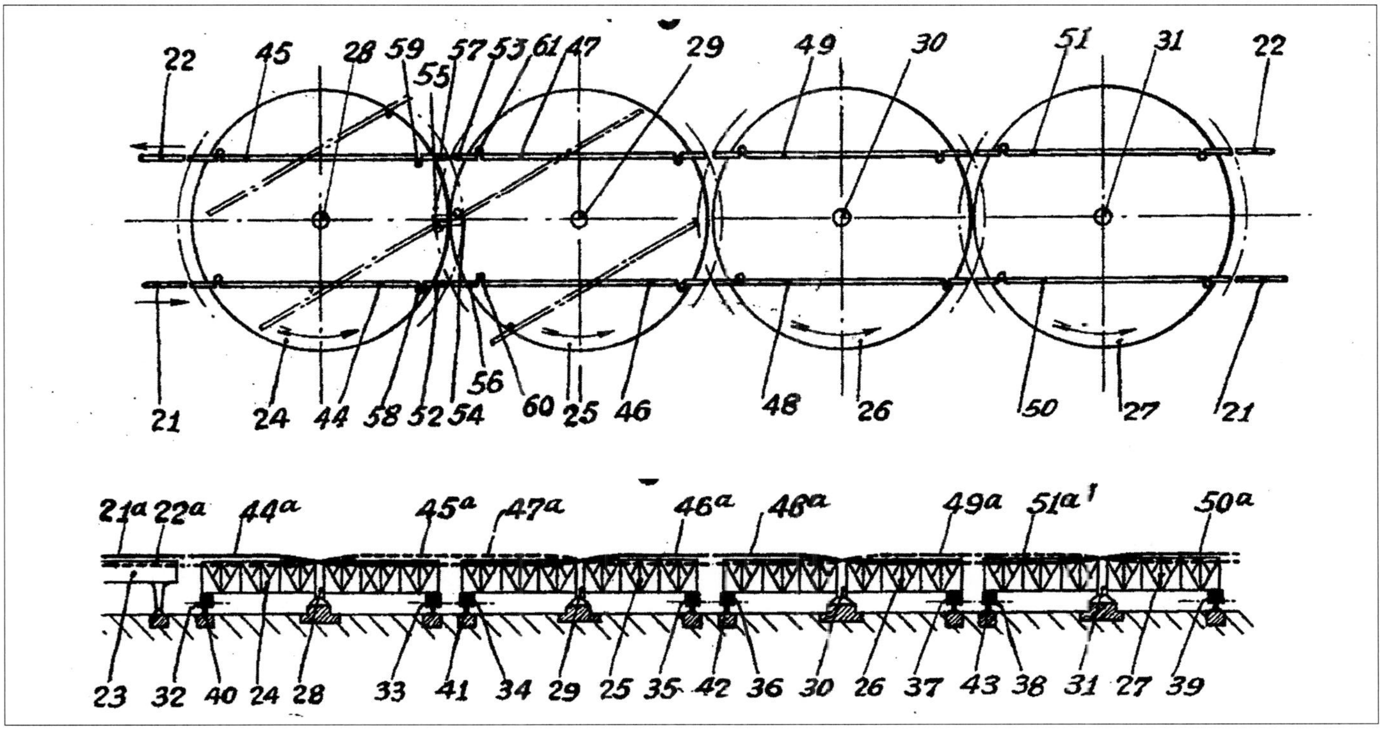

Stedefeld and Black's solution to turning trains at termini was to involve a series of turntables which rotated in unison so that all carriages were turned at the same time rather like dancers in a ballet. *US Patent No. 1825683*

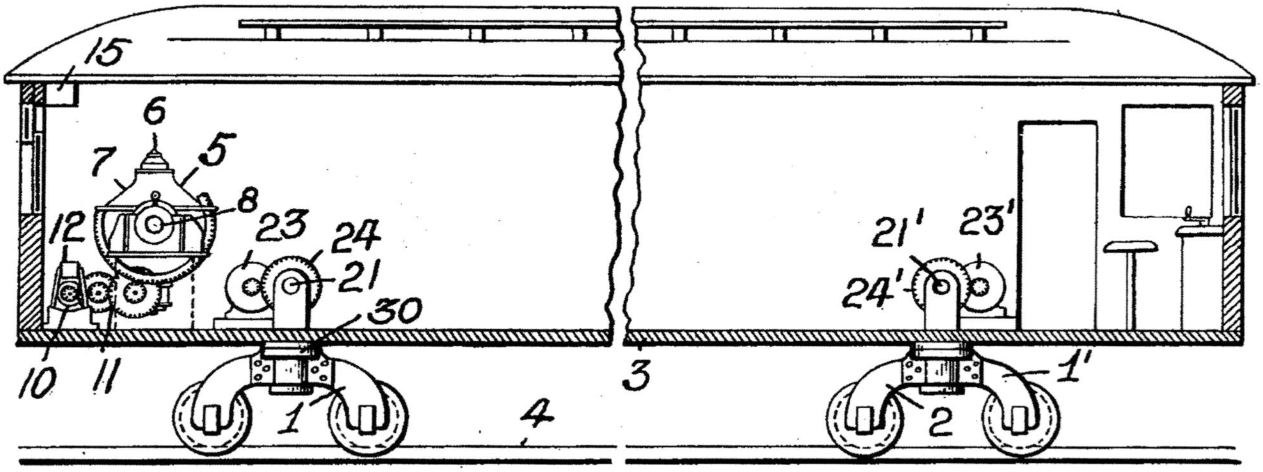

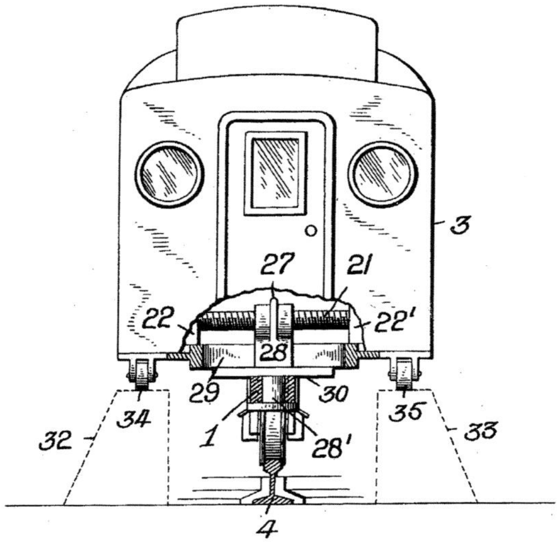

The side elevation from US Patent No. 1947119 shows the gyroscope mechanism at the left hand end of the vehicle whilst the end elevation shows the leadscrew, labelled 21, and nut, labelled 28, which would be used to move the whole body laterally. This might have been useful in taking up the effect of unbalanced loads but would have been impossibly slow and cumbersome if attempted for use to help the general stability of the vehicle.

1934

Sperry Gyroscope Company
Inventor **Hollis Walter** (USA)
Type: Gyroscopic
US Patent no. 1947119 Date of Grant 13 February 1934
Walter was based in Baldwin, New York, and assigned his patent to the Sperry Gyroscope Company, probably his employer. He proposed a monorail with gyroscope(s) to maintain stability supplemented by a means of laterally shifting the centre of gravity of the vehicle. This latter approach was hardly a new (or good) idea. Chandler McWayne had already taken out US Patent No. 163227 in 1875 applying the same idea to a conventional A frame monorail.

1935

Inventor: **George R. Napier** (USA)
Type: Unique
US Patent No. 1986845 Date of Grant 8 January 1935
Napier of Cleveland Heights, Ohio, claimed to have invented two new ways of stabilizing a monorail vehicle running on a central lower rail. The first was to add a large vane to the roof of the vehicle which '…acts somewhat like the rudder of a ship, but not for the purpose of steering the vehicle, because its motion is governed entirely by the rail to which it is confined by the flanges of wheels, but said vane acts as a stabilizer for maintaining the vehicle upright.' Napier then added a propeller both to provide motion to the vehicle and to act as a further stabilizer by rotating its direction around the vertical.

The patent suggests the driver may directly control these features, an interesting job, or "If desired, the vane and propeller, or either thereof, if used alone, may be automatically controlled by any suitable mechanism, preferably one which is controlled by the direction of movement of the vehicle."

1939

Inventor: **Rudolf Steiner**
Type: Bicycle
UK Patent No. 502136 Date of Grant 13 March 1939
Steiner was a Hungarian living in Vienna, Austria. His patent states "This invention relates to monorail railways of the kind in which the car is driven by air propellers and, is supported upon a track by means of a plurality of running wheel units arranged one behind the other in swivel frames at the bottom of the car, guides for instance guide wheels, rollers, stops or the like being provided at the top of the car which co-operate with a guide monorail."

The drawing accompanying the patent showed a vehicle similar to those designed by Bennie and precursors, the novel feature being that the lower bogies and upper guide wheels were to be connected by a vertical shaft so that they turned together.

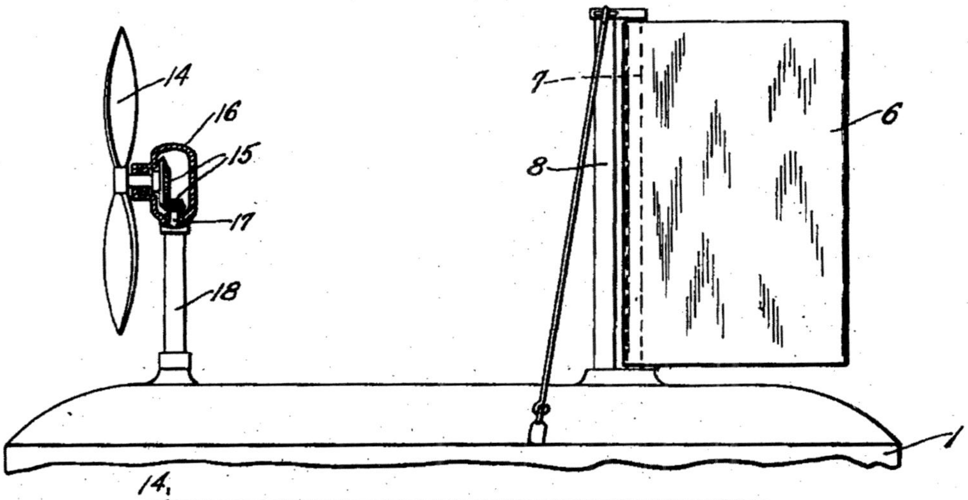

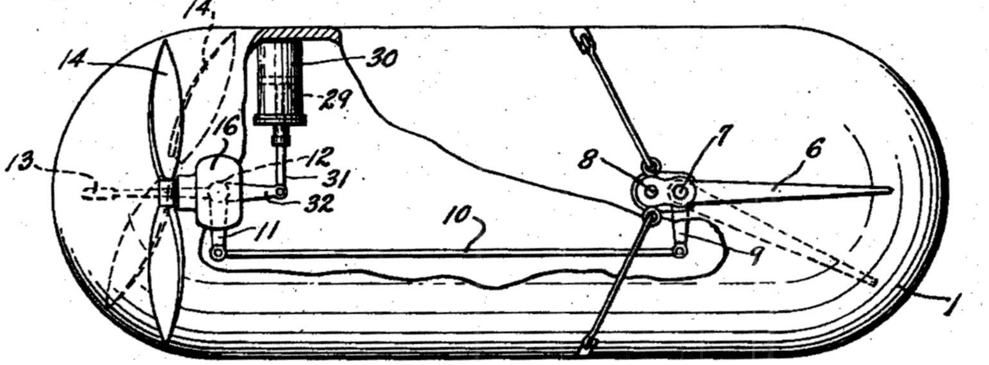

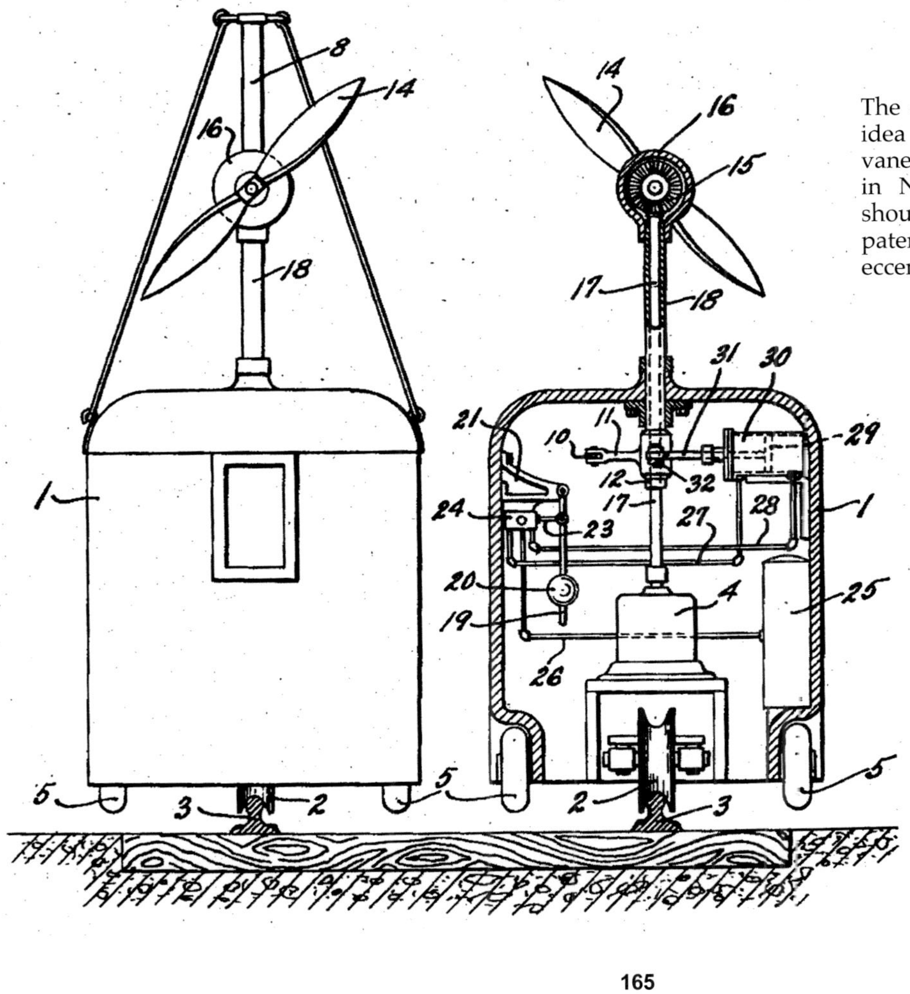

The author finds it surprising that the idea of stabilizing a monorail using a vane and pivoted propeller as shown in Napier's US Patent No. 1986845 should be proposed as late as 1935. This patent was granted in the twilight of the eccentric monorail era.

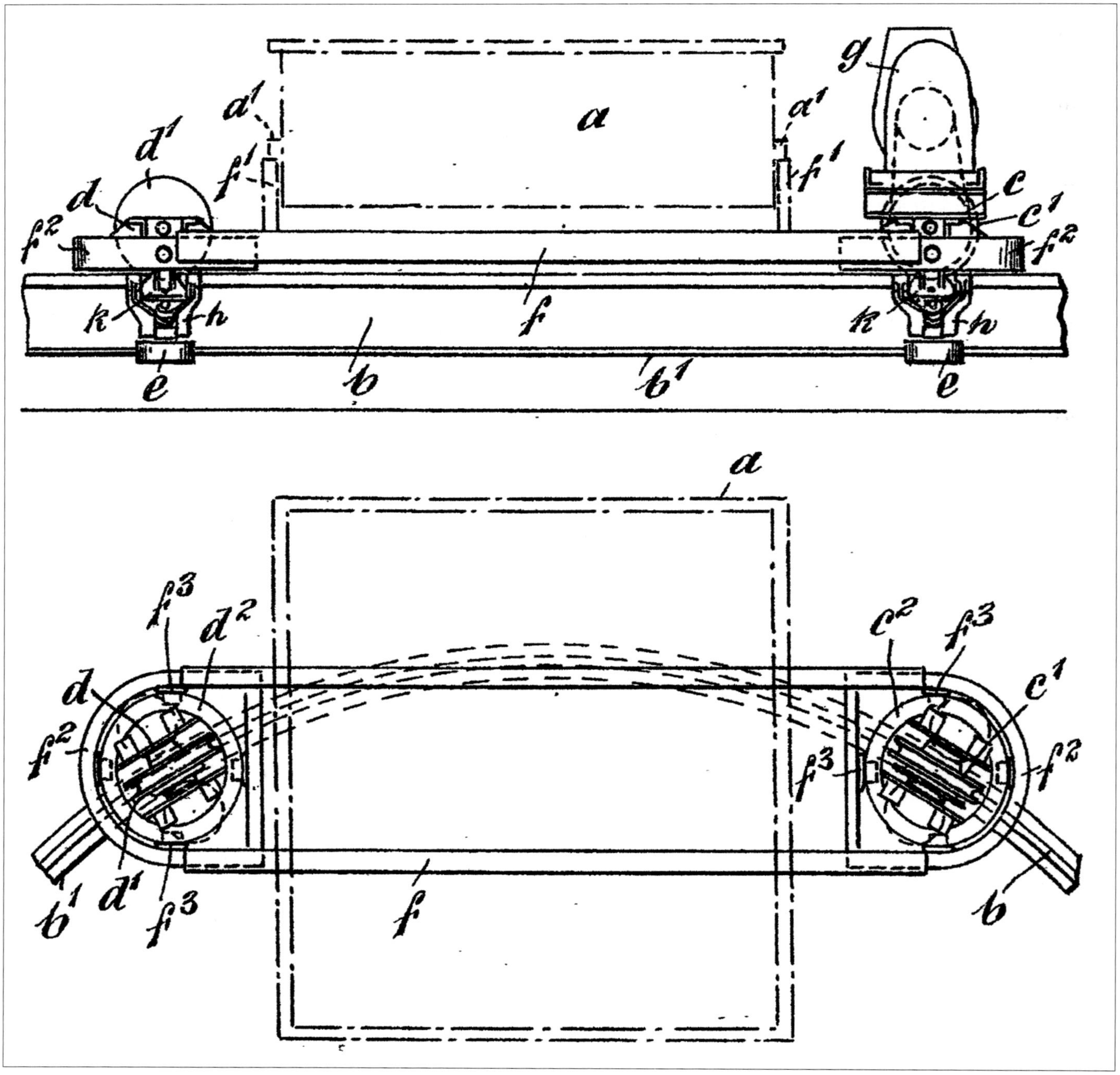

UK Patent No. 583760 taken out by Noel Green jointly with Aveling Barford in 1946 showed a skip running on a single rail with a power unit above one wheel (right).

1946

Inventor: **Noel Dutton Green**
Type: Unique

UK Patent No.	Date of Grant
577882	4 June 1946
583760	30 December 1946

Engineer Vol. 188, 9 December 1949, pp684-685.
Mono-Rail by David Voice, 2011.

Entrepreneurial monorail development virtually ceased with the beginning of the Second World War. The above two applications for patents were made on 30th November 1944, about a year before hostilities ceased. They represent the more realistic and commercial approach to development which followed the end of the war. The inventor Noel Green lived in West Wickham, Kent, and was a consultant to the manufacturer Aveling Barford Ltd which was based at its Invicta Works in Grantham. The patent applications were made jointly by Noel Green, Aveling Barford Ltd and an employee named Oscar Styles Penn.

These patents made no claims for high speed. The design was aimed at the practical issue of transporting materials around factories and building sites in a transferable container or skip using either a propulsive unit or just gravity.

Whilst Aveling Barford Ltd toyed with the possibility of developing the system no prototype was publicly displayed and the idea could have died.

Post script

Just at the point where this book finishes the ideas of Green's design were taken up by Road Machines (Drayton) Ltd, of Horton Parade, West Drayton, Middlesex. This company had been set up by William Muir Robb in 1946 to capitalise on the opportunities for reconstruction of London and other cities devastated by the effects of the war. Learning that Aveling Barford Ltd did not wish to develop their monorail design further, Road Machines (Drayton) Ltd acquired the rights which it renamed 'Mono-Rail'. The company exhibited their full size operational prototype for the first time at 'Building Week' held in Tunbridge Wells, Kent, in late 1949.

The prototype exhibited consisted of a driverless train of two side tipping wagons each 8ft long by 4ft wide overall, with a hopper capacity of 13 cubic feet. They ran on a steel rail mounted on aluminium alloy stands with adjustable jack feet. The train could negotiate curves of 12ft radius and a 1 in 18 gradient. The rails were in 15ft lengths some 7½in. deep and of welded construction (quoted in the *Engineer* as weighing 1½cwt per 12ft length). The curves were in 6ft lengths and had a 12ft radius. 8ft long pedal operated points were also shown. The track was assembled using spigot and socket mountings without fishplates or nuts and bolts.

The train was powered by a 3 horse power air-cooled petrol engine with a double plate clutch and chain drive to the running wheel. An automatic stop could be bolted to the track to control the train.

The timing of this display fitted perfectly with the needs of the construction industry after the war. The 'Mono-Rail' was a success. Road Machines (Drayton) Ltd. went on to supply the system to many hundreds of users in the UK alone. During the 1950s they applied for a series of patents for improvements to the design of both the track and the vehicles which were granted in the UK, USA, Europe and elsewhere.

Following Robb's death in 1965, the rights to produce 'Mono-Rail' were purchased by Metalair Ltd, Wokingham, Buckinghamshire, which continued manufacture until 1977 by which time the construction industry had become more reliant on cranes. Six years later, in 1983, Richard Morris acquired the rights, equipment and spares for preservation. A detailed history of the system post 1950 is provided in David Voice's book, above.

A preserved section of Road Machines (Drayton) Ltd. track with a ride on petrol engine powered locomotive operating on a temporary track at the Festiniog Railway's Fifty Year celebrations in 2005. The seat is an addition to this non-passenger system as is the embellishment of a Welsh Dragon. The simple rail joints supported by adjustable height feet is unchanged from its industrial days *Author*

The reality of 21st century monorails; a train arrives at Harbour Front Station, Singapore, from Sentosa Island on the 11th January 2015. These two car units provide a frequent service for visitors to this popular beach and resort. *Author*

The eccentricity of monorails continues to appeal; Richard Morris, who acquired the rights to the designs of Road Machines (Drayton) Ltd (Chapter 8), commissioned Century Millwrights to build Monoloco to run on Road Machines type track. This small 0-2-0ST locomotive was completed in 1998 and has a 6ft wheelbase and 3½in. bore by 4½in. stroke cylinders. A fitting tribute to the pioneers of monorail railways. *Author*

EPILOGUE

Monorails of the 19th Century together with this book provide a history of the development of the monorail from its birth in the 1820s through to maturity in the mid twentieth century.

The majority of the monorail designs were a mix of the eccentric together with a disregard of commercial reality or the basics of engineering and physics. Most got no further than the drawing board or patent office. Some, despite the odds against their success, came to fruition and proved their failure.

Amongst those ideas, however, there were successes. For example Palmer's original monorail was simple but solved a problem at both the Royal Naval Victualling Yard in Deptford and at Gibb's Brickworks in Cheshunt. Duchamp's monorail in Lyon only ran during an exhibition but during that period it was a commercial success as was General Roy Stone's at the Philadelphia Centennial Exhibition. Lartigue's agricultural lines were also a great success but these, like that by General Roy Stone, should never have been developed further into a public railway system. The only long term success to emerge was the Langen system used on the Wuppertalbahn and Loschwitz Schwebebahn in Germany. Both these lines continue to operate and provide much needed transport.

It is very clear, however, that the designers of monorails were open to the use of latest technology. Designs incorporated fixed and variable pitch propellers as well as wings and air brakes long before successful flight was achieved. They also included the use of electricity and gyroscopes before these became common place. Probably unaware, some inventors mentioned in passing ideas that would later become successful. The use of pneumatic tyres on trains by Theodore Roghmanns in his 1931 patent is an example.

Following all this nearly uninhibited experimentation, a new commercial reality emerged after the Second World War which required new monorails to be financially viable rather than just innovative. It is perhaps not chance that the very successful design marketed by Road Machines (Drayton) Ltd from the 1950s onwards had exactly same purpose as that patented by Henry Palmer some one hundred and seventy years before. The story of the monorail had come full circle.

From then on, the need for a monorail rather than some other mode of transport has become the driver. Many monorails are now installed as novelties and are fun in theme parks, they can rise above the ground and allow occupants to look down into zoos and they can provide transport above already crowded streets such as in Las Vegas or between terminals at airports. But perhaps because their installation is now based on commercial need and logic they no longer have quite the same eccentric charm.

An epitaph to the monorails that failed to be commercially successful; the remains of the American Magnesium Company's monorail at Wingate Wash in 2007. Compared to the picture of the track on the title page, a surprising amount of the wood remains thanks to the mainly dry conditions.
Alexander. K. Rogers

Locomotive No. 4 built by Alan Keef in 2000, Works No. 62, awaits departure on a sunny afternoon on 6th August 2015.

Author

APPENDICES

APPENDIX 1

AN UPDATE ON THE LARTIGUE MONORAILS

The history of these monorails was included in Monorails of the 19th Century. A full size replica of the Listowel and Ballybunion Railway now operates at Listowel, together with a museum of artifacts from the original line, and the route of the Feurs to Panissières Railway has been converted into a walking route. A little more has also emerged about the proposed high speed line from Liverpool to Manchester. An update on these developments is appropriate.

Listowel & Ballybunion Railway reborn

This 9¼ mile long line was opened on Thursday 1st March 1888 and ran for thirty six years until its closure on Tuesday 14th October 1924. Thomas W. Ward was appointed to demolish the railway. The locomotives, rolling stock and track were sold as scrap.

A few items missed the eye of the demolition team and were kept by those nostalgic about the line or remained buried in the earth. In particular Michael Barry of Ballingowan, Lisselton, Co. Kerry, searched out items including lengths of track from barns, buildings and fences over a period of forty years from the 1950s in the hope of forming a museum[1].

Mr Sean Quilan, writing in *The Kingdom* on the 3rd July 1984 said[2]:

> "Michael and Sheila [Barry] have put a lot of time and effort into restructuring and protecting a part of our heritage and it is time that somebody somewhere stands up and on behalf of this and future generations says 'thank you'. This paper does now!"

In 1988 to commemorate one hundred years since the line was opened the Lartigue Centenary Committee was set up with Michael Guerin as Secretary. In addition to acting as Secretary Michael Guerin wrote and published a book to coincide with the celebrations[3]. The Committee actively encouraged a number of local activities including an exhibition of relics and photographs, local slide shows and screening of the short film of the line. Thanks to these efforts visitors to the area to see what remained increased and when Michael Foster updated the book by A. T.

Thomas W. Ward left few traces of the monorail but this bridge over the line just outside Listowel Station where the track turned towards the sea survived and has been preserved. *Author*

On an area of land to the side of the new museum at Listowel the concrete bases of two rotating points remain together with part of the foundations of the long gone carriage shed. The corrugated iron clad goods shed also remains (2015) but is on private land. *Author*

Newham in 1989 he included a feasibility report on the line's reconstruction.

In summary Foster's report found:

- Much of the land originally used was available but some had been built on. Any reconstruction would need to minimize inconvenience to people's homes.
- The cost of the manufacturing process of rolling rail identical to the original size was prohibitive but standard C.I.É. rail might be useable, albeit over size. Identical angle iron 'A' frames could, however, be constructed from stock material and the work could be carried out by apprentices gaining skills in drilling, welding and assembly.
- Locomotives similar in outline to the originals could be constructed. Following an approach to Severn Lamb Ltd in 1984, the firm had responded that in their view an Internal Combustion / Hydraulic Drive system built

A short section of the original track mounted on its steel sleepers is displayed in the Listowel & Ballybunion Railway Museum at Listowel. Its preservation is thanks to the efforts of Michael Barry. *Author*

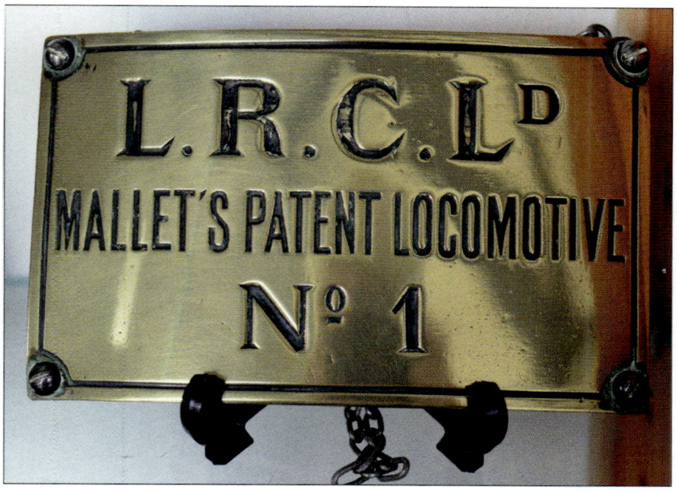

Amazingly the original brass plate from the twin vertical boiler locomotive built by La Métallurgique, Tubize, Belgium has survived. This locomotive was used to demonstrate the Lartigue system in London before it was shipped to Ireland to help construct the Listowel & Ballybunion Railway. It is now displayed in the museum. *Author*

into a locomotive cosmetically and dimensionally the same as the original would be commercially viable. The high capital cost and operational cost would probably rule out an operational steam locomotive. They estimated the cost of an I.C./Hydraulic locomotive to be in the region of UK£60,000.

- The Hunslet Engine Company was also approached. The company still had the records and drawings of the original locomotives they had built in 1887 and they estimated that the cost of manufacture of a replica steam locomotive would be UK£125,000.
- The drawings of the original carriages and wagons built by the Falcon Engine & Car Company of Loughborough had been lost but carriages not dissimilar could be constructed. To operate a rebuilt line three trains, of some six carriages each, would be required.

No immediate action occurred but the idea of reconstructing part of the railway gained momentum as the millennium approached and the Lartigue Monorail Restoration Committee was formed in 1998 to promote the project. Whilst Foster's feasibility report had considered reconstruction of the whole line, the reality of the cost involved was recognized and a more modest but realistic aim pursued. In June 2000 the *Limerick Leader*[4] reported that Fine Gael's Deputy Jimmy Deenihan, MP for Kerry North, who had been appointed chairman of the restoration committee, optimistically considered that a short section of the line would be back in operation by the end of 2000. The project planned to restore half a kilometre of track with a replica steam engine and two carriages seating forty passengers. The site was to include a platform. turntable and storage area with an interpretive centre and museum being built as a second phase. The cost was estimated at IR£850,000 and Deenihan reported that the project was in the fund raising stage.

The breakdown of the estimated costs published in the promotion material[5] was:

	Cost IR£
Full size replica locomotive	99,360
Two carriages – replica 3rd Class	27,780
- replica 3rd Class/Guards	29,580
500 metres of track	45,000
Five turntable type points	30,912
Site acquisition	50,000
Storage areas, fencing, site works	100,000
Building renovation	220,679
Interpretive Centre, Museum & café	150,000
Contingency	100,000
Total cost	853,311
(All figures exclude VAT)	

The project was officially launched by the government Chief Whip, Seamus Brennan, on Thursday 8th June 2000 and was backed by the Millennium Committee which had pledged IR£175,000. The site for the new Lartigue monorail was announced to be land previously occupied by Listowel station of the CIÉ which had closed to freight in 1977 and had previously formed part of the Great Southern and Western Railway broad gauge line from Tralee to Limerick. This land had been purchased by the Listowel Urban District Council after the broad gauge closed and was leased to the project by the Council, effectively a contribution of IR£50,000. Further funding was being sought from Shannon Development (the local tourist organization), FÁS (Irish National training and Employment Authority), Tuatha Chiarrai (the European funded Kerry development agency), Kerry County Council and Iarnród Éireann (Irish Rail).

The project was a rapid success and a formal order for a steam outline diesel locomotive and 500 metres of track was placed with Alan Keef Ltd, Ross-on-Wye in August 2000[6 & 7]. A first section of track was displayed at an open day at their works on the 9th September 2000 and the track completed within six months. The outbreak of foot and mouth disease, however, delayed shipment to Listowel until May 2001.

As suggested by Foster, the cost of rolling prototypical rail would have been prohibitive. Alan Keef Ltd therefore opted to use conventional 30lb per yard rail for the main rail and S7 section light continental rail material for the side rails.

During this period the final design of the locomotive was also resolved. The original 0-3-0 wheel arrangement of the Hunslet steam locomotives was simplified to 0-2-0 and not provided with power. Instead the tender, also an 0-2-0, is powered by a 3 cylinder 100 Series Perkins type diesel engine mounted on the right hand side of the tender driving a Linde BPV 50 hydraulic pump. This in turn drives a Chinese built Poclain MS08 hydraulic piston motor which is coupled to both the front and rear double flanged wheels of the tender by a roller link chain. The direction of flow of the hydraulic fluid, to allow both forward and reverse motion, is controlled by an electrically operated reverser switch. Interestingly the original steam locomotives had cylinders in the tender connected by a flexible steam pipe to the locomotive boilers. These were intended to provide additional power but were not used due to lack of steam and sufficient power being available from the locomotive cylinders. Powering the replica from the tender is thus not so far from the original.

The new Lartigue locomotive under construction at Alan Keef's works.
David Smith

The locomotive weighs 2.76 tons and the powered tender 3.25 tons. As the length of the line is short the fuel tank only contains 30 litres.

By January 2002 grants and individual donations had brought the total to within IR£80,000 of fruition. The site for the new Lartigue monorail, the former broad gauge Listowel station, was cleared and 10,200 tonnes of ballast delivered and modern industrial type buildings erected to protect the locomotive and carriages. The Great Southern & Western Railway's goods shed was kept and earmarked to be the visitor centre and museum at an expected cost of about IR£400,000.

The locomotive was delivered on 20th March 2002 and commissioned the following day[8]. By December 2002 all items were on site at which time the Chairman of the project, Deputy Jimmy Deenihan, said that the standard of worksmanship by Alan Keef Ltd was excellent and he went on to thank FÁS, especially Tom Roche and his fellow workers Tom O'Connor, William Keane, Simon O'Brien, Tom Blennerhassett, Joe Reidy, Timmy Billman and Moss Heaphy for their commitment to the project[9].

He also praised the assistance and support from:

The Millennium Committee
Kerry County Enterprise Board
ESB (Electricity Supply Board, Ireland)
The Peace and Reconciliation Fund of the Department of Foreign Affairs
Spectra Laboratories
Shannon Ferries
Kerry Group
Ardfert Quarries
J. J. Galvin & Sons
Tuatha Chiarrai
Kostal Ireland

A short time later, in January 2003, Deputy Deenihan said that he anticipated that phase one of the project would

The driver's side of the cab. The whistle lever is just below the cab window with string attached. The wooden handle to the right controls the engine throttle. The direction is controlled by the black handle to its right whilst the brake handle is mounted on the side panelling. Brakes on both the locomotive and carriages work at 70lbs per sq. in.
Author

The Perkins engine and hydraulic pump is accessed through a side panel on the right of the tender. *Author*

Balance is maintained by double flanged side wheels with axles mounted on cranks connected by a long rod. This is identical to the original locomotives. *Author*

be completed by April 2003 and would be operational during the summer tourist season. The latest estimate of the cost of phase one was €750,000 of which €600,000 had been raised. (Note: Ireland changed currency to the Euro on the 1st January 2002) A series of initiatives were announced to raise the final €150,000 including a fund raising event at the Shelbourne Murray Hill Hotel in New York, a Lartigue Supporters Draw, a sale of 'Sleepers' and a Lartigue Patrons Circle[10].

The rebuilt Lartigue monorail was completed and opened to the public on Friday 18th July 2003[11].

This success reflects well on the efforts of the members of the Lartigue Monorail Restoration Committee that governed the project, many of whom had been involved since the beginning. By 2003 the Committee had needed to become a corporate body, the Lartigue Monorail Restoration Limited, and its members were:

Chairman: Jimmy Deenihan TD
Vice Chairman: Maurice O'Sullivan, Solicitor
Secretary: Michael Guerin
Patron: Senator Maurice Hayes
President: Jack McKenna
Vice President: Michael Barry
Other members: Maurice Heaphy, Christy Holyoake, Ursula Leslie, Cara Trant, Cllr. Tim O'Leary, Pat Brodin & Cllr. Pat Loughnane.

In August 2004 the National Heritage Award was bestowed on the project as part of the Tidy Towns national competition and during its first full year of regular daily runs in 2004 over 3000 visitors travelled on the line. The award and fares had reduced the outstanding debt to €30,000[12].

The official opening took place on the 14th October 2005. Both the British and French ambassadors were present reflecting the input from nationals from these countries to the original railway and the ceremony was conducted by the President of Ireland, Mary McAleese[13]. In 2007 a museum was opened in the former Great Southern & Western Railway's goods shed. The line now operates throughout the summer and all readers are strongly encouraged to visit.

More than one hundred years after the Lartigue railways had been built in Ireland and France they are still having an impact. The towns of Listowel and Panissières hold regular twinning activities to celebrate their monorails.

Two carriages have been built by Alan Keef for the museum line to designs representative of the originals but with modern safety standards. Not yet numbered, this carriage is a cross between the original guards vans B1 and B2. It has three doors, steps at one end and a birdcage (but without windows) type roof. Seats face outwards. *Author*

To meet modern safety standards a pneumatic piston operates an external rod locking all doors before a train departs. The compressed air for both the brakes and the door locking system is generated by a 12V electric compressor in the locomotive tender. *Author*

Above: The other carriage represents the pannier type carriages of the original line which consisted of two half sections affixed to a central chassis. Neither of the new carriages has windows and thus avoids the need for expensive safety glass. *Author*

The structure of the two bogies with the half section carriage bodies is identical to the design of the original. The modern plastic piping is for the pneumatic brake and door lock systems. *Author*

Left: Listowel Station and shed as seen from the museum. Note the curved nature of the track needed to cope with the rotating points.

Below: Whilst not steam, the replica locomotive captures the feel of the original railway with the large locomotive headlamp. The museum, formerly the goods shed of the Great Southern & Western Railway at Listowel, is behind the train.

both Author

Although the museum line is short, Locomotive No. 4 is turned for the return journey. As on the original railway, there is only one turntable at each end of the line. On the rebuilt line these sturdy structures are supported at their outer ends by three wheels running on a circular track. The rotating points, which superficially appear to be similar to the rotating turntables, are lighter and have only two support wheels at each end. The original rotating points designed by Bocandé had only a short arc of supporting rail where the rails joined. The replica rotating points with their full circle of support rail make for easier and safer operation. *Author*

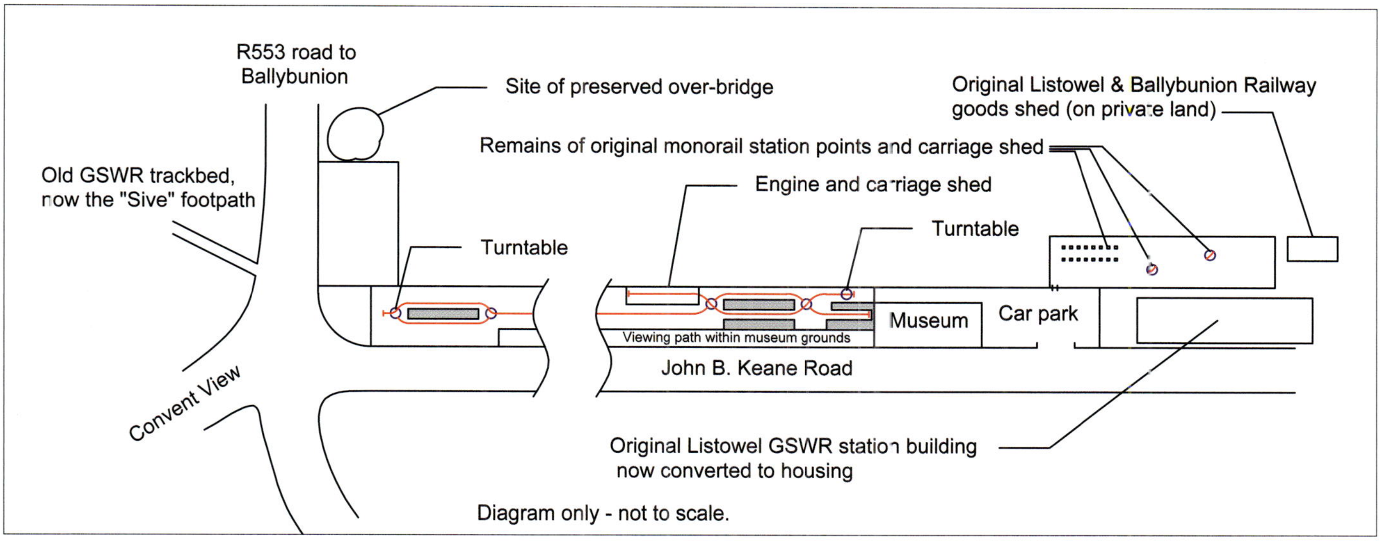

The curved shape of the rotating point designed and patented by Olivier B. Bocandé for the original railway is clearly seen as the point is rotated to allow Locomotive No. 4 to join its train. *Author*

A walk from Feurs to Panissières

The monorail from Feurs to Panissières near Lyon in France was never opened to the public. Construction started in 1894 and repeated attempts were made to bring the track up to the standard required for public safety. The costs involved ensured that the line was not viable to operate and it was closed on the 26th August 1898. Whilst the track was sold for scrap in 1902, many of the earth works and civil engineering structures remain. The local authorities have turned most of the track bed into a very attractive walk with illustrations of the line and explanations of its working on posts along the route.

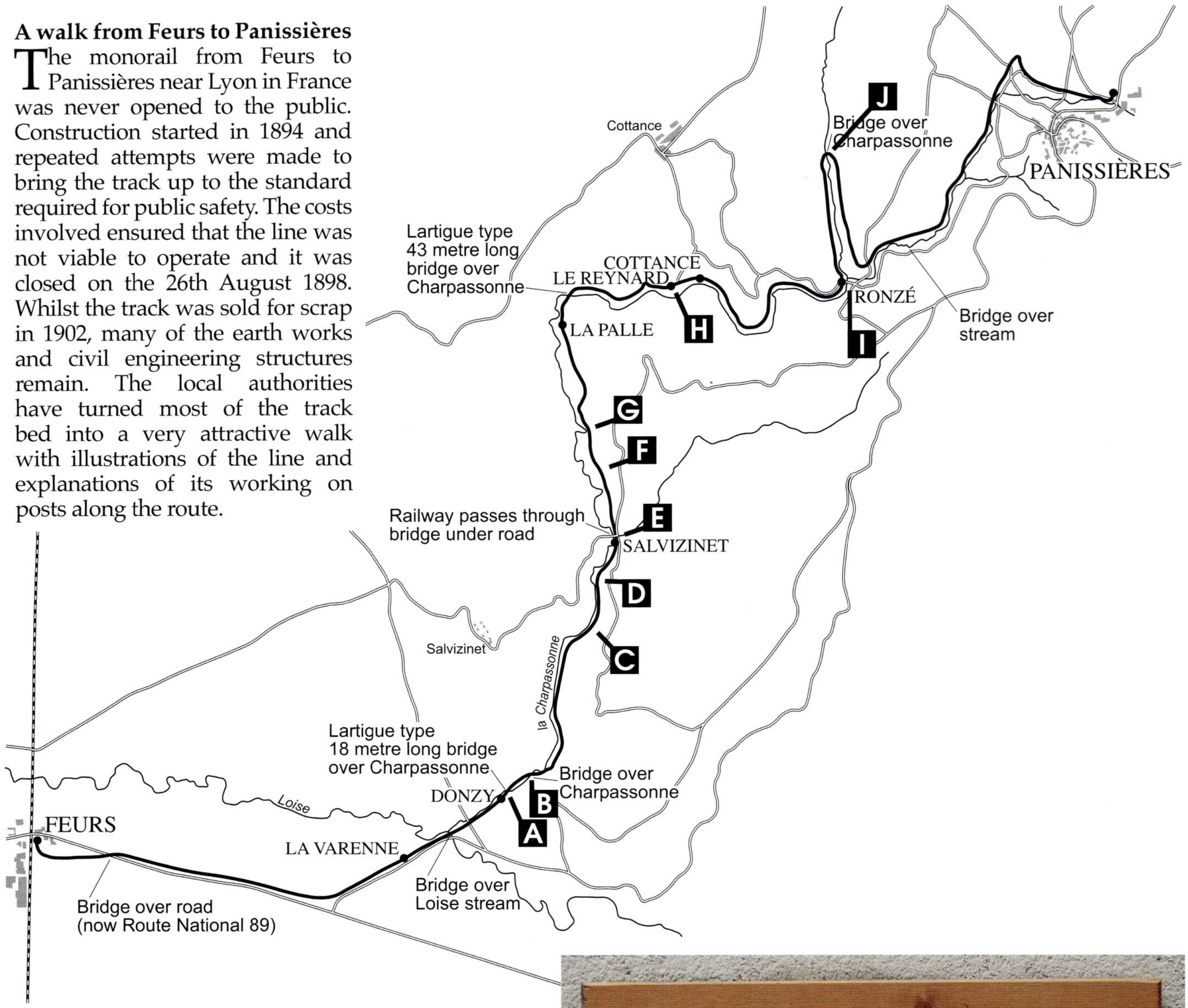

The walk starts to the north west of the village of Salt-en-Donzy near where the original station of La Varenne was sited. The first 3km of trackbed from Feurs to this point has been lost to redevelopment. The remaining monorail track bed is now part of a network of walks. The distance of 25km shown on the sign represents a hiking loop. It is a pity that a conventional railway engine is depicted. *Author*

Shortly after starting the walk are the remains of railway bridge (**A**). The railway passed over the path to Les Ruins (a ruined castle) and continued on a stone faced embankment to a bridge across the Charpassonne in the far left of the picture.
Author

After bypassing Les Ruins, the railway returned across the Charpassonne via an 18 metre bridge (**B**) to the east bank. This area is now overgrown but the stone abutments can still be seen. The photograph was taken from the south.
Author

Taken in the 1890s, the 18 metre railway bridge over the Charpassonne. Unlike the view above this picture was taken from the north on higher ground (now private) and shows Les Ruins in the background. The 'A' frames have had metal plates riveted to them to improve rigidity.

The line climbed through very hilly country with many bridges provided for farmers. Crossing bridge (**C**) over the track bed is typical of those that remain. *Author*

The earthworks for the bridges with stone facings were substantial. The spans were, however, simple girder constructions. The wooden planking has long been removed or rotted. *Author*

Maintaining a steady climb necessitated deep cuttings, many with stone facing such as this near La Valette (**D**). *Author*

Above: The station of Salvizinet was near to a bridge under the main road. The road has now been rerouted and obliterated part of the old track bed but just to the north the original road bridge remains as an outdoor area for a local café (**E**). *Author*

Left: Taken during the construction of the line, the unusually large 'I' beam indicates that this bridge was not a farmers crossing. It may be the bridge shown above.

Below: The remains of a crossing bridge (**F**). The countryside just to the north of Salvizinet is more open. The earthworks either side of the stonework has been removed. *Author*

Crossing bridge (**G**) viewed from the north. The post on the left shows one of the many signs giving a history of the line in both French and English. *Author*

The route of the line is nearly lost in this field at Le Reynard. The dip in the ground is the old track bed and inside the trees is yet another over bridge (**H**). The railway followed the river around to the right of this picture and then continued its climb up the hills seen in the distance. *Author*

At Moulin Ronzy the line turned north to climb up one side of a valley and then returned down the other side whilst continuing to climb. The train from Feurs would have come from the distant right under this bridge which supports the main road from Feurs to Panissières (**I**). *Author*

At the top of the Charpassone valley the line crossed the river and turned 180 degrees on an embankment to head south on its climb to Panissières (**J**). After nearly one hundred and twenty years trees grow over much of the embankment. *Author*

An unidentified site but this picture shows the hilly nature of the terrain that the monorail had to climb.

The driver and fireman next to the only locomotive delivered, No. 1, *Feurs*. The picture illustrates how the 'A' frames were extended to cope with the contours of the ground. The upper rail nearest the camera was probably more than two metres above the ground.
Author's collection

The mockup of locomotive No. 2, *Panissières*, beside the main road in the town of Panissières. Whilst both the track and locomotive are inaccurate in many details, it gives a feel as to how it would have looked. *Author*

Liverpool to Manchester proposal

The Act of Parliament to allow this line to be built received Royal Assent on the 17th August 1901. The Manchester and Liverpool Electric Express Railway Company, however, never raised sufficient capital for construction to proceed.

Considerable effort had, however, gone into its design including automatic signalling as described in Monorails of the 19th Century. An illustration has now been found of a model constructed for the promoters of the Liverpool to Manchester railway to demonstrate the safety of the proposed automatic signalling system.

Whilst the bodies of the carriages were no more than cigar shaped boxes, the model of the automatic signalling system built for the promotors of the Liverpool to Manchester monorail ran prototypically using two of the four side rails on each track for current collection. Just visible on the roof of each model carriage (top left of nearest vehicle, far right on furthest vehicle) was a small projection which tripped the signals as they passed by. This was a simplified version of that proposed for the prototype.

Illustrated London News *Vol. 119, 13 July 1901, p63*

References

1 *Railway Magazine* November 1988, p705.
2 *The Listowel & Ballybunion Railway* compiled by Michael Foster and incorporating the original booklet by the late A. T. Newham. Oakwood Press, 1989.
3 *The Lartigue* by Michael Guerin, 1988.
4 *Limerick Leader* 10 June 2000.
5 *The Listowel Lartigue Monorail Project: an exciting opportunity to contribute.*
6 *Steam Railway* No. 252, 8 December 2000 – 4 January 2001, p26.
7 *Railway Magazine* January 2002, pp26-31.
8 *Narrow Gauge News* No. 251, July 2002, p8. (Narrow Gauge Railway Society publication)
9 *The Kingdom* 24 December 2002.
10 *The Kingdom* 7 January 2003.
11 *Steam Railway* No.288, 12 September – 9 October 2003, p26.
12 *Irish Independent* 7 October 2004.
13 *Backtrack* May 2008, pp295-299.

At the far end of the line Locomotive No. 4 runs around the train ready for its return journey to Listowel Station. *Author*

The new stock delivered to the Wuppertal Schwebebahn in 1950. The rounded ends of the 50 series cars reflected the new modernism of the period. *Author's collection*

APPENDIX 2

A POSTSCRIPT TO *MONORAILS OF THE 19TH CENTURY*

Since publication in 2011 a little more information has come to light.

PANARMONION GARDENS RAILWAY

John R. Day refers to this railway in his writings about monorails[1] and his comments have since been quoted in a number of books and articles. As earlier sources verifying or adding to the details written by Day had not been traced, this monorail was excluded from the earlier volume. Recent research indicates that one reason these could not be traced was due to a spelling error – Day refers to 'Panarmonium' – and subsequent works have continued this error.

This monorail is, however, worthy of inclusion. It was probably the first self-propelled, albeit man powered, monorail and it was also the first truly suspended monorail.

In the early 1800s the area now known as Kings Cross, London, was known as Battle Bridge as it was a crossing point over the River Fleet and a tradition had built up that this area was the site of a battle between the Romans and Boadicea. Part of this area, just south of the current King's Cross Station, had been used to deposit waste and ashes from fires and in 1820s these were cleared to leave a large vacant space bounded by New Road (now Euston Road) to the north, Liverpool Street (a small road running at right angles to New Road) to the East, a parallel side road called Argyll Street to the West and Manchester Road to the South. A prospectus to subscribe for about £20,000 for its development was issued by a company promoted by Signor Gesualdo Lanza in 1829. Lanza presided over a school for singing and acting and he proposed a great 'Panarmonion Institution' consisting of a theatre, concert hall, hotel, restaurant, library etc.[2].

The gardens opened on the 4th March 1830 but the venture was unsuccessful with little of Lanza's ideas being realised. The site and building supplies of bricks etc. were subsequently sold in early 1832. The theatre, however, had been completed and was variously named the Royal Clarence Theatre, the King's Cross Theatre and in 1897 became part of a dining room of a restaurant. One aspect was a temporary success. A Mr H. Thorrington had invented

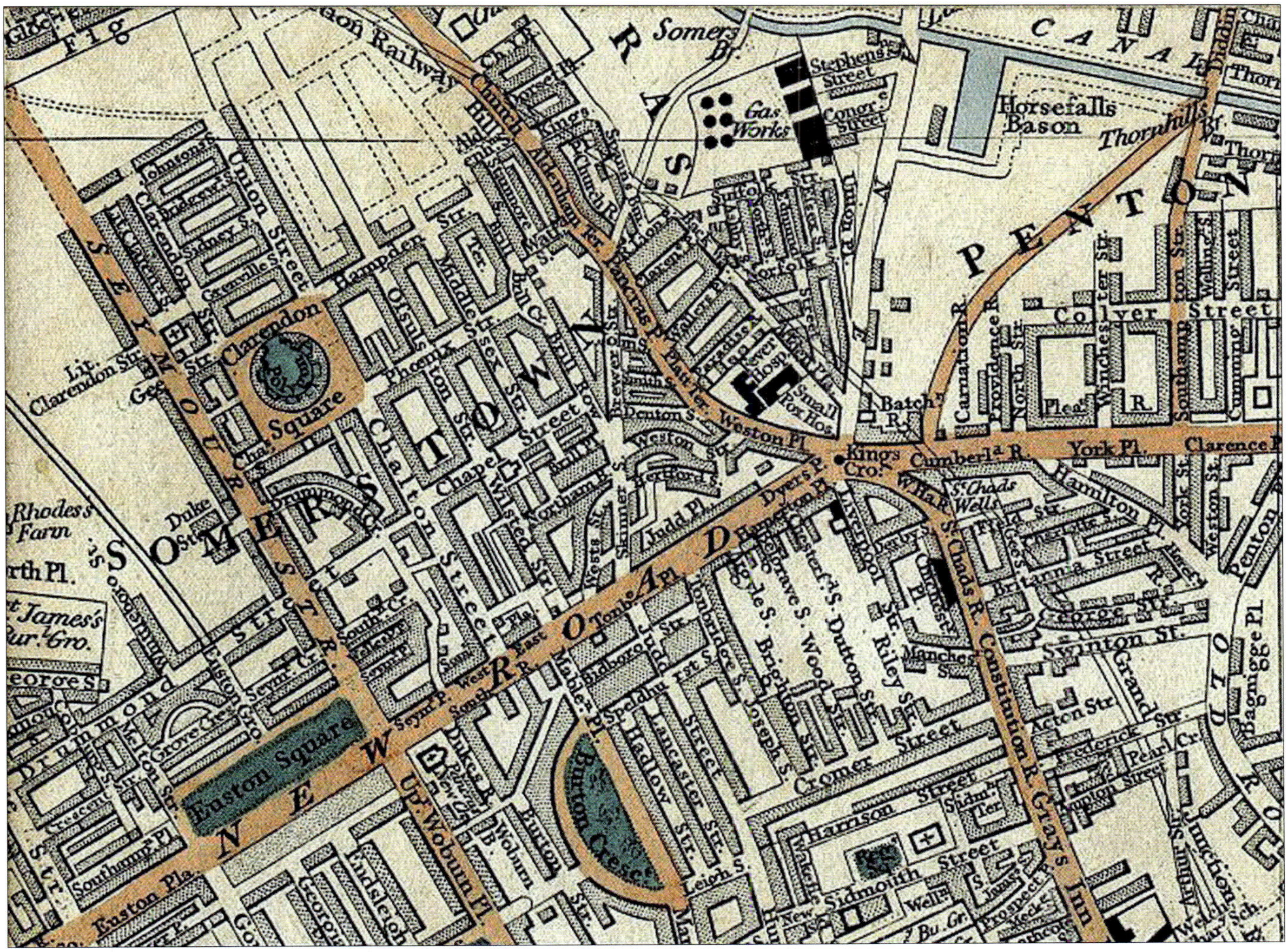

Cary's New Plan of London and its Vicinity in 1837 shows the undeveloped roads on the site of the short lived Panarmonion Gardens. The 'Kings Cross' monument at the end of what was then called New Road is shown as a black dot on this map.

Looking somewhat like a suspended gondola, Thorrington's William the Fourth monorail car.
Cremorne and the Later London Gardens *by Warwick Wroth, 1907*

and installed his suspension railway during the period the gardens had been open allowing a tour of some of the grounds. The railway was described by George Clinch[3]:

"The invention seems to have consisted in suspending a boat shaped car from a substantial level bar, along which it travelled upon small wheels. The motive power was supplied from the car by means of a wheel which was worked by hand, and by which means the rate of progression was regulated. 'No one can believe,' says a contemporary account, 'that this Car travels with such ease and rapidity without being a witness of the fact. The idea is a very ingenious one, and does great credit to Mr. H. Thorrington, who is the inventor. The admittance to the Gardens is One Shilling each Person, entitling the parties to ride round the gardens in the Car, or on the Hobby Horse. On Sunday, 6d each person to walk in the Gardens.'"

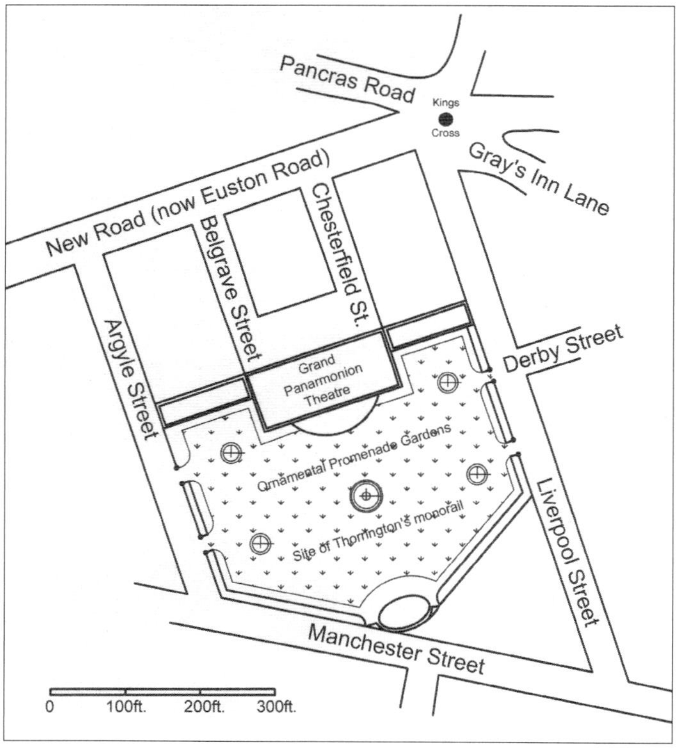

The ground plan of Signor Gesualdo Lanza's Panarmonion Gardens. The monorail formed a loop around the grass covered gardens in front of the planned theatre (redrawn from information in the British Library).

Wroth[2] suggested that the 'Hobby Horses' were rudimentary cycles suspended from the bar and worked the same way as the boat.

The suspended monorail car was named William the Fourth in honour of King William IV who was crowned in 1830, the year the gardens opened. The change in name of the area to Kings Cross arose from the monument to King George IV erected in 1830 following his death on the 26th June 1830.

Unfortunately the inventor, Thorrington, did not patent his ideas which might have provided more detail. The system certainly predates the designs of both Enos and Langen.

Rails at Ground Level

Lisbon Steam Tramways (Chapter 3)

As recorded in the earlier volume, sixteen locomotives using the Larmanjat system were ordered from Sharp Stewart & Co., Atlas Works, Manchester for these tramways. Following trials in England at Buckhurst Hill at least three of the locomotives, No. 1 *Lisboa*, No. 2 *Cintra* and *Lumiar* (number not known) were delivered to Portugal. The line from Lisbon to Cintra opened on the 5th July 1873 and the line from Lisbon to Torres Vedras opened on the 6th September 1873. The project, however, was a disaster with many shareholders losing the money they had invested when the company was launched in 1871 by the time trains were suspended on the 8th April 1875.

A recently found report in *Iron*[4] published in 1874 suggests that the line might have had some short term success or perhaps the correspondent from *The Times* had been persuaded to give a positive report:

"***Occasional Notes***
Steam Tramways on the Highways: A correspondent of the Times states that for more than twelve months locomotive engines, drawing trains of carriages and waggons, have been running on a tramway laid on public roads in Portugal. The running speed has been from eight to ten miles an hour, but in special cases a speed equal to twenty or twenty five miles an hour had been attained. The gradients or hills over which the trains are taken have a rise of 1 in 20 and the curves or corners around which they run have a radius of twenty yards. Trains consisting of seven closely-packed carriages have been successfully worked under the above exceptional conditions between Lisbon and Cintra, and also between Lisbon and Torres Vedras, and in local districts near Lisbon still longer trains have been run. They are under perfect control on the steepest hills, and are worked among the ordinary public road traffic with a wonderful freedom from accident."

The locomotives, carriages and track delivered to Portugal were previously assumed to have been scrapped. It now appears, however, that some of the locomotives that had not been shipped from the UK were rebuilt by Merryweather's steam tramway works at Greenwich to operate on conventional standard gauge. They were then sold to contractors Lucas & Aird for use on the construction of the Tilbury Docks near London for the East & West India Dock Company and also the Hull & Barnsley Railway[5].

Zipernowsky's balancing tram (Chapter 13)

Patented in 1889 and demonstrated in Budapest in 1891, Zipernowsky's monorail tram never gained commercial success.

Whilst the prototype was scrapped, a large scale model built during its development has been preserved in the Hungarian Technical and Transportation Museum, Budapest.

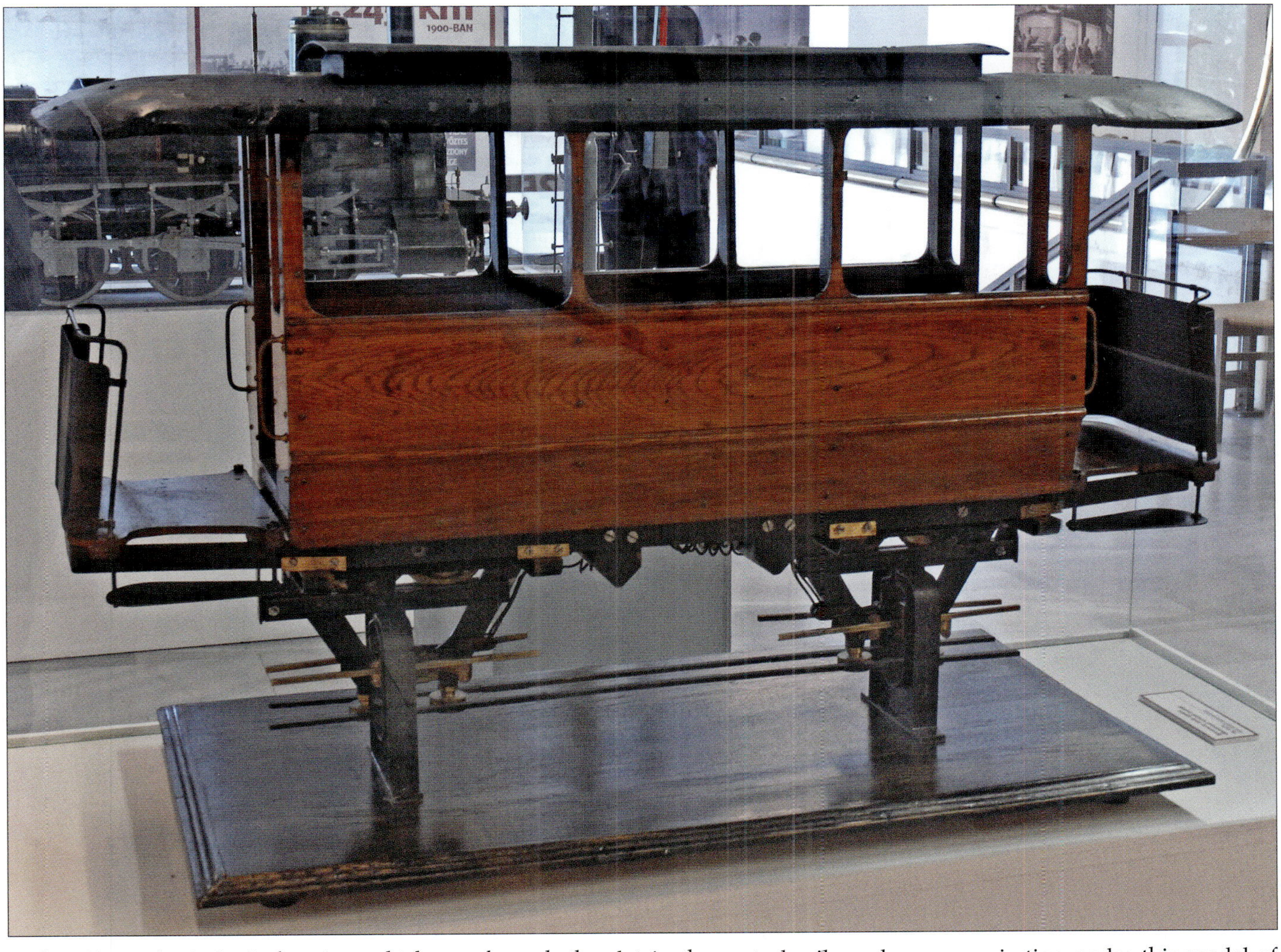

Rather like a ship's keel, the plate which ran through the slot in the central rail can be seen projecting under this model of Zipernowsky's tram. The rail slot was not dissimilar to the conduit system adopted by London's trams but underneath it provided not only the power supply but also rails for the balancing wheels. *Author*

Ewing's system (Chapter 14)

As recorded in the earlier volume, two traction engines were used to haul Ewing type monorail carts between Luzira and Kampala in Uganda around 1910 following the heavy mortality of cattle as motive power. The traction engines were not modified in any way and remained strictly road vehicles.

Ewing proposed, however, that a traction engine could be converted for dedicated single rail use by replacing the front road wheels with two double flanged rail wheels in a bogie to provide guidance and took out a patent for the arrangement which was granted on the 9th July 1903. This was not a true monorail as the rail did not bear the main weight of the traction engine. It was essentially a single rail guidance system for road vehicles.

At the time of writing the earlier volume there was no evidence that this system had been tried but it is now known that one, or possibly two, traction engines were converted to this form of operation. They were originally built by Wallis & Steevens at their works in Basingstoke to their 3 ton tractor design and had been ordered by the Crown Agents for use in South Africa. The precise date is uncertain but Hutchinson suggests[6] that they were probably Works No's 2517 and/or 2518, both of which were supplied around 1900. Subsequently one or more special bogies were ordered by the Crown Agents. Again the date is not known but the plans made by the drawing office at Wallis & Steevens were dated the 7th June 1904, just a year after the grant of Ewing's patent.

The concept of using tractors in this fashion was new and to test the design Wallis & Steevens fitted one of the bogies to their works tractor for testing. This tractor had been built in 1898 (Works No. 2410) as the 3-ton prototype and was identical to those that had been shipped to South Africa. Being the prototype it was no doubt used for various trials.

After proving the arrangement on a short length of track at Basingstoke the 'monorail' bogie on the works tractor was replaced with the normal road wheel arrangement and the tractor continued its regular duties until being sold in 1915. The bogie(s) were presumably shipped to South Africa for fitting locally.

Little is known about the success of the design or where the Ewing type monorail line operated in South Africa. It is clear, however, that the two wheeled rail bogie on the tractor could rotate so it is doubtful that the tractor could have been used in reverse as any uneven grip by the large rear driving wheels would have caused it to wander to one side.

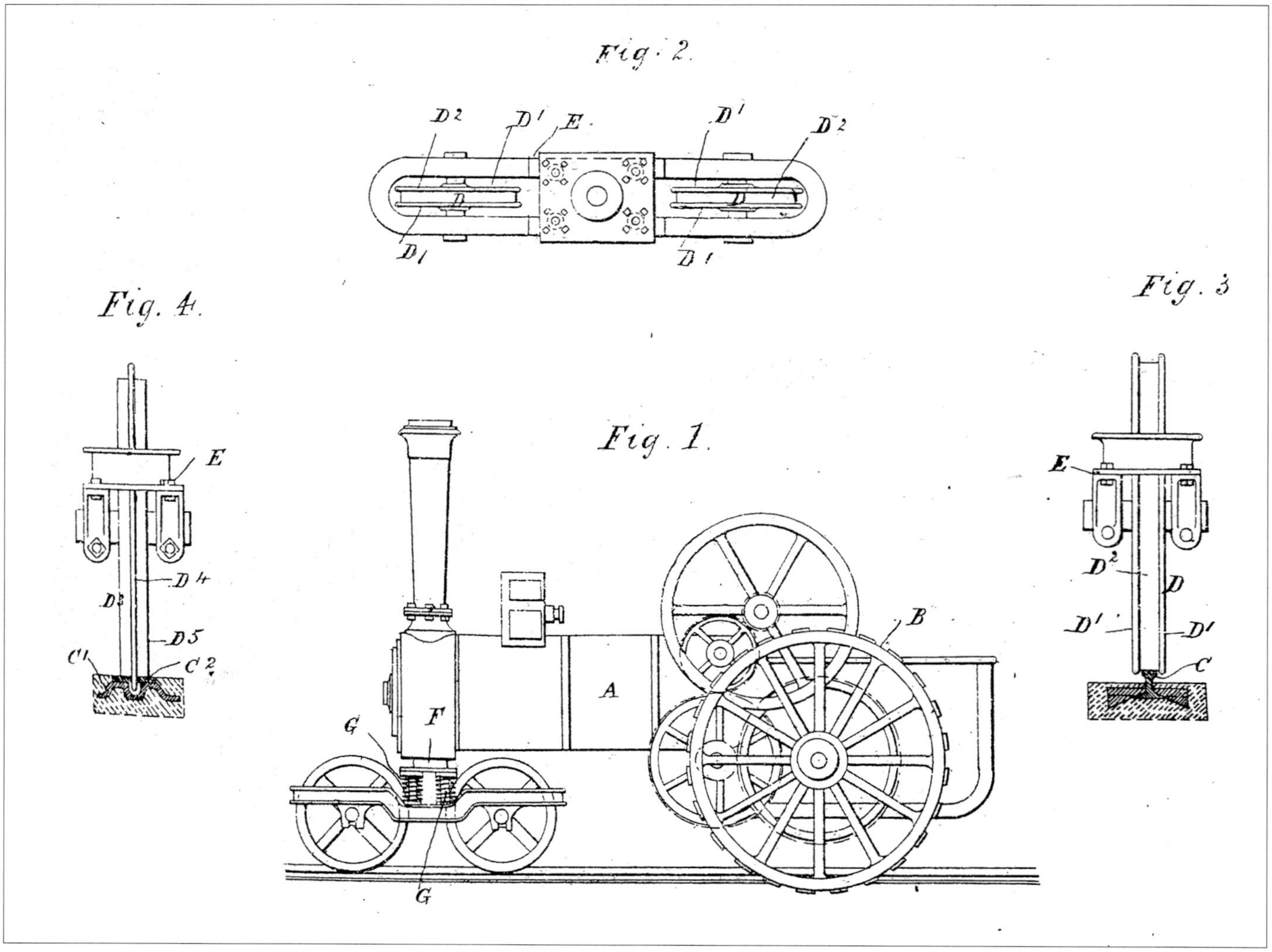

Ewing's UK Patent No. 19904 granted in 1903 for a system of steering traction engines.

The Wallis & Steevens 3-ton traction engine was a light weight engine used for road haulage and farm use. An example is *Little Olga*, seen here at the Great Dorset Steam Fair. Built in 1903 she worked mainly around Alton and Farnham in Hampshire. *Author*

In the 1920s *Little Olga* was temporarily converted to a road roller and used on airfields. The conversion required removal of the front wheel assembly from the bracket beneath the smokebox. The conversion for use on a monorail would have been similarly effected with the two wheeled bogie being secured as shown on the accompanying drawing. *Author*

The Wallis & Steevens works tractor temporarily converted for monorail use. The monorail bogie looks flimsy even for use on this light 3-ton traction engine. Industrial Railway Record *1967, Issue 14 courtesy of the Industrial Railway Record Society*

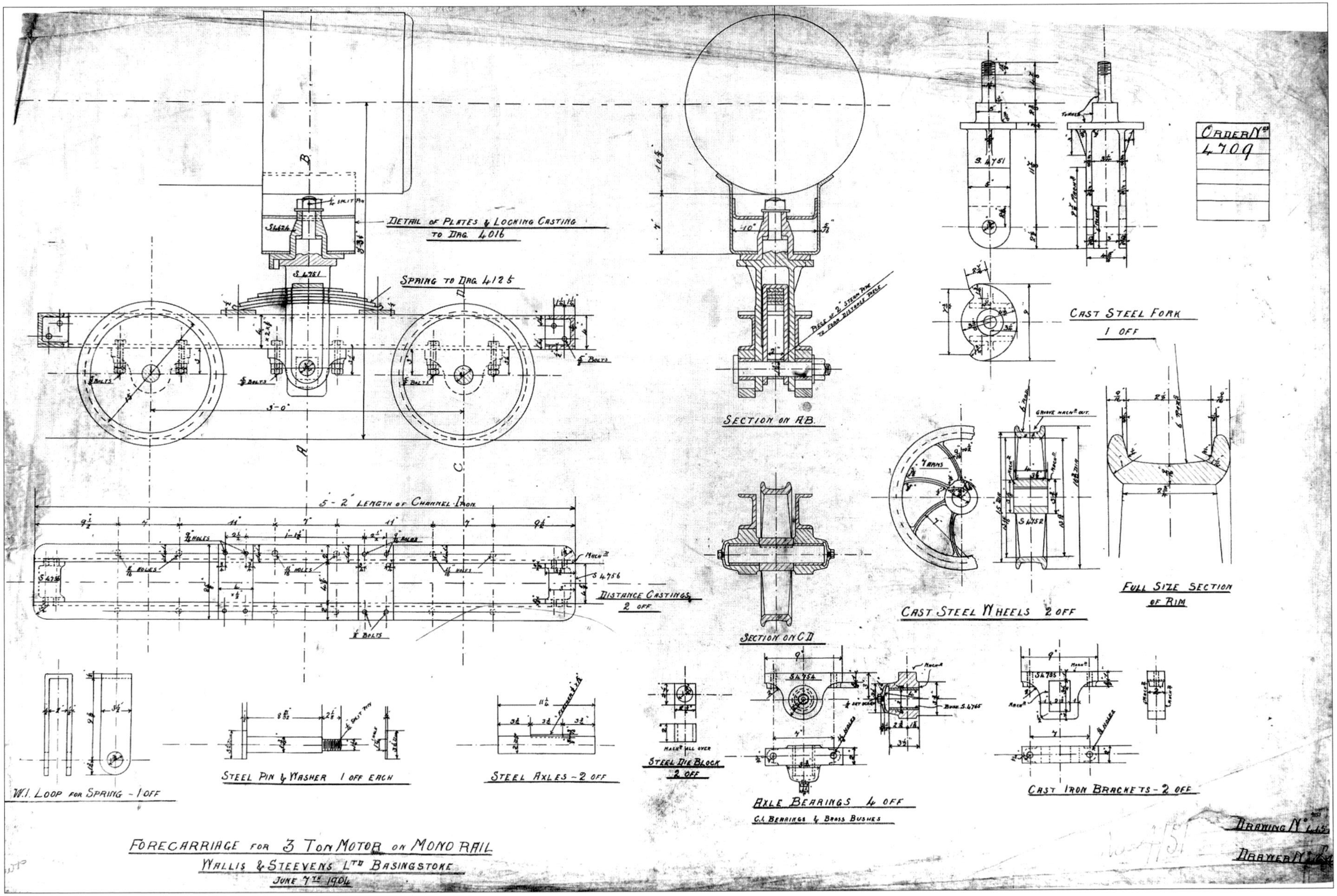

Forecarriage drawing for the 3-ton steam tractor by Wallis and Steevens. *Museum of English Rural Life, University of Reading. Drawing No. TR WAL D01/1/4151*

Whilst not a true monorail (and thus outside the scope of this book) the concept of using a single rail to provide guidance to road vehicles continues to be reinvented every now and then. For example in 1932 C. Skelton, an Indian consulting engineer, developed the Guide Rail System intended to provide cheap transport in remote areas This was further promoted after the Second World War in 1946 as the Guideway System. The rail served merely to locate vehicles on a narrow road which could be surfaced in the narrowest of strips. Each vehicle carried a pair of roller bearing guide pins on each bogie to keep it in the centre of the guideway[7]. A very similar system was designed and promoted by J. Brockhouse and Co. Ltd. as the Uniline in the early 1950s[8]. Both of these systems allowed vehicles to be reversed, unlike that designed by Ewing.

Right: The Skelton Guideway system was a road guidance system rather than a true monorail but followed from the ideas of Ewing. Modern Transport *Vol. 55, 4 May 1946*

Langen's 'Schwebebahn' or swinging railway (Chapter 15)

Wuppertal Schwebebahn

Without question this is the most successful monorail, as following the opening of the full length of the line on 27th June 1903, it has been and remains a vital form of transport in this densely populated valley. At the time of writing (2016) new rolling stock is to be delivered by the end of the year. A full description of the original rolling stock was given in *Monorails of the 19th Century*. A summary and an update of rolling stock operated up to 1950 and subsequently shows the success of the original design:

98 series: Two carriages, run as a pair, were supplied by Van der Zypen und Charlier in September 1898 to test the line. They are identifiable in early photographs (see *Monorails of the 19th Century*) by their ten narrow passenger windows plus four air vents at each end above the main compartments. They had doors at each end of the carriage. These carriages were never classified into a numbering system and probably not used in service.

00 series: Twenty six carriages were constructed by Van der Zypen und Charlier in 1900. Numbered 1-26, they are identifiable by the four large passenger compartment windows and end doors. Many of these vehicles continued in service for some seventy years until 1973-75 when they were replaced. Carriages numbers 5 and 22 survive and form the 'Kaiserwagen' historic train.

03 series: Eight, three car trains consisting of one driving carriage and two trailer carriages, were constructed by Van der Zypen und Charlier in 1903. They were numbered 27-50 and are identifiable in photographs (see Monorails of the 19th Century) by the position of the passenger doors about one third of the way from the front of the carriage. The low mounted motor with its vertical shaft driving bevel gearing was not as resistant to wear as the spur gearing on the 00 series and they were retired in the 1950s and 1960s.

Two of the 00 series carriages, leading carriage No. 5 and trailing carriage No. 22, have been preserved to form the 'Kaiserwagen' historic train seen here on Sunday 19th July 2015 about to enter Zoo station with the special 11.00 train from Vohwinkel. *Author*

12 series: Six further carriages were delivered by Van der Zypen und Charlier in 1912 to the 00 series design. They were numbered 51-56. Five of these vehicles continued in service until 1973-74.

30 series: Two new carriages, numbered 57 and 58, were constructed in 1930 by Vereinigte Westdeutsche Waggonfabriken AG., the successor company to Van der Zypen und Charlier following its amalgamation into a group with other smaller companies.

Whilst many of the stations have been modernized to cope with passenger numbers, Landgericht station has been maintained in its original art nouveau style. Remove the modern car and road signs and this scene would be little changed from the time the line opened. *Author*

The preserved carriage No. 5 retains the original drive system using transverse motors and spur gears to the front spoked wheel. This drive has a distinct growl sound. The 'Kaiserwagen' historic train operates (2015) three trains a day at weekends and can be hired for weddings. It is always fully booked. *Author*

The bodies had steel framing and external panel plates and were equipped with separate twin centre outside sliding doors for each saloon which provided a 1,100mm opening. The doors were electrically interlocked and were operated pneumatically from the driver's compartment. The locking was so arranged that the driver could not set the train in motion before all the doors had closed. The electrical equipment was supplied by Siemens-Schuckert-Werke A.G. and, unlike the original carriages which had fourteen power and seven brake notches, these carriages had electromagnetic multiple unit control with nine power and six brake notches. In normal service only electric braking was employed. The control apparatus was located in a box in front of the driving position.

The main dimensions were:

Length over body:	11.450m
Width over body:	2.100m
Length of 2nd class saloon:	4.267m
Length of 3rd class saloon:	7.183m
Motor on each bogie:	35Kw operating at 600V DC

Inside the carriages the panels were of varnished ash wood with seats made from stamped light metal mounted on one side only of the carriage thereby allowing room for 48 standing passengers. The 16 seats in the 3rd Class saloon were finished in leather. The 11 seats in the 2nd Class saloon were finished in plush. The main windows were fixed but the upper part allowed ventilation and both saloons had electric lighting. As expected in the 1930s, one carriage provided for smoking, and the other for non-smoking passengers.

The internal ceilings were enameled white and externally the carriages were painted red with a yellow band. The upper part of the paneling was painted brown[9].

41 series: Carriages No. 14 (00 series) and No. 53 (12 series) were rebuilt in 1941 as a trial. They were withdrawn in 1974.

50 series: Twenty carriages to a new post war design were constructed by Vereinigte Westdeutsche Waggonfabriken AG., Köln with electrics by Siemens-Schuckert in 1950. They are easily recognized in photographs by their 1950s rounded design. They were introduced to provide greater capacity but be lighter in weight. The use of the system during the First World War followed by the boom years 1926-29 had placed a strain on the track. The heavy damage by air raids on the 30th May and the 25th June 1943 during the Second World War had added to this strain and had temporarily closed the line until the 19th December 1944, following which it was attacked and closed again by another air raid. After hostilities had finished the line reopened on the 21st April 1946 (Easter Day) but for reasons of safety the pre-war three carriage trains were suspended. Regulations forbade overcrowding, again due to weight, and queues at the main stations became prevalent[10].

Prior to building the two 30 series carriages, two of the bodies of the earlier 03 series carriages were converted to test the external sliding doors.
Locomotive *Vol. 40, 14 April 1934*

30 Series carriage number 58 under construction at the works of Vereinigte Westdeutsche Waggonfabriken AG. The design appears to have been unsuccessful as only two carriages of this type were built. Electric Railway Traction *Vol. 60, 9 February 1934*

The inside of the 3rd Class compartment of 30 series carriage number 58 had plain padded seats. Just visible at the end is the 2nd Class compartment with what appear to be chesterfield type padded seats. Electric Railway Traction *Vol. 60, 9 February 1934*

These new two carriage sets were of all steel construction with pressed profiles and light weight paneling. Their tare weight was 11 tonnes allowing some overcrowding. They were permitted to carry eighty passengers. Each carriage had a 2nd and 3rd Class saloon, entrance to the former was by one door only, there were two doors for the latter. A sliding door separated the saloons. The seats, for three passengers, were upholstered on the inner side of the carriage in both the 2nd and 3rd Class saloons. The sliding doors were operated by compressed air controlled by the driver and for safety the dead man's handle only operated when all the doors were closed. One axle of each bogie was driven by a 45Kw motor through a worm gear which made for very quiet running. They were numbered 59-78.

72 series: Twenty eight three part carriages were delivered by Vereinigte Westdeutsche Waggonfabriken AG. during the years 1973-74. These replaced the service of all (except for two preserved carriages) of the aging carriage stock and a new numbering sequence was started – they were numbered 1-28. Sometimes colloquially described as 'two rooms and a bath' configuration, they consisted of two 34ft (approx.) long carriages flexibly connected to a 10ft long (approx.) central section with concertina sides. With an unladen tare weight of 21 tons they could carry up to 120 passengers.

72 Series carriage sets No's 22 and 14 pass above the Wupper river. Most of the deep sided valley is industrial with the exception of a short section near Zoo station where the monorail turns to continue its journey to Oberbarmen above the river. *Author*

Above: The Schwebebahn or Swinging Railway was aptly named. Series 72 carriage set No. 8 rounds the corner near Alter Markt station with a full load in July 2015. *Author*

Left: The 72 Series bogies had the motors mounted in line with the track with a worm and wheel drive to both disc wheels providing very quiet running. *Author*

The newly arrived stock is prepared in the Wuppertal Schwebebahn workshops in January 2016.
Courtesy © WSW Wuppertaler Stadtwerke GmbH

Generation 15 Series: On the 10th November 2011 Wuppertaler Stadtwerke GmbH. signed a contract for €122m for thirty one articulated carriages to replace the ageing 72 series rolling stock. The carriages were designed by Büro+Staubach GmbH., Berlin and they are currently (August 2016) being assembled by Vossloh Kiepe GmbH. at its Spanish plant in Albuixech, near Valencia, from sections made throughout Europe. The main structure and chassis for each vehicle is being constructed in Austria, the train safety equipment is being made in Belgium and the traction equipment is being supplied by Vossloh Kiepe from Dűsseldorf. The windows and door mechanisms are being provided from Turkey and fitted to the vehicles in Germany. The Swiss firm of Prose Ltd which specializes in engineering and testing services of railway rolling stock, is providing vehicle development and manufacturing support services.

The trains are 24m long, 2.2m wide and weigh 25 tonnes. The sleek design has 48 padded wooden seats to the far side of the carriages to allow room for standing passengers, very necessary during the rush hours, together with areas at each end for pushchairs and wheelchairs. Passengers will also benefit from LED lighting, air-conditioning and information displays. To keep weight to a minimum, the carriages are formed from welded aluminum. The power supply for the line is being changed from 600V DC to 750V alternating current and the new carriages will be provided with four longitudinal three-phase asynchronous motors with a capacity of 60 Kw. The change is anticipated to reduce maintenance costs and to enable peak headways to be reduced by two minutes due to the faster acceleration. Whilst the new trains will be capable of accelerating to 65km per hour, the maximum permitted speed will be 60km per hour[11].

The first section of the new carriages, still mounted on the lorry that had delivered the vehicle from the factory in Spain, was unveiled in Wuppertal on Saturday the 14th November 2015 by the Mayor of Wuppertal, Herr Andreas Mucke. Engineering trials commenced in early 2016.

The new (2016) carriages on the Schwebebahn pass the Evangelical Church at Sonnborn where the line turns away from the streets to follow the river up the Wupper Valley towards Oberbarmen.
Courtesy © WSW Wuppertaler Stadtwerke GmbH – 012AVM

This rear view of the new rolling stock on the Schwebebahn shows the panoramic window at each end of the carriages as they leave Oberbarmen station on their journey to Vohwinkel.

Courtesy © WSW Wuppertaler Stadtwerke GmbH – 012AVM

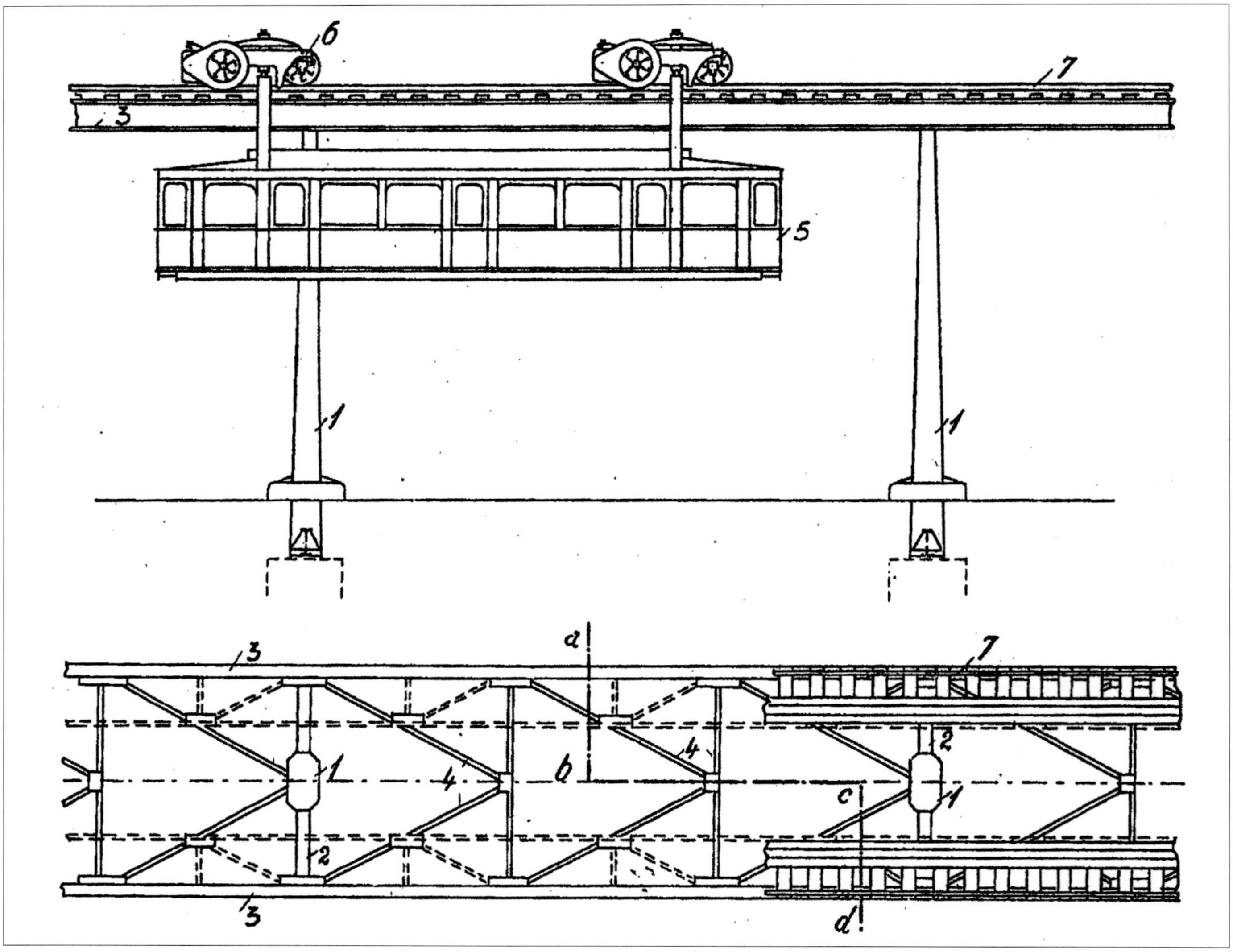

The use of Rieppel beams and related supports was not practical in the already built up streets of Berlin. Petersen therefore designed a system to support Langen 'Schwebebahn' type cars using this girder construction. *US Patent No. 935859*

Proposal for Berlin

In 1905 Continentale Gesellschaft für Elektrische Unternehmungen, the company founded by Carl Eugen Langen to develop his suspended monorail system, which was so successful in the Wupper Valley, proposed a similar system for Berlin. The project was led by their chief engineer, Richard Petersen.

In the Wupper Valley the monorail was constructed to run above a road that had not been developed and then to run above the river where it passed through the already built up area. As shops and buildings were developed along the road section, account was taken of the already existing monorail supports. In Berlin, the route was not to be above a river or an undeveloped road. Instead it had to be designed to run overhead of traffic on existing roads. To solve this problem, Petersen patented[12] a design of rail structure based on a lattice supported by substantial central supports. The design included expansion joints, very necessary given the range of temperatures in Berlin, and the lattice construction together with the vertical supports were optimized to allow for the stresses of trains that swing freely.

Despite the work on designing these supports, no monorail was constructed.

Proposals plain and exotic (Chapter 16)

Joseph de Baader (née Joseph von Baader)

Joseph von Baader was a Bavarian and the earlier volume stated that he had taken out Patent No. 3959 in Bavaria. This is incorrect – the patent was taken out in England under the French translation of his name to Joseph de Baader, Patent No. 3959. The application was made and signed on the 25th January 1816 and the patent 'inrolled' on the 6th May 1816.

The date of the 14th November 1815 in reference[13] cited in the earlier volume relating to UK Patent No. 3959 is incorrect but it might refer to the date another patent was granted, possibly in Bavaria.

Baader's patent is probably the earliest taken out for a monorail in the UK. It predates Palmer's monorail patent by five years but no evidence has been traced that a railway was built to Joseph von Baader's system. To quote from the patent:

> "…I place my rails (generally cast of one piece) a good deal nearer together, from twenty-four to five inches, or I make but one single line of rails, and I cause the men, horses or other animals employed for drawing

the carriages to walk without and on one side of the said double or single line of rails, or on both sides of them if more than one animal be employed…

…The rails (which may be constructed of cast or wrought iron, or of any other hard or fit substance) are fixed upon and supported by a proper foundation of stone or wood, upon blocks, pillars, or posts, placed at proper distances, but a good deal more elevated above the ground than in the usual way, that is to say, from five to ten inches and upwards…

…The plates of my rails are provided with a vertical or inclined rest or support below, cast or joined in one piece with them, which forms a lateral line of rails, the flat or plain surface of the upper rails or plates projecting a little on each side of the said lateral plates or supports....

…The carriages which are to be used on my said improved railroads, and the size, shape, and body of which may be varied according to the quantity and nature of articles to be transported, or according to the convenience and taste of the persons which are to be conveyed, are provided each with four vertical wheels if the line of the rails be double, or with two wheels, one placed behind the other, if there is but a single line of rails. These wheels have a projecting rim or flange to keep them upon the rails, but every carriage is provided with two or four horizontal or inclined wheels (constructed of iron, brass, or any other fit substance) placed on both sides of the carriage, or in the middle of the same, turning round their vertical or inclined axles, and working against the afore-mentioned lateral rails on the outer side, or in the middle between the two upper rails and below their projecting horizontal plates. By this new arrangement the lateral dragging friction of the wheels, which upon a common tram or railroads is very considerable, is totally avoided, and at the same time the carriages, however broad their bodies may be, and notwithstanding their vertical or principal wheels being placed so near together, or quite in the centre of gravity, are kept in such a steady position that they can neither overset nor get off the railway."

John Kyte Collett

Collett's patent of the 7th November 1879 (UK Patent No. 4540) described a steam hauled suspended monorail and included illustrations of the railway hanging from a rail secured to beams across a deep ravine. A report recently found in *Illustrated London News* states that Collett thought the system would have been useful in war time and included two illustrations of the proposed system in less dramatic terrain[14].

Collett's system would have allowed vehicles to swing on curves but did not include any safety measures to ensure it did not derail. Illustrated London News *Vol. 119, 13 July 1901*

The locomotive cylinders were to drive a shaft with pulleys mounted under the boiler just in front of the firebox. A belt was to connect these to a further shaft between the upper wheels. Further pulleys were to connect this shaft to the two large upper wheels. Illustrated London News *Vol. 119, 13 July 1901*

Lucian F. Cook

A recent article in *News Tribune*[15] reported that in 1892, in parallel with Cook applying for the US patents detailed in *Monorails of the 19th Century*, Cook had constructed a working model of his elevated electric powered monorail which was displayed at the Tacoma Post Office. The carriage was suspended from the upper track and stabilized by rollers bearing on either side of a rail underneath the carriage. It is not clear if this was a true monorail as some of the patent drawings envisaged the use of two (narrow gauge) upper rails.

Cook estimated that it would cost about US$15,000 a mile to construct a thirty seven mile long line from Tacoma's Commencement Bay to Seattle's Elliott Bay and the trip would take twenty minutes. He raised sufficient finance to allow a full size experimental track about a quarter of a mile long, together with a carriage just 3ft. wide seating ten passengers in single file, to be built on the waterfront below the Tacoma Hotel. Test runs were made on Friday 26th November 1892 with the engineer Henry Shaw acting as motorman. The ride would hardly have been pleasant as there was no system to control the current, just a simple on/off switch, so starting and stopping was abrupt.

Cook announced that he thought the upper limit of speed of his invention would be 200 miles per hour and that it could be used to connect Tacoma and New York. The idea got no further as a collapse in share markets (the 'Panic of 1893') killed any possibility of raising finance for this project.

Maxwell Dick & others

A number of articles and books over the last fifty years have suggested that the patent by Maxwell Dick (UK Patent No. 5790, applied for on 17th November 1829 and inrolled on the 21st November 1829) was a monorail design. This is incorrect and it is likely that the authors have repeated an earlier incorrect source. In Dick's patent of 1829 he certainly refers to Palmer's monorail but Dick states 'My invention, however, differs entirely from Mr. Palmer's, mine having four rails, as shown in the drawing, two of which are bearing and two as safety rails.' The only similarity with a true monorail is that the vehicles were to be suspended from these rails.

The following designs are also sometimes incorrectly quoted as monorails:

Nicholas Kirchner: US Patent No. 355826, granted 11 January 1887.
Thomas J. Myall: US Patent Nos. 381401, 381403, 381405, 382267, 384054 & 384921. All granted in 1888.
Lorenzo Joseph Cody: US Patent Nos. 410577 granted 10 September 1889 & 415617 granted 19 November 1889.
L. D. Girard: References including *Engineering* Vol. 48, 27 September 1889 p362.

Girard's design was for a form of water glide railway whilst the others were designs for two rail suspended railways. None were constructed.

References

1 *More Unusual Railways* by John R. Day published Frederick Muller Ltd., 1960.
2 *Cremorne and the Later London Gardens* by Warwick Wroth, 1907.
3 *Marylebone and St. Pancras* by George Clinch published by Truslove and Shirley, 1890.
4 *Iron* Vol. 4, 15 August 1874, p204.
5 *Industrial Railway Record* Vol. 3, No. 32, August 1970 pp306-308, article A Merryweather Metamorphosis by K. P. Plant. The article states the original source as the contemporary journal, *Iron*, 4 April 1884, but searches have not revealed the precise reference.
6 *Traction Engine Locomotives* by Ian Hutchinson. Published by the Road Locomotive Society, 1981.
7 *Modern Transport* Vol. 55, 4 May 1946, p21.
8 *Modern Transport* Vol. 64, 14 April 1951, p3.
9 *Railway Gazette*, Electric Railway Traction Supplement, Vol. 60, 9 February 1934, pp242-243 & Locomotive Vol. 40, 14 April 1934, p128.
10 *Railway Gazette* Vol. 94, 29 June 1951, p723 & *Railway Magazine* Vol. 97, August 1951, pp538-540 & 561-563.
11 *Railway Magazine* August 2013, pp32-35 and website www.schwebebahn.de
12 UK Patent No. 21826 Date of Grant 29 April 1909
US Patent No. 935859 Date of Grant 5 October 1909
13 *Monorail to Maglev* – Part 2 by Brian and Roy Wilson, The Friends of the National Railway Museum Newsletter, No. 66, February 1994, p21.
14 *Illustrated London News* Vol. 119, 13 July 1901, p63.
15 *New Tribune* 7 September 1995

APPENDIX 3

INDEX OF INVENTORS AND DESIGNERS

Name	Monorails of the 19th Century	Monorails of the Early 20th Century
Francis Laur		188
Albert P. Lee		158
R. V. Leeson		104
Albert Lehmann		146
Berthold Lindemann		157
Edward Locher	276	
John B. Mahana	279	
M. Mähl		157
Anatole Mallet	75	
William Maloney		154
William H. Martin	283	
Chandler McWayne	271	164
Charles Mehring		150
Joe V. Meigs	159	
Milinaire frères	275	
Ernst Mittag		153
Thomas J. Myall		206
George R. Napier		164
John B. Newbough	270	
William Newton	268	
E. Obleight	59	
Emilio Oliviera	59	
Robert T. Oney	278	
A. Oppenheimer	273	
Howe Paige	278	
Henry R. Palmer	13	
Richard Petersen		204
Henry S. Pruyn	274	
Joseph T. Pullon	276	
Joseph O. Raymond		150
William K. Reynolds	270	
Jeddiah Richards	268	
Anton Rieppel	244	
W. Willshire Riley	271	
Robert Roach	278	
William M. Robb		167
Benjamin Roberts	281	
Theodor Roghmanns		162
Hippolyte W. Romanoff		75
Frederick J. Rowan	281	
Henry Sargeant	19	
Robert C. Sayer		147

Name	Monorails of the 19th Century	Monorails of the Early 20th Century
Max Scheftel		154
August H. F. Scherl		33
Pierre Schilovsky		38
William T. Shaffer	280	
William H. Shepard		154
Richard W. Shoemaker		158
Alfred Speer	276	
Thomas C. Spelling		156
Curt Stedefeld		162
Rudolf Steiner		164
George Stevenson	271	
James Stimpson	268	
Roy Stone	43	
J. Langdon Sullivan	267	
James P. Taylor	213	
Florian Tentschert	283	
Robert E. Terry		150
Robert R. Thom		63
H. Thorrington		189
Vyacheslav P. Tichotsky		98
Howard H. Tunis		49
Ephraim M. Turner	213	
Walter D. Valentine		156
John N. Valley	278	
Volderauer	238	
Rudolf Wagner		160
S. Waldner		100
Hollis Walter		164
Elijah S. Watson	275	
Adam A. Welsh		145
Alexander A. Welsh		145
John Westcott	271	
Cassius I. White		149
Reynolds T. White	277	
Erwin F. von Wilmowsky		77
Major Wilson		94
William P. Wood	278	
George W. Wright	278	
Thomas H. Wright		103
John E. Wyman	276	
Károly Zipernowsky	207	191
Steven Zsinko		155